A QUEST FOR HOME
Reading Robert Southey

LIVERPOOL ENGLISH TEXTS AND STUDIES

General editors: JONATHAN BATE and BERNARD BEATTY

This long-established series has a primary emphasis on close reading, critical exegesis and textual scholarship. Studies of a wide range of works are included, although the list has particular strengths in the Renaissance, and in Romanticism and its continuations.

A QUEST FOR HOME

Reading Robert Southey

CHRISTOPHER J. P. SMITH

LIVERPOOL UNIVERSITY PRESS

First published 1997 by
LIVERPOOL UNIVERSITY PRESS
Senate House, Abercromby Square, Liverpool, L69 3BX

British Library Cataloguing-in-Publication Data
A British Library CIP Record is available for this book
ISBN 0–85323–511–2 *cased*
0–85323–521–X *paper*

Set in Linotron 202 Garamond by
Wilmaset Limited, Birkenhead, Wirral
Printed and bound in the European Union by
Bell & Bain Ltd, Glasgow

To Julie Anne Slater
without whose help this book
would not have been written

Robert Hancock (1739–1817), *Robert Southey*, 1797; by
courtesy of City of Bristol Museum and Art Gallery

Contents

Acknowledgements

Professor Jonathan Bate for guidance in turning a thesis into a book. Professor M. Wynn Thomas and Dr John Turner for inspirational lectures in Romanticism, supervision, suggestions, ideas, encouragement.

Professor Kenneth Curry, Professor Marilyn Butler, and Professor M. H. Abrams for their suggestions and advice. Professor Francis Warner for hospitality at St Peter's College, and guidance during the consultations of manuscripts and first editions in Oxford.

The courtesy and efficiency of the staff of Swansea and Sheffield University libraries, of Duke Humphrey's library and the Upper Reading Rooms of the Bodleian. To Elizabeth Freebairn of the Special Collections Department of the Newberry Library Chicago, for prompt recovery of an elusive sonnet.

Glyn Purseglove, Swansea's *Poetry Man*, and Dr Parvin Loloi, expert in Eastern literatures, for ten years of sustaining friendship and bibliophilia. Johanna Procter for the generous gift of the 1853 Southey *Complete Poetical Works*. Christopher Weeks and Jon Meah of *Babbage Design* for advice upon sources and textual management. Gerald Moore, Nigel, Elaine, Katherine, and Jonathan Smith, convivial guides throughout the literary places of the South West. Duncan Wu, editor of *The Charles Lamb Bulletin*, for encouragement and textual surgery. Dr John Morgan for help with Classical references.

Special thanks are also due to Dr Simon Baker, Dr Nick Potter, Dr Steven Vine, Dr Jeni Williams, Mary Davies, Anne Pye, Sarah Hoyles, Dee Gilmore, Philip Jones, Dr Huw Price,

Gillian Bazovsky, Leon Eakins, Melanie Thomas, Dr Carol Borrill.

This book is also inscribed to the memory of my dear friend Anthony Somerset Gibbs, whose hospitality was of considerable help to me during the reading of periodicals and first editions in London, and who guided me to the prints of Vivares:

ον οι θεοι φιλουσιν αποθνησκει νεος

Abbreviations

AA   *The Annual Anthology*, ed. Robert Southey,
               2 vols (Bristol: Biggs for Longman London, I
               1799, II 1800).

BL   Samuel Taylor Coleridge, *The Collected
               Works 7, Biographia Literaria,* J. Engel and
               W. Jackson Bate eds (London: Routledge
               and Kegan Paul, 1983).

B   Edmund Burke, *Reflections on the Revolution
               in France*, ed. Conor Cruise O'Brien
               (Harmondsworth: Penguin, 1968).

CA   Geoffrey Carnall, *Robert Southey and his Age*
               (Oxford: Clarendon, 1960).

CB   *Southey's Common-Place Book,* ed. J. W.
               Warter (London: Longman, Brown, Green,
               and Longmans, 1850), Fourth Series.

CP   Samuel Taylor Coleridge, *Poetical Works*,
               ed. Ernest Hartley Coleridge (London:
               Oxford University Press, 1969).

Everest   Kelvin Everest, *Coleridge's Secret Ministry*
               (Sussex: Harvester, 1979).

F   *Poems of Robert Southey,* ed. M. H. Fitz-
               gerald (London: Oxford University Press,
               1909).

Griggs   *Collected Letters of Samuel Taylor Coleridge*,
               6 vols, ed. E. L. Griggs (Oxford: Clarendon,
               1956).

G   Geoffrey Grigson, *A Choice of Southey's
               Verse* (London: Faber and Faber, 1970).

Hazlitt   *The Complete Works of William Hazlitt*, 21
               vols, ed. P. P. Howe (London: J. M. Dent,
               1930).

J	*The Letters of Robert Southey to John May 1797 to 1838*, ed. Charles Ramos (Austin, TX: Jenkins Publishing Company, The Pemberton Press, 1976).
JAC	Mary Jacobus, *Tradition and Experiment in Wordsworth's Lyrical Ballads (1798)* (Oxford: Clarendon, 1976).
K	Ernest Bernhardt-Kabisch, *Robert Southey* (Boston: Twayne, 1977).
L	Molly Lefebure, *The Bondage of Love* (New York: W. W. Norton, 1987).
LC	*The Life and Correspondence of Robert Southey*, ed. C. C. Southey, 6 vols, 2nd edn (London: Longman, Brown, Green and Longmans, 1849–50).
M	*Robert Southey. The Critical Heritage*, ed. Lionel Madden (London: Routledge, 1972).
MP	*The Contributions of Robert Southey to the Morning Post*, ed. Kenneth Curry (Alabama: University of Alabama Press, 1984).
N	Hoxie Neale Fairchild, *The Noble Savage: A Study In Romantic Naturalism* (New York: Russell and Russell, 1928).
NL	*New Letters of Robert Southey*, 2 vols, ed. Kenneth Curry (New York and London: Columbia University Press, 1965).
Poems 1795	*Poems: Containing The Retrospect, Odes, Elegies, Sonnets, &c.*, by Robert Lovell, and Robert Southey, of Baliol College, Oxford, (Bath: R. Crutwell, 1795).
Poems 1797	*Poems by Robert Southey*, 1st edn (Bristol: J. Cottle, 1797); facsimile (Oxford: Woodstock Books, 1989).
Poems 1799	*Poems By Robert Southey*, The Second Volume (Bristol: Biggs and Cottle, 1799).

PW   *The Poetical Works of Robert Southey, Collec-
            ted by Himself*, 10 vols (London: Longman,
            Orme, Brown, Green, & Longmans, 1843–
            45).

R   *A Memoir Of The Life And Writings Of The
            Late William Taylor Of Norwich*, 2 vols, ed.
            J. W. Robberds (London: John Murray,
            1843).

RA   Jean Raimond, *Robert Southey* (Paris: Didier,
            1969).

RO   Derek Roper, *Reviewing Before the Edin-
            burgh 1788–1802* (London: Methuen, 1978).

S   Robert Southey, *Letters Written during a Short
            Residence in Spain and Portugal*, 2nd edn
            (Bristol: 1799).

Simmons   Jack Simmons, *Southey* (London: Collins,
            1945).

W   *Selections From The Letters of Robert Southey*,
            edited by his son-in-law John Wood Warter,
            in four vols (London: Longmans, 1856).

WH   George Whalley, 'The Bristol Library Bor-
            rowings of Southey and Coleridge 1793–98',
            Library 5th Ser., 4, 1949, pp. 114–32).

Woodring   Carl R. Woodring, *Politics in the Poetry of
            Coleridge* (Madison: The University of
            Wisconsin Press, 1961).

WP   *The Poetical Works of William Wordsworth*,
            ed. E. de Selincourt and H. Darbishire, 5 vols
            (Oxford: Clarendon, 1940–49).

Introduction

Robert Southey: The Quest for Home

1

No study of Robert Southey's early career can evade the sense of change natural in the life of a youth responding to the momentous provocations of the post-revolutionary years. I have chosen to examine part of that change by focusing upon poetry preoccupied with home in its literal, political and psychological senses, and to show how this personal drive was related to his emerging literary reputation. I also wish to put forward the case for a new edition of the early work of this poet, as this would be invaluable from the point of view of its relevance to the emergence of *Lyrical Ballads* alone.

This book is in effect a critical anthology of Robert Southey's early poetry designed to follow the poet's search for home, to throw open readings of the selected poems and to join in with 'the reassessment of this poet's career and achievement already underway'.[1] I wish to link Southey's work to the poetic projects of Wordsworth and Coleridge, where this is appropriate, and where I feel that collaborations, parallels, imitations, parodies and debates exist between the rival texts of the sibling Lakers as they came to be known. Lack of sympathetic criticism in Southey's direction (with notable exceptions, such as the work of Jean Raimond) has sometimes made this a difficult task. Hostility to Southey is frequent, especially in Coleridgean criticism where the same anecdotes are told over and over again (but nothing else) about Sara Fricker and Pantisocracy. Worse than this is the general refusal (again with exceptions) to *look at the poetry itself*, to

revise critical attitudes, where they exist, in respect to what is a
very large and interesting body of work.

In his lifetime, Southey commented on the incessant attacks
upon his reputation. Having read the review in *The Examiner*
of his *Colloquies* (*LC* VI, pp. 48–49, 8 July 1829) he said:

> . . . it is evident that the constant hostility of newspapers
> and journals must act upon an author's reputation, like
> continued rain upon grass which is intended to be cut for
> hay; it beats to the ground and ruins the harvest, though
> the root may remain unhurt.

It is the nature of that root which I hope to lay bare in this
study, amongst the wreckage of a ruined harvest. But by using
the word 'quest' in my title, to describe the 'purposeful
journey, nowadays tendentiously spiritualized',[2] I have no
wish to represent the international Southey as another vates of
Romanticism, another heroic national figure like Wordsworth, who continues to serve as the grand exemplum in many
different aspects of literary discussion. My interest lies in the
active part Southey played during the late 1790s in English
poetry and how a privileged selection of his textual work
reveals to us one of his most central desires, the search for
home. In this, I am following up remarks made by Kenneth
Curry, in his *Southey*,[3] who states:

> Much can be understood about Southey if the struggle of
> the early years can be remembered. Although of short
> duration, the precariousness of his situation in life was
> early brought home to him. A dominant theme in his
> letters and his occasional poetry is the desire for a settled
> home, peace, and security. These things he never had in
> childhood or young manhood.

The quest for home in Southey's poetry as I am anthologizing
it takes place in its most poignant sense between the years 1793
and 1799, roughly between the death of his father and the

quittal of 'Martin Hall' at Westbury-Upon-Trym near Bristol. The year at Westbury was, according to Grigson:

> . . . the first perfect year, perhaps, of recovered and repaired childhood, the first year of the domesticity which the lack of domesticity in that broken childhood always compelled him to value so highly . . . (*G* p. 18)

But we do not have to accept Grigson's views on this; the facts speak for themselves. The enormous quantity of poetry produced during the Westbury period shows the freeing-up of the poet's muse and a temporary freeing from those anxieties of fracture which marred his previous life. But his stay in Westbury, emblematized by the migratory martins, had a kind of doomed brevity.

Following Coleridge up to the Lakes, to Greta Hall, was an expedient move, a retreat, away from the beloved area around Bristol with its melancholy associations, but was in some ways a negative act. The heroic yet claustrophobic drudgery to which Southey was subjected at Keswick has a vivid poignancy reflected inversely by the lack of esteem in which his poetical writings are now held. Keswick was home, but it was also a barrier. In the words of Jean Raimond (*RA* p. 577), 'l'isolement géographique est le symbole de l'isolement dans le monde des lettres. Southey se situe en marge du grand romantisme.' Keith Feiling puts this succinctly:

> In sum, Southey lived for forty years in a wilderness with an adoring community of cats and mortals, a library, and commonplace books.[4]

At the age of fifty-five Southey thought of his writing as 'the voice of one crying in the mountains' (*LC* VI, p. 52, 12 July 1829), yet still that of a would-be good shepherd of society, like an unacknowledged legislator in a Coleridgean-style clerisy. His fatherly opinions extended from his family circle at Greta Hall out onto the national stage, where he expected to see at any moment the next revolution besieging him with violence. As he grew older he saw the circles of friendship of the past shrinking alarmingly, and the occupants of Greta Hall itself thinning out. Southey's book-world increasingly took over his life, as he admitted (*LC* VI, p. 230, 16 January 1834):

> As my household diminishes, there will be room for more books. These I shall probably continue to collect, as long as I can; living in the past, and conversing with the dead,—and The Doctor.

Southey's early poetry in this study is often in conversation with the dead and he displays an 'intertextual range'[5] which this study can only hint at, and which no edition of his work explores. The obtrusive presence of both the living and the dead in his work may shed light upon not just Southey, but the literary vocabularies and methods of composition of other figures of the period. As Marilyn Butler notes in the case of Wordsworth:

> by stripping him of almost all his own contemporaries and associates . . . we do not learn his natural vocabulary of thought and feeling.[6]

A close, open-minded reading of Southey may, at the very least, aid the understanding of him as poet, his contemporaries, and the 'natural vocabulary' of the period. A proper edition or anthology of Southey's poetry would certainly invigorate any discussion of eighteenth- and nineteenth-century poetical discourse, especially in regard to the careers of Coleridge and Wordsworth.

My own critical anthology consists of poetry (and drama) which I am reading thematically and with any critical tools that seem appropriate. I have concentrated largely upon the shorter poems, in which at least Lionel Madden (*M* p. 9) sees strengths more clearly revealed than in the epics. Hazlitt also supports this choice:

> By far the best of his works are some of his shorter personal compositions, in which there is an ironical

mixture of the quaint and serious, such as his lines on a
picture of Gaspar Poussin, the fine tale of Gualberto, his
description of a Pig, and the Holly-tree, which is an
affecting, beautiful, and modest retrospect on his own
character. (*Hazlitt* V, p. 164)

Following the example of Francis Jeffrey in his famous review
of *Thalaba* in the *Edinburgh Review* (1802, i, pp. 63–83), I
have looked at what seems to be a natural tendency in
Southey's poetry, the reiteration of versions and visions of
home:

All the productions of this author, it appears to us, bear
very distinctly the impression of an amiable mind, a
cultivated fancy, and a perverted taste. His genius seems
naturally to delight in the representation of domestic
virtues and pleasures, and the brilliant delineation of
external nature. In both these departments, he is frequently very successful . . . (*M* p. 90)

In this account, I have not always chosen (in Jeffrey's words
above) Southey's 'successful' poetry, or poetry that represents
'domestic virtues and pleasures' directly, but my poetic
examples also often relate to these qualities by virtue of
concealed desire. In the case of the epic *Madoc*, Southey's
unacknowledged revision of *Joan of Arc* 1796, domestic ideals
are translated into national ideology. The gradual reconciliation of the private ideal of home with the public (even
vulgar) voice of saleable poetry is interesting to behold in a
young poet and it is the realization of that voice which
concerns me here. The excavating of Southeyan tesserae
represents the act of opening textual ground for a further
repossession of historical and cultural clues.

2
Hence Your Rites Domestic Gods, Arose

Such feelings Nature prompts, and hence your rites
DOMESTIC GODS! arose. When for his son
With ceaseless grief Syrophanes bewail'd,
Mourning his age left childless, and his wealth
Heapt for an alien, he with fixed eye
Still on the imaged marble of the dead
Dwelt, pampering sorrow. Thither from his wrath
A safe asylum, fled the offending slave,
And garlanded the statue and implored
His young Lord to save: Remembrance then
Softened the father, and he loved to see
The votive wreath renewed, and the rich smoke
Curl from the costly censer slow and sweet.

(Poems 1797, p. 216)

If Thomas McFarland[7] had chosen to include Southey in his book in any other fragmentary, ruined form but that of the textual example or footnote, that mere fact, let alone the result, might have surprised us. Though not a strong poet in Bloom's sense,[8] nor very often the victor in the struggle between ephebe and precursor, Southey is the perfect candidate for a study of diasparaction, of being torn to shreds, broken to fragments.

His own response to adversity, or what McFarland thinks of as (Heideggerian) *Verfallen*, 'the sense within life of its continuing ruin',[9] was the cultivation of a stoical mind—in control of a problematic nervous agitation and irritation. Thomas Carlyle perceived this even in the aged Southey who visited him in London:

> . . . I had a good deal of talk with him, in the circle of the others; and had again more than once to notice the singular readiness of the blushes; amiable red blush, beautiful like a young girl's, when you touched genially

the pleasant theme; and serpent-like flash of blue or black blush (this far, very far, the rarer kind, though it did recur too) when you struck upon the opposite. All details of the evening, except that primary one, are clean gone; but the effect was interesting, pleasantly stimulating and surprising. I said to myself, 'How has this man contrived, with such a nervous system, to keep alive for near sixty years? Now blushing under his grey hairs, rosy like a maiden of fifteen; now slaty almost, like a rattle-snake or fiery serpent? How has he not been torn to pieces long since, under such furious pulling this way and that? He must have somewhere a great deal of methodic virtue in him; I suppose, too, his heart is thoroughly honest, which helps considerably!'[10]

One expression that Geoffrey Carnall includes in his excellent book (*CA* p. 12, from *LC* I, p. 23) on Southey's political development, describes the poet's character-to-be (gleaned from an astrological prediction) whose keynote is 'a gloomy capability of walking through desolation'. We might add this to Carlyle's account. It is a note frequently sounded in the poetry when the poet considers himself and humanity or the city, though it is often balanced by Southey's humorous side, giving the impression of a Carlylean tug-of-war. My anthology examines aspects of this gloomily-cheerful walking home, this test of endurance, in the 1790s. The price of old Southey's stoical endurance of the ordeal by text was also spotted by Carlyle, when he and Southey were discussing Shelley some days later:

> At some point of the dialogue I said to Southey, 'a haggard existence that of his.' I remember Southey's pause, and the tone and air with which he answered, 'It is a haggard existence!' His look, at this moment, was unusually gloomy and heavy-laden, full of confused distress;—as if in retrospect of his own existence, and the haggard battle it too had been.[11]

The poet's life was a process of abrasion and erosion by writing—like Walter Scott's heroic efforts to clear his burden of debts after 1826, but beginning much earlier in his career.

Southey's diasparactive quest for home was the result of other pullings-apart, fragmentations in childhood. The youth's fatherlessness is one quality at least which binds him to the other Lakers and, as Malcolm Elwin remarked, Southey had 'no more paternal influence than his fellow poets'.[12] His father was neither a support nor a role-model for the boy, and his death put paid to many problems:

> My father is now in heaven. On Monday week I attended him to the grave. Who knows but my next visit thither may be final—. I ought to have written to you before but the subject was painful and you will excuse me. He had long been declining evident however as this was I still deceived myself. When I passed thro Bath to Oxford I staid at my father's and saw him in his bed—he prest my hand with affection and for the only time in his life blest me . . . To his loss I am resigned. I am even thankful for it when I consider how grevious a burden is a heart opprest by injustice and misfortune . . . I have however resources in my own reflections and solitude I have never found irksome—one book succeeds another. I take the pen for relaxation and at least possess negative happiness. (*NL* I, p. 12. Bristol, 26 December 1792)

Yet the expression of 'negative happiness' surfaced in the Southeyan poetics of the lost son, the wanderer (clutching his pen, his books) without a father, looking to father-figures to remake the fragmented home. Southey's own sense of the dramatic fully supported this wandering posture, convinced of its rightness and the eventual goal of its desires:

> Amid the pelting of the pitiless storm did I, Robert Southey, the Apostle of Pantisocracy, depart from the city of Bristol, my natal place—at the hour of five in a wet

windy evening on the 17th of October, 1794, wrapped up
in my father's old greatcoat and my own cogitations.[13]

Southey had to assume very quickly his 'father's old greatcoat'
which enveloped him in the comfortless folds of absence. The
lost son, dressed in a dead man's clothes, thrust out from
acceptance and respectability on to the road. This incident
could serve very simply as a metaphor of his life in the
chronology of this study.

In the epigraph above, I quoted a passage from Southey's
Hymn to the Penates of 1796, which tells how the worship of
domestic gods began through the erection of an idol to the lost
son. This enshrinement of the dead prodigal in the heart of a
household, as the founding point of the rites of domesticity, is
a dramatic emblem of Southey's own relationship to his father.
The image of the offending slave garlanding the statue, causing
the softening remembrance in the father, is brimful of
Southey's lack.

'Syrophanes'[14] though, at least in the Southey poem, is at
the centre of an anti-idyll, childless, wealthless, an inversion
of Southey's own family story, the father mourning the son.
He would have liked to have been mourned by his poor ruined
father, and to make his re-appearance into the arms of the
family. But because the father was gone, domesticity, something else to love, becomes the goal:

> Racked between the *father* (cadaverous *body*, arousing to
> the point of defaecation) and *death* (empty *axis*, stirring
> to the point of transcendence), a man has a hard time
> finding something else to love. He could hardly venture
> in that direction unless he were confronted with an
> undifferentiated woman, tenacious and silent . . . This
> will then be the only love . . . *banishment-love*.[15]

My anthology is, it goes without saying, another 'thrust to
unity' (McFarland, ibid., p. xi) whose 'necessary complement'
is the murderous dissection of a life.[16] The ceaseless movement

of desire, almost halted at Westbury, begins with the confrontation in the drama of banishment love of that 'undifferentiated woman' Southey's 'Ariste' and superimposed upon her, the retrospective and prospective story of home, poetic style and literary reputation.

NOTES

1. *The Year's Work in English Studies* Vol. 70 (Oxford: Basil Blackwell, 1989), p. 406.

2 Marilyn Butler, 'Repossessing the Past: The Case for an Open Literary History', in *Rethinking Historicism*, ed. Levinson, Butler, McGann and Hamilton (Oxford: Basil Blackwell, 1989), p. 82.

3 Kenneth Currey, *Southey* (London: Routledge and Kegan Paul, 1975), p. 20.

4 Keith Feiling, *Sketches in Nineteenth Century Biography* (London: Longmans, Green & Co., 1930), pp. 73–74.

5 Butler, *op. cit.*, p. 74.

6 Marilyn Butler, 'Plotting the Revolution: The Political Narratives of Romantic Poetry and Criticism', in *Romantic Revolutions: Criticism and Theory* (Bloomington: Indiana University Press, 1990), p. 137.

7 Thomas McFarland, *Romanticism and the Forms of Ruin* (Princeton: Princeton University Press, 1981).

8 Harold Bloom, *The Anxiety of Influence* (London, Oxford and New York: Oxford University Press, 1975).

9 McFarland, *op. cit.*, p. 5.

10 *Reminiscences*, ed. J. A. Froude, 2 vols (London: Longmans, Green & Co., 1881), Vol. 2, appendix, p. 317.

11 *Ibid.*, pp. 325–26.

12 Malcolm Elwin, *The First Romantics* (London: Methuen, 1947), p. 95.

13 Quoted in *ibid.*, p. 125.

14 The story of Syrophanes may be found in *Fulgentius, The Mythographer*, trans. from the Latin, with introductions, by George Whitehead (Columbuso: Ohio State University Press, 1971), p. 48:

> He was devoted to his son, heir to vast wealth, with an affection beyond words, beyond anything required of a father; and when the son was taken from him by a bitter blow of fate, the announcement of

a double bereavement for the father left him cruelly stricken, in that the perpetual support of offspring had been denied him and he had met an unexpected check to the further expanding of his wealth. What use to him now was either his prosperity as a father, now condemned to barrenness, or delightful possessions, now curtailed of succession? . . . Then, in the grip of grief which always endeavours to relieve its need, he set up an effigy of his son in his household . . . for he did not realize that forgetting is the true healer of distress . . . This is called an idol, that is *idos dolu*, which in Latin we call appearance of grief.

The story also appeared in John Gower's *Confessio Amantis: The Complete Works of John Gower*, 4 vols, ed. G. C. Macaulay (Oxford: Clarendon, 1899–1902), Works in English, Vol. II, 1901, p. 444ff, where the statue is 'sette . . . in the market place', rather than the home.

15 Julia Kristeva, *Desire in Language*, trans. Leon S. Roudiez, ed. T. Gora, A. Jardine and L. S. Roudiez (Oxford: Basil Blackwell, 1989), p. 149: 'what the banished man needs most from a woman is simply someone to accompany him into Death's void'. *Ibid.*, p. 152.

16 McFarland, *op. cit.*, p. xl.

Chapter One

Janus in a Claude-Glass: Southey's *The Retrospect*

When the first emotions of despair have subsided, and sorrow has softened into melancholy, she amuses with a retrospect of innocent pleasures, and inspires that noble confidence which results from the consciousness of having acted well.[1]

I have lately read the Man of Feeling—if you have never yet read it— do it now from my recommendation—few books have ever pleased me so painfully or so much—it is very strange that man should be delighted with the highest pain that can be produced—I even begin to think that pain and pleasure exist only in idea but this must not be affirmed, the first twitch of the toothache or retrospective glance will undeceive me with a vengeance.[2]

1
Critical Débuts: The Posture of Melancholy

No modern critic, as far as I know, has ever made a full-length study of *The Retrospect*. In various ways it has parallels with Wordsworth's *An Evening Walk*, published in 1793. Both poems are addressed to young women, in heroic couplets, and set out memories of youth within familiar landscapes informed by other writings. What Stephen Gill says of Wordsworth's poem goes equally well for Southey's:

Melancholy reflection on past and present, the lament for past joys, the mind accordant to the promptings of Nature, the address to an absent loved one—these are such common tropes of later eighteenth-century poetry that one suspects Wordsworth conceived of the poem's dominant tone just by turning the leaves of his favourite authors. But one has to recognize, too, that no matter how much was poetical stock-in-trade, the poem does bring into focus what were currently the most painful and inchoate aspects of Wordsworth's life.[3]

Wordsworth looks to authors of the Picturesque to valorize what he was already profoundly familiar with, and claimed (*WP* I, p. 318) that there was 'not an image in it which I have not observed'. Southey imitates the retrospective poetry of the time to buttress his own experience, to legitimize the début of his personal life as poetry. Wordsworth links sensibility and Memory much in the same way that Southey would:

> While, Memory at my side, I wander here,
> Starts at the simplest sight th' unbidden tear . . .
> (*WP* I, p. 6, ll. 43–44)

The movement of *An Evening Walk* runs from the avowed pains of memory through a conflated, if finely observed, picturesque tour of the Lakeland, to a vision (*WP* I, p. 36, l. 407) of 'Hope' enshrined in an emblem of domesticity, the cottage (*WP* I, p. 38, l. 416), 'Sole bourn, sole wish, sole object of my way'. Southey anticipates domestic bliss with his new bride. Both poets look to domesticity as a goal, though the final points of the poems, Southey's 'love' (*The Retrospect*, p. 15) and Wordsworth's 'lonely hound' (*WP* I, p. 38, l. 445) are, in terms of mood, very different *places* indeed. Southey's landscape is not the rugged and 'idealized' (*WP* I, p. 319) mountainous region of Wordsworth's poem, but a more intimate episode which is revisited compulsively. Wordsworth comes close in the early part of his poem to the revisiting desire of *The Retrospect*:

> Return Delights! with whom my road begun,
> When Life rear'd laughing up her morning sun;
> When Transport kiss'd away my April tear,

'Rocking as in a dream the tedious year;'
When link'd with thoughtless mirth I cours'd the plain,
And hope itself was all I knew of pain.
For then, ev'n then, the little heart would beat
At times, while young Content forsook her seat,
And wild Impatience, panting upward show'd
Where tipp'd with gold the mountain summits glow'd.
(*WP* I, p. 6, ll. 26–36)

The above passage may be compared with the opening lines of Southey's poem and to other points within. And this is how *The Retrospect* is usually left, as an example of a fashion, a footnote only. In 1795, however, the volume of *Poems: Containing the Retrospect, Odes, Elegies, Sonnets, &c.* by Southey and Lovell drew some critical interest. No less than five Reviews ran articles on the book, and *The English Review* mentioned it both in March *and* May. Their writers did not approve of undergraduates printing poetry at all, and damned *The Retrospect* in March (pp. 232–33) for lack of originality:

> Nothing, indeed, argues so incontestably a defective imagination as the poverty of language appearing in the frequent recurrence of the same words and phrases . . . The author is fond of alliteration . . . but we do not approve of 'the bright brown boarded hall.'

In May they also sneered alliteratively (p. 391) at Southey's sonnets to his prospective bride Edith Fricker: 'for if Ariste is a girl of taste, she will certainly reject the suit of such a sorry sonneteer as the writer of the first three sonnets'. *The Critical Review* of April 1795 found that *The Retrospect* lacked novelty (p. 420) because it followed the well-beaten poetical motif of the adult visiting the scenes of youth, and Thomas Holcroft in *The Monthly Review* of July thought Southey's verses frequently exhibited 'the vice of despondency'. All was not lost, however. *The Analytical Review* for February 1795 (p. 179) was, restrainedly, in approval:

> The general character both of the sentiments and lan-
> guage are purity, and simplicity; the versification is
> harmonious; and the general air of classical elegance runs
> through the pieces, sufficient to prove, that the authors
> have been no strangers to the ancient models. So much of
> the plaintive and tender is dispersed throughout these
> poems, that the authors are justified in assuming the
> signatures of Bion and Moschus.

At least the authors were classically educated. Southey's odes,
they said, marked him out as the better poet. Later, in August,
the *British Critic* found (p. 185) that their compositions were
'chaste, harmonious, and correct' and quoted from *The
Retrospect*, but thought erroneously that Lovell had written
most of the poems in the volume. It is interesting (*RO*, pp. 22–
23) that Southey had drawn praise from *The Analytical*
(founded in 1788), whose opinions were 'more radical both in
politics and religion than any other journal' *and* the *British
Critic* launched in May 1793, canvassed by Tory churchmen
and 'backed by the subscriptions of well-wishers and by Pitt's
secret-service money'.

According to these Reviews then, there was in 1795 a taste
for the mingling of classical material with the well-used
innovations of sensibility. This, it seems to me, is one reason
for choosing to examine *The Retrospect* in its original form.
Though to us it *is* a derivative and affected piece, it is of further
interest because it is the earliest long poem in Southey's work
to set out autobiographical concerns which run up to 1799 at
least. For any reader of Romantic discourse, this poem
demonstrates clearly the major poetic influences of a young
poet in the mid-1790s. It is almost a cultural index for the
composer of verse of that time.

The Retrospect is Southey's first published major poem, an
unstable mixture of melancholy and love, finally seeking the
stability of a new home. Autobiographical passages set into its
structure make up an early survey of a poet upon the quest for

home, questing through the dangerous manipulation of memory. Here, fashionable retrospects and compulsions of repetition seem to the cynical reader mere poses and to the post-Freudian reader consolatory actions of loss. The homeless poet (through the ventriloquism of Bion the pastoral poet) effects his selective harrowing of memory to bring the future under control. I want to retain Freud's picture of the child in the cot here as a useful model of a troubled individual making an act of control and in effect playing with the boundaries of its personal world. If this may be translated into adult terms, we might apply the model interestingly here to Southey's compulsive poeticizing of the past and the present, the neurotic anxiety about his *place* in the world, his vision of home. *The Retrospect* gives us a glimpse of his creed, an ideology of home. His big gamble with the poem lies in this hallucinatory play factor, this fashionable (and therefore mutable) demand for attention.

The poem itself poses some difficulties, because of its thematic variety. Can Southey the man appear for serious consideration (as he attempts to) through the prosopopeia of 'Bion'? In innovator's terms, does the dressing-up (of moments of pleasure, crisis, love and fracture) in 'atavistic' (*Woodring* p. 118) post-Popeian heroic couplets devalue their worth? Does the traditional form of the poem act as disguise or burial of emotion? Are the allusive and imitatory passages of the poem merely the act of a fatherless youth dressing up in the old clothes of his poetic fathers, while his own father's death is accorded a brief tear? Could Southey's melancholy stance, his willing self-exposure, be interpreted in part as an active grieving? Some of these questions are the necessary subject of this study.

2
The Work of Mourning, the Scenes of Writing

Southey had written *The Retrospect*[4] by 6 June 1794,[5] and he considered that this poem was (*NL* I, p. 72) the best piece he had ever written. Many of the literary motifs he employed in *The Retrospect* were adapted from the most famous poems of the century, as the critic of the *English Review* for May 1795 (p. 389), pointed out:

> In 'The Retrospect' we are often reminded of Goldsmith's 'Deserted Village,' Rogers' 'Pleasures of Memory,' and Gray's 'Ode on a Distant Prospect of Eton College,' as well as his 'Elegy written in a Country Churchyard' . . . For 'The Pleasures of Memory' we may trace Mr. Southey almost everywhere in 'The Snow' of Rogers.

Of course the *retrospective* qualities of all the above authors were fair game for a young poet learning to write, making out an account of his life, and, in Southey's case, his days at Corston school.[6] His determination to write *fashionably* seemed to some to detract from what was not merely retrospective verse, but a dedication to future love. Holcroft (no lover of the school of Bowles), in *The Monthly Review* Vol. 17, for July 1795 said:

> We particularly object to a certain woe-begone and debilitating affectation of fine feeling . . . a propensity to bewail instead of to remedy misfortune has too long been supposed a test of superiority of mind, and of uncommon delicacy of sentiment. (p. 355)

Yet we could say that Southey was seeking a 'remedy' in *The Retrospect*, through a faith in refound domesticity and love. The poem delves backwards into the past, where lurk fracture, loss and pain mingled with resonantly pleasurable memories (though memory is a 'torturer', l. 276), and the poem proposes a future where happiness in love is expected. Thus it appears to act as a kind of literary threshold, it is Janus-headed, looking before and behind, and fittingly, under the eyes of that god, marks a new beginning.

Retrospection was evidently a feature of the 'college gloom' (p. 13) of Balliol, as Southey locates the poem in 'Oxford 1794' (*PW* II, p. 270) where he is not surveying the general aspect of the world with a wide historical vision, as had Johnson, but selectively turning to survey his formative memories. *The Retrospect* is certainly what Mary Jacobus (*JAC* p. 113) calls a ' "revisit" poem—the most popular elegiac vehicle of the period'. Yet the poem which initially invokes a display of 'memory', seems to end with a longing for escape from certain memories of fracture. The poem itself breaks off, or turns away from the past at the very moment when the past (seen as a storm) rises to annihilate the voice of 'Bion'.

Christopher Salvesen[7] draws attention to the word 'retrospect' as used by William Gilpin in 1770[8] to describe the act of surveying the landscape just quitted by the picturesque traveller-tourist, often with the aid of a Claude glass. The act of retrospection, in the rational (and highly selective) search for a formula of harmony, when metaphorically applied to the poeticizing of the memory, borrows the language of the picturesque. From the Bristol Library records, we know that Southey was familiar with some of Gilpin's work by 1793 (*WH* p. 117), and presumably the Wye tour, with its comments on the area of Bristol,[9] was also known to him. In *The Retrospect*, Southey's dependence upon what we could loosely call picturesque attitudes and language applied to the self, appears to founder. The selective control over the visual promised by such as Gilpin breaks down and the poet becomes impatient of wilfully looking back, being tormented by memory. The spectator of his own past runs the danger of becoming a spectator in his own past, menaced by it as well as gaining pleasure from it. Southey's picturesque tour of the self does not seem to synthesize past and present, but contem-

plates the painful gap between time present and time past. It is
in the un-Gilpinesque details that the dangers lurk. Southey
appears to have produced a picture of a fragmented self, or
selves, in the attempt at autobiographical unity.

The autobiographical parts of the poem[10] reveal both a
distaste for authority and an avowed faith in love. If these are
typical concerns of youth, what is untypical here is that
Southey took the trouble to publish this long poem and revise
it for inclusion in the final edition of his poetical works. He
refers to himself as 'Bion'[11] in the poem, dedicating it to
'Ariste', Edith Fricker (see NL I, p. 86, note 2), to whom he
was engaged as early as spring 1794 (NL I, p. 194), and he goes
on to describe 'Alston',[12] which is his name for the village
of Corston outside Bath. At Corston, the seven-year-old
Southey had spent a year at school in 1781, and this place is
reflected in the glass of memory.

To The Retrospect is prefixed a quotation from William
Bowles.[13] Southey had a copy of Bowles' poetry by 13 April
1794, transcribed by 'a friend' (NL I, pp. 52–53) who is not
named—perhaps this 'friend' was a friend of Coleridge, who
appeared in June of 1794 in Oxford. Perhaps Coleridge had
sent Allen, his contemporary from Christ's Hospital, now at
Oxford, a copy of Bowles' work in advance? Whatever the
answer to this might be, Bowles' poem, To a Friend largely
summarizes The Retrospect and Southey pursues two main
Bowlesian themes of sensibility from this sonnet; the journey
of life and the comfort gained from poetry. Memory, feeling
and place are therefore rapidly mixed together.

Southey's poem is an apostrophe to memory, where the
poet, looking at his own past, recognizes the force of the
fracture between what is and what was. He is fascinated by the
distance and the strangeness between (at least) four worlds
emergent in the poem (Southey and Corston as they were, and
Southey and Corston as they are) and seeks for some control
over these coordinates by writing. The struggle to associate
himself with his memories also becomes a determination to

inure himself to, or flee from, those areas of painful experience in childhood which threaten the present. The heroic couplets clothe the 'da' ('there') of memory in a reliable and familiar structure. They are almost a valedictory gesture to the school of Pope. And as I have already noted, their subject-matter indicates Southey's ear for fashion.

In 1792 Samuel Rogers had published his immensely successful *The Pleasures of Memory*, in which reflection and memory (set in heroic couplets) combine to produce a pleasantly melancholy effect. Rogers' fashionable model of memory is a sentimental faculty switched on or off at will, and does not possess that 'autonomous urgency' or 'compulsive emotion' of response to the past later displayed by such as Wordsworth,[14] and where Rogers' quiet melancholy is soothing and untroubled, Southey's confessional poem somewhere in the middle of these poles, boldly dressed in its apophradic cast-offs, is the scarecrow of memory, the spectre of his heart.

Within *The Retrospect* Southey depicts himself as the traveller, the wanderer seeking the home that was (and the home that is to be), travelling through his past, a past before (and after) grief appeared making necessary the controlling relief found in poetry. 'Reflection and misery are with me the same' (*NL* I, p. 40), claimed the youth back in December 1793, thinking over the seemingly impossible *prospect* before him—the war, family troubles—he thought his mother was going to die, he even believed that he was about to go mad. The discrepancy between what he wanted the world to be like and what his personal world had become,[15] shows in part why *The Retrospect* was written: it helped in the attempt to order and control the past, and even to deaden the pain of loss. If we regard the poem as an active gesture of unloading, a restoration of health in hope, we might agree with Freud[16] that 'when the work of mourning is completed the ego becomes free again'. Southey's active grief over a poor and empty world is poeticized through his own melancholia which travels towards that freedom.

The poem's beginning includes a paragraph (pp. 3–4) of Thomsonian landscape, dawn breaking upon the 'pilgrim' as the dawn of life breaks upon the child. It evokes the 'prospect' of life, as if the life-journey were a painting about to be planned out by reason. Memory wields a 'vivid pencil'[17] (p. 3), after the inadequate delicacy of the picturesque. Southey dedicates memory's 'pensive song' (p. 4) to 'ARISTE' (Gk. 'the best or noblest one'), who appears later in several sonnets of the 1795 volume. He portrays himself as her 'minstrel'[18] and calls Edith 'the mistress of my future days' (p. 3), making the poem at once a mixture of memory and love. The fashionable melancholy of retrospection is therefore quickly undermined in the poem and memory is presented as a gift of the self to a prospective bride.

Mary Jacobus (*JAC* p. 113, note 3) states that both Southey and Rogers 'draw on Goldsmith's method to lament change within themselves rather than a village'. This is true, but Southey's fascination with the lost scenic coordinates of place lays stress upon the provocative importance of the objective site lying in wait for him as if it were a disfigured text. The changes are both inside and outside. In Goldsmith's *The Traveller* (subtitled 'A Prospect of Society')[19] we encounter what would become a key Southeyan theme in *The Retrospect* and in other poems. Goldsmith's dedication to Auburn (Lissoy in Ireland) in *The Deserted Village* is emulated by Southey in his apostrophe to 'Alston'. Southey avoids imitation of Goldsmith's politics, favouring instead an imitation of the homely vignettes of the schoolmaster and the mansion. Rogers' poem also follows Goldsmith in exploring the past:

> The Poem begins with the description of an obscure village, and of the pleasing melancholy which it excites on being revisited after a long absence. This mixed sensation is an effect of the Memory. (Rogers p. v)

Southey's retrospective observations reach for these feelings of 'pleasing melancholy' but focus upon the 'opening mind'

(p. 4) and the bittersweet associations of place at the village school in Corston. Rogers' description of the rational associative quality of memory which binds the individual to local and personal points of experience, seems to stress the gentle pleasures of memory rather than the possibility of the individual finding himself caught between the wreckage of the past and the incomprehensibility of the present and the future. And *The Retrospect*, like *The Pleasures of Memory*, is not a stridently political poem, because, as Freud[20] says: 'pathological distrust of rulers and monarchs' is 'repressed at times when compassion for parents is active—at times of their illness or death'. Politics and the work of mourning are not brought together, but political hostility is put away under the cloak of melancholy.

The posture of melancholy found in *The Retrospect* is the shadow of the poet's nervous problems, which would have found any associative transferral difficult. Southey's sensibility was excitable and problematic, but he dealt with excesses of feeling by trying to develop a stoical mind and immersing himself in writing. His continual recommendation of Epictetus,[21] whom he began reading in 1793, played no small part in his coping with feelings about death, friendship and the growing sense of alienation in England. The war with France in 1793, following hard on the heels of Southey's expulsion from Westminster in 1792, lent bad associations to his life at this time, as he was a French sympathizer and had republican views. This feeling persisted with him until the Peace of Amiens in 1802, of which he said:

> It restored in me the English feeling which had been deadened; it placed me in sympathy with my country, bringing me thus into that natural and healthy state of mind upon which time, and knowledge, and reflection were sure to produce their proper and salutary effect. (W III, p. 320)

The Retrospect actively seeks out a formulation of 'that natural and healthy state of mind', in adverse times. The poem was prompted by a visit to Corston in 1793 (*Simmons* p. 14, and *LC* I, p. 46). Southey returned again when he was 62 years old in 1836, to show his son Cuthbert the area, which indicates the haunting attraction this period of his past had for him. Life at Corston, as shown in the poem, included unpleasant moments, but the child was essentially happy in its little world. The schoolhouse itself, the 'mansion' that once held the quasi-chivalric world of the squire and his pack of hounds, was now ruled by the despotism of reason in the form of the schoolmaster who arrives to succeed him:

> For now, in petty greatness o'er the school,
> The mighty master held despotic rule:
> With trembling silence all his deeds we saw,
> His look a mandate, and his word a law;
> Severe his voice, severely grave his mien,
> And wond'rous strict he was, and wond'rous wise, I
>   ween. (p. 6)

Southey, in his first allusive 'da' (there is the absent past), borrowed contentedly from one of his poetic fathers, recalls the famous picture of the village schoolmaster in Goldsmith's *The Deserted Village*.[22] The schoolmaster figure had a special significance for the poet at this time. Two years earlier he had been expelled from Westminster (a factual suppression here) for his article on flogging as an invention of the Devil in the magazine *The Flagellant*. Southey spent some time setting down his thoughts about this incident in doggerel verse, as the following example shows from 30 December 1792, just before he went to Balliol:

> Exild from Westminster is Southey seen
> Expelld from school rejected by the Dean—
> & shall I strive the glorious truth to hide
> Which conscience owns & only owns with pride?

True I attacked the beastly rod & true
Held horrible indecency to view
But Satan feard Ithuriels potent touch
And Power as usual provd for Right too much—
Power held the sevenfold shield to Dulness head
I am expelld the Flagellant is dead
Christ Church rejects as though the itch possest
But Baliol takes & Basil is at rest.
Nor I alone in this eventful year
Of wicked libels and sedition hear
To hope that Truth would shelter me how vain
When Truth & Eloquence both faild for Paine!
                    (Bodleian MSS. Eng. Letters, c. 22, f. 41)

I quote this passage at length because it provides an insight into the young man's faith in his own rectitude. He rarely questions the appropriateness of his actions, or considers the possibility of holding back his opinions. He links his rebellious schoolboy deeds[23] with the experiences of Paine who had fled arrest in 1792 after *The Rights of Man* had been published.

In the above passage Southey was playing with ideas of his own persecution, and allying himself with republicanism, already having cause to mistrust figures of power, be they schoolmasters, lords or politicians. He articulates power-struggles in the language of another poetic father. Here Milton's angel and Satan are combatants in what is for Southey a black and white case, Truth against Untruth. He had acted well against authority. He links together power-figures and the theme of loss, of leaving his home (p. 6) in *The Retrospect*. Separation from home and from the weeping mother, the child's idea of truth and stability, forms a compound emotion of pain transferred eventually into blame put upon the new figures of authority.

The pain which is felt when we are first transplanted from our native soil—when the living branch is cut from the parent tree—is one of the most poignant which we have

to endure through life. There are after-griefs which
wound more deeply, which leave behind them scars
never to be effaced, which bruise the spirit, and sometimes break the heart: but never, never do we feel so
keenly the want of love, the necessity of being loved, and
the sense of utter desertion, as when we first leave the
haven of home, and are, as it were, pushed off upon the
stream of life.[24]

So it is that Southey (p. 6) began to regard his life as a series of
expulsions, beginning with one most painful expulsion, being
sent to a boarding school nine miles from Bristol, and looks to
the day when he can arrest this process by creating the security
of a home. He represents the 'mistress' and 'master' of the
school as counterfeit parents who betray the child's naive
trust, and connects this betrayal with the child's tearful
farewell (p. 7) to his father implicating him in this bad
moment. Memory becomes a kind of pleasurable pain, which
the poet yet prefers to the immediate situation:

> Ill fares the wanderer in this vale of life,
> When each new stage affords succeeding strife;
> In every stage he feels supremely curst
> Yet still the present evil seems the worst:
> On as he goes the vision'd prospect flies
> And, grasping still at bliss, unblest at last he dies.
> (pp. 7–8)

This little pretend death yields to echoes of Gray's *Ode on a
Distant Prospect of Eton College* in the next stanza (ll. 115–
24), where Southey sees the days of childhood fraught with
petty worries, which remain as such until the dawn of reason
in the child. Reason's 'saddening power' (p. 8) gives an
increasing and distressful understanding of time. Southey,
echoing Gray's famous lines, looks back with some fondness
(p. 8) upon the time 'When even ignorance was happiness'.
Gray's fatherly presence leads to the second 'da' of the poem.

Recalling the pictures of the school's routine at Corston, such as the morning wash in the nearby brook, or the picking of fruit, provoked Southey into an imitation of Bowles.[25] In a letter of 13 April 1794 (*NL* I, p. 52), he tells Bedford that he has passed the brook where at school he used to perform his ablutions. He quotes Bowles' sonnet *To the River Itchin near Winton* and speaks of the 'pleasing melancholy' that childhood memories give. Bowles' poem finds sorrow and pleasure joined in the river scene, like being parted from and reunited with a friend, and he considers the passing of time and the passing of the hopes and dreams of youth, which bring to mind the faces of lost companions. Later in November 1794 Southey follows up Bowles' idea in a letter to Horace Walpole Bedford (*NL* I, p. 87) when he writes out his own sonnet, *To a Brooklet near Alston*. This poem appears in a different form, called simply *Corston*, in the final edition of his poems. In the letter, Southey has been enthusing over Bowles' poetry whilst longing for the scheme of emigration to America to be realized, itself just outside the chronology of *The Retrospect*:

> As thus I bend me oer thy babbling stream
> And watch thy current Memory's hand pourtrays
> The faint-formd scenes of the departed days,
> Like the far forest by the moons pale beam
> Dimly descried yet lovely. I have worn
> Upon thy banks the livelong hour away
> When sportive childhood wantond thro the day
> Joyed at the opening splendour of the morn
> Or as the evening darkend heard the sigh
> Thinkd of distant home, as down my cheek
> At the fond thought slow-stealing on would speak
> The silent eloquence of the full eye.
> Dim are the long-past days—yet still they please
> As thy soft sounds half heard borne on the inconstant breeze.
> (Bodleian MSS. Eng. Letters, c. 22, f. 136)

The connections between this poem and *The Retrospect* are obviously strong (Southey mentions both poems together, *NL* 1, p. 87), as the sonnet uses 'Memory' to reanimate the past. The simple picture of the animated 'brooklet', symbolizing the fledgling world and the fledgling mind, is made romantic by likening these memories to 'the far forest by the moons pale beam / Dimly descried but lovely' or to 'thy soft sounds half heard'. Southey's alliterative and yearning phrases 'faint-formd', 'far forest', 'dimly descried', 'distant home', would suggest that although here he is essentially talking about the past, thoughts of the present and the future (the Janus-headed threshold) fill the sonnet. The idyll of the brook, containing stasis and movement, sets up by its lachrymose and oxymoronic 'silent eloquence' a yearning for completeness or closure. Southey's longing for 'home' babbles constantly in his mind like the play of memory set in the sounds of the stream 'borne on the inconstant breeze'.

Within *The Retrospect* he views these 'trifling pastimes' (p. 8) as memories which compose his character, which 'still remain imprest'. He illustrates this idea, the organic growth of the mind, with an appropriate simile of the 'rustic hind' (p. 9) who carves 'the rude legend' in the bark of a tree and lives on to watch the letters expand. This picture is itself buried in the centre of the poem at the halfway point. Like Corston the revisited place of memory, the inscription marks a point in time, but grows away from that time, a distorted reminder of the moment of inscription. The letters remain deep in the trunk of the tree, surviving the storms and winters that besiege it.[26] Memory endures like the inscription, though its absolute presence is never guaranteed because the action alone of the poetic 'fort/da' of wilful retrospection casts its cotton-line through layers and coordinates of other memories. The past cannot step out clean. Nevertheless, he expresses his introspection as a determined Grand Tour of the mind, his own past:

Whilst letter'd travellers delight to roam,
The time-torn temple and demolish'd dome;
Stray with the Arab o'er the wreck of time,
Where erst Palmyra's towers arose sublime;
Or mark the lazy Turk's lethargic pride,
And Grecian slavery on Illyssus' side:
Oh! be it mine to flee from empire's strife,
And mark the changes of domestic life;
See the fall'n scenes where once I bore my part,
Where every change of fortune strikes the heart.

Southey validates his own landscape of memory in contrast with the romantic eastern vistas. His own 'wreck of time'[27] assumes an importance parallel with exotic grandeur, a kind of living inscription like the peasant's tree. He turns (pp. 9–10) from the classical east to the landscape of home, the 'fall'n scenes' which he links with friends fallen in war.[28] He implies that warfare (promoted by the great), in its very largeness and impersonality, runs against nature, or at least that nature which binds communities of friends and relatives together. Threading his own wreck of time, Southey contrasts the monuments of the great and famous (p. 10) such as the Gothic tombs of heroes, kings[29] and minstrels, castles and convents, with the area around his 'Alston'. The third 'da' of the past is a direct apostrophe to place:

Yet never had my bosom felt such pain
As, ALSTON, when I saw thy scenes again!
For every long-lost pleasure rush'd to view,
For every long-past sorrow rose anew;
Where whilome all were friends, I stood alone,
Unknowing all I saw, of all I saw unknown. (p. 10)

Alston reappears, like the 'expanded legend' on the peasant's tree. Southey's mind acts as the connecting 'tree' in the chain of memory, the (painful) 'fort/da' jerking the poet back into a past-as-present. 'Alston' (p. 176ff) is a place of sacred pilgrimage along the track of memory. Childhood at 'Alston' is a picture of exuberant summer (p. 10), where the boy runs in play with a democracy of 'equals'—that very play which had been denied to the young Southey by his imperious aunt Tyler and her phobias (*Simmons* p. 11) of dirt.

But the last sight of 'Alston' appropriately enough is on a cold morning in winter when the poet exclaims: 'It seemed as tho' the world were chang'd, like me!' Both 'Bion' and Corston have changed, and spectral memories play across the present world, setting up an imbalance vital to the melancholy frisson of the poem. Alienation proceeds from the wreck of time. As with the hind's inscription, both inside and upon the bark of the tree (both are distorted by time), the world of child's play in memory fails to give back an objective presence. The past is never *there* in reality, the 'da' always strung along with 'fort' in the act of versification. Southey's little retrospective vignettes now become mixtures of 'there' and 'gone', reversing the game of 'fort/da' into 'da/fort', or even superimposing the action into 'there/not-there in gone/not-gone'. This mixing and blurring of sensibility is depicted by the metaphorical play of the child's garden:

> There, where my little hands were wont to rear
> With pride the earliest sallad of the year;
> Where never idle weed to grow was seen,
> There the rank nettle rear'd its head obscene.
> I too have felt the hand of fate severe—
> In those calm days I never knew to fear;
> No future views alarm'd my gloomy breast,
> No anxious pangs my sickening soul possest;
> No grief consum'd me, for I did not know
> Increase of reason was increase of woe. (pp. 11–12).

At this point Southey invokes another poetical father, Shakespeare,[30] in speaking of the metaphorical garden of weeds, which signifies the present state of the poet's melancholy mind. Southey's 'rank nettle' underlines the adverse soil upon which ideas of worldly permanence or even comfort, struggle for growth. Even the poet's own garden rejects him, turns him out into the homeless world with only echoes and pains of nostalgia for comfort—what the child took for granted as permanence, the adult now (p. 12) perceives as transience and ruin, a 'fall'n dwelling'. And yet the *spot* still yields its little pictures of the past around the ever-moving stream:

> Once more my soul delighted to survey
> The brook that murmured on its wonted way;
> Obedient to the master's dread commands,
> Where every morn we wash'd our face and hands;
> Where, when the tempest raged along the air,
> I wont to rear the dam with eager care;
> And eft and aye return'd with joy to find
> The neighbouring orchard's fruit shook down by war-
> ring wind.

Southey charts the known history of the house at Corston as a background for his own personal history. 'How art thou chang'd!' he exclaims, addressing the house as if he were also addressing himself in a mirror. The riotous squire and his huntsmen cede the house to reason and learning, then it becomes a farmhouse where Southey hopes (pp. 12–13) the labourer will experience 'joys domestic'. The farmer represents the virtues of the simple life and values enshrined at the heart of the imminent American scheme. Southey or 'Bion' bids 'Alston' farewell here (p. 13), leaving the past and perhaps the future in the farmer's hands. Southey's 'fort/da' games of verse-memory seek for the closure of 'fort' and the reclamation of 'now':

> Seat of my earlier, happier years, farewell!
> Thy memory still in BION'S breast shall dwell:
> Still as he journeys life's rough road along,
> Or sojourns sad, this college gloom along,

Will fond remembrance paint those careless days,
When all he wish'd was speedy holy days!

The persona of *The Retrospect* is a mixture: a Greek ghost, the
weary traveller, and the pensive Oxford scholar yearning for the
bitter-sweet days of childhood. 'Alston' is seen as a kind of
child-Eden (pp. 13–14) from which the child was naively glad to
escape, and having done so, it becomes the point of entry into
the world of care. To emphasize this Southey links departure
from Corston or 'Alston' (in 1781) with his father's death:

I knew not even the comfort of a tear
O'er a beloved father's timeless bier;
His clay-cold limbs I saw the grave inclose,
And blest that fate which snatch'd him from his woes.[31]

His father died in 1792, when the boy was eighteen, just after
he had been denied a place at Christ Church, because of his
expulsion from Westminster, and had managed to matriculate
at Balliol. This chronological leap within the poem marks
another incident of fracture[32] in the poet's life and looks to the
premature closure of the poem. The theme of expulsion runs
through *The Retrospect* and the poet continues in this vein
even as late as 1797, when he sets down a poem in which he not
only sees himself as an exile from his father's house, but from
Bristol itself, the perimeter of a larger circle of melancholy
associations.[33]   Southey finishes his retrospective account
with more Thomsonian landscape, the 'cheerful pilgrim'
amongst woods and fountains, an idyll which is then broken
up by a sublimely fierce storm. The pilgrim becomes the
'mariner' waiting for oblivion, but cheered by the lights that
signal rescue. Thus the final point of the poem is another
departure, another dedication to 'ARISTE', or to love itself
and, of course, hope in love. 'Ariste' signifies the future and
the possibility of domestic bliss, which Southey appears to
believe will break the pattern of expulsion and sorrow:

ARISTE! so when memory's painful sway
Recalls the sorrow of the distant day;
When the soft soother turns at length to thee,
The gloom disperses, and the shadows flee;
Grief's cankering pangs no more my bosom move,
That beating bosom only bounds to Love.

The Retrospect ends with partial release from the past, even a partial 'release from time'[34] arrived at by way of a dangerous manipulation of memory. But his exploration of the prelusive wreck of time began a process of re-writing and self-recovery which continued well into the next century and which did not lay the ghost of Corston to rest until the poet's own mental decay and death. What has simply been seen as an exercise in literary fashion by some critics haunted Southey's mind for the rest of his life. As a first step upon the quest for home, the poem (like a scarecrow in Southey's field of writing) collects up all the rags of loss and sets them upon the crossed sticks of desire. The melancholy, in its shabbiness, is real enough, being an oblique expression of the difficulty of the youth's attempt at reconciliation with the past. Southey's theory in *The Retrospect* is the theory of the self, the mind, the home. It genuflects to the fathers of poetry, not to France, and its politics are the politics of the backward glance rather than the millennial vision, which is the subject of the next chapter.

So *The Retrospect* and indeed most of the work in *Poems* 1795 employs the classical forms and the artistic predilections of the establishment. At the publication of this volume, he and Lovell do court the establishment audience. Southey's avowed republicanism remains well-hidden. If Coleridge had assessed the implications of *The Retrospect* more dispassionately, then he might have perceived the nature of the domestic rather than millennial desires in Southey's ideology of home, but he was deceived. Blinded by his own longings for domesticity, a family circle (theological and theoretical) to which he could affectionately belong, Coleridge placed his own ideological desires over

Southey's fragmentary retrospective autobiography. *The Retrospect* was to him 'a most lovely Poem' (*Griggs* I, p. 133, 11 December 1794) that would in the next edition of Southey's works 'be a perfect one', which also sounds like a desire for the perfecting of his sturdy republican intimate. He enshrined his idea of Southey awkwardly among other worthies, like a Bowlesian-classical bust, in: *To Robert Southey of Baliol College Oxford, Author of 'The Retrospect', and other Poems.* But Southey *had* written like a soulmate, and had touched, not for the first time, an area close to Coleridge's heart:

> But O! more thrill'd, I prize
> Thy sadder strains, that bid in MEMORY'S Dream
> The faded forms of past Delight arise;
> Then soft, on Love's pale cheek, the tearful gleam
> Of Pleasure smiles—as faint yet beauteous lies
> The imag'd Rainbow on a willowy stream. (*CP* p. 87)

Coleridge had his own vision of 'Memory's Dream' and 'past Delight' eventually theorized into Pantisocratic law. Carl Woodring remarks on the more straightforward Southeyan 'happiness' (*The Retrospect* p. 4) and indeed on Southey's whole vehicle of expression:

> Backward glances filled the melancholy air, as in Southey's poem *The Retrospect*, on days 'ere yet I knew Or grief or care, or happiness and you'; but Coleridge found no place for 'happiness and you' until he met the eudemonic ethic in Godwin's version of the greatest-happiness principle. (*Woodring* pp. 45–46)

Woodring underlines the distance between the two men, a distance which was composed of two ideologies, two versions of Pantisocracy, which for a time seemed to run in the same direction. After the crash of theory and ideology which broke Pantisocracy into aspheterists and non-aspheterists, and famously drew from Coleridge in November 1795 his disgust about becoming 'Partners in a petty Farming Trade' (*Griggs* I,

p. 165), another remark surfaced. Coleridge (*Griggs* I, p. 171) bridled at 'those accounts of your Mother & Family, which had drawn easy tears down wrinkled Cheeks'. This, as a rejection of Southey and Southey's relationship to his family, is born of jealousy, but it is also by extension a rejection of the melancholy aspects of such poems as *The Retrospect*, refusing to validate it as a process of grieving, leaving it, in his eyes at least, merely as 'easy tears', an insincere familial picture from his erstwhile friend who had given up Pantisocratic theory, virtue, and Coleridge.

NOTES

1 Samuel Rogers, *The Pleasures of Memory with Some Other Poems*, 5th Edition (London: T. Cadell & C. Dilly, 1793), p. 38 (hereafter 'Rogers').

2 Bodleian MSS. Eng. Letters, c. 22, f. 51, 4 April 1793. It seems to me that Southey's wilful and controlling glances back into the past in *The Retrospect* can be usefully described by the adapted Freudian terms 'fort/da', loosely rendered as 'gone' and 'there'. See Sigmund Freud's *Beyond the Pleasure Principle*, trans. C. J. M. Hubback and ed. Ernest Jones, in *The International Psycho-Analytical Library* No. 4 (London and Vienna: The International Psycho-Analytical Press, 1922), pp. 12–14. By making a game out of memory, as in *The Retrospect*, it is to be wondered to what extent Southey's past constitutes him, and how much of that past is forever sealed away.

3 *William Wordsworth: A Life*, (Oxford: Clarendon, 1989), pp. 42–43.

4 The version of *The Retrospect* under discussion is that found in the volume *Poems: containing The Retrospect, Odes, Elegies, Sonnets & c. by Robert Lovell, and Robert Southey, of Baliol College, Oxford* (Bath: R. Crutwell, 1795), pp. 3–15. *Simmons* (p. 233, note 66) explains that, according to Southey, the poems appeared in the autumn of 1794, despite the title-page dated 1795. I refer to the poem by page numbers.

5 Bodleian MSS. Eng. Letters, c. 22, f. 113.

6 An interesting account of the localities mentioned in many poems by Southey, including those pertinent to *The Retrospect*, may be found in Berta Lawrence's 'Southey And Somerset' in *The Charles Lamb Society Bulletin* New Series, no. 7 (London: Stanhope Press, July 1974), pp. 133–41. She notes that Southey visited the South West in 1836 with his son Cuthbert on a

farewell tour of the scenes of his youth (*W* IV, p. 494). An engraving of the Corston schoolhouse may be found in *PW* vol. II, as a frontispiece, and this, alongside the fact that *The Retrospect* was the only poem salvaged (and re-written) from the volume of *Poems* 1795, stresses its importance to the poet. (In *NL* 1, p. 125 Southey is thinking of including *The Retrospect* in *Poems* 1797, omitting some poems for its sake and correcting it.)

7 Christopher Salvesen, *The Landscape of Memory* (London: E. Arnold, 1970), p. 56.

8 William Gilpin, *Observations On The River Wye* (Richmond: Richmond Publishing Company, 1973), pp. 19, 68 and 92. Derek Roper describes the 1795 *Poems* as 'a slim volume treating picturesque and nostalgic themes in conventional verse'. *RO* p. 101.

9 Gilpin, *op. cit.*, pp. 89–92.

10 'He had, indeed, in early life often contemplated "writing the history of his own mind" ', *LC* I, p. 160. See also *The Wordsworth Circle* Vol. V, No. 2, Spring 1974: 'Southey and the Art of Autobiography' by Michael Staunton, pp. 113–19.

11 In the 1795 volume of poems, Lovell took the pen-name 'Moschus' and Southey 'Bion'. Coleridge's opinion of this device, and of the 1795 *Poems*, may be found in *Griggs* I, pp. 133–35 particularly. Coleridge's aversion to classical names was instilled in him by Boyer at Christ's Hospital (*BL* p. 4), whose preference for the particular object or image in poetry composition obviously had an important effect upon Romantic poetry.

12 The name 'Alston' is of interest in this poem because it suggests Southey's preoccupation with his father's death. Southey's grandmother Hill had relatives who farmed at a place called Ashton (now Long Ashton) and his father was buried in Ashton churchyard. The two names 'Alston' and 'Ashton' seem to indicate a connection. In the Bedford correspondence, there is to be found a monochrome sketch by Southey of the church at Ashton (Bodleian MSS. Eng. Letters, c. 22, f. 29) dated November 1792, and Southey refers to this again in *LC* Vol. III, p. 35, when reconstructing his early life for Bedford.

13 William Bowles, *Sonnets Written Chiefly on Picturesque Spots During a Tour* 2nd edn (Bath: R. Cruttwell, 1789), pp. 9–10 *To A Friend*.

14 Salvesen, *op. cit.*, p. 43.

15 Southey had even made a will in November 1793. Bodleian MSS. Eng. Letters, c. 22, f. 80.

16 *Mourning and Melancholia* in *Collected Papers* by Sigmund Freud, trans. Joan Riviere (London: The Hogarth Press, 1925), Vol. 10, p. 154.

17 Gilpin's language of art is here used to describe the impressions of memory. The pencil sketch aided Gilpin in his quest for the picturesque view, often supplying the general framework and parts of a scene which

could perhaps be reassembled and harmonized later. And Gilpin himself was of course not ignorant of the connections between picturesque detail and poetry itself: 'The maladies of trees are greatly subservient to the uses of the pencil . . . Even the poet will sometimes deign to array his tree with these picturesque ornaments. I am always glad of his authority, . . . and I have seen a poetical oak garnished in a way, that the painter might copy from' (*Remarks On Forest Scenery And Other Woodland Views* Vol. I [London: R. Blamire, 1791]). Southey borrowed this particular volume in 1793 from Bristol library.

18 He had lent Bedford a copy of Beattie's poetry, which included *The Minstrel*, and was asking for them early in 1794. *NL* I, p. 45.

19 *The Poems of Thomas Gray, William Collins, Oliver Goldsmith*, ed. Roger Lonsdale (London: Longman, 1969), p. 565.

20 *The Standard Freud*, trans. James Strachey (London: The Hogarth Press, 1966), Vol. I, pp. 254–55.

21 The following extracts give some idea of the importance of the tenets of Epictetan stoicism for Southey. Epictetus offered him freedom of mind, praise of virtue, abstinence and endurance, and was a tranquil influence:

> Early admiration, almost adoration of Leonidas, early principles of stoicism derived from the habitual study of Epictetus, and the French Revolution at its height when I was just eighteen,—by these my mind was moulded. (*R* II, p. 82, 9 April 1805)

> Twelve years ago I carried Epictetus in my pocket, til my very heart was ingrained with it, as pig's bones become red by feeding him upon madder . . . I am convinced that Stoicism, properly understood, is the best and noblest system of morals. (*W* I, p. 400, December 1806)

> Did you ever read Mrs. Carter's 'Epictetus'? Next to the Bible, it is the best *practitional* book and the truest philosophy in existence. (*W* II, p. 1, 10 April 1807)

> Christian stoicism is wholesome for all minds; were I your confessor, I should enjoin you to throw aside Rousseau, and make Epictetus your manual. (To Landor, 2 May 1808, *LC* I, p. 144)

However, Jean Raimond (*RA*, p. 538) emphasizes that the Christian coloration of Spenser's poetry, beloved by Southey, preceded his reading of Epictetus. As a boy Southey wanted to complete *The Faerie Queen* (*LC* IV, p. 192).

22 *The Poems of Thomas Gray, William Collins, Oliver Goldsmith*, pp. 684–85.

23 Dr Vincent, who had expelled him, ironically enough, was also a contributor (*RO* p. 23) to the *British Critic*.

24 Southey, *Life Of Nelson* (London: Oxford University Press, 1911), pp. 16–17.

25 See *Poems* 1797, p. 112, *To a BROOK near the Village of Corston* (1794). The different aspects of 'Memory' in this sonnet and sonnet number IV (p. 110) may be compared. Sonnet IV describes the faculty of memory as 'Inhuman'. See also Thomas Warton the Younger's sonnet *To the River Lodon*, in *The Three Wartons*, ed. Eric Partridge (London: The Scholartis Press, 1927), p. 129, with its mildly amazed retrospective evocation of memory. Along with Bowles', Warton's influence was formative for Southey.

26 Interestingly, Southey gives the impression that his idea of mental growth carries with it an anxiety about inscripsive life after death, as if the peasant figure had carved a living epitaph. This is borne out by the final revised version of the poem (*PW* II, p. 268) where the 'rude inscription uneffaced will last / Unalter'd by the storm or wintry blast'.

27 He adopts one key phrase from Rogers' poem (my emphasis):

So TULLY paus'd, amid *the wrecks of Time*,
On the rude stone to trace the truth sublime;
When at his feet, in honour'd dust disclos'd,
The immortal Sage of Syracuse repos'd.
(Rogers, p. 25)

28 Coleridge (*CP* p. 65) in his poem *To a Young Lady with a Poem on the French Revolution* of September 1794, adapts a line from *The Retrospect*. Where Southey writes: 'And suffering nature grieve that one should die' (p. 10), Coleridge substitutes 'And suffering Nature wept that *one* should die!' Southey briefly notes how the effects of war (the loss of a friend) blight the news of victory. Coleridge's poem describes the pity he feels on hearing the death-knell of any person, and also the pity he feels for the 'Tyrant' (Robespierre?) cut down by 'Mercy'. Coleridge's poem also speaks of the desire for retreat into virtue. He offered this poem, along with a copy of *The Fall of Robespierre*, to a Miss Brunton (see *Woodring* pp. 62–63). Coleridge, of course, awkwardly enshrined Southey in his Pantheon of heroes and heroines *Sonnets On Eminent Characters* (*CP* pp. 79–90), in a poem (*CP* p. 87) entitled *To Robert Southey of Baliol College, Oxford, Author of the 'Retrospect', and Other Poems*.

29 See *NL* I, p. 34 and note 8: 'Wandering over cathedrals is apt to make me melancholy, but when I tread upon the rotten relics of royalty I feel proud and satisfied'. The republican sentiments here expressed are allied to the general imaginative sense of history possessed by Southey when he writes poetry of place. Politics and the poetry of place are merged in the *Inscriptions*.

30 Southey recalls *Hamlet* I, ii, ll. 135–36: 'Fie on't! O fie! 'tis an

unweeded garden, / That grow to seed; things rank and gross in nature / Possess it merely'.

31 This passage may be compared with one from Wordsworth's juvenilia (*WP* Vol. I, pp. 279–80) which records the death of his father in 1783:

> Long, long, my swimming eyes did roam
> For little Horse to bear me home,
> To bear me—what avails my tear?
> To sorrow o'er a Father's bier. (ll. 424–27)

Coincidentally both poets use exactly the same rhymes in their brief descriptions. See Salvesen, *op. cit.*, p. 51.

32 Jean Raimond, in a fascinating psychoanalytic study *Southey et la peur de l'Eros* in *Romantisme anglais et Eros*, ed. C. La Cassagnere (Clermont-Ferrand: Université de Clermont-Ferrand II, 1982), pp. 30–31, suggests that Southey's relationship with his father was not one of admiration. He suffered from lack of fatherly care and saw his father in prison for debt, after which the man shortly died (*NL* I, p. 12). Raimond (p. 31) detects Southey's 'satisfaction' in this death (though Southey does write tenderly about his father), and a desire to purge off his father's memory. Hence perhaps the inclusion in *The Retrospect* of so many poetic 'fathers' and Southey's gravitation towards fatherly friends.

33   Bristol! I die! not on thy well-known towers
> Turn my last look without one natural pang.
> My heart remembered all the peaceful years
> Of childhood, and was sad. Me many cares
> Have changed. I may revisit thee again,
> But never with that eager glow of joy
> As when from Corston to my mother's arms
> I hastened with unmingled happiness,
> Returning from first absence. Thy old towers
> Again may from the hill-top meet my view,
> But I shall see them dimly thro the tear.
> There is a stranger in my father's house,
> And where my evil fortunes found a home
> From the hard world, the gate has closed upon me,
> And the poor spaniel that did love me lies
> Deep in the whelming waters. Fare thee well
> O pleasant place! 'I had been well content
> 'To see no other earthly home beside!'
>
> (*NL* I, p. 153 and *CB* IV, p. 38)

34 Salvesen, *op. cit.*, p. 178.

Chapter Two

Theorizing for Another State: *The Fall of Robespierre* and the American Scheme

'Perish these mighty ones,'
Cried Conrade, 'these prime ministers of death,
Who stalk elated o'er their fields of fame,
And count the thousands they have massacred . . .
(*Joan of Arc* BK.V, ll. 160–63)

Time has justified all your prophecies with regard to my French friends. The Jacobins, the Sans Culottes, and the fishwomen carry everything before them. Every thing that is respectable, every barrier that is sacred, is swept away by the ungovernable torrent.

The people have changed tyrants, and, for the mild irresolute Louis, bow to the savage, the unrelenting Petion. After so open a declaration of abhorrence, you may perhaps expect that all the sanguine dreams of romantic liberty are gone for ever. It is true, I have seen the difficulty of saying to the mob, 'thus far, no farther.' I have seen a structure raised by the hand of wisdom, and defended by the sword of liberty, undermined by innovation, hurled from its basis by faction, and insulted by the proud abuse of despotism. Is it less respectable for its misfortunes? These horrid barbarities, however, have rendered me totally indifferent to the fate of France, and I have only to hope that Fayette will be safe. (*W* I, pp. 3–4, College Green, Bristol, 1792)

1

In the previous chapter, I examined *The Retrospect*, a poem which Southey finished in the early summer of 1794, whose melancholy elegiacism gives little indication of the loud democratic voice he was soon to assume in his work. Yet the central section of the poem includes a brief political comment: that the poet wants to turn away from 'empire's strife' (p. 9) to look towards his own domestic future, the quest for home enlightened by the examination of his own past. By the time of *The Retrospect*, Southey was already showing a desire for retreat into simple and sustaining domesticity. The poem makes a journey of retreat into the past, and looks forward to the prospect of marital bliss, but it also depicts a wrecked emotional and psychological landscape. Love is seen as salvation from the trials of the past and the present emotional and political turmoil. But love needs a place of enactment and a theory of longevity, and these common problems are the focus of this chapter. By the summer of 1794, Southey already had plans for an ideal society where he (and now 'Ariste') could thrive. Inextricably linked to this are questions of power and rule. *The Fall of Robespierre*, a three-act play (act I by Coleridge and acts II–III by Southey) is a study of French power, republican power which fails to liberate a Revolutionary society seemingly always already corrupted by the spectres of monarchy and caught in a cycle of repetitive decay. The problem of power and the desire for regeneration at the play's end are key elements in Southey's (and Coleridge's) contemporary thinking which can be woven into their scheme of emigration to America of 1794–95, called Pantisocracy. Before attempting this, I will sketch Southey's political observations up to 1794.

Watching the accounts of the French political scene in the newspaper reports as early as 1792, the youth must have sensed that 'sanguine dreams of romantic liberty' (see above) might never be realized in France. The political events of 1792 to which he seems to be referring, include the storming of the Tuileries by the mob (10 August) and the consequent overthrow of the monarchy.[1] For Southey, it was one thing to support ideas of liberty and another to behold all the recognizable structures and limits of a nation being obliterated. Southey's idea of respectability forms the sacred barrier beyond which his own disgust is aroused, and he was not alone in this. He had hoped, as others had, that tyranny would succumb to the rise of liberty, whose 'structure' (above) in its wisdom would override 'faction' and 'despotism' forever.

Also in the above extract are clues which show how the eighteen-year-old poet saw the members of the states of France. Two main blocks of stereotype are suggested by 'people' and 'mob'. The former evoking solidarity and sense, the latter merely the pejorative image of the 'ungovernable torrent' upon which any claims or values of rationality are void. Ideas of 'structure' and 'barrier' here echo Burke in his *Reflections* of 1790, criticizing any attempts to tamper with age-old institutions:

> But now all is to be changed. All the pleasing illusions, which made power gentle, and obedience liberal, which harmonized the different shades of life, and which, by a bland assimilation, incorporated into politics the sentiments which beautify and soften private society, are to be dissolved by this new conquering empire of light and reason. All the decent drapery of life is to be rudely torn off. All the super-added ideas, furnished from the wardrobe of a moral imagination, which the heart owns, and the understanding ratifies, as necessary to cover the defects of our naked shivering nature, and raise it to dignity in our own estimation, are to be exploded as a ridiculous, absurd, and antiquated fashion. (*B* p. 171)

But Southey has, like Paine, an eye for both the plumage and the dying bird, and moreover, his avowed *indifference* to the state of France and its ideals is contradicted by his subsequent writing. So by 14 July 1793 (*NL* I, p. 29), he is excitedly hoping 'to hear of the fall of Marat Robespierre Thuriot and David'. Coincidentally, Marat had been assassinated on 13 July of that year, when Southey was making his first draft of *Joan of Arc*. But it was the death in October 1793 (*LC* I,

p. 189) of the Girondist Brissot, who advocated a form of federal republic, which more affected him:

> I am sick of this world, and discontented with every one in it. The murder of Brissot has completely harrowed up my faculties, and I begin to believe that virtue can only aspire to content in obscurity . . . (Bodleian MSS. Eng. Letters, c. 22, f. 77, 11 November 1793)

This passage is frequently quoted to illustrate Southey's incipient misanthropy, but it also needs to be pointed out that he is drawing upon the language of *Hamlet* (Act I, Scene V, ll. 12–23) where the ghostly Old Hamlet reveals his murder to his son. Southey's lament for the death of virtue in the form of Brissot rests therefore on a most resonant literary allusion, the youth's personal psychological turmoil being articulated through Shakespearean vocabulary. Southey makes Brissot into a kind of spiritual father whose death provokes a kind of madness in him in misanthropic posturing.

Fixing millennial hopes upon individual names seems to have been one of Southey's favourite ploys, perhaps as a natural reaction against the inchoate nature of the political situation. And Robespierre himself, after Brissot, took on something of the role of millennial champion for Southey, and his name is linked with Southey's father during an infamous episode at Stowey.[2] The news of Robespierre's death caught up with the young Pantisocrats on a visit to Thomas Poole's house. Southey appeared 'more violent in his principles than even Coleridge himself'.[3] The narrator is, however, unclear as to whether Southey's pro-Gallican sentiments are uttered for effect or whether he means what he says:

> . . . two young men, introduced to him by the names of Coleridge and Southey . . . not only did not show the feelings any right-thinking people might have been expected to manifest at such a piece of intelligence, but one of them—Southey—actually laid his head down

upon his arms and exclaimed, 'I had rather have heard of the death of my own father.'[4]

Of course, Southey's father had been dead since 1792, so this was something of an empty gesture, and as I noted in the last chapter, Southey's relationship with his father was problematic. Robespierre, though, was mourned:

> Poor Robespierre! Coleridge and I wrote a tragedy upon his death in the space of two days! so good that he has it now in town to get printed. If you ask my opinion of this great man, I will tell you.
>
> I believe him to have been sacrificed to the despair of fools and cow[ards.] Coleridge says 'he was a man whose great bad actions cast a dis[. . .] lustre over his name.' He is now inclined to think with me that the [. . .] of a man so situated must not be judged by common laws, that Robespierre was the benefactor of mankind and that we should lament his death as the greatest misfortune Europe could have sustained—the situation of Europe is surely most melancholy—it presents to the eye of humanity a prospect of carnage from which it shrinks with horror. (*NL* I, pp. 72–73, 22 August 1794)

In this passage, Robespierre assumes a portentous and tragic status, rather like Southey's Joan of Arc, a sacrificial offering, taking on impossible odds for the good of 'mankind'. As a father-figure (a paragon and a warning to the textual sons and daughters of Pantisocracy), Robespierre held out guidance to Europe, in Southey's opinion at least, providing a face to represent France, instead of the many faces of faction.

> The death of Robespierre is one of those events on which it is hardly possible to speak with certainty. The charges brought against him after his execution are most futile and contemptible; on the other hand I see much to commend in the Convention. They debate freely and set

many prisoners at liberty. Tallien in one day delivered
700. Coleridge and I wrote a tragedy upon the subject in
24 hours, which he has in London now, either to sell or
print on our account. (*NL* I, pp. 75–76, 7 September
1794)

By elevating Robespierre to the status of tragic literary hero,
Southey is able to represent the wayward political theatre in
understandable terms. If the seeds of his discontent with
France began as he says in 1792, then perhaps Robespierre's
death confirmed for him that a nation which perversely
murdered such a leader, and helped to destabilize Europe, was
practically a lost cause. French ideals, the genius of liberty,
volatile and desirable, were what might be salvaged from the
ruins. The same ideals might also inform his American dream.

Brissot's death in 1793 seems to have thrown Southey into
one of his misanthropic phases from which the Pantisocratic
scheme briefly rescued him. By 1796, and the publication of
Joan of Arc, he came to see the volatile Parisians as part of a
'headstrong mutable ferocious race' and Paris itself as the seat
of bloodshed:

> Ill-fated scene!
> Thro' many a dark age drench'd with innocent blood
> And one day doom'd to know the damning guilt
> Of BRISSOT murder'd, and the blameless wife
> Of ROLAND! Martyr'd patriots—spirits pure,
> Wept by the good ye fell! (*Joan of Arc*, p. 94)

Neither Southey nor Coleridge visited Revolutionary
France, and so their role-models for a literary re-enactment of
Robespierre's fall had to be lifted from books and placed
inside 'An Historic Drama' as their play was entitled—it
should be remembered that they were not eye-witnesses of the
Terror, as was Wordsworth. French politics were for them as
much of a dramatic performance of the mind as were Burke's
Reflections and of course by 1794, and the aftermath of the

Terror, at least something in Burke's predictive 'drama' could be seen to be substantiated. So apart from the bare *reported* facts about the fall of Robespierre, both Southey and Coleridge mainly draw upon Shakespearean imagery, tone, and gesture to describe the political stage of France. The theatre (then an expanding medium), being a prime seat of popular entertainment in the late eighteenth century, could serve political ends equally well.

On the London stage[5] such plays as *Macbeth* and *Hamlet* were acted each year: *Julius Caesar*, with its bloodthirsty republicanism, seems to have fallen out of vogue by 1780. In fact, *Julius Caesar* was the perfect model for re-enacting political faction of a similar nature to that taking place in France. Gary Taylor sees writing in the eighteenth century moving back from books into actions,[6] enacting the philosophy of the Enlightenment, although such critics as Burke became appalled at the tragic consequences of the ensuing action.

Coleridge and Southey's work tries to re-enclose actions within text, and despite the pro-French flourishes, the reviews of the play are mild. The *Critical Review* (*Madden* p. 37) for November 1794 (possibly George Dyer) drew attention to the quality of the writing:

> . . . we mean not to under-rate Mr. Coleridge's historical drama. It affords ample testimony, that the writer is a genuine votary of the Muse, and several parts of it will afford much pleasure to those who can relish the beauties of poetry. Indeed a writer who could produce so much beauty in so little time, must possess powers that are capable of raising him to a distinguished place among the English poets.

He adds: 'The third act closes beautifully'. Even the *British Critic* for May 1795 (v, pp. 539–40) laid stress upon the future possibilities for the writer:

Mr. Coleridge has aimed at giving a dramatic air to a detail of Conventional speeches, which they were scarcely capable of receiving. The sentiments, however, in many instances are naturally, though boldly conceived, and expressed in language, which gives us reason to think the Author might, after some probation, become no unsuccessful wooer of the tragic muse.

The writing of poetical works it seems, even in the increasingly tense political atmosphere of 1794, lent some immunity to authorial views.

2

The Fall of Robespierre was a hasty exercise in versifying contemporary events wherein both poets make statements which do not pull equally in one direction as at least one critic believed.[7] In this reading, my intention is to try to suggest the meaning of 'home' for Coleridge and for Southey, viewed through the medium of this joint production and other contemporary events. To begin with, I want to examine two major aspects of Coleridge's thought which lie in Act I of the play, namely his attitude to the revolutionary powers, and his Pantisocratic yearnings, which have been already thoroughly discussed by critics such as Everest.[8]

In Act I Coleridge depicts Robespierre as the supernatural leader (an Ossianic shade), whose elemental nature is a central cause of fear:

> Barrere:I fear the Tyrant's *soul*—
> Sudden in action, fertile in resource,
> And rising awful 'mid impending ruins;
> In splendour gloomy, as the midnight meteor,
> That fearless thwarts the elemental war.
>
> (Act I, ll. 3–7)

Robespierre's 'soul' is the volatile quintessence of tyranny, easily passed from him to some other bearer.[9] The above quote is echoed in Southey's picture of regenerate France at the end of the play. Domination of the many by the evil tyrant was one of the problems of corrupt society that Pantisocracy would eradicate. Robespierre serves and epitomizes the abstract *genius* of tyranny here rather than the equally abstract 'Liberty' which he purports to uphold. The acts of 'Liberty' are privileged over those of tyranny and come to mean liberty for Robespierre the individual rather than 'Liberty' for the French nation. As Legendre says (Act I, Scene I, ll. 40–41), 'O what a precious name is Liberty / To scare or cheat the simple into slaves!' In serving 'Liberty' Robespierre has taken upon himself the dangerous and uncontrollable burden of the apparent presence of that term. Tallien sees Robespierre as the man of science who has experimented upon the volatile 'Liberty', confined it within his own parameters, and is now facing the consequences:

> All—all is ours! e'en now the vital air
> Of Liberty, condens'd awhile, is bursting
> (Force irresistible!) from its compressure—
> To shatter the arch chemist in the explosion!
> (Act I, ll. 251–54)

Perhaps Coleridge had in mind here the esteemed scientist and Unitarian Joseph Priestley,[10] who had been hounded out of England in 1794 as a supporter of the French. Priestley (in a different sense to Robespierre) is a figure of power, an architect of enlightenment, a victim of the people he is working for.

Robespierre's self-serving principles, however, tyrannize over the people. Coleridge does not have to look far for a literary model in which to express this. At line 61, thinking over his bloody successes, the tyrant exclaims: 'What! did th' assasin's dagger aim its point / Vain, as a *dream* of murder, at my bosom?' Coleridge's emphasis on the dream of murder,

obviously recalls *Macbeth*[11] (Act II, Sene II, ll. 33ff) where
Macbeth contemplates killing the king. Robespierre gloats
over the fact that (unlike a Duncan or a Louis) he has cheated
death. He will continue to elude the assassin, in a sense,
because he is evidence of a corruption deeply seated in, or
produced by, sophisticated society. Robespierre may perish,
but in the present fallen state of society other Robespierres
will certainly follow. Here the text links with Southey's own
long-held unease over the transgression of 'sacred barriers',
releasing into the world powers such as this tyrant, contained
only by the shifting parameters of 'Liberty', a liberty soaked
in blood. Robespierre Junior, the tyrant's brother, acts upon
him as a kind of conscience, someone who like Macbeth (Act
III, Scene IV, ll. 136ff) is 'Stepp'd' in human gore:

> Nay—I am sick of blood; my aching heart
> Reviews the long, long train of hideous horrors
> That still have gloom'd the rise of the Republic.
> (Act I, Scene I, ll. 95–97)

Coleridge's word 'train' suggests the show of kings in *Macbeth* (Act IV, Scene I), the 'long, long train' of rightful
monarchs (in contrast to the 'horrors' of the Republic) who
are attended by the bloody ghost of Banquo, proudly showing
his lineage in continuance. Here lies the implicit unease that
Coleridge, like Southey, feels towards the brutal tampering
with existent social structures. The answer was not to remove
the king (as the Macbeths did), simply giving rise to such as
Robespierre and the worst viciousness of human nature, but to
review the very foundations of society itself.

Act I is a complex and vicious struggle for power, effectively presented by Coleridge as the opposite of Pantisocracy.
As St Just says:

> The state is not yet purified: and though
> The stream runs clear, yet at the bottom lies

The thick black sediment of all the factions . . .
(I, ll. 71–73)

Robespierre can officially 'clear' the waters of his state, as can any government, yet the 'sediment' of the factions will affect the already dubious Liberty and Equality with their own versions of these terms, and as St Just adds (Act I, l. 74) 'It needs no magic hand to stir it up!'

It was at the political 'sediment' or rather the bedrock of the human race that Coleridge aimed his socially purifying version of the theoretically egalitarian Pantisocracy. Hence his disgust over Southey's intentions of taking servants to America with them, as these individuals smacked too much of the 'sediment' in the sense that they were already formed by all the prejudices of another society, as of course were the two poets themselves. Thomas Poole was of a similar mind:

> These are the outlines of their plan . . . could they realise them they would, indeed, realise the age of reason; but, however perfectible human nature may be, I fear it is not yet perfect enough to exist long under the regulations of such a system, particularly when the Executors of the plan are taken from a society in a high degree civilised and corrupted. America is certainly a desirable country, so desirable in my eye that, were it not for some insuperable reasons, I would certainly settle there . . . But I think a man would do well first to see the country and his future hopes before he removes his connections or any large portion of his property there.[12]

Southey had decided to take his aunt's servant Shadrach Weeks and the man's family to America, not as Pantisocratic equals, but in the role of servants. This was actually a gesture of care, which Coleridge admitted, but nevertheless it was a flaw in their plan. Coleridge quotes Southey back at himself:

> 'Shad's children will be educated as ours—and the Education we shall give them will be such as to render

them incapable of blushing at the want of it in their Parents.'—PERHAPS! With this one word would every Lilliputian Reasoner demolish the System. Wherever men *can* be vicious, some *will* be. The leading Idea of Pantisocracy is to make men necessarily virtuous by removing all Motives to Evil—all possible Temptations. 'Let them dine with us and be treated with as much equality as they would wish—but perform that part of Labor for which their Education has fitted them.'— *Southey* should not have written this Sentence . . . Is every Family to possess one of these Unequal Equals.? (*Griggs* I, p. 114)

The inclusion of the 'Shad' contingent would simply infect Pantisocracy with the habit of inequality, and this is exactly what Coleridge thought should be left behind. Rousseau and Godwin would have agreed, blaming corruption upon the advance of civilization. Godwin emphasizes that if the citizen becomes used to the hypocrisy of institutions, then communal ideas will always fail. Profound change was needed:

Simplify the social system, in the manner which every motive, but those of usurpation and ambition powerfully recommends; render the plain dictates of justice level to every capacity; remove the necessity of implicit faith; and we may expect the whole species to become reasonable and virtuous.[13]

Both Coleridge and Godwin put what seems a naive faith in the human race—nurture is all-important. Godwin thinks radical change to the present system will effect regeneration, Coleridge thinks that if motives to evil and temptations are removed from sight or from reach, they will lose their power over human ideas. Somehow what is begun right will remain right and no one will want servants in the Pantisocracy if servants are not in evidence? But the servant issue (23 October 1794) was not the only thing on Coleridge's mind. He wrote again to Southey, prompted by a six-hour discussion at the invitation of a certain Dr Edwards (a Grecian of Cambridge) upon the principles of Pantisocracy.

> In conclusion, Lushington & Edwards declared the System impregnable, supposing the assigned Quantum of Virtue and Genius in the first Individuals. (*Griggs* I, p. 119)

Concern about the 'first Individuals' inevitably led to questions (see *Everest* pp. 80ff) about the women and their offspring:

> Are they saturated with the Divinity of Truth sufficiently to be always wakeful? In the present state of their minds . . . is it not probable, that the *Mothers* will tinge the Minds of the Infants with prejudications? . . . These children—the little Frickers for instance and *your* Brothers—Are they not already *deeply* tinged with the prejudices and errors of Society? . . . *How* are we to prevent them from infecting the minds of *our* Children? . . . *How* can we ensure their silence concerning *God &c-*? . . . But *must* our System be thus necessarily imperfect? I ask the Question that I may know whether or not I should write the Book of Pantisocracy . . . (*Griggs* I, pp. 119–20)

Coleridge's intense desire for an agreement with Southey over the basic tenets of the system is plainly stated in the letter; they must decide on the rules before the book can be written. The old society, present in this discourse under the metaphor of disease, must be guarded against. Coleridge was dogged by the spectre of failure just as he had seen his way forward:

> Southey! I am fearful that Lushington's prophecy may not be altogether vain—'Your System, Coleridge! appears strong to the head and lovely to the Heart—but depend upon it you will never give your *women* suffi-

cient strength of mind, liberality of heart, or vigilance of Attention—*They* will spoil it! (*Griggs* I, p. 122)

Once again, the foundations of the scheme are examined. The reasoning behind Pantisocracy is betrayed by lack of faith in the building bricks of the new nation:

> I wish, Southey! in the stern severity of Judgement, that the two mothers were *not* to go and that the children stayed with them—Are you wounded by my want of feeling? No! how highly must I think of your rectitude of Soul, that I should dare to say this to so affectionate a Son! *That* Mrs Fricker—we shall have her teaching the infants *Christianity*,—I mean—that mongrel whelp that goes under its name—teaching them by stealth in some ague-fit of Superstition! (*Griggs* I, p. 123)

It was of course vital that the teaching of the Pantisocratic children should be most carefully monitored so that they in their turn could be capable of prolonging the system. It is appropriate that Coleridge talks of Christianity (the Fricker version) as 'that mongrel whelp', underlining the need for the *pure* birth of Pantisocracy into a medium of nurture that disallows the half-bred, half-conceived or half-understood notions of religion and communal living which, in his eyes, a mere mother such as Mrs Fricker would hold, if at all. Perhaps Coleridge was influenced here by the Platonic model for society:

> And shall we just carelessly allow children to hear any casual tales which may be devised by casual persons, and to receive into their minds ideas for the most part the very opposite of those which we should wish them to have when they are grown up?
>
> We cannot.
>
> Then the first thing will be to establish a censorship of the writers of fiction, and let the censors receive any tale of fiction which is good, and reject the bad; and we will

persuade mothers and nurses to tell their children the authorized ones only. Let them fashion the mind with such tales, even more fondly than they mould the body with their hands . . . it is most important that the tales which the young first hear should be models of virtuous thoughts.[14]

So Pantisocracy was not to be thrown together by 'casual persons' with their equally casual ideas, but held in place by censorship and the authorized tales of virtue. What Coleridge dreams of is the perfected human society, a concert of desires all pulling in one direction. But sinister overtones are born with the idea of Utopian perfectibility as Karl Popper intimates:

Plato . . . believed that all change . . . is decay . . . Accordingly his Utopian blueprint aims at arresting all change; it is what would nowadays be called 'static'.

This 'static' condition which Coleridge idealized as a cottaged vale, was the projected locus wherein the 'Utopian engineer' would attempt to 'suppress unreasonable objections' to his schemes, but:

with them he must invariably suppress reasonable criticism too. And the mere fact that expressions of dissatisfaction will have to be curbed reduces even the most enthusiastic expression of satisfaction to insignificance.[15]

This brings us to the second scene of Act I of *The Fall of Robespierre* (ll. 197–201), whose action takes place appropriately enough in the quiet of a household (a 'static' environment), where Adelaide, the mistress of Tallien, reviews the virtues of domesticity in comparison with the vicious renegade actions of Liberty:

O this new freedom! at how dear a price
We've bought the seeming good! The peaceful virtues

> And every blandishment of private life,
> The father's cares, the mother's fond endearment,
> All sacrificed to liberty's wild riot.

Liberty in this instance unseats the harmonious flow of private familial life by its 'wild riot' of individual faction. The state lacks a coherent set of guiding principles, which were for Coleridge founded upon the model of the family group. But this in itself was not enough, as Coleridge's comments on the Fricker family show—the 'seeming good' in that case being undermined by mongrel religion and half-formed, half-heard, ideas. Society demands a good shepherd, a group of good shepherds, who collude to ensure that liberty is eventually known to all by an instinctive general will, which serves to prolong the life of that society. If the right tale is told in the first instance, it will continue to be told. The originators of Pantisocracy seemed in no doubt that they knew, as Robespierre himself knew (identifying himself with the people and their virtue in one idea), that their plans and rules were the right ones.

In *The Fall of Robespierre*, Coleridge enshrines his vision of 'domestic peace', fundamental to his vision of Pantisocracy, in the harmonies of a song. This *Song* grows out of the domestic tranquillity and love amidst the noise of faction and evokes the picture of a society with one general theme at its heart serving all its members (the motive power of each metaphorical Aeolian harp), and is in radical contrast to Robespierre's republic of the self. Coleridge hoped that, by starting the scheme with the right people, no dissent or faction would emerge to cast him and others in the light of tyrants. Because if it did, there would always be someone, like Tallien in Act II here, who would say:

> If the trembling members
> Even for a moment hold his fate suspended,
> I swear by the holy poniard, that stabbed Caesar,
> This dagger probes his heart! (ll. 271–74)

The allusion to Julius Caesar (and again to Shakespeare) exaggeratedly dramatizes the political issues in this play. Once more the theme of killing the ruler (be he king, dictator, or tyrant) is underscored, and also the nature of *Song* (domestic peace as a political alternative) is brought to the fore, backing up Everest's comments.[16] Coleridge seeks a bloodless despotism in his version of Pantisocracy, and this play underlines his fears about the tainted 'stock' of the political world. He shows the men guiding the mob and the machine of the French government remain in a fallen state, carrying their imperfections into the world of (and the word of) liberty. America seemed to offer a haven from this theatre of repetitions.

In *Song*, Coleridge poeticizes and politicizes the desire for retreat from revolution. The noise of revolution is present both in *Song* itself and in the house of Adelaide, which is only a temporary haven or 'static' environment. *Kubla Khan* of 1798 (*CP* p. 298) seems to repeat this de-stabilizing invasion of the idyll where the vision of the pleasure garden is troubled by 'Ancestral voices prophesying war!' Perhaps even the planned flight to America would not be far enough to salvage the new 'family' from the inevitably corrupting cycle of the old order, the Robespierrian flaw.

3

By contrast, Southey in Act II dramatizes the character of Robespierre as the lone figure espousing his truth as a prophet amongst enemies, bragging of the king's death:

> Mouldering in the grave
> Sleeps Capet's caitiff corse; my daring hand
> Levelled to earth his blood-cemented throne,
> My voice declared his guilt, and stirred up France
> To call for vengeance. (Act II, ll. 7–11)

This kind of melodramatic posturing (not the Southey of *The Retrospect* or of *Poems* 1795) has been seen as the source that drew from Coleridge his own 'full-blooded republicanism' which Everest dates from the meeting with Southey in June 1794 (*Everest* pp. 17–18), and is heard 'for the first time in his first letter to Southey, written on 6 July 1794'. Perhaps Southey's influence is exaggerated: there is no doubt that some mutual encouragement to republican excess took place.

Whatever the case, Southey's Robespierre is the tragic figure before lesser men, the superhuman figure (like Coriolanus) not to be judged as if he were an ordinary mortal. Robespierre's qualities (prophetic of Southey's later epic heroes) are those of the hero-philosopher in action, the near-Satanic genius, righting what he considers to be the wrongs of the republic and dealing out the blank resolution of death. His convictions about his own rectitude are undaunted, even (l. 12) over the deaths of the Girondists. Their 'labyrinth of words' (l. 17) is what Robespierre opposed and overthrew, substituting his own maze of evasion and slippage. He remembers with pride his exposure of faction amongst the political groups of France, such as:

> those, who long
> Mask'd treason's form in liberty's fair garb,
> Long deluged France with blood, and durst defy
> Omnipotence! (Act II. ll. 26–29)

This speech recalls Satan's shame in Milton's *Paradise Lost*[17] and Robespierre, in allying himself with 'Omnipotence', takes on the aura of a supreme deity, ironically boasting of his power over the forces of evil. It seems that all knowledge of what liberty is and what it is not is lost in this debate. Robespierre both condemns and exonerates himself and is presented as a latter-day Caesar, surrounded by the conspirators.

> I stand here
> An isolated patriot—hemmed around
> By faction's noisy pack; beset and bay'd
> By the foul hell-hounds who know no escape
> From Justice' outstretched arm, but by the force
> That pierces through her breast. (Act II, ll. 61–66)[18]

Southey recalls Shakespeare's *Julius Caesar* (Act III, Scene I, l. 204): 'Here wast thou bay'd, brave hart; / Here didst thou fall; and here thy hunters stand . . .' where Mark Antony reviews Caesar's corpse. Antony calls him 'the ruins of the noblest man / That ever lived' (Act II, Scene I, ll. 256–57), a statement which looks forward to his pronouncement in Act V, Scene V, l. 68, that Brutus was 'the noblest Roman of them all'.

In *The Fall of Robespierre*, there is a similar play of notions about what it means to be a noble man and what it means to be a noble Roman. The former serves his own state, yet may engender love in his followers, and the latter serves the republic or his ideals 'in a general honest thought / And common good to all . . .' (*Julius Caesar* Act V, Scene V, ll. 71–72). The character of Robespierre is a confusion of noble man and noble Roman in Southey's eyes it seems. In France itself, the Romanizing of public festivals and the classical themes of both plays and paintings forged links with the ancient Roman world. The Revolutionary patriot employed the vocabulary of the Roman republic. Southey above, in describing Robespierre as 'an isolated patriot' perhaps gives us a direct clue as to why he appears to idolize and deplore the man at the same time.

The notion of patriotism became more radical in England as the eighteenth century advanced. The radical patriot sat in opposition to the government and the King, especially if there was a sense that the delicate balance between monarchy, aristocracy and democracy (King, Lords and Commons) was under threat—that is, if one section had more than its fair share of influence over another. A radical reading of English history might conclude that most governments since the imposition of the so-called Norman Yoke were corrupt and that oppositional stances were intrinsically patriotic. Liberty for the people meant looking to the past for a model, as Robespierre looked to ancient Rome. But of course, after the Revolution in France, opposition to English government carried with it a pro-French colouring, whether openly stated or implied, even ideas of Liberty, indeed the word Liberty itself, so valued by the English, had been enshrined by the French revolutionaries as the first word in their triadic creed, and Wordsworth, an eye-witness to the period of the Terror, shows his fears about where French Liberté was leading:

> That Liberty, and Life, and Death would soon . . .
> Lie in the arbitrement of those who ruled
> The capital City . . .[19]

Patriotism and Liberty could of course be invoked by Whig, Tory and Radical. 'The rhetoric of patriotism was one to which appeal was as likely to be made by the government and its supporters as by the opposition.'[20] But for the Pantisocrats, patriotism of course leant heavily towards a new people and away from all who were perceived as tyrants, be they French or English:

> When he applies himself more specifically to the Con-
> stitution, the late eighteenth-century radical seeks to
> extend the democratic element in the system, which is
> notionally held to be a balance between monarch, aris-
> tocracy, and commons. Typically, then, the radical
> criticizes the monarch, or the aristocracy, or both, and
> represents these institutions as encroaching upon the
> populace or upon its preserve . . . He sees the existing
> government as not truly tripartite, but aristocratic.[21]

Their emerging creed was indeed anti-monarchical, but it was a patriotism which sought to shake off the old structures of government, not even to look back to Saxon liberty as a

model, but to make something entirely new. Southey's Robespierre had come close to this renewal, this true patriotism,
before being infected and corrupted by power. Southey and
Coleridge saw in leaders such as Brissot and Robespierre the
potential for a true patriotism whose *patria* is not England or
France, but the universal family of the world, the new
Brotherhood of Mankind, their 'Family of Soul' (*Griggs* I,
p. 102) as Coleridge liked to say. Robespierre is beleaguered
in the attempt to purge the state of France and betrays the fact
that, despite what he says, his heart was not all 'Given to the
People'[22] in a patriot's zeal, but self-centred. The germ of
dissent, of personal ambition, grows up in emulation of
Robespierre, even if like Southey, one has sympathy with the
larger ambitions of his actions (Act II, ll. 110–11) upon the
'dangerous path / Of virtue'. Faction amongst the citizens of
France is 'hydra-headed' (l. 84) or a 'brood' (l. 31), suggesting
that executions alone will never cure the Republic's ills.

The story of Julius Caesar continues to inhabit the textual
play of the factions hostile to Robespierre, and Robespierre
himself. His enemies see him as 'Caesar-like' (Act II, l. 141)
dividing up the kingdom of France for himself, and he,
remembering Danton (Act II, l. 166), regrets 'That I kill'd
Caesar and spar'd Antony', Antony here being represented by
'Legendre', a mere name, as are most of the unformed
characters in the play. But it is unfair to dismiss Southey's
revolutionaries so quickly. The character of St Just, though
playing a small part in the action, is based upon reasonably
accurate facts and potent allusions to the act of ruling the
perfect state. St Just was, according to J. M. Thompson, a
flatterer of Robespierre[23] and responsible for introducing the
new word 'vertu' in a political pamphlet 'Esprit de la Révol-
ution et de la Constitution de France'. This 'vertu' linked St
Just with the ancient world as he saw it,[24] and with Robespierre (who took it from Rousseau). Barère said of him that:
'If he had lived in the age of the Greek Republics . . . he would
have been a Spartan',[25] yet in this drama Southey makes him

allude not to Sparta, but to ancient Athens, where the two
stoical leaders Aristides (the Just) and Phocion (the Good)
served 'vertu' at the expense of personal ambition. And from
what Southey said of Robespierre himself, quoted earlier in
this chapter, such stoical and virtuous figures would form
role-models for the Southeyan Republic. Yet if Robespierre
cannot be judged by the laws of ordinary men, then he has no
place in governing them, and he is no better than a monarch, as
Tallien says:

> O citizens of France
> I weep for you—I weep for my poor country—
> I tremble for the cause of Liberty,
> When individuals shall assume the sway,
> And with more insolence than kingly pride
> Rule the Republic. (Act II, ll. 217–22)

Tallien sums up Robespierre's career as that of a man (like
Caesar) who has reached the point where only the name of
'King' (l. 263) is lacking. Tallien takes upon himself the duty
of saviour of France and invokes the 'avenging arm' (l. 277) of
Brutus to complete his duty. Robespierre and 'Caesar' become
interchangeable terms in Act III where Southey makes it plain
that the tyrant has taken on all the bad aspects of kingship.
Robespierre rules with poison like the 'baneful tree of Java'[26]
(l. 1) and is 'worse than Cromwell' (l. 3) in Collot d'Herbois'
words. Robespierre's apparent 'vertu' made him a fearful idol,
once the scourge of kings and now king in all but name. Ideal
principles, the actions of pure 'vertu', inform Southey's
'sanguine dreams of romantic liberty' (see epigraph) which are
in fact an enduring belief in the principles of the Revolution
and its ability to re-emerge after the Terror. Southey dramatizes this at the end of the play:

> *Tallien.* I hear, I hear the soul-inspiring sounds,
> France shall be saved! her generous sons attached
> To principles, not persons, spurn the idol

They worshipp'd once. Yes Robespierre shall fall
As Capet fell! Oh! never let us deem
That France shall crouch beneath a tyrant's throne,
That the almighty people who have broke
On their oppressors' heads the oppressive chain,
Will court again their fetters! easier it were
To hurl the cloud-capt mountain from its base,
Than force the bonds of slavery on men
Determined to be free! (Act III, ll. 64–75)

Here Southey is directly paraphrasing Paine:

> Notwithstanding Mr Burke's horrid paintings, when the
> French Revolution is compared with the revolutions of
> other countries, the astonishment will be, that it is
> marked with so few sacrifices; but this astonishment will
> cease when we reflect that *principles*, and not *persons*,
> were the meditated objects of destruction. The mind of
> the nation was acted upon by a higher stimulus than what
> the consideration of persons could inspire . . .[27]

This is the stance that Robespierre himself liked to adopt, as
quoted by Noel Parker: 'His opinion, he swears, is "independant, isolated; neither my cause nor my principles have ever
been attached, nor are attached to anyone". In this way he
aligns himself with virtue against all egoism.'[28] It seems that
this very shifting idea of 'virtue' was Robespierre's downfall.
The writer for *Felix Farley's Bristol Journal* of Saturday 23
August 1794 shows how widely this belief was spread,
claiming that: 'The French people . . . are attached neither to
Robespierre, nor any other individual—Liberty is alone the
object of their affections'. Tellingly at the end of the play
'Barrère' contrasts the 'idol' Robespierre with the true nature
of liberty:

In the goodly soil
Of Freedom, the foul tree of treason struck

Its deep-fix'd roots, and dropt the dews of death
On all who slumber'd in its specious shade.
He wove the web of treachery. He caught
The listening crowd by his wild eloquence,
His cool ferocity that persuaded murder,
Even whilst it spake of mercy!—never, never
Shall this regenerated country wear
The despot yoke. Though myriads round assail,
And with worse fury urge this new crusade
Than savages have known; though the leagued despots
Depopulate all Europe, so to pour
The accumulated mass upon our coasts,
Sublime amid the storm shall France arise,
And like the rock amid surrounding waves
Repel the rushing ocean.—She shall wield
The thunder-bolt of vengeance—she shall blast
The despot's pride, and liberate the world!
                              (Act III, ll. 195–213)

The enthusiasm of Barrère's speech upon 'this regenerated country' alongside the imagery of a monolithic giant, the nation of France itself, rising up in Ossianic magnificence 'sublime amid the storm', strikes the key note of the political thinking of the 1790s. M. H. Abrams[29] regarded the spirit of the French revolution as the most vital hope of contemporary writers and thinkers concerned with the regeneration of the earth and William Taylor of Norwich (*R* I, p. 68) gives us an idea of how France was revered in the early part of the revolutionary period. Writing from Paris on 14 May 1790 he says:

> I am at length in the neighbourhood of the National Assembly . . . whose pure streams are now overflowing the fairest country upon earth, and will soon be sluiced off into the other realms of Europe, fertilizing all with the living energy of its waters.

Southey's dramatic flourish at the end of this play clings to the belief in such a spirit, even after the Robespierrian tyranny. The poetic monolith that is France is seen here as the symbol of a regenerate earth, a genius of vengeance and liberty rising in defiance of tyranny. Wordsworth, like many others, had similar expectations about post-Robespierrian France which he included in *The Prelude*:[30]

> Great was my glee of spirit, great my joy
> In vengeance, and eternal justice, thus
> Made manifest. 'Come now ye golden times.'
> Said I.

The personification of regenerate France once more shaking off oppression may be interpreted as being cognate with Southey's own personal desire for renewal, intimately connected with the Pantisocratic scheme. Yet Southey's work in *The Fall of Robespierre* throws grave doubts upon the future of France, just as the final speech in the mouth of the dubious character of Barrère (see *Woodring* p. 195) seems ironically self-undermining. It might also be noted that neither Coleridge, nor Southey himself (despite his avowed willingness to risk death in France [*NL* I, p. 40]), express desires to experiment with Pantisocracy in France. France itself was soaked in the blood of political change, and despite Southey's flourish at the play's end it is hard to believe that he had convinced himself about the future of Liberty upon tainted ground. Perhaps for him the same uneasiness would hang over Pantisocracy.

4

Southey's notions of regeneration had really always involved himself alone or his version of the small community. This extract from *Poems* 1795 is an example of the kind of patriarchal idyll that Southey also set into *Joan of Arc*. His

wish to 'train the future race' is coupled with the desire for
melancholy self-obliteration, dying unknown and forgotten,
as if he longs for the release from the line of his socially-
conditioned past, and of the society around it:

> Be mine to taste the humbler joys of life
> Lull'd in oblivion's lap to wear away,
> And flee from grandeur's scenes of vice and strife,
> And flee from fickle fashion's empty sway:
> Be mine, in age's drooping hour, to see
> The lisping children climb their grandsire's knee,
> And train the future race to live and act like me.
> Then, when the inexorable hour shall come
> To tell my death, let no deep requiem toll,
> No hireling sexton dig the venal tomb,
> Nor priest be paid to hymn my parted soul;
> But let my children, near their little cot,
> Lay my old bones beneath the turfy spot:
> So let me live unknown, so let me die forgot.
> (*To Lycon*, in *Poems* 1795, p. 84)[31]

In effect, Southey allies himself with the nameless dead of the
sort found in Gray's *Elegy*. By writing a poem in this vein he
admits his own desire for retreat and self-erasure, which
amounts to a strong disgust with the world. Paradoxically the
self is preserved in the poem, its desires made known and
perpetuated.

Southey had ideas of retreat, not to France but to America,
at least as early as 1793 writing to Grosvenor Bedford
(Bodleian MSS. Eng. Letters, c. 22, f. 43) in January 1793:
'Thebes Sparta & Athens & Carthage have been. America is.'
It is clear that America, as well as Greece which in the same
letter he dreamed of repopulating with 'ten thousand people
visionary as myself', is, in Southey's mind, the place where
either retreat or the new colony of 'Southeyopolis' might be
built. He wants the new state to be as great as the famous cities
of the ancient world, but to have that democratic vigour which

America already possessed. By November of that year his views of the world had taken on a strong misanthropic tone and he felt that Balliol was little more than a prison for his real needs and desires. Yet his letters to Bedford often show a mixture of humour alongside the sense of persecution and injustice he feels he has suffered from a tyrannous world. Dreams of escape are never very far away. Disgust with human endeavour is interwoven with dreams about American idylls, and as above, some thought about training the 'future race'. Southey considers an escape-route from England through the literary motif of retreat:

> It was the favourite intention of Cowley to retire with his books to a cottage in America & seek that happiness in solitude which he could not find in society. My asylum would be sought there for different reasons, (and no prospect in life gives me half the pleasure this visionary one affords) . . . (*LC* I, p. 193)

The allusion to the Cowleyan model was rather unfortunate, because as in the case of Cowley, emigration was to remain a cherished dream only. Cowley, in his preface to the *Poems* of 1656, quotes Horace (*Odes* III, no. 26), who claims he is going to give up love and poetry himself, and he continues:

> this resolution of mine does the more befit me, because my desire has been for some years past (though the execution has been accidentally diverted) and does still vehemently continue, to retire myself to some of our *American Plantations*, not to seek for *Gold*, or enrich myself with the traffique of those parts (which is the end of most men that travel thither . . .) But to forsake this world for ever, with all the *vanities* and *Vexations* of it, and bury my self in some obscure retreat there (but not without the consolation of *Letters* and *Philosophy* . . .[32]

Cowley's prospective retreat is that of the individual scholar with no ideas of creating a new Greece or a new colony of philosophical like minds. His intention was simply to 'bury' himself away from the world and inside his studies.

> In his boyhood he had pretended to envy Horace and his Sabine cottage. But he had yielded to his academic and patriotic ambitions. During his French exile he had meditated an escape to the American colonies, where he had thought that life could be nourished by reading poetry and philosophy. But when Will Davenant had started on his expedition to the New World, Cowley was not found as a passenger, a member of the crew, or a stowaway.[33]

Cowley wrote his preface ten years after the end of the Civil War in England, when he had become confused and disgusted with the political climate and concerned for his own lack of reward for his services. Dr Johnson, in his *Rambler* No. 6, picks upon this escape-desire and sees as its cause the internal turmoil of the individual, coupled with a lack of perception:

> If he had proceeded in his project, and fixed his habitation in the most delightful part of the new world, it may be doubted, whether his distance from the 'vanities' of life would have enabled him to keep away the 'vexations.' It is common for a man, who feels pain, to fancy that he could bear it better in any other part. Cowley having known the troubles and perplexities of a particular condition, readily persuaded himself that nothing worse was to be found, and that every alteration would bring some improvement; he never suspected the cause of his unhappiness was within, that his own passions were not sufficiently regulated, and that he was harassed by his own impatience, which could never be without something to awaken it, would accompany him over the sea, and find its way to his American elysium. He would, upon the tryal, have been soon convinced, that the fountain of content must spring up in the mind; and that

> he, who has so little knowledge of human nature, as to
> seek knowledge by changing any thing, but his own
> dispositions, will waste his life in fruitless efforts, and
> multiply the griefs which he purposes to remove.[34]

Johnson had no illusions about changing the world by moving
away from others and finding 'delightful' surroundings. He
locates the Cowleyan problem as essentially an attitude of
mind: like Milton's Satan, the would-be émigré will carry his
own hell with him to whichever hiding place he chooses to
seek out. *The Rambler* argues for the status quo, as if all
discontent could be diagnosed as simply a misguided attitude.
The place of retreat can easily be found in one's native land
according to Johnson, and supposing that the perfectly quiet
life is found, then will it not pall soon enough for lack of
contrast with noise and intrusion? Furthermore, the pursuit of
retreat is, as D. H. Lawrence believed, indicative of the extent
to which humans are trapped and confined:

> Men are less free than they imagine; ah, far less free.
> Men are free when they are in a living homeland, not
> when they are straying and breaking away. Men are free
> when they are obeying some deep, inward voice of
> religious belief. Obeying from within. Men are free when
> they belong to a living, organic, *believing* community,
> active in fulfilling some unfulfilled, perhaps unrealized,
> purpose. Not when they are escaping to some wild west.
> The most unfree souls go west, and shout of freedom.
> The shout is a rattling of chains, always was.[35]

According to Lawrence (and despite the Coleridgean echoes
here) the mere desire for escape correspondingly indicates the
bonding or bondage of the individual to the past or the present
social and political state. The measure of Southey's own
entrapment in his impecunious home situation with a con-
sumptive mother, may be judged from a letter of 12 December
1793:

> I could bear single misery with more resignation—not
> only bear it but fly from it—but two brothers almost
> infants chain me to England. I must and will protect
> them. Otherwise the first vessel that sails for America
> should bear with it one more emigrant. (*NL* I, p. 39, 12
> December 1793)

America rose correspondingly in the estimation of many
alarmed at the course of French politics or alienated from
England. And in America land might be bought cheaply, land
upon which liberty might thrive.

Southey's alienation and alarm in England certainly fed his
misanthropy, and there also crept into his mind a mistrust of
the French democracy. In the period just before he met
Coleridge, his faith in France, England, his education, and, to
an extent, his faith in himself, was shaken. He readily
associated his own conflicts with authority with ideas of
oppressed truth and virtue, as if he himself were victim to
monarchical excesses exercised through men like Dr Vincent.
So the misanthropic Cowleyan idyll had its appeal, being I
suppose a rather typical youthful response to the pressures of
the established adult world, and as the Lawrence passage
states, merely sounded 'a rattling of chains'. Yet it is hard to
tell whether in the December of 1793 Southey's ideas are
merely idle fantasies or serious schemes; it is more than likely
that there is a combination of the serious with the kind of self-
burlesque that Southey often demonstrates in his letters:

> now if you are in the mood for a reverie—fancy me in
> America. imagine my ground uncultivated since the
> creation & see me wielding the axe now to cut down the
> tree & now the snake that nestles in it. then see me
> grubbing up the roots and building a nice snug little dairy
> with them. three rooms in my cottage & my only
> companion some poor negro whom I have bought on
> purpose to emancipate. after a hard days toil see me sleep
> upon rushes, & in very bad weather take out my casette

& write to you, for you shall positively write to me in America. do not imagine I shall leave rhyming or philosophising. so thus your friend will realize the romance of Cowley & even outdo the seclusion of Rousseau, till at last comes an ill-looking Indian with a tomahawk & scalps me—a most melancholy proof that society is very bad & that I shall have done very little to improve it! So Vanity Vanity will come from my life—& poor Southey will either be cooked for a Cherokee or oysterized by a tyger. (Bodleian MSS. Eng. Letters, c. 22, f. 88, received 20 December 1793)[36]

Beneath the comedy is a picture of society in embryo, the potential for solitude, and also, the intrusion upon this potential of the Edenic snake, the emancipated negro and the murderous Indian. These figures are common literary types in the poetry of the time, in Cowper or Blake for example. The negro is of further interest because s/he symbolizes Southey's philanthropic concerns in an exercise of power and their dubious nature—is s/he regarded as a companion here or, with a further rattling of chains, a servant? As for the Indian, he is a member of a primitive society, already corrupt (according to Rousseau) and therefore aggressive. In envisaging his own death Southey hints at the general corruption of human societies. Southey's 'axe' is the signifier of the distance between him and the savage of Rousseau's *Discours sur l'origine de l'inégalité*: Rousseau's savage needed no such implement. The aggressive cruelty of the Cherokee indicates that he is far removed from ideas of an 'original' savage. Like Southey and his plot of land, the Indian is in a fallen state, yet a perfect literary type.

Cowley's idea is 'romance' for the young poet, yet it does contain that uneasy germ of wisdom that a new beginning, a new colony, can only build itself securely upon selective philosophies and ideas. Certain things must be artificially excluded. Southey would presumably plan a new state, rationally, with centuries of enlightenment to help him along, from which he could select the information most useful to him. Under the triteness of the literary idyll of retreat, he stresses the need for special conditions in which the scheme could flourish, secure not just from the Indian, but from the destabilizing presence of 'society' even in its most primitive form. The fledgling reformed race would need to exist beyond the marauding whims of the indigenous peoples and the spectre of received ideas, to test the experiment fully.

By the end of 1793, Southey was in need of some shaping or consummating influence in his life. He had found something of this, as I have indicated, in his reading of Epictetus the stoic[37] and in the company of one Edmund Seward, a morally severe individual who was, like Southey himself, then destined for the Church. Southey never forgot Seward (who died in June 1795), whom he regarded as a kind of human paragon, someone who could live by a code, as indeed the Pantisocrats would have had to:

> Edmund Seward says the man who pursues literary studies merely for the gratification they afford, is as little entitled to respect as the libertine or the glutton. (Bodleian MSS. Eng. Letters, c. 22, f. 80, November 1793)

Unfortunately Southey seems to have disagreed with Seward over the formalities of acceptance into the Church:

> Edmund Seward is preparing for orders & I cannot persuade him that the testament only should qualify him. the fathers were either mere men or below mere men— human authority is not to be followed with passive obedience: but Seward is as fearful of heterodoxy, as oppression is of truth. what is to become of me at ordination heaven only knows. after keeping the straight path so long, the test act will be a stumbling block to honesty. (Bodleian MSS Eng. Letters, c. 22, f. 80, November 1793)

Southey eventually abandoned the idea of taking orders, because even Seward failed to persuade him that the Christian religion was more than simply a refined code of morals. Seward was one of the authorities that Southey looked to for support in the scheme of Pantisocracy and was, apparently, to be one of the chosen group. At first he was willing to join, but withdrew as Simmons says because he did not think it right to leave his mother alone, and in any case he saw through the scheme. He writes to their mutual friend Lightfoot (*Simmons* p. 48) on 3 October 1794: 'Southey seems to look upon my retraction from the scheme as a dereliction of Christianity itself'. This is certainly how it would have seemed to Southey, under the eventual influence of Coleridge's ideas:

> Christ's disciples formed the original model for Coleridge's ideal community of familial equality, a point which emphasises the Christian basis of Pantisocracy and its successive forms, and the millennial quality of its value. (*Everest* p. 89)

It is hard to imagine how Southey reconciled all the different philosophies and emotions that came to a head in the shape of Coleridge. In December 1793, Godwin's *Political Justice* (see *WH* p. 116) had given Southey new fuel for his condemnation of the society of 'mere men', a society which by making its 'artificial distinctions' (*NL* I, p. 40) effectively ensured that poverty and want, and therefore crime, would flourish. He saw himself caught in the trap of inequality, even poverty, but refused to compromise his principles, preferring to emigrate (*NL* I, p. 54) rather than to be seen as a 'villain'. By June 1794, Southey looked gloomily and indifferently to a projected future 'in England in America or among the convicts of New Holland' (*NL* I, p. 57), and his contemplation of convict life had already been put into verse in January of 1794, in the first of the *Botany Bay Eclogues*.

Coleridge, freshly discharged as 'insane' from the Dragoons on 10 April 1794, arrived in Oxford in June to clarify

Southey's position. They would write their way to America. Indeed, *Joan of Arc* (first drafted in 1793) would if successful (*NL* I, p. 61) 'carry me over and get me some few acres a spade and a plough'. The same letter speaks of the 'storm' (*ibid.*, p. 61) which he expects will engulf England in some nameless apocalypse and in this he captures the mood of the times vividly. Joseph Priestley (who departed for America early in 1794) preached his sermon *The Present State of Europe compared with Antient Prophecies*[38] in late February of that year. Priestley sees revolution and war as indicative of the end of the world, the approach of the kingdom of God:

> The aspect of things, it cannot be denied, is, in the highest degree, alarming, making life, and every thing in it, peculiarly uncertain. What could have been more unexpected than the events of any one of the last four years, at the beginning of it? What a total revolution in the ideas, and conduct of a whole nation! What a total subversion of principles, what reverses of fortune, and what a waste of life! in how bloody and eventful a war are we engaged, how inconsiderable in its beginning, how rapid and wide in its progress, and how dark with respect to its termination! At first it resembled Elijah's cloud, appearing no bigger than a *man's hand*; but now it covers, and darkens, the whole European hemisphere![39]

The terrible prophetic voice of doom made urgent 'peace and independance in America' (*NL* I, p. 63) seem the only way out, and the Pantisocrats seem to take on the aura of Noah's own sons and daughters. Southey begins to write sonnets about the journey:

> To the distant shore
> Where Freedom spurns Oppression's iron reign
> I go. (*NL* I, p. 65)

Initially, the plan was to arrive in Kentucky to establish the community. Southey had moved from the position of single

Cowleyan misanthrope, and taken on Godwin's ideas, particularly Book VIII of *Political Justice* which deals with
property. But what did he make of the condemning of
marriage in the same book, or the part of Chapter II
containing the famous assessment of human (and parental)
worth in the example of Fénelon's valet? He seems to have just
conveniently ignored them.

But he was certainly no absolute Godwinian. He wanted to
marry Edith Fricker, he felt a loving duty to his mother and
brothers which was far from the coldly rational Godwinian
stance. Southey's Pantisocracy, his perfect (but not perfect-
ible) new home seems to have emerged as a replica of the old
patriarchal home which Godwin's philosophy supposedly
taught him to revile (see *Everest* p. 70), and furthermore he
had dutifully taken his father's place in it. Or was his domestic
paradise a repressed matriarchy in disguise? The women were
of course the vital and almost voiceless element in this picture:

> August 5. Every thing smiles upon me. My Mother is
> fully convinced of the propriety of our resolution. She
> admires the plan, she goes with us. Never did so
> delightful a prospect of happiness open upon my view
> before. To go with all I love—to go with all my friends
> except your family and Wynn! to live with them in the
> most agreeable and most honourable employment, to eat
> the fruits I have raised, and see every face happy around
> me, my Mother sheltered in her declining years from the
> anxieties which have pursued her, my brothers educated
> to be useful and virtuous. (*NL* I, pp. 67–68)

Southey's 'delightful prospect' of regeneration (echoed in the
last act of *The Fall of Robespierre*) also continues the domestic
vision of *The Retrospect* by fondly enshrining the parent and
the parental home at the centre of his life. Southey could boast
(*NL* I, pp. 70–71): 'my Mother accompanies me, who will not
be the only Mrs Southey. The woman whom I love has
consented to go with her sisters.' Would this make the

foundation of a regenerated society, now envisaged on the banks of the Susquehanna? Would it not, as Coleridge perceived, simply invite a repetition of the old ills? How would the line of influence be broken between the grand-mothers, the mothers and the new generation of perfected children of Pantisocracy?

> The regulations relating to the females strike them as the most difficult; whether the marriage contract shall be dissolved if agreeable to one or both parties, and many other circumstances are not yet determined. The employments of the women are to be the care of infant children, and other occupations suited to their strength; at the same time the greatest attention is to be paid to the cultivation of their minds.[40]

This brief manifesto provides a glimpse of some form of liberation for the woman on the scheme. But she would inevitably be expected to nurse children, to remain in the maternal role, whether married or not. Marriage still implied ownership by the male, and passive obedience to the male. David Punter in *The Romantic Unconscious* comments upon the implications of this dumb subservience:

> Coleridge and Southey in the Pantisocratic experiment appear to be experimenting with the possibility of clon-ing, which would in turn entail a denial of the individ-uality of women.[41]

Other roles 'suited to their strength' would be found. Who would judge this 'strength', and who would fit the role of 'cultivator of minds'? The phrase itself implies that the women's minds are, like the American lands, fertile and ready for the Pantisocratic seed, lying passive and silent. Molly Lefebure (*L* p. 37) recognizes the convenience of the Fricker sisters as the nucleus of the Pantisocratic 'distaff side' and how they were apparently not positively consulted in the planning. Only Martha Fricker refused to be 'a wife in a hurry'.

Martha's comment, breaking the female silence, speaks volumes.

March 1795 was to be the month of departure (*NL* I, p. 76) and Coleridge was now in London trying to sell *The Fall of Robespierre*.[42] Southey wrote to his brother Thomas (*NL* I, p. 81):

> We are now twenty seven adventurers . . . You shall not remain longer in the navy than January . . . Think of America! . . . This Pantisocratic system has given me new life new hope new energy.

Southey was flung out of doors by his inhospitable aunt Tyler on 17 October 1794, an event which upset his mother considerably. Miss Tyler despised Southey's plans for America and for marriage, and had a pernicious hold (see *Simmons* p. 29) over his mother. Jean Raimond sees Southey's aunt plausibly as a 'femme phallique' (*RA* p. 560), a repressing dominatrix who embodied Southey's unconscious fear of (financial and social?) castration. Her rooted respectability had more power over him than he knew. Having bailed out the Southeys in 1792 (when his father was in prison for debt), Miss Tyler exercised her respectable and prohibiting powers over Southey's mother, and through her over Southey himself. The dubiously 'secure' (*Everest* p. 72) position Southey enjoyed in his family, as compared with that of Coleridge himself, bore with it the inevitable and imprisoning weight of socio-political attitudes from its centre of power. The conservatism of Johnson caught up with him before he even paid his passage.

Southey preferred to see women as he saw Miss Fricker (*NL* I, p. 84): 'like the lilly [sic] of the valley lovely in humility'. White and green, the colours of purity, virginity and renewal are suggested in this description. It was perhaps to be hoped that every Pantisocratic bride would epitomize these qualities. The pure woman, and the untouched, uncorrupting plot of ground (see *Everest* pp. 75 and 79) were vital components of the scheme; after all, it was through ownership of the women and the land that this essence of purity (schematized by the males) could be transferred to the new race. From the divinely natural condition of American soil also, would emanate the source, or the nature of renewal. The white virgin became the symbol of this new nature, which was attempting to come into being, to break with England, with Europe and all the old doomed natures and doomed political structures.

But even Godwin's evident approval of the scheme (*NL* I, p. 86) did not prevent Southey from some emotional confusion when his mother decided against the plan, and Edith took some re-persuading:

> my heart strings have been sadly jarrd. I had depended on my Mothers going. Ariste did the same—and her mothers accompanying us depended on that. My Mother seemed to change her resolution. Horace the question was—will you abandon all your relations for me—or me for your sisters and mother? . . . Heaven surely has no higher delight than I experienced at last from the answer . . . Linen drying by the fire! one person clear starching—one ironing—and one reading aloud in the room—a blessed scene to write in! Oh for my transatlantic log house! (*NL* I, pp. 86–87, 12 November 1794)

It is obvious that the inmates of this 'transatlantic log house' replicate the functions of domesticity (and the implied innate conservatism) that Southey enjoyed in England. Southey's reveries merely transplant domestic nuclei into fancies which perpetuate the old life. Neither his mother nor 'Ariste' (both so equally vital to his dream) were likely to be doing the writing, nor he himself the 'ironing'. Real equality, if it were possible, would come in the future generations of Pantisocracy, but only if the women were educated alongside the men, and if the men allowed the women freedom from the infant heirs of Pantisocracy. Perhaps it was his mother's decision to quit among other things that prompted Southey to suggest the Welsh farm scheme as an alternative to America:

> If we go into Wales it will be exactly upon the same plan
> as America that of establishing among ourselves the
> generalization of property and the equalization of
> labour. My Mother will go with us when this house is
> disposed of. (*NL* I, p. 90, 3 January 1795)

This farm would raise the money to make the trip to America
possible: it also carried Southey's mother on the first stage of
the journey to the American dream. Southey could still say in
March 1795:

> If Coleridge and I can get 150m pounds a year between
> us, we purpose marrying, and retiring into the country,
> as our literary business can be carried on there, and
> practising agriculture till we can raise money for Amer-
> ica—still the grand object in view. (*NL* I, p. 93)

During March he also gave his historical lectures in Bristol[43]
and spent much of the year revising *Joan of Arc* for the press,
with money-making in mind. But Southey never reached
America; it remained 'the grand object' in his writing only, as
his epic *Madoc* (begun in 1794) and his many poems on the
American Indians testify.[44]

Southey was caught between the enthusiastic belief in
regeneration and the duty to his family, especially his mother,
who stands for the past, a living nucleus of home, the mother-
country. Even in courting Edith Fricker, Southey is binding
himself to the past, as his family had had intimate connections
with the Frickers (see *L* p. 26ff) for many years, his projected
domesticity being a repeat of what was, recalling family ties.
By October 1795 (*LC* I, p. 81) Southey had rejected Godwin,
who he said 'theorizes for another state'. This confirms both
the practical nature of Southey's wants and their conservative
essence. America was in fact more of a way back than a way
out, and the yearning expressed in the *Madoc* of 1794 would
perhaps never really be satisfied:

Madoc, thou hast not told us yet what land
So long estrangd thee from us? hast thou found
Those distant realms beyond the vasty reign
Of Ocean, which thy Fancy picturd forth?[45]

NOTES

1 Lafayette (who had, incidentally, proposed a new American-style constitution) was a prisoner of the Austrians by 20 August, having fled from his army and defected, and he remained so until 1796.

2 See Mrs Henry Sandford, *Thomas Poole and His Friends* (London: Macmillan, 1888) pp. 100–07.

3 *Ibid.*, p. 97.

4 *Ibid.*, pp. 100–01.

5 See C. B. Hogan, *Shakespeare in the Theatre 1701–1800* (Oxford: Clarendon, 1957), pp. 319, 228, 391.

6 Gary Taylor, *Reinventing Shakespeare* (London: The Hogarth Press, 1990), p. 109.

7 Kelvin Everest discusses the political nature of Coleridge's 'Domestic Peace', from *The Fall of Robespierre*, and quotes Geoffrey Carnall who believes that the poem 'indicates where the deepest sympathies of both poets lay' (*Everest* p. 58). I am attempting to give colour to the two differing notions of this domestic ideal.

8 Many accounts of Pantisocracy have been written including: Sister Eugenia Logan, 'Coleridge's Scheme of Pantisocracy and American Travel Accounts', *PMLA* 45, pp. 1069–84; H. N. Fairchild, 'The Pantisocratic Phase' in *The Romantic Quest* (New York: Columbia University Press, 1931), pp. 50–69; and J. R. MacGillivray, 'The Pantisocratic Scheme and its Immediate Background', *Studies in English by Members of University College* (Toronto: University of Toronto Press, 1931), pp. 131–69. Kelvin Everest supplies the most thorough and stimulating modern account in his study (*Everest* ch. 3). Southey's involvement is explored in *The Politics of Nature* by Nicholas Roe (Basingstoke: Macmillan, 1992), chapter II, 'Robert Southey and the Origins of Pantisocracy', pp. 36–55.

9 At line 153 of Act I, Coleridge hints again at worldly powers which defy containment. His 'secret-sapping gold' recalls Pope's *Moral Essays* III, ll. 37–38, 'In vain may Heroes fight, and Patriots rave: / If secret Gold saps

on from knave to knave'. *The Poems of Alexander Pope*, ed. John Butt (London: Methuen, 1968), p. 573.

   10 Sister E. Logan, *op. cit.*, p. 1073.

   11 Note also Wordsworth's employment of Shakespeare in his allusion to *Macbeth* Act II, Scene II: 'Methought I heard a voice cry "Sleep no more!" ' in *The Prelude* Bk X, ll. 76–77: 'Until I seem'd to hear a voice that cried, / To the whole City, "Sleep no more" '. Ed. Ernest de Selincourt and Stephen Gill (Oxford: Oxford University Press, 1986), p. 179.

   12 Mrs Henry Sandford, *op. cit.*, pp. 98–99.

   13 See *Burke, Paine, Godwin, and the Revolution Controversy*, ed. Marilyn Butler (Cambridge: Cambridge University Press, 1984), p. 166.

   14 See *The Dialogues of Plato*, 4th edn, 4 vols, trans. B. Jowett (Oxford: Clarendon, 1953), Vol. II, *Republic* Bk II, pp. 221–23.

   15 Coleridge, *The Poverty of Historicism* (London: Routledge, 1957, repr. 1991), p. 73 and p. 89.

   16 Everest disagrees with Carl Woodring (*Woodring* p. 197) who claims that Pantisocracy (as viewed through 'Song') has a 'strong anti-political hue'. He says, '. . . it is difficult to see how Pantisocracy, a theory of social organization, could be regarded as "anti-political". It certainly assimilates Coleridge's stress on the values of friendship and familial community, but this argues for the politicality that developed in these values, rather than for Coleridge's resort to these values as an alternative, transcending social and political issues, to involvement in the life of his times. Coleridge felt that personal problems, and the problems created by his relation to English society in the 1790s, could both be resolved in a single way' (*Everest* pp. 58–59).

   17 Bk IV, ll. 81ff: 'boasting I could subdue / Th'Omnipotent'.

   18 Noel Parker in *Portrayals of Revolution* (London: Harvester Wheatsheaf, 1990), p. 44, notes the appropriate theme of Voltaire's *Brutus* (performed 31 times) as applied to the revolutionary period when it was often produced. 'It situated in classical history a tragic conflict between duty towards the public good and private passion and ambition . . . In the early 1790s, the parallel between the situation of Rome and France . . . can only have reinforced its effectiveness . . .' The red cap of liberty itself was 'a neo-classical allusion to the practice of freed Roman slaves' (Parker, ibid., p. 92).

   19 *The Prelude*, *op. cit.*, Bk X, ll. 108–11, p. 180.

   20 See *Patriotism: The Making and Unmaking of the British National Identity*, Vol. I, ed. R. Samuel (London/New York: Routledge, 1989), p. 60.

   21 See Marilyn Butler, *Romantics, Rebels and Reactionaries* (Oxford: Oxford University Press, 1981), pp. 3–4.

   22 *The Prelude*, *op. cit.*, Bk IX, l. 126, p. 154.

23 J. M. Thompson, *Leaders of the French Revolution* (Oxford: Basil Blackwell, 1988).

24 *Ibid.*, p. 191.

25 *Ibid.*, p. 209.

26 In Geoffrey Grigson's *The Harp of Aeolus* (London: Routledge, 1947), there is a chapter on the Upas tree (pp. 56–65) and its development into one major Romantic symbol.

27 See Thomas Paine, *Rights of Man* (Harmondsworth: Penguin American Library, 1984), p. 50.

28 Parker, *op. cit.*, p. 27.

29 See 'English Romanticism' in *Romanticism Reconsidered*, ed. Northrop Frye (New York and London: Columbia University Press, 1963), pp. 30–37.

30 *Ibid.*, Bk X, ll. 539–42.

31 Compare this with the Horatian sentiments of Pope's *Ode on Solitude* st. V, in *The Poems of Alexander Pope*, ed. John Butt (London: Methuen, 1965), p. 265:

> Thus let me live, unseen, unknown:
> Thus unlamented let me dye;
> Steal from the world, and not a stone
> Tell where I lye.

32 Abraham Cowley, *The Essays and other Prose Writings*, ed. A. B. Gough (Oxford: Clarendon, 1915), p. 7.

33 Arthur H. Nethercot, *Abraham Cowley The Muse's Hannibal* (New York: Russell and Russell, 1931/1967), p. 232.

34 *The Yale Edition of the Works of Samuel Johnson* Vol. III, *The Rambler*, ed. W. J. Bate and Albrecht B. Strauss (New Haven and London: Yale University Press, 1969), p. 35.

35 *Studies in Classic American Literature* (London: Martin Secker, 1933), p. 12. Lawrence's own desire for the ideal community or rananim, something he continually sought for throughout his life, is well known. Kenneth Young, *D. H. Lawrence*, Writers and Their Works No. 31 (London: Longman, 1963), p. 11, called this 'rananim' 'but the old Coleridge "pantisocracy" '.

36 I fail to see how this can be, in the words of Nicholas Roe, entirely a 'comfortable reverie' when the admittedly playful passage ends in despair about society and death. See *The Politics of Nature* (Basingstoke: Macmillan, 1992), p. 48.

37 'Rousseau and Epictetus, in fact, battled for the possession of Southey's mind to the end of his days' (*N* p. 210).

38 Joseph Priestley, *The Present State of Europe compared with Antient Prophecies* (London: J. Johnson, 1794).

39 *Ibid.*, p. 31.

40 Mrs Henry Sandford, *Thomas Poole and his Friends* (London: Macmillan, 1888), p. 98.

41 David Punter, *The Romantic Unconscious* (Hemel Hempstead: Harvester Wheatsheaf, 1989), p. 50.

42 See *Griggs* I, pp. 98, 101 and 117 for details of Coleridge's involvement of George Dyer in the publication and distribution of the play. Later on 6 November 1794 Southey was composing his *Wat Tyler*, an anti-monarchical play with much the same heated atmosphere as *The Fall of Robespierre*.

43 See *The Collected Works of Samuel Taylor Coleridge* No. I, ed. Lewis Patton and Peter Mann (Princeton: Princeton University Press, 1971), pp. xii, xxxiii–xxxv.

44 Various 'Songs of the American Indians' were written by Southey in 1799, and as Fairchild (*N* p. 452) says: 'Their outstanding feature is an unusual desire to find romance *in* the Indian instead of imposing romance *upon* him'. (See also *N* pp. 202–04 and 452–53.)

45 Kenneth Curry, 'Southey's *Madoc*: The Manuscript of 1794', *Philological Quarterly*, Vol. XXII, No. IV, October 1943, p. 360, ll. 353–56.

Chapter Three

Joan of Arc: The First Edition, 1796: True Patriots of the Hearth

Homer is the Poet for the Warrior—Milton for the Religionist—
Tasso for Women—Robert Southey for the Patriot. (*Griggs* I, p. 258)

It has been established as a necessary rule for the Epic, that the subject
be national. To this rule I have acted in direct opposition, and chosen
for the subject of my poem the defeat of my country. (*Joan of Arc*,
Preface, p. vii)

By interweaving *The Fall of Robespierre* and the Pantisocratic
scheme I hoped to show how Southey's views upon the
regeneration of France were shadows of his own personal
desires, and also how his deep-rooted sense of love and duty to
his own family thwarted the radical perfectibility envisaged by
Coleridge. The pressure of the past, which Southey admitted
and enshrined in *The Retrospect*, was carried forward through
the regenerative bragging in *The Fall of Robespierre* and into
Pantisocracy itself. Yet Southey's *Joan of Arc* displays a
continued philanthropic interest in some idea of the Universal
Family, which, if not exactly Pantisocratic, contains a *patriotism* in the radical sense of 'a loyalty to the welfare of mankind'[1]
boldly stated.

In *Joan of Arc*, Southey again examines aspects of renewal,
both national and personal. The leader of this regenerative
impulse is a woman who embodies purity, liberty and
strength, and who brings peace by conquering the English in
the epic. 'En célébrant la grandeur de Jeanne d'Arc, Southey
exalt la femme en général. L'image qu'il nous donne de Jeanne
séduirait les partisans du feminisme.' The rather patronizing
and seductive empowering (*RA* p. 197) of a female entity, a

85

female voice for democratic purposes may have raised eye-
brows in some quarters, despite the universally-acceptable
anti-war message of the poem. Yet as Bernhardt-Kabisch says:

> In other respects, Southey's choice of heroine was
> brilliant, and it anticipated by a whole decade the Maid's
> promotion to the rank of national heroine under Napo-
> leon as well as Schiller's treatment of her legend in *Die
> Jungfrau von Orleans*. In accordance with Classical
> precedent, Joan lent Southey's theme the authority of
> age. At the same time, she was a radically modern
> protagonist. For although there had been a long line of
> literary Amazons—Virgil's Camilla, Tasso's Clorinda,
> Spenser's Britomart—the theory that a woman could be
> the hero of an epic had not hitherto been put to a serious
> test. Southey's poem would boldly oppose the spirit of
> equality to the tyranny of decorum and the humane
> commonsense of Mary Wollstonecraft to the 'despotism
> of Aristotle' and Le Bossu. (*K* p. 31)

Southey employs two main strands of argument in the poem.
Joan herself, the heroine leading regeneration through warfare, and the little pictures of domesticity around which this
war is enacted. Regeneration and domestic stasis are literally at
war in the text, as I will demonstrate, and by the date of the
poem's publication Southey had partially resolved the
problem of this dialectical struggle, within himself at least.
The long gestation period of the poem was in effect the
gestation of Southey's own struggle with these poles. Here I
want to examine briefly the poem's genesis, thoroughly lay
bare its pro-domestic message—which, I will suggest, is not
essentially Burkean—and draw attention finally to the critical
reception the poem received and the implications of this.

Joan of Arc was originally drafted out in 1793, at the
Bedford's residence at Brixton Causeway, then revised and
reworked until Joseph Cottle published it in 1796. Back in
July 1793 Southey wanted not so much to write a national epic

but rather to 'deserve popularity' (*NL* I, pp. 28–29), even if this meant satisfying a few friends only for the time being, anticipating the responses of a larger audience. He goes on: 'my Joan is a great democrat or rather will be', and hopes to join her symbolically to the 'Genius of Liberty'. Clearly Southey had large ambitions here.

> The enormous fecundity of Southey's heroic muse and his long-lived ambition to devote an epic to each of the major religions were not just products of an impulsive and headlong nature but the single most voluminous precipitation of what was generally in the air. More immediately, of course, the Romantic and Southeyan epic got its impetus from the revolutionary fervor of the period. Great ages had always demanded great song to embody their spirit. What, then, could be plainer than the duty of a poet, especially a young one, to officiate as the bard of democracy, to sing the wrath of the People, to depict in epic form the fall of Louis the Last, the advent of the Millennium, and the regeneration of the human race? There was only one difficulty: the traditional epic had rested heavily on the very concepts of hierarchy, aristocracy, and precedent which the Revolution attacked . . . Southey sensed the problem . . . but he never quite made the break with Classicism . . . Short of writing a 'para-epic,' or modern *Pharsalia*, about the fall of Albion or of withdrawing into remote historical analogues, the English bard had no alternative but the unheard-of one of hymning the cause of the national enemy. (*K* pp. 29–30)

And, as Southey explains in his preface (*Joan of Arc*, p. v), in epic poetry generally, the reader often cannot sympathize with the heroes depicted, so:

> to engage the unprejudiced, there must be more of human feelings than is generally to be found in the

character of Warriors: from this objection the Odyssey
alone may be excepted. Ulysses appears as the father and
the husband, and the affections are enlisted on his side
. . . it is the poem of nature . . . The good Eumaeus is
worth a thousand heroes!

If he chose to act in 'direct opposition' to the accepted rule of
epic then he at least hoped that, as he says of Glover's poems
(p. vii), 'the young heart will feel itself warmed by the struggle
and success of free men'. If Joan herself was a democrat in a
thin disguise, at least everyone could sympathize with her
humanity.

In 1793, and of course more fully in 1794–95, Southey's
mind was intent upon emigration to America, or at least upon
escape from England, and *Joan of Arc* in fact reached America
(see *M* p. 23) as Southey did not, being published there in
Boston soon after the English edition was released. Yet it is
not America, but Portugal that he alludes to on page ix of the
Preface: 'Such as it is, the poem is before the world. I shall not
witness its reception, and it will not be long before the tidings
will reach me in a distant part of Europe.' American Pantisocracy was over by then, but the quest for home remained
inscribed in the heart of the epic.

Scattered throughout *Joan of Arc* are Southey's little idylls
of desire for retreat, domesticity, a longing for mankind to be
welcomed back from the city and the rule of kings into the
small circles of association under the sway of some beneficent
god of nature. Wordsworth commented upon these moments
in the epic, in a letter to William Mathews, 21 March 1796, as
'some passages' in the poem 'of first-rate excellence'.[2] Charles
Lamb followed suit in a letter to Coleridge, 10 June 1796:

The anecdotes interspersed among the battles refresh the
mind very agreeably, and I am delighted with the very
many passages of simple pathos abounding throughout
the poem—passages which the author of 'Crazy Kate'
might have written.[3]

It is Coleridge, however, who criticizes the epic in the greatest detail, perhaps because he had something of a vested interest in his by then estranged friend's work. As Southey noted in his *Preface*:

> The 450 lines at the beginning of the second book, were written by S.T. COLERIDGE. But from this part must be excepted the lines 141, 142, 143; and the whole intermediate passage from 148 to 222. The lines from 226 to 272 are, likewise mine, and the lines from 286 to 291. (p. vi)

One can perhaps sense the animosity of the poet in the exact way he delineates Coleridge's contribution.[4] Coleridge gave his opinions of the poem as a whole in a letter (*Griggs* I, pp. 293–94) to John Thelwall of 31 December 1796. He could find something to praise in the smaller moments of the poem even if Southey in his eyes did not display 'that *toil* of thinking' which led to the grand harmony of wholeness so important to him.

> I think, that an admirable Poet might be made by *amalgamating him & me*. I think too much for a *Poet*; he too little for a *great* Poet. But he abjures *thinking* & lays the whole stress of excellence—on *feeling*.—Now (as you say) they must go together.

Southey's accent on feeling certainly leads to a see-sawing motion between the idylls of simplicity and the melodramatic portrayals of war. Coleridge also notices the idyll-making which will form the basis of this discussion. 'In language at once natural, perspicuous, & dignified, in manly pathos, in soothing & sonnet-like description . . . Southey is unrivalled.' It is this sonnet-like description, these little rooms in the text that I want to centre my reading around, not the least because they are the sheet-anchor of the Maid's psychology.

2
The Patriot's Textscape of Feeling: A Descriptive Tour

> Seize then my Soul! from Freedom's trophied Dome
> The Harp which hanging high between the shields
> Of Brutus and Leonidas, oft gives
> A fitful music to the breezy touch
> Of patriot Spirits that demand their fame.
>
> (*Joan*, p. 39, by Coleridge)

Southey's Maid springs up out of this landscape of feeling, to fight against what were thought to be invincible forces invested in the English monarchy. Yet she lives only to be betrayed by monarchical forces:

> Her family was ennobled by Charles (the French king), but it should not be forgotten in the history of this monarch, that in the hour of misfortune he abandoned to her fate, the woman who had saved his kingdom. (*Joan*, p. xi)

Southey finally stops short of the martyrdom of the Maid, at the coronation of Charles, where Joan exhorts him (Bk X) against the oppression of his people. She hopes (Bk X, ll. 747–48) that 'the ALL-JUST' may always 'Give to the arms of FREEDOM such success'. He allows his heroine to found a new order of kings, a curious but historically sound twist, given his own anti-monarchical views in the 1790s. However, he does imply that the good king, the benevolent ruler, like a Pantisocratic father re-aligned with the God of love, is preferable to the Robespierrian chaos of political faction. And as Joan says to Richemont in Book X:

> He best
> Performs the Patriot's and the Good Man's part,
> Who, in the ear of Rage and Faction, breathes
> The healing words of Love. (*Joan*, p. 381)

In June 1814, Coleridge (*Griggs* III, p. 510) called Southey's Joan 'Tom Paine in petticoats', a remark that echoes Horace Walpole's verdict upon Mary Wollstonecraft.[5] Southey's political alignment with Painite democracy and early feminism, performing in epic manner the 'Patriot's and the Good Man's part', is obvious. Yet there is textual evidence to suggest that Southey projects something of his own character through that of the Maid, although writers such as Ingvald Raknem[6] see the character of Conrade as Southey's voice in the poem. The main correspondences are the Maid's reverence for natural purity, and the fact that she has lost her father in a time of trauma. Both fathers' deaths are associated with city affairs, war and commerce, and look back to the epitaphic *The Retrospect* of 1794 in this theme alone. Southey and his Maid are displaced from their respective hearths, and set upon their respective quests in time of war:

> Seat of my earliest years!
> Still busy Fancy loves with fairy touch
> To paint its faded scenes: even now mine eye
> Darts thro' the past in retrospective glance,
> And calls to view each haunt of sportive youth,
> Each long-lost haunt I lov'd: the woodbin'd wall,
> The jasmine that around the straw-roof'd cot
> Its fragrant branches wreath'd, beneath whose shade
> I wont to sit and mark the setting sun
> And hear the redbreast's lay. Nor far remote
> As o'er the landskip round I gaz'd,
> The towr's of Harfleur rose upon the view.
> A foreign master holds my father's home!
> I, far away, remember the past years,
> And weep. (*Joan*, pp. 10–11)

Joan's origins are the small community, not the city, and the cot (reminiscent of Coleridge's Clevedon retreat, *CP* p. 106) wreathed in fragrant flowers, suggesting the harmonious balance between the human and the natural non-human world. Southey is also preaching an obvious democratic message:

> The poem is the creation of a poet who was at logger-heads with his age, i.e. with the policy of oppression pursued by the die-hard Tories of the 1790's and later.[7]

Warfare in the epic is the effect of misrule by monarchs whose city power-bases create and perpetuate the evils which spring up when the citizen is separated from beneficent nature. Church and state suffer alike from city corruption, but those who suffer the most are the common people, perhaps soldiers recruited from their rural homes, forced into combat unwillingly, leaving behind the broken circles of domestic association. Joan is the champion of these people.[8]

Joan's early memories are of invasion by the English forces and the flight from home, leaving 'Silent the hamlet haunts of Innocence' (p. 11). The fracture of good associations marks the Maid's mind with 'bleeding memory' from this point. Jean Raimond (*RA* pp. 197–98) regards this deprivation of parental affection in Joan's life as a root of her recourse to stoical values, which of course links her directly with Southey. The fracture from home-life is brutal:

> The shrieks of anguish and the yell of war
> And Death's deep groan, yet vibrate upon my heart,
> Yet wake the strings of grief! (*Joan*, p. 13)

Joan calls upon the spirit of her father to watch over her as she quits the domestic joys of the hamlet to fulfil her destiny, and in her description of the scattering of the community after Harfleur, she recalls the Miltonic expulsion from Eden:

> Suddenly all was still: anon burst forth
> The shout of conquest: from their long lov'd homes
> Thrust forth, the unhappy natives wander o'er
> The wasted plain, in want and wretchedness.
> (*Joan*, pp. 14–15)

The man of nature, a hermit called Bizardo, looks after the
Maid in the seclusion of his cave-dwelling:

> Rude was Bizardo's cell; the beetling rock
> Frown'd o'er its ivied entrance; the hewn stone
> Form'd his rough seat, and on a bed of leaves
> The aged hermit took his nightly rest.
> A pure stream welling from the mossy rock
> Crept murmuring thro' the wood, and many a flow'r
> Drank on its side the genial sap of life. (*Joan*, p. 16)

As in Joan's first home, the natural forces envelop and
embrace the dwelling, which is bedded in adamant rock away
from the monarchical forces of war. Unlike her wandering
kinsfolk, Joan has found the special opening of the natural
landscape, the rock cell, from which the source of life, the
'pure stream', emerges into the world of fallen man (p. 18)
mentioned by Bizardo. Cave and stream are two common
motifs associated with retreat and melancholy in the poetry of
the eighteenth century, but are modified here to form the
natural basis for social reform. Bizardo is another of Southey's
father-figures, the hermit or sage, whose welcoming arms and
secure cave are the places where society has its boundaries. As
a liminal figure, he is sensitive to the needs of those who, as
victims of that society, fly to him for help. He represents that
strand of eighteenth-century thought which saw city life as a
great evil, which anticipated reform, regeneration for
mankind. Carl Woodring links the hatred of cities to Pantisocracy:

> However diverse, all primitivists wanted London
> unmade. Pantisocracy, looking like a temple to Nature,
> rose partly from the need to exorcise the diabolical forces
> of the city. Convinced by the Hartleian psychology that
> the mental associations of the child determine the moral
> character and nearly all else of the adult . . . Coleridge
> wished to gather a few enlightened, benevolent fathers

together in a rural setting so that their children would develop as far removed as possible from men in their civilised, fallen state. (*Woodring* p. 66)[9]

Bizardo's cave is, however, a specific allusion to an image in the poetry of Spenser, in *The Faerie Queene*, Bk I, canto I, no. 34:

> A little lowly hermitage it was,
> Down in a dale, hard by a forest's side,
> Far from resort of people, that did pas
> In travel to and froe: a little wyde
> There was an holy Chappell edifyde,
> Wherein the Hermit dewly wont to say
> His holy things each morne and eventyde:
> Thereby a Christall streame did gently play,
> Which from a sacred fountaine welled forth alway.

The hermit as a poetic motif proliferates in the eighteenth century,[10] and in Southey's poem his purpose is to join the politicized ideas of retreat and simplicity with closeness to the divine. Bizardo's 'melancholy' points out the true path towards the divine which has been lost within the cities of men. Joan's own melancholy aversion to cities is the white melancholy which looks to a millennium directly connected to the purity which feeds the Maid as it feeds the flowers. Bizardo himself instructs her in the natural lore of the forest:

> Of every herb that blooms amid the grove,
> Or on the high cliff drinks a purer air
> He bade me know the virtue. (*Joan*, p. 17)

Joan's purity feeds from the very root-source of the landscape, a landscape like that of the American dream. Southey is at pains to show this aspect of Joan throughout the epic, as here in Book III where she stands before the corrupt Doctors and the representatives of the Church:

So have I seen the simple snow-drop rise
Amid the russet leaves that hide the earth
In early spring, so seen its gentle bend
Of modest loveliness amid the waste
Of desolation. (*Joan*, p. 107)

This continues the depiction of woman as purity to which I alluded in the previous chapter. Once again Southey employs the colours white and green, set here amongst brown leaves symbolizing the fallen nature of the church and recalling the fallen angels of Milton's *Paradise Lost* (Bk I, l. 302ff). Joan brings the hope of a second democratic spring (as the snow-drop is a spring flower) for her people under the desolate misrule of the monarchs. But before this can happen, Joan must be pushed closer to the war.

Bizardo and the Maid take in Theodore, a wounded youth, and nurse him. Then the hermit, Joan's spiritual father, dies, signalling another departure for the heroine, another expulsion from home. They journey to Theodore's village, where again the Maid tastes the settled daily life of peace:

Sometimes at morn
With pleasing toil to drive the woolly flock
To verdant mead or stream, sometimes to ease
The lowing cattle of their milky load,
My grateful task. (Bk I, p. 24)

Southey inserts his descriptive pastoral idylls into the poem with a rather plaintive frequency, recalling the classical georgic, and, like the *Georgics* of Virgil particularly, countering the harmonious pictures of farm life with forces of adversity. Southey's adverse powers are not found in the climate especially, but in the unnatural political activities of men fired by ambition and greed. Joan is alerted to these evils, as manifest in war, by her meeting with Conrade who comes inside Theodore's house to shelter from a storm (natural and

political) raging outside. Conrade serves the French cause
mindful of the cares of his own domesticity, having left his
aged mother behind. Joan's comment 'I never dreamt of what
the wretched feel' (p. 25), recalls King Lear's own exposure to
the elements upon the heath, and the subsequent review of his
status. The Maid is set to unite a fractured kingdom—unlike
the aged Lear, the symbol of decayed monarchy, a man who
gave his own kingdom away to the vicious mercies of faction
and personal ambition. Conrade's words seem to provoke her
visionary determination to lead her country's regeneration.
Joan has her first vision (p. 33) in natural seclusion. Like the
cave, the 'dingle' here has divine or magical connotations, and
is another significant eighteenth-century emblem of communion with the larger universe.

> Down in the dingles depth there is a brook
> That makes its way between the craggy stones
> Murmuring hoarse murmurs. On an aged oak
> Whose root uptorn by tempests overhangs
> The stream, I sat, and mark'd the deep red clouds
> Gather before the wind, whilst the rude dash
> Of waters rock'd my senses, and the mists
> Rose round . . .

The Maid sits like a figure from Ossianic mythology upon her
emblem, the tempest-shaken oak, which itself links her to
ideas of endurance, of victory (oak leaves), the natural world
and her own struggle. Death and madness are present here as
well, half hidden in the allusion to Ophelia's reported death in
Shakespeare's *Hamlet* (Act IV, Scene VII, ll. 167ff). Purity
challenged or destroyed by worldly, or more precisely kingly,
powers, is what Southey is trying to evoke. The Maid is, like
Ophelia, quite alone in her situation, both in the court and by
the brook. Joan is Nature's child, as Dunois remarks to the
King in Book III, p. 110: 'She has liv'd retir'd . . . ignorant of
courts . . .', the very places (p. 128) where lurk the 'foul
corruption-gender'd swarm of state'. Joan herself describes

her attitude to the external natural world and the powers therein:

> I saw th' eternal energy pervade
> The boundless range of nature, with the Sun
> Pour radiance from his flamy path,
> And on the lowliest flowret in the field
> The kindly dew-drops shed. All nature's voice
> Proclaim'd the all-good Parent; nor myself
> Deem'd I by him neglected. This good Power
> My more than Father taught my youth to know,
> Knowing to love, and loving to adore. (*Joan*, pp. 110–11)

One of the French priests who comes to examine Joan demands to know whether nature taught her religion, and has therefore deluded her into sin. She replies (p. 114): 'It is not Nature that can teach to sin; / Nature is all Benevolence—all Love'. Bearing in mind Raymond Williams' remarks[11] on how different social and political models of the world are often constructed around different ideas of Nature, we can once again detect Southey's underlying interest in ideas of political purity springing up in an unblemished natural landscape. Southey advocates a politicality seated in a cleansed landscape, a true patriotism of sisterly and fraternal love. Further to this, Marina Warner[12] views Southey's heroine as an embodiment of the unspoiled culture of the soil, a Rousseauesque pre-industrial figure. Joan's visions, rooted in the relative purity of her home landscape, devalue the attitudes of medieval super-stition (which, it is implied, is still functioning in 1796), shown in the epic as priestly corruption. Joan's supernatural abilities come to her as Warner says 'like weather' and derive from her closeness with the uncorrupted natural world, and therefore from her direct correspondence with the deity who created it. Southey, then, appears to be taking care not to censure the Christian God, whilst at the same time condemn-ing the priesthood. Joan's personal voices cause her to act on behalf of the people, but paradoxically, whilst serving her

God, she invokes the very system of power which has been used to chain and subdue them. Bernhardt-Kabisch notes that:

> In revising the poem in 1798, Southey joined the critical opposition to machinery in the epic: he eliminated the supernatural element and, at about the time that Words-worth passed Milton's angel-thronged cosmos for the vaster and more awesome regions within the Mind of Man, inserted the following palinode into his preface: 'The aid of angels and devils is not necessary to raise [Joan] above mankind; she has no gods to lackey her . . . [She] acts wholly from the workings of her own mind . . . The palpable agency of superior powers would destroy the obscurity of her character. (*K* p. 32)

But in the years 1793–96, the poet, with some awareness of his market, defers to authorities and influences which respect the Classical epic form, to religious ideas, and to the commercial system which would print and circulate, and, importantly for the struggling young poet, buy up his work. As we have seen, Southey wanted to escape the tyrannies of Bristolian commerce, which had ruined his father, for 'peace amid the dearest joys of home' as described by Theodore (p. 29), but realized that, like Conrade, he would have to leave 'an aged mother' (p. 27) and a family now dependent upon him for financial help in the long term. In fact the problems of emigration, the castrating forces of retrospective memory, and deferral to social and literary authorities provoke the writing of what is in effect an epic of defacement. We might even say that Southey is writing a defaced autobiography, one of his books of Pantisocracy. If, as Paul de Man says, 'Prosopopeia is the trope of autobiography',[13] then Southey's Joan, speaking his own biography, places his voice inside the puppet and in the past, trapping it in text. This trapped voice, or voices, can only repeat Southey's message that an evil or unenlightened ruler infects the nation with discordant misery. The poem is fertile in examples of this kind of misrule. In Book II,

Joan is entertained by Old Bertram, who escaped having
escaped death at Agincourt, was released by his English
captors:

> Them louting low with rustic courtesy
> He welcom'd in, on the white-ember'd hearth
> Then heapt fresh fuel, and with friendly care
> Spread the homely board: fatigued they eat
> The country cakes and quaff the nut-brown bowl.
> (*Joan*, p. 66)[14]

Bertram entertains (p. 73) his children from his store of tales
about war: 'I lov'd around the cheerful hearth / To tell of all
the perils I had known: / My children they would sit and listen
eager, / And bless the all-good Father who preserv'd me'.
Tales of war are put into the positive context of children's
stories. But added to this, and more to the purposes of
democratic propaganda, is the adult tale of the cruelty of the
English King Henry V, who at the siege of Rouen, had driven
out French citizens from their homes into the midwinter cold
to starve to death. Southey's anathema is embodied in this
unfeeling guardian of the common folk, a treacherous *father*
of a nation, acting without remorse:

> I did think
> There was not on this earth a heart so hard
> Could hear a famish'd woman cry for bread,
> And know no pity. (*Joan*, p. 79)

The aged Bertram is to be torn from his hearth again to do his
duty in war. Characters like Bertram, with his own simple and
instinctive sense of patriotism, are meant to emphasize the
anti-Christian, anti-domestic horrors of war, and the corruption of monarchs. Kings who have lost touch with a people
whose relative closeness to the natural world endows their
little circles of domesticity with the mark of the universal
family of God. It is left to Joan herself to bring the court and
the powers of God-in-nature together, with a demonstration

of divine intervention, a sign from God, before the Doctors at the end of Book III. Book IV sees her in among the licentious courtiers (who buzz like bees), the text once again linking her with the natural world:

> As o'er some flowery field the busy bees
> Pour their deep music, pleasant melody
> To the tired traveller, under some oak
> Stretch'd in the chequer'd shade; or as the sound
> Of far-off waters down the craggy steep
> Dash'd with loud uproar, rose the murmer [sic] round
> Of admiration. Every gazing eye
> Dwelt on the mission'd Maid. (*Joan*, p. 128)

The naturalizing epic simile reclaims for a moment the lost and corrupted society of the court. This simile recalls Virgil's fourth *Georgic*, the bee-society hard at work in the service of its monarch, and the monarch of the bees itself serving its republic. Yet the bee-republics fight amongst themselves to the detriment of both societies, as France and England fight here. Virgil states the care needed by the bee-keeper over his charge, just as the monarch should look to the welfare of the people. Joan herself, like the 'tired traveller' in the simile, listens to the hum of the court, and the common people, and especially to the voice of the God speaking to the individual who has retired into the contemplation of divine work.

The isolated and decadent French king Charles (p. 131), cannot understand the Maid's interest in being: 'Devoted for the King-curst realm of France!'. Joan's duty leads her to take up the old armour of the hero Orlando from his tomb to invest her purpose with past glory. She reminds the withdrawn and sensual king that he is responsible for the subjects he commands and ultimately for their patriotic actions:

> They wait thy will to quit their peaceful homes,
> To quit the comforts of domestic life,

For the camp's dissonance, the clang of arms,
The banquet of destruction. (*Joan*, p. 148)

> Believe me, king,
> If thou didst know the untold misery
> When from the bosom of domestic Love
> But one—one victim goes! if that thine heart
> Be human, it would bleed! (*Joan*, p. 151)

Charles' response to the impending arousal of the nation for war is to decree a fast, for which the Maid rebukes him. His subjects, especially if poor, need to be fed to fight properly. Book V describes the march to Orleans, the first city that the Maid is to liberate. As a warrior-figure, Joan is surely cognate with the revolutionary figure of Liberty, the championess of virtue. But she is also a distressed heroine, an immensely popular figure in the literature of the 1790s. And Southey has other distressed and oppressed women in his epic—figures that serve both political *and* fashionable literary ends.

Joan and the warrior Dunois encounter one of these women, Isabel, called 'The Wanderer', who has been outcast from Orleans, and rescued by Conrade, who comments:

> But little cause to love the mighty ones
> Has the low cottager! for with its shade
> Does POWER, a barren death-dew-dropping tree,
> Blast ev'ry herb beneath its baleful boughs! (*Joan*, p. 162)

Conrade's presentation of the abstract 'POWER' as an Upas-tree, suggests the direct opposite of the revolutionary liberty-tree. Power—here as kingly power—an abstract vice serving an individual's ambition, spreads its poison down through the ranks of its subjects, whose local and particular lives are of no consequence to it, but grouped together as a nation support its very fabric, and it is obvious how usefully such an image could be employed in a radical critique of monarchy:

There is a tree in the island of Java, called the Upas, or
poison-tree . . . The Upas grows . . . in a plain surrounded by rocky mountains; the whole of which plain,
containing a circle of ten, or twelve miles round the tree,
is totally barren. Nothing, that breathes, or vegetates,
can live within it's [sic] influence. The bird, that flies over
it, drops down dead. The beast, that wanders into it,
expires. The whole dreadful area is covered with sand,
over which lie scattered loose flints, and whitening
bones.[15]

Conrade has another grievance against the Upas-monarch
Charles, namely that he took Agnes, Conrade's intended, for
his mistress. Conrade thinks over what might have been if
Agnes had remained with him, and he looks back to a pastoral
age of domestic association which at once suggests Southey's
American or domestic utopia:

> 'Oh happy age!'
> He cried, 'when all the family of man
> Freely enjoyed the goodly earth he gave,
> And only bow'd the knee in prayer to God!
> Calm flow'd the unruffled stream of years along,
> Till o'er the peaceful rustic's head, grew grey
> The hairs in full of time. Then he would sit
> Beneath the coetaneous oak, whilst round,
> Sons, grandsons, and their offspring join'd to form
> The blameless merriment; and learnt of him
> What time to yoke the oxen to the plough,
> What hollow moanings of the western wind
> Foretel [sic] the storm, and in what lurid clouds
> The embryo lightning lies. Well-pleas'd, he taught,
> The heart-smile glowing on his aged cheek,
> Mild as decaying light of summer sun.
> Thus calmly constant flowed the stream of life
> Till lost at length amid that shoreless sea,
> Eternity.' (*Joan*, p. 243)[16]

Southey echoes the poet Gray here, whose rustic swains teach the quiet pleasures of retirement and homely life. The 'coetaneous oak' being the symbol for the uninterrupted growth of body, mind, and familial circles. This may be compared with the inscribed tree-trunk in the discussion of *The Retrospect* (p. 9), itself linked to growth, even distortion, but not violent change. Southey's picturesque tree-imagery works with many symbolic interpretations, such as the human mind, the duration of human life, and liberty itself. Earlier in this chapter we saw Joan sitting upon an oak in what is in effect a painterly description. Her oak then symbolized the uprooting of the state:

> The *blasted tree* has often a fine effect both in natural and artificial landscape. In some scenes it is almost essential. When the dreary heath is spread before the eye, and ideas of wildness and desolation are required, what more suitable accompaniment can be imagined, than the blasted oak, ragged, scathed, and leafless; shooting it's [sic] peeled, white branches athwart the gathering blackness of some rising storm?

William Gilpin[17] here takes note of the adaptability of the oak to landscape views, especially those constructed in the picturesque fashion. The oak seemed to Gilpin to provide a universally convenient motif; it could never seem out of place in the painter's work. Carl Woodring comments (*Woodring* p. 136) that the 'oak, if it represents most narrowly the Whig party, absorbs the traditional meaning of "the British oak", the state, the constitution, and more, as in Southey's poem *The Oak of Our Fathers*, first published in the *Annual Anthology*, 1799'. He draws attention to Burke's picture of a national oak (*B* p. 181), under whose shadow 'thousands of great cattle . . . chew the cud and are silent'. Burke's picture of the British subject as a placid beast of the field, under the oak of state (swine in other places), is of interest not simply because of Burke's rather condescending view of the ordinary

subject, which is what Carl Woodring fixes upon, but for the
kind of landscape picture that Burke chooses.

His is no romantic dell, shut away from the spies of the
state, where all manner of plots and schemes may be hatched.
Burke's field and the summer mood of his grasshoppers
suggest the Italian-inspired calm of the painter Claude Lorraine (1600–82), or the cattle-paintings of the Dutchman
Albert Cuyp (1620–91). Both artists would have been well
represented by their paintings and prints in England by the
late eighteenth century. But most importantly, Burke's political idyll is not really picturesque, if we take the key virtue of
that word to be roughness. His smooth, Italianate calm, a
never-ending summer mood reflecting a nation's dormant
power, has a classical stateliness, even an indifference, before
which the revolutionary grasshoppers chirrup in vain. Burke's
little picture entirely supports his views concerning the
dangers of radical political change. Where Burke is at pains to
show the unified nation indifferent to change, Southey in *Joan
of Arc* presents a differing picture, the fragmentation of the
simple family unit, the very building-blocks of Burke's
general vision. Southey's aforementioned Isabel is a victim of
the monarchical Upas-tree. Her tale may be seen as a glimpse
of Pantisocracy if the domestic idyll described is viewed as a
model for society:

> Of lowly line
> Not far from Jenville, dwelt my sire.
> Two brethren form'd our family of love.
> Humble we were, but happy. Honest toil
> Procur'd our homely sustenance. Our herds
> Duly at morn and evening to my hand
> Gave their full stores. The vineyard he had rear'd
> Purpled its clusters in the southern sun;
> And plenteous produce of my father's toil
> The yellow harvest billow'd o'er the plain.
> We were content and envied not the great;

We fear'd them not, for we were innocent.
How chearful seated round the blazing hearth
When all the labour of the day was done,
We past the ev'ning hours! for they would sing
Or chearful roundelay, or ditty sad . . .
. . . the while my spinning wheel
Humm'd not unpleasant round! (*Joan*, p. 162)

Southey presents his cottagers (worthy inhabitants of his
projected transatlantic log cabin, *and* of his later poetry) as
innocent families dwelling in simplicity. Innocence and
simplicity and the honest work of self-sufficiency are presented as the model tenets of an ideal life. But these values
were also literary commonplaces, as Jean Raimond admits
(*RA* p. 201) when quoting from the above passage. He regards
this picture as being entirely representative of eighteenth-
century sensibility after Thomson, Gray and Collins, aiming
at the reader's sympathy. Yet, as I have said, when set in the
context of war, these pastoral images serve the propaganda of
republicanism. For the idyll is wrested from Isabel by an
English invasion, her own father must fight, and she must seek
the protection of the Church:

Then did I look on our forsaken home,
And almost sob my very soul away!
For all my hopes of happiness were fled,
Like a vain dream! (*Joan*, p. 166)

Orleans itself is reduced to a 'melancholy waste' (p. 170) with
'many a ruined dwelling' where Isabel has fled finding no help
in the deserted monasteries. But the city is the wrong place to
be in times of disaster.[18] The problems of the crowded
conditions are exacerbated by war, where famine and disease
soon follow. Southey's descriptions of the war often contain
the word 'storm' pointed out in the previous chapter as the
motif he associates with warfare, or imminent invasion. Isabel
describes the English attack upon Orleans thus:

> The iron storm of death
> Clash'd in the sky. From the strong engines hurl'd
> Huge rocks with tempest force convuls'd the air.
> (*Joan*, p. 179)

And the campaign to retake Orleans is also seen in this way:

> O'er the host
> Howl'd the deep wind that ominous of storms
> Roll'd on the lurid clouds. The blacken'd night
> Frown'd, and the thunder from the troubled sky
> Roar'd hollow. (*Joan*, p. 207)

But here Southey has to show Joan in command of the forces of victory, and superior to the 'storm' if not the embodiment of the storm of liberty itself. She fights in conventional epic tradition as the divine amazon, invincible so long as her mission for France has its duration upon earth.

> Her flamy falchion thro' the troops,
> That like a thunderbolt, where'er it fell,
> Scattered the trembling ranks. (*Joan*, p. 206)

The power to annihilate enemies in this epic fashion recalls the divine or semi-divine heroes of Homer (Southey was reading Cowper's translation in December of 1793 [*WH* p. 117]), or Milton's war in heaven in *Paradise Lost*. Joan is described as being 'Like as the Angel of the Lord' (p. 206), God's instrument upon earth for the advancement of the kingdom of love 'amidst the waste of war . . .', and as I suggested earlier, surely Southey had republican iconography in mind in the character Joan of Arc. Joan neatly suggests the French incarnation of Liberty, often depicted as militant simplicity, purity and vulnerability (closely allied to the image of the ideal Pantisocratic bride), who was still represented as late as 1830 (*Liberty Leading the People*, Louvre, Paris) by Delacroix, with naked breast, heading the advance of revolutionary power.

But though Southey presents Joan as the virginal divine instrument, her message to her followers, and indeed the ever-repeated message of the epic, focuses upon the peaceful domestic roots of the common people.[19] Before the attack on the English forts that besiege Orleans she reminds the troops of what the war has done to their city:

> Look round. Your holy buildings and your homes—
> Ruins that choke the way! your populous town—
> One open sepulchre! (*Joan*, p. 222)

The French have suffered grievously in this conflict, but Southey develops his message about war by viewing both sides of the conflict from the point of view of the common soldier. Conrade (likened to Turnus of Virgil's *Aeneid* in Book VII, p. 239)[20] hurls a spear at an English knight, but kills instead an unnamed man. This episode gives Southey the chance to tell the man's story in brief, or what he has left behind him in England:

> At her cottage door,
> The wretched one shall sit, and with dim eye
> Gaze o'er the plain, where on his parting steps
> Her last look hung. Nor ever shall she know
> Her husband dead, but tortur'd with vain hope,
> Gaze on—then heart-sick turn to her poor babe
> And weep it fatherless! (*Joan*, p. 237)

This paragraph sums up the main plot of Wordsworth's *The Ruined Cottage*, which was begun coincidentally in 1795, the year when he and Southey met in Bristol. Wordsworth's account is disturbing in its intensity, and demonstrates that poet's ability to feel and suffer with his subject:

> Yet still
> She loved this wretched spot, nor would for worlds
> Have parted hence; and still that length of road
> And this rude bench one torturing hope endeared,

Fast rooted at her heart, and here, my friend,
In sickness she remained, and here she died,
Last human tenant of these ruined walls.[21]

Southey revised this portion of his epic (the story of Joan's
friend Madelon) for the 1798 edition taking Wordsworth's
poem into account:

Heavily the summer pass'd

To her a joyless one, expecting still
Some tidings from the war; and as at eve
She with her mother by the cottage door
Sat in the sunshine, I have seen her eye,
If one appear'd along the distant path,
Shape to the form she loved his lineaments,
Her cheek faint-flush'd by hope, that made her heart
Seem as it sunk within her . . .

. . . she pined and pined away. (*Joan* 1798, pp. 110–12)

This smallest and most vulnerable facet of society is at risk in
time of war, those unnamed ones (as above, *Joan* 1796, p. 237)
who support the royal cause but gain no reciprocal help.
Southey unfortunately here defeats his readers by giving no
name to the family and by denying the reader the detailed
information necessary for the formation of imaginative
strands of sympathy, details that Wordsworth supplied so
fully. Yet at times he succeeds by the very opposite course,
lifting the reader's mind out of the main narrative completely
and resting it upon the idylls of the hearth. He took the hearth
for his main subject in a piece called *Hospitality*, from *Poems*
1795, showing this social quality as the essence of the truly
enlightened society, supporting the very fabric of the nation
and consequently its culture. Working against hospitality are
kings (such as Henry VIII) and lords, proudly excluding their
fellows from looking over their art treasures. Arthur himself,
the 'patriot monarch', is fallen from proper commemoration:

Thou, AVALON! in whose polluted womb
The patriot monarch found his narrow tomb;
Where now thy solemn pile, whose antique head
With niche-fraught turrets awe-inspiring spread,
Stood the memorial of the pious age?
Where wont the hospitable fire
In cheering volumes to aspire,
And with its cheering warmth the pilgrim's woes
  assuage.
Low lie thy turrets now,
The desart ivy clasps the joyless hearth;
The dome which luxury yrear'd,
Though Hospitality was there rever'd,
Now from its shatter'd brow,
With mouldering ruins loads the unfrequented earth.
(*Poems* 1795, pp. 51–52)

Southey's language of pollution by luxury and the fall from piety, suggests the inhospitable onset of the Norman Yoke, implicating contemporary events. Interestingly, in the third stanza Southey sees the 'minstrel throng', the poets or bards, from Thule to Cambria, with no hospitable places to perform, as the king or aristocrat keeps his doors shut against them. Poets are thrown out of sympathy with their own lands, their songs unheard. But the brotherliness of hospitality exists in foreign lands, with the Arab and the Indian, as a matter of course, because of these cultures' proximity to the natural world. The welcoming hospitable hearth is then in the poet's eyes, another aspect of true patriotism—a patriotism binding together the domestic nuclei of a nation.

Hospitality is also a feature of the story of Gargrave, an Englishman who perished in the war, and this sketch, although brief, has the pleasantly relaxed quality of a fashionable landscape:

On the sunny brow
Of a fair hill, wood-circled, stood his home,

> A pleasant dwelling, when the ample ken
> Gaz'd o'er subjected distance, and surveyed
> Streams, hills, and forests, fair variety!
> The traveller knew its hospitable towers,
> For open were the gates, and blazed for all
> The friendly fire. (*Joan*, p. 275)

Such resting-points in the narrative strongly evoke the South-eyan desire for the quiet wholeness of domestic community. But now warfare and the threat of invasion are ever-present in England itself, which he views as the wreck of a once hospitable land. The metaphorical closing of the hosts' doors in the faces of their fellow-men signals the fragmentation of vital society, from which the disinherited bard seeks escape. Southey's little pictures speak eloquently of that desire, even in this example, which although describing the action of a battering-ram in a siege, intimates other things:

> so rolls the swelling sea
> Its curly billows to the unmoved foot
> Of some huge promontory, whose broad base
> Breaks the rough wave; the shiver'd surge rolls back,
> Till, by the coming billow borne, it bursts
> Again, and foams with ceaseless violence.
> The Wanderer, on the sunny clift outstrech'd,
> Harks to the roaring surges, as they rock
> His weary sense to forgetfulness. (*Joan*, p. 277)

Resting places in the text, such as this simile, resist the forward action of the main narrative and of the historical dénouement itself. They attempt to break from history, or inevitability, setting up emblems of virtue as the points of assessment which criticize society. Southey's wanderer is a liminal figure poised at rest between the ceaseless changeability of the sea and the weariness of his own past. Like Southey himself in the mid-1790s, this wanderer is domestically alienated. He is set between two worlds: of solid land, his own nation, and the powers of change or ruin whose sea lullaby seems to promise escape. The simile recalls Bowles' sonnet *On Dover Cliffs*, which I quote in full:

> On these white cliffs, that calm above the flood
> Rear their o'er-shadowing heads, and at their feet
> Scarce hear the surge that has for ages beat,
> Sure many a lonely wanderer has stood;
> And, whilst the lifted murmur met his ear,
> And o'er the distant billows the still Eve
> Sail'd slow, has thought of all his heart must leave
> To-morrow-of the friends he lov'd most dear,—
> Of social scenes, from which he wept to part:—
> But if, like me, he knew how fruitless all
> The thoughts, that would full fain the past recall,
> Soon would he quell the risings of his heart,
> And brave the wild winds and unhearing tide,
> The World his country, and God his guide.[22]

Once anti-domestic pictures like the above are politicized, then their mere sensibility is transformed. Dover itself, being the closest point to France on the English mainland, has been a frequent place of conflict in literature. In Shakespeare's *King Lear* (Act IV, Scene VI), Gloucester undertakes his imaginary cliff-jumping, whilst Lear himself, the symbol of a kingdom in turmoil, awaits French help brought by the virtuous Cordelia. If this is a resonant allusion when we link it to the discussion of regeneration in *Joan of Arc*, then it also brings along with it the note of doom, because the involvement with France was futile, with the failure of the plan to rescue Lear. Coleridge uses Dover cliffs as the place where Liberty stands to look across at France in order to call Famine to her aid, as Famine makes Liberty more eloquent in the cause of humanity.[23] All in all, Southey's little simile calls up not only his personal situation, but allusively, a politicized history of national conflicts. Joan (p. 288) lays blame upon the monarchical powers as instigators of the wrecking changes that lead their subjects astray.

Soldiers and dispossessed villagers all inhabit a metaphorical cliff-top. She feels that the English prisoners are but 'Misguided men, led from their little homes, / The victims of the mighty!' And quitting home is equal to quitting God, and as one of the English troopers says (p. 297):

> I marvel not that the Most High
> Hath hid his face from England! Wherefore thus
> Quitting the comforts of domestic life,
> Swarm we to desolate this goodly land.

It is obvious that the small man, the ordinary soldier, can perceive the wrongs of war, because after all he is fighting against people who are essentially of his own class and kind. Confronted by Joan herself he is fighting against God's representative. This same trooper squarely blames the Church for giving bad advice to the king about France. Military and *religious* imperialism are the root-causes of worldly evil as much in this quasi-medieval world as in the revolutionary one.

Southey's little theatre of war extended into the punishment of kings. (How different this was from the sentiments of the 1821 *A Vision of Judgement*, when he adopted a more sensitive approach.) Book IX deals with the 'Vision of the Maid' in which Joan encounters a repentant monarch, none other than Henry V, who is condemned to be a prisoner (pp. 353–54) in a sort of underworld until 'the whole human race, /. . . shall form ONE BROTHERHOOD. / "ONE UNIVERSAL FAMILY OF LOVE." ' This message is reinforced by that of Theodore, who was killed by the English hero Talbot at the end of Book VII, and who is now a ghostly shade, a prophet of millennium. Theodore's visionary predictions of the regenerate earth are expressed in the abstract nouns of popular verse:

> OPPRESSION shall be chain'd, and POVERTY
> Die, and with her, her Brood of Miseries;
> And VIRTUE and EQUALITY preserve
> The reign of LOVE, and Earth shall once again

Be Paradise, whilst WISDOM shall secure
The state of bliss which IGNORANCE betrayed.
(*Joan*, p. 360)

This vision of paradisal existence also seemed to be offered by the vastness of the American landscape, which had since 1776 been free from the tyranny of the English monarchs. But Southey's epic, as already mentioned, perversely crowns another king. Before this, Joan rouses her soldiers with more sentiments of fraternity.

Amid the plain
There was a little eminence, of old
Piled o'er some honoured Chieftain's narrow house.
His praise the song had ceas'd to celebrate,
And many an unknown age had the long grass
Waved o'er the nameless mound, tho' barren now
Beneath the frequent tread of multitudes.
There, elevate, the Martial Maiden stood. (*Joan*, p. 372)

Joan identifies herself with the warriors of the past here, but at the same time stands above the warrior code, treading down its despotic associations. In the millennium, those old deeds of blood symbolized by the long-dead warrior will, like the bardic songs that praised them, finally be defunct. Part of Joan's speech had already served another purpose, as the author himself admits in the *Preface*:

From line 121 to 131 in the tenth Book, of my writing, has been seen already by the public in another work; but as it is at present out of print and improbable that another edition will appear: on account of the appropriate sentiments they contained, I did not scruple to place them in their present situation. (p. ix)

The lines in fact derive from *The Fall of Robespierre* Act III, giving a picture of the sublimely regenerate nation of France, casting back adversaries. But they do not harmonize with

Joan's asking the freshly-crowned Charles to be a good king, in the sense that millennial forces are not dependent upon monarchs for their being. Southey's re-assertion of the message from *The Fall of Robespierre* feels hollow when set alongside his rather conceited and polite preface. Which 'public' was he addressing? By allying himself with France he had produced a book which could be seen as treasonable. By including in his book the escape or retreat idylls, he effectively scorned the society to which he presented his work.

3
Critical Receptions

The first edition of *Joan* was published by Joseph Cottle of Bristol who gave Southey fifty free copies, and offered fifty guineas for the script. The book was grandly printed and the prefatory remarks especially irritated Wordsworth:

> You were right about Southey, he is certainly a coxcomb, and has proved it completely by the preface to *his Joan of Arc*, an *epic* poem which he has just published. This preface is indeed a very conceited performance . . .[24]

We might imagine Wordsworth's scorn grew not simply from Southey's conceitedness, but from a sense that in boldly stating his own social and political views in poetry, Southey was doing, however badly, what he himself ought to be doing and of course would do with *The Prelude* and *The Excursion*. Perhaps this Southeyan advance began the subdued rivalry between them. Southey's *Preface* caught the eyes of the reviewers too. John Aikin in the *Monthly Review* for April 1796 queried the way this haste of composition ran against the author's education:

> We were sorry to observe, in the preface to this work, certain facts stated in order to display the extreme rapidity with which it was written. An epic poem in 12

books finished in six weeks, and, on its improved plan in 10 books, almost entirely recomposed during the time of printing! Is it possible that a person of classical education can have so slight an opinion of (perhaps) the most arduous effort of human invention, as to suffer the fervour and confidence of youth to hurry him in such a manner through a design which may fix the reputation of a whole life? . . . To *run a race with the press, in an epic poem*, is an idea so extravagant, that Mr.S. must excuse us if it has exorted from us these animadversions. (*M* p. 41)

Southey is mildly chastized, like a rebellious schoolboy who has gone against historical precedent, good manners and good taste. But if Aikin's ideas of correctness are offended, then Southey's anti-establishment pose had in part (though perhaps in the wrong part) succeeded, and he had, of course, published the first viable literary epic since Glover. The *Analytical Review* began from a similar position to Aikin, that of astonished schoolmasterly interest:

Among the classes of poetry, the epic has commonly been allowed the first place . . . When we read that Virgil, after devoting eleven years to his *Aeneid*, left it at last unfinished, and that an interval of about twelve years passed between the commencement and the completion of the *Paradise Lost*, we learn with astonishment, that *Joan of Arc*, in its first form, in twelve books, was, except the first three hundred lines, finished in *six weeks*; and that, afterwards, when the author, upon receiving the first proof from the printer, seeing its faults, formed a resolution to new-model the work, although, with the exception of the first three hundred and forty lines, the plan of the whole was changed, and not a thousand lines remained as they were originally written, the rest was composed while the printing went on. We feel ourselves little disposed to concur with the author of this poem in the contempt which . . . he casts upon the Horatian precept, *Nonum prematur in annum*,[25] or to flatter an ill-placed vanity by applauding the rapidity with which this poem was written. Nevertheless, we would by no means allow a circumstance so perfectly adventitious any weight in the scale of criticism against the merit of the work.

Indeed, the general consensus seems to have been that it was rather outrageous for a youth to have produced an *epic* poem, especially a hasty and opinionated youth, but as it was available it demanded attention. Only the *British Critic* (Vol. 8) of October 1796 was essentially unfavourable, hoping that 'he will employ more care and deliberation on his promised epic poem on Madoc'. The *Critical Review* of June 1796 did however look at Southey's use of language, and brought out problems that would haunt the poet's work:

> Mr. Southey sometimes uses quaint and antiquated expressions. We allow that a word, not in general use, may sometimes be safely adopted in poetry; and that an old word which has been disused may sometimes be happily restored . . . It may be allowed a poet also . . . to enrich his verse by new expressions, formed on the principles of his own language, or fairly derived from others. This practice, however, requires judgement, and, by a young writer, should be followed with caution. (*M* pp. 44–45)

This observation is absolutely central to the evaluation of the poet's work. When he attempts 'historical' discourse, Southey spoils lines and scenes by the almost perverse relish taken in antiquarian or obscure words and phrases, or worse, the love of what comes close to being semi-nonsense. In letters or works like *The Doctor*, this is acceptable, but not in serious poetry. Aikin, in the *Monthly Review* (*M* p. 42), added to this list of defects with his criticism of 'harsh sounds or images in harsh versification', false pronunciation of French names, the 'frequency of alliteration' and the 'licentious coinage of new verbs out of nouns, in which our poet, in common with many other modern lovers of novelty, too much indulges'. However, the *Monthly Magazine* of July 1796 (*M* p. 46), along with most of the other reviews, thought *Joan* worthy of praise despite blemishes, and:

> . . . viewed as a whole, the performance has singular merit. It abounds in lofty conceptions, vigorous sentiments, rich imagery, and all the sublimer graces of poetry. The author possesses uncommon powers of poetic invention; and with diligence of study, and severity of correction, to which genius so reluctantly submits, may become a poet of the first order.

Most of the reviews looked to some future point at which Southey would make his mature achievements and be received more wholeheartedly, no doubt, into English life. Southey's political stance in *Joan*, partly described (*M* p. 48) by the *Analytical* as, 'the noble spirit of freedom, which is evidently the poet's inspiring muse', seems to have been very tolerantly dealt with, even if it was a moral 'lesson . . . taught at the expense of the author's native country', for 'he who wishes success to injustice because his countrymen support it, is a traitor to human kind'. But nevertheless, Southey's choice of subject was the source of some interest; how could it not be in such politically sensitive times?

> Some suspicion may at first arise, that Mr. Southey has chosen a subject scarcely suited to the dignity of epic poetry. His prudence may at least be called in question. How can he expect to interest the English nation in the fortunes of a heroine who was an active champion against his own countrymen . . .? Many of his readers will undoubtedly ask these questions,—and at a time when the course of public opinion is more than ordinarily

influenced by recent occurrences, will not be over
forward to compliment his patriotism.

As to ourselves, we profess to accord in sentiment with
those who think the cause of truth of higher importance
than any particular interest,—that national claims may be
ill-founded, and that patriotism is something worse than
enthusiasm, unless guided by moderation, and settling in
justice.—That the English, in the instance before us . . .
cannot . . . be vindicated . . .

The above cautionary approval from the *Critical Review* (*M*
pp. 43–44), underlines Southey's political and commercial
situation very well. Patriotism in their sense, or patriotic
adherence to the national flag *on any issue* certainly did not
have Southey's (or their) approval. But Southey's 'prudence'
was now certainly in question, and not merely because he
might lose a few sales. John Aikin (*M* p. 42), though
supportive to the grand feelings of the epic, inserts a warning
into his high-flown review:

With respect to the sentiments, they are less adapted to
the age in which the events took place, than to that of the
writer; being uniformly noble, liberal, enlightened, and
breathing the purest spirit of general benevolence and
regard to the rights and claims of human kind. In many
parts, a strong allusion to later characters and events is
manifest; and we know not where the ingenuity of a
crown lawyer would stop, were he employed to make
out a list of innuendos. In particular, War, and the lust of
conquest, are every where painted in the strongest
colours of abhorrence.—Far be it from us to check or
blame even the excesses of generous ardour in a youthful
breast! Powerful antidotes are necessary to the corrupt
selfishness and indifference of the age.

As a champion of liberty and peace, Southey could be
tolerated. As a champion of French history and a scourge of

English historical oppression he might yet be allowed a voice. But as a critic of national policy in time of war he must watch his step. Even if Southey was then 'utterly unconnected with any party, or club, or society', as Coleridge later admitted (*Griggs* II, p. 1001), that would not prevent the metaphorical arrest and punishment of his Muse.

NOTES

1 Editor's Introduction to *The Watchman*, *The Collected Works of Samuel Taylor Coleridge*, ed. Lewis Patton (Princeton: Routledge & Kegan Paul, 1970), p. xxxix.

2 *The Letters of Dorothy and William Wordsworth 1787–1805*, 2nd edn, revised by C. L. Shaver (Oxford: Clarendon, 1967), p. 169.

3 *The Letters of Charles and Mary Lamb*, ed. Edwin W. Marrs Jr (Ithaca and London: Cornell University Press, 1975), Vol. I, p. 16.

4 Coleridge worked this section into 'The Destiny of Nations' (*CP* pp. 131–48).

5 Walpole described Mrs Wollstonecraft as 'that hyena in petticoats'. *Horace Walpole's Correspondence*, ed. W. S. Lewis and A. Dale Wallace, 48 vols (London: Oxford University Press, 1937), Vol. 31, p. 397.

6 Ingvald Raknem, *Joan of Arc in History, Legend and Literature* (Bergen: Universitetsforlaget, 1971), p. 81.

7 *Ibid.*, p. 76.

8 Coleridge had of course in 1793 been the champion of another anti-war figure, William Frend. Although Southey claimed (*NL* I, p. 31, July 1793) to despise the conduct of the man, it may be that some of the pacifist sentiments of Frend's early pamphlet *Peace and Union* fed into *Joan of Arc*.

9 See also *Poems* by J. Hucks, AM, fellow of Catharine Hall, Cambridge (B. Flower, 1798), p. 150; 'Lines Addressed to S. T. Coleridge':

> Pleasant are the paths,
> And sweet the simple bowers, that in the vale
> Of humble life, peace with no niggard hand,
> And meek content have form'd: to them unknown,
> The feverish hours, tumultuous hopes and fears,

The war of struggling passions, wan disease,
Inbred of Cities; pale disastrous want,
Wealth's feeble offspring; vice and fell remorse.

Hucks accompanied Coleridge on a tour of North Wales in 1794, when both met Southey at Oxford. Hucks' poem, though published in 1789, continues this theme of the hatred of cities, and looks toward some of the sentiments of Keats' Nightingale ode.

10 See for example *The Pleasures of Melancholy* by Thomas Warton the Younger. *The Three Wartons*, ed. Eric Partridge (London: The Scholartis Press, 1927), p. 110.

11 Raymond Williams, *Problems in Materialism and Culture* (London: Verso, 1980), 'Ideas Of Nature', pp. 67–85.

12 Marina Warner, *Joan of Arc and the Image of Female Heroism* (York: A. A. Knopf, 1981), p. 243.

13 'Autobiography as Defacement', *MLN* 94, 1979, p. 926.

14 Note Southey's use of Spenserian language here, as a source for quasi-medieval language in *Joan*. The expression 'Louting low' may be found in *The Faerie Queene*, Bk I, canto I, no. 30, and in Bk II, canto III, no. 13.

15 William Gilpin, *Remarks on Forest Scenery* Vol. I (London: R. Blamire, 1791), pp. 56–57. Southey had come across this book in 1793 (*WH* p. 117). See also Geoffrey Grigson's *The Harp of Aeolus* (London: Routledge, 1947), 'The Upas Tree', pp. 56–65.

16 Compare the allegorical ending of this piece with that of *For the Banks of the Hampshire Avon* in   I, pp. 67–68.

17 William Gilpin, *Remarks on Forest Scenery* Vol. I, *op. cit.*, p. 14.

18 Rousseau's famous letter to Voltaire (18 August 1756) concerning the earthquake in Lisbon put forward the view that the large numbers of people *unnaturally* concentrated in one place had exacerbated the effects of the disaster. See *Correspondance Complète de Jean Jaques Rousseau*, ed. R. A. Leigh (Geneva: Institut et Musée Voltaire, 1967), Vol. IV, letter 424, pp. 37–50.

19 Late in 1793, Southey had read Mary Wollstonecraft's *A Vindication of the Rights of Women* (1792) in which similar anti-war views are found (see *WH* p. 117). 'Yet, if defensive war, the only justifiable war, in the present advanced state of society . . . were alone to be adopted as just and glorious, the true heroism of antiquity might again animate female bosoms.' *The Works of Mary Wollstonecraft*, ed. J. Todd and M. Butler (London: William Pickering, 1989), Vol. 5, p. 216. Wollstonecraft adds: 'I am not going to advise them to turn their distaff into a musket' (*ibid.*, p. 216).

20 Conrade is likened to Turnus 'Slaughtering the robber emigrants of Troy' (Bk VII, p. 239), implying that he takes sides against *heartless* piety like that of Aeneas.

21 See *The Ruined Cottage* and *The Pedlar*, ed. James Butler (Ithaca: Cornell University Press, 1979), p. 72. MS. B.

22 *Fourteen Sonnets* (Bath: R. Cruttwell, 1789), p. 11.

23 See 'A Letter from Liberty' in *Consciones ad Populum* delivered in February 1795: *Lectures 1795: On Politics and Religion*, ed. Peter Mann and Lewis Patton (Princeton and London: Routledge & Kegan Paul, 1971), p. 31.

24 See *The Letters of William and Dorothy Wordsworth, 1787–1805, op. cit.*, p. 169.

25 *M* p. 47, note: 'Let it be kept quiet until the ninth year'. Horace, *Ars Poetica*.

Chapter Four

Poems 1797: From Mediocrity to Progressive Genius

1

In the last chapter, I illustrated the problems Southey faced when writing *Joan of Arc*. Firstly his poem was pro-French and pacifistic in a time of war against France. Secondly it was purportedly *anti-monarchical* and yet crowned a king. Thirdly it exposed the Southeyan desire for the simple domestic or Pantisocratic life (suggested by the medieval hamlet life in the epic) which only a peaceful land could sustain. The message of regeneration for France, intimately linked to Pantisocratic ideals, carried over from *The Fall of Robespierre*, and set into the tenth book of *Joan of Arc*, was like Pantisocracy a fading dream by the time the epic was ready for the press.

In *Joan of Arc* Southey tries to speak for the Pantisocratic nation, to write in his own style a politicized book of Pantisocracy, with the insistent use of the domestic idyll as his key image. His poetic notion of home and nation derives in part from the pastorals of Pope, which are classical patriarchies, rather than from any serious readings of Godwin. Southey both quests for retreat and courts a paying audience. Pantisocracy, once it collapsed, left the main problems it could have solved behind, namely where to live and how to live. And Southey was rapidly coming to realize that he might live by writing and pursue the modest, but burgeoning fame that his publications were gaining for him. His facility in verse was, however, both a blessing and a curse, as the publication of

Poems 1797[1] would show. Coleridge's comments to Cottle in April 1797 (*Griggs* I, p. 320) explore this tension perceptively:

> I see they have reviewed Southey's *Poems* and my *Ode* in the *Monthly Review*. Notwithstanding the Reviews, I, who in the sincerity of my heart am *jealous* for Robert Southey's fame, regret the publication of that volume. Wordsworth complains, with justice, that Southey writes *too much at his ease*—that he seldom 'feels his burthend breast
>
> Heaving beneath th' incumbent Deity.'
>
> He certainly will make literature more *profitable to him* from the fluency with which he writes, and the facility with which he pleases himself. But I fear, that to posterity his wreath will look unseemly—here an ever-living amaranth, and close by its side some weed of an hour, sere, yellow, and shapeless—his exquisite beauties will lose half their effect from the bad company they keep.

The volume of *Poems* 1797 serves as a developmental chart of Southey's poetry from the early to mid-1790s. Coleridge's grouping of the poems in *Griggs* I, pp. 296–300 (6 January 1797) advances under three headings: namely poems that 'do not rise much above mediocrity', poems that 'are worthy of the author of Joan of Arc', and the *Musings on a Landscape of Gaspar Poussin* with *Hymn to the Penates* which he thought of as 'proofs of a *progressive* genius'. The *British Critic* Vol. 10, for July 1797 (unconsciously following up what Coleridge said), was of the opinion that Southey needed to be more ruthless in his editing:

> There is every appearance that Mr. Southey writes at all times, and on all occasions, and publishes all that he writes. He certainly is not without poetic talents; but till he shall have learned, that times for correction are as

necessary, to the most brilliant genius, as leisure for writing, he never will achieve the legitimate title of a poet.

So the variety of the volume, the light and heavy mixture of the work, found no praise with them, nor perhaps the politics which they do not mention. Further doubts about Southey's editing judgements, and indeed his attitude to poetry, were picked up in an earlier article from the *Monthly Review* for March 1797, by John Aikin. He notices that Southey in his preface 'speaks in terms of disparagement' about the ode as a poetic form which leads him to wonder why the poems should have been included at all. Aikin recommended the volume, but stated that 'Poetry is a trifle to trifling poets and trifling readers:—but no one ever excelled in it who treated it as a trifle'. So publication for publication's sake was condemned along with the poet's casual attitude to at least some of the things he had set in print. In the various responses to his work these doubts about Southey's poetic sincerity were coupled with doubts about his political attitudes. His poetic fame was quickly turning to poetic infamy.

2
Outcasts of the Hearth:
The Politics of Literary Fashion in Southey's Female Wanderers

A human being, in the lowest state of penury and distress, is a treasure to a reasoner of this cast—He contemplates, he examines, he turns him in every possible light, with a view of extracting from the variety of his wretchedness, new topics of invective against the pride of property. He indeed (if he is a true Jacobin) refrains from *relieving* the object of his compassionate contemplation; as well knowing that every diminution from the general

mass of human misery, must proportionately diminish
the force of his argument.[2]

During a break from polishing his Bristol historical lectures
and further thoughts on ways of earning money for Pantisocracy early in 1795, Southey may have been reading the
Critical Review for 13 April. Inside, he would have taken in
(perhaps with some pride) the review of his *Poems* 1795 on
pages 420–21. As I have said earlier, the reviewer gave
examples of his work from *The Retrospect*—but along with
this, made note of another poem *The Death of Mattathias*:

> Many bold attempts have been made to free our poetry
> from the shackles of rhyme, or rather our poets from the
> trouble of seeking for it, Dr. Sayers has given us some
> beautiful specimens of this kind in his Sketches of
> Northern Mythology; but still we are of the opinion, that
> our language does not possess harmony enough to gratify
> the ear in any great degree without the assistance of that
> Gothic ornament, unless it could be made to run more
> into dactyls, which the structure and genius of it does not
> easily admit. (p. 421)

Perhaps it was Southey's ear for fashion, here flattered and
challenged by an early review and his growing awareness of his
own poetic status, that led to the dactylics in question. If in
1795 he was out of tune with English political life, he certainly
tried to remain in tune with the public that bought his poetry.
And if he heard that dactylic verse was needed, then dactylics
he would write. In a letter to Grosvenor Bedford of 12 May
1795 (*NL* I, p. 95), Southey sent a series of poems for his
friend's approval, three of which (*Elinor*, the first of the
Botany Bay Eclogues; *The Outcast* and *The Soldier's Wife*) fall
into the category of poems of humanitarian concern. The last
two of these were joint productions by Southey and Coleridge. The two men had lived together in Bristol from the
February of 1795 in order to write for Pantisocratic funds, and

this was, according to Simmons (p. 51), the 'most fruitful period of their collaboration'. Southey included *The Soldier's Wife* and another related poem *The Widow* in *Poems* 1797. Both are famous only because they were parodied by *The Anti-Jacobin*—*The Widow* came under fire on 27 November 1797, and *The Soldier's Wife* on 11 and 18 December.

These small poems need to be read against the historical background of that particular year, with its social unrest and repressive Pittite acts of Parliament. But they also focus upon wives and widows, broken elements of domestic nuclei suffering from the effects of the war. They could also be dismissed as mere exercises in fashionable taste, for as Robert Mayo[3] says: 'Bereaved mothers and deserted females were almost a rage in the poetry departments of the 1790s'. Southey had made his debut as a magazine poet in the autumn of 1794 when Coleridge (*Simmons* p. 47) had placed a copy of Southey's first *Botany Bay Eclogue* in the *Morning Chronicle*. Southey had adopted the eclogue form from Collin's use of it (in his *Persian Eclogues*) but Collin's moralizing is replaced by Southeyan humanitarianism—and Elinor herself (see *Poems 1797*, p. 78) is another 'Outcast—unbeloved and unbewail'd'.

The crucial approach to such poetry should come through a feeling for the subject, and the poet tries to force the point by making his situations as grim as possible, and by the frequent use of the exclamatory apostrophe. But his excess of feeling for, rather than feeling with, the subject led Geoffrey Grigson to claim (*G* p. 15) that if Southey

> could easily be parodied, one feels, in poem after poem, even poems mainly serious, that he stations himself deliberately on the verge of self-parody, in rhythm and movement and in statement . . .

This is perhaps the single most interesting remark I have encountered so far upon the quality of Southey's poetic output. Indeed, after drafting out *The Soldier's Wife* for Bedford, Southey remarks (*NL* I, p. 95): 'Written with

Coleridge. Read this aloud and accent it.' Does this statement merely reduce the poem to merely a late schoolboy exercise in scansion, with its dactyls tripping lightly forward (*Poems* 1797, p. 145) against the sense of the picture of his 'Weary way-wanderer . . . Travelling painfully'?

The choice of subject is interesting if only as an indication of contemporary politics and contemporary taste. The soldier's wife is little more than a motif, a mother and children travelling in a void. No information is supplied concerning her destination or her home. The poets make her situation utterly hopeless: without her husband, she is rendered emotionally and materially without support, and the snow pathetically emphasizes her own adversity. If Southey's metrics are suspect in places, at least one key dactyl, 'wanderer' is sound enough. No conversation is allowed to the suffering woman, she literally *becomes* apostrophe and she is placed in the kind of desperate environment essential to such works as Wordsworth's *Ruined Cottage*, but at a much greater distance from help. She is not so much narrated as voyeuristically condemned:

> Thy husband will never return from the war again,
> Cold is thy hopeless heart even as Charity—
> Cold are thy famish'd babes—God help thee, widow'd
> One! (*Poems* 1797, p. 146)

She has achieved almost total social insignificance, and has become not only the pathetic obverse of the idyll of home life, but the symbol and signifier of the ill-effects of the war against France. The poem is certainly dramatic, and does have an atmosphere of tangible despair, but is undermined by the fact that the metre does not support the sense of the poem.

Charles Lamb reacted to the sheer misery of the imagery and the absurdity of the metre with his own corrective laughter, which must accord him a secure place in the assessment of Southey's verse. Lamb's own dactylics are also written in the manner of a schoolboy exercise, but their import should have been taken to heart by both Coleridge and Southey. If only we could say plainly that *The Soldier's Wife* had been written as a wholehearted parody in the first place, and not a poem which in effect inhabited both the camp of reform or protest, and that of fashionable magazinish band-wagon-jumping, we might be left thinking that the poem literally does not know what it is.

Lamb was frequently in touch with Coleridge during the May of 1796 (the month that Southey returned from his first Portugal trip), sending him many long letters upon personal and literary topics. He was enduring worry and exhaustion, and was in desperate need of a holiday, preferably with Coleridge. We might regard him as an eighteenth-century version of a 'carer', but one strung between work and home, worn down, unsupported. The collaborators' poem *may* ultimately have struck a very deep personal chord in Lamb's world. Suffering, especially female suffering, was no light matter, and perhaps Lamb even felt something of his own situation in that marooned and isolated figure in the poem, though if he did, he would have laughed it to extinction. Whatever the case, he went on to beat *The Anti-Jacobin* to a parody of these metrics in a letter to Coleridge of 1 July 1796:

> What shall I say to your Dactyls? They are what you would call good per se but a parody on some of 'em is just now suggesting itself & you shall have it rough & unlicked. I mark with figures the lines parodied.

> 4 Sorely your Dactyls do drag along limp-footed.
> 5 Sad is the measure that hangs a clog round 'em so.
> 6 Meagre, & languid, proclaiming its wretchedness.
> 1 Weary, unsatisfied, not a little sick of 'em.
> 11 Cold is my tired heart, I have no charity.
> 2 Painfully trav'lling thus over the rugged road.
> 7 O begone, Measure, half Latin, half English, then.
> 12 Dismal, your Dactyls are, God help ye, rhyming Ones.[4]

Lamb (using the linguistic guise of Touchstone from *As You Like It*) parodies only one of Coleridge's lines compared with seven of Southey's, a heavily adverse ratio, even if Coleridge only supplied three out of twelve lines in the poem. It is interesting that he picks out the strained emotional content of the poem, and parodies its metrical arrangement, which is, as I have said, out of key with the weary pace one would expect from the woman in the snow. We might add to Pope's[5] dictum that 'The *Sound* must seem an *Eccho* to the *Sense*', a few further comments upon the appropriateness of metre. Lamb's Shakespearean voice can be overheard commenting upon Coleridge's involvement in a project which fails to respond seriously to its subject-matter:

> For your Dactyls I am sorry you are so sore about 'em—a very Sir Fretful—. In good troth the Dactyls are good Dactyls, but their measure is naught. Be not yourself 'half anger half agony' if I pronounce your darling lines not to be the best you ever wrote in all your life,—you have written much.[6]

Lamb's perceptive punning around the word 'measure' almost exactly predicts the focus of the *Anti-Jacobin*'s attacks upon the irritating display of metre without content, or, rather, irritating metre with the wrong political content. Southey was using classical learning, classical metre, the property of the establishment, against that establishment, which the *British Critic* at least saw as 'folly'.

Another of Southey's wanderers, *The Widow*, is similarly beleaguered by winter snows and the indifference of society, with 'no home . . . no shelter' against the cold. For this poem Southey chose Sapphics, appropriately enough (almost) in a woman's lament, but again using classical metre for radical purposes. We are not told whether the widow was married to a soldier or not, but as Southey (with Coleridge's help) had been preparing the anti-war *Joan of Arc* early in 1795, there is no doubt that the effects of the war with France were centrally important to him at that time. Certain passages in *Joan* deal with the subject of warfare and widowhood, as here in the description of the capture of Harfleur:

> . . . fertile fields laid waste,
> Dispeopled hamlets, the lorn widow's groan,
> And the pale orphans feeble cry for bread. (*Joan*, p. 20)

After the seige of Rouen, certain inhabitants of the town, being considered useless, are sent out to die in the cold:

> Fainter they grew, for the cold wintry wind
> Blew weak; fainter they grew, and at the last
> All was still, save that ever and anon
> Some mother shriek'd o'er her expiring child
> The shriek of frenzying anguish. (*Joan*, p. 81)

This passage in particular has similar vocabulary and imagery to the poems in this discussion, and this motif of the frozen mother and child is again used by the poet in *To Horror* in *Poems* 1797, p. 143. Southey notes that the image was taken 'from the campaign of 1794 and 1795 . . . during the retreat from Deventer'. This may be so, but it was a fashionable motif which Wordsworth had also used in *An Evening Walk*, of the wretched wandering woman (widowed by the American war) who 'dragg'd her babes along this weary way' until death overtakes them all. Southey's Widow is passed by both a 'horseman' and a 'chariot':

> Fast o'er the bleak heath rattling drove a chariot,
> 'Pity me!' feebly cried the poor night wanderer.
> 'Pity me Strangers! lest with cold and hunger
>   Here I should perish.

> 'Once I had friends,—but they have all forsook me!
> 'Once I had parents,—but they are now in Heaven!
> 'I had a home once—I had once a husband—
>   'Pity me Strangers!

I had a home once—I had once a husband—
'I am a Widow poor and broken-hearted!'
Loud blew the wind, unheard was her complaining,
    On drove the chariot.

The inclusion of the 'chariot' is of further cultural and political interest to Southey's theme because it constitutes a thinly-veiled swipe at those people who could afford the (jolting) comfort of wheels, the aristocrats. The 'Travelling Charriot' (sic) was a type of post-chaise privately-owned by the nobility or by high-ranking officers, and was often used for touring the Continent, on the first and last stages of the journey. It typically carried a crest on the doors, and a sword-case at the rear. It was the sort of carriage that democratic pedestrians like Southey and Coleridge abhorred. Coleridge had versified his disgust in a poem called *Perspiration: A Travelling Eclogue* of 1794:

    The dust flies smothering, as on clatt'ring wheel
    Loath'd Aristocracy careers along . . . (*CP* p. 56)

The 'chariot' underlines the depiction of the aristocrat or officer as uncaring, unseeing—speeding through a landscape, but never pausing to communicate with that landscape, or with its widows—the essentially slow walking pace of Wordsworth's *Ruined Cottage* might also be brought to mind here. It was this class-born blindness to poverty that Coleridge deplored in his companion Joseph Hucks during their walk through Wales in 1794. Coleridge (burlesquing Hucks) shows how Aristocratic manners impede reforms:

    It is *wrong* Southey! for a little Girl with a half-famished sickly Baby in her arms to put her head in at the window of an Inn—'Pray give me a bit of Bread and Meat'! from a Party dining on Lamb, Green Pease and Sallad—Why?? Because it is *impertinent* & and *obtrusive*—I am a

Gentleman!—and wherefore should the clamorous Voice
of Woe *intrude* upon mine Ear!?

My companion is a Man of cultivated, tho' not
vigorous, understanding—his feelings are all on the side
of humanity—yet such are the unfeeling remarks, which
the lingering Remains of Aristocracy occasionally
prompt.[7]

Coleridge's little girl was an example from life of the voice of
woe, set into apostrophic text. Southey's poem is only a short
step from the inscription tradition, the voice of the subject
calling to the passers-by in an attempt to gain sympathy or
give information. But his woman is no graveyard stone (as in
the poetry of Gray) or inscribed tablet; she is meant to be
viewed as a homeless deserted wanderer, a rootless social
casualty in the wake of the Revolution and war with France,
and:

> As the wits of the Anti-Jacobin knew, however, such
> way-wandering humanitarianism as Southey's and
> Wordsworth's, if not increasing, was increasingly parti-
> san and ought to be damned. England's war against the
> Revolution changed an age of sentiment to an age of
> politics, as one sees in Southey's movement from the
> elegiac cluster of *Poems* 1795, around frail Emma, a
> flower plucked and destroyed by an ungrateful seducer,
> to the clusters in *Poems*, 1797, around slaves worn with
> toil, soldiers' wives and widows, and deserters trans-
> ported to Botany Bay, and on to *Poems*, 1799: 'The
> Sailor who had Served in the Slave Trade.'[8]

If the *Critical Review* for March 1797 could praise Southey's
sonnets on the slave trade as pleasing to 'every friend of
humanity',[9] the *Anti-Jacobin* thought that Southey's poetry[10]
was written for the purpose of 'aggravating discontent in the
inferior orders'. It regarded the poems as designed to expose
the contempt and tyranny of the rich over the poor, or to

subvert 'those orders and gradations of Society, which are the natural result of the original difference of talents and industry among mankind'.[11] But *The Anti-Jacobin* voice (with its Burkean overtones) is really a cry of failure, even the sound of 'beating a dead snake'[12] for by 1797, Southey's pro-French stance had cooled off. If he was interested in revolutionary reform at all, then it was not through social uprising.

The humour of the magazine (showing an alertness to the phraseology of contemporary review work), though devastating, rests upon contempt for and fear of the social reformer and the unrelieved poor. The individual is blamed for self-degradation, rather than society for beating him or her down. The lower classes are the butt of these parodies and are seen as harmless, to be patronized by the magazine audience, presumably of a higher class. The 'Needy Knife-grinder' (*Anti-Jacobin* I, p. 71) is a drunken brawling simpleton, the 'little Drummer Boy' (*Anti-Jacobin* I, p. 169)[13] is a gullible child, and the 'Wearisome Sonneteer' (*AJ* I, p. 201) is merely moon-mad and ill-educated. Southey had tried hard to create an underclass of liminal figures, dispossessed of home, friends and hope. The widow's grief is perhaps for the soldier she recently married, her poverty indicative of society's neglect. Perhaps the soldier's wife saw her husband pressed into service, leaving her bereaved, to cope with an England hostile to poverty and suspicious of any voice of complaint.

In this brave attempt Southey was an easy target, as Jonathan Wordsworth notes in the preface to the 1989 reprint of *Poems* 1797: 'his earnest tones are captured, his sympathy is debased'. But as the epigraph to this chapter insists, Southey's widows operate in an artificial void, sorely trying to our ability to suspend disbelief. As Lamb hinted when he noted the dismal nature of the dactylics, Southey fails to excite lasting compassion because he does not allow the reader close enough to his characters. Instead of investigating the psychology of his widows, he presents us with two-dimensional figures, rather like wood-engravings,[14] and leaves the final judgement to divine agency where as in *Joan of Arc* (p. 83) 'God shall hear / The widow's groan'. This implied indifference is taken up by *The Anti-Jacobin*:

> We think we see him fumbling in the pocket of his blue pantaloons;—that the splendid Shilling is about to make its appearance, to glitter in the eyes, and glad the heart, of the poor Sufferer.—But no such thing—the Bard very calmly contemplates her situation, which he describes in a pair of very pathetical Stanzas; and . . . concludes by leaving her to Providence. (*Anti-Jacobin* I, p. 168)

In the attempt to write humanitarian poetry, Southey had produced a series of what are rather half-hearted, even melodramatic postures. His women appear to be tragic stage heroines, whose measure is naught. Lamb (as Coleridge's Fool) sits in judgement between the politics and metrics of Coleridge and Southey, and the politics, parodies, and contempt of *The Anti-Jacobin*. His laughter is the sane point between opposed and extreme political stances, the real voice of feeling, born of experience. I have no evidence that Southey ever read Lamb's critique of the dactyls. If he had read and acted upon the advice, he might have saved himself one of the larger knocks that punctuated his career as a poet. Knocks that from 1797 onwards would come with some regularity, not in the least because of the exertions of *The Anti-Jacobin*.

NOTES

1 Southey had his copies of the first edition by 19 December 1796. For an excellent account of the *two* editions of *Poems* 1797, see the Bodleian Library Record, Vol. vi, 1957–61, pp. 620–24.

2 *The Anti-Jacobin* (4th edn, 2 vols, 1799) (hearafter *AJ*), i. 70, 27 November 1797.

3 'The Contemporaneity of the *Lyrical Ballads*', *PMLA* 69 (1954), pp. 486–522, p. 496.

4 *The Letters of Charles and Mary Anne Lamb*, ed. Edwin W. Marrs Jr, 3 vols (Ithaca and London: Cornell University Press, 1975), Vol. I, pp. 34–35.

5 'An Essay on Criticism', *The Poems of Alexander Pope*, ed. John Butt (London: Methuen, 1968), p. 155.

6 Marrs, *op. cit.*, I, p. 41.

7 *A Pedestrian Tour through North Wales, in a Series of Letters*, by J. Hucks, BA (1795), ed. Alun Jones and William Tydeman (Cardiff: University of Wales Press, 1979), p. 92. See Coleridge's letter to Southey, 6 July 1794.

8 Carl Woodring, *Politics in English Romantic Poetry* (Cambridge, Mass.: Harvard University Press, 1970), p. 87.

9 Notice how this is twisted around in the *Anti-Jacobin*'s parody of *The Widow* (The Friend of Humanity and the Knife-Grinder) of 27 November 1797.

10 *Anti-Jacobin* I, p. 70, 27 November 1797.

11 *Ibid.* I, pp. 69–70.

12 H. N. Fairchild, *The Romantic Quest* (Philadelphia: Albert Saifer, Columbia University Press, 1931), p. 49.

13 The *Anti-Jacobin* quoted the words 'fiddledum, diddledum' from the *British Critic* of July 1797 in their parody of *The Soldier's Wife*, 11 December 1797.

14 A. D. Harvey in the excellent *English Poetry in a Changing Society* (London: Alison and Busby, 1980), p. 62, sees the poems as 'episodes of lower class life . . . converted into free-standing vignettes', close to the ballad tradition which relies upon action and speech rather than description.

Chapter Five

Breaking the Idyll:
On a Landscape of Gaspar Poussin,
Bath 1795

Prospect-painting then began with the decoration of walls of rooms, as if man was born to live abroad, and can only banish from his home the idea of its being a prison, by giving to its boundaries a semblance of the horizon of nature.[1]

Would that we could wander with her under the azure skies and golden sunsets of Claude Lorraine . . . or repose in Gaspar Poussin's cool grottos, or on his breezy summits, or by his sparkling water-falls!—but we must not indulge too long in these delightful dreams. (*Hazlitt* Vol. 16, p. 308)

> While Fancy loves apart to dwell,
> Scarce thro' the wicker of her cell
> Dares shoot one timorous winking eye
> (*WP* I, p. 277, ll. 554–56).

1

If the wits of the *Anti-Jacobin* had looked hard at the miscellany that was Southey's *Poems* of 1797, they might have noted alongside what they perceived as the poet's Jacobinical stance the beginnings of a retreat from, or mistrust of the idealisms spawned by the Revolution. Southey's politics became increasingly centred around the personal and the domestic, rather than the revolutionary—if they had ever really been such at all. *Musings on a Landscape of Gaspar Poussin* depicts the failure of Southey's idealism, the temporary arrestation and confounding of his fraternal poetic impulses, and marks an impasse from which he emerged in a different key.

Musings is a poem of wonder, loneliness and dejection, which apparently catches the poet just at the point when Pantisocracy has failed him. It is included here as an important flashback to the period when Southey had finished, or was finishing, his correction of *Joan of Arc*. The sense of loss in the poem is very strong, as is the sense that Southey's political vigour is cooling off. William Haller[2] sees the poem in this way:

> Though pantisocracy was by that time an abandoned hope, the poem shows the desire for a home in retirement which was the abiding aspiration behind that project in the poet's mind.

Haller is certainly correct in his view, but it needs to be added that 'home' for Southey had seriously to take literature into account as I have said, and the implied readership which that included. Retreat, 'the abiding aspiration', was unsurprisingly a recoil from cities, but a retreat from whose vantage the poet would seek publication and a city audience.

Musings on a Landscape of GASPAR POUSSIN appeared in *Poems* 1797 (pp. 154–58) and is dated 'Bath 1795' by Southey in his *Complete Poetical Works*. The year 1795 with its changes, losses and monumental quarrel, was an exciting episode in Southey's life, ending in the trip to Portugal which in effect enabled him to view his own country very differently.

The year opened with Southey's famous pursuit of Coleridge in London and the return of both men to Bristol (*Simmons* p. 51) for the 'most fruitful period of their collaboration'. Joseph Cottle, introduced to Southey at the end of 1794 by the third major Pantisocrat Robert Lovell, took on the publication of work by the collaborators, though it was usually Southey who made a profit for him. The political, theological and historical lectures given by Coleridge and Southey date from this period. Southey's lectures (see *LC* I,

pp. 234–35 and *Simmons* p. 233, note 71) were finished by
May, leaving him time to think about other literary ventures,
such as *Joan of Arc* or the new edition of poems he had
discussed (*NL* I, p. 92) with Cottle back in March, in which
Musings was to appear. Southey's prolific output and con-
scientious delivery of work (and lectures) threw Coleridge
into a poor light in the eyes of Cottle, and was one of the
reasons for the bickering between the poets that ended in the
fracture of relations between them. Coleridge's long hysterical
letter of 13 November 1795, on the very eve of Southey's
wedding, is most virulent upon the subject of collaborative
projects: most damning of Southey's attitude to money and his
abandonment of Pantisocracy. Southey may have abandoned
Pantisocracy in the idealistic and theoretical sense, but the
quest for the Pantisocratic virtue of domestic stability
remained as a central theme in his life and his poetry.

He was offered an annuity by his friend C. W. W. Wynn in
late summer 1795, which would commence when he came of
age in October 1796. His uncle had also sought him out in
person during August to repeat the invitation to Portugal, and
to discuss again the taking of Holy Orders, a move which his
honest conscience, in the face of the Test Act, recoiled from.
His friend Seward died on 10 June, an event which he said (*RA*
p. 43) left 'a strange vacancy in my heart. The sun shines
as usual, but there is a blank in existence to me'. He uses
Milton's language of blindness (*Paradise Lost* Bk III, l. 48) to
express this loss, as if it were a separation from the sun itself,
but, along with this, the tragic pose of the young Werther:

> Ach, diese Lücke! Diese entsetzliche Lücke, die ich hier
> in meinem Busen fühle!—Ich denke oft, wenn du sie nur
> Einmal, nur Einmal an dieses Herz drücken könntest,
> diese ganze Lücke würde ausgefüllt sein.[3]

Seward's death doubtlessly destroyed much of the enthusiasm
which Southey still felt for Pantisocracy. He and Coleridge

lived together until the end of August when the joint rooms at College Street in Bristol were abandoned. Coleridge went to prepare the cottage at Clevedon for his marriage, and Southey went to stay with his mother at Bath.

I suggest that *Musings* sprang out of Southey's bewilderment at that time. The poem itself examines life and art, the real and the ideal, the attractions of 'Fancy' and the unease generated by the superimposition of Fancy and the commercial and imperial world. Southey reads the work of Gaspar Poussin in a way similar to that in which John Keats was to contemplate the Urn, and describes a state of entrapment which Mallarmé brought to a nightmarish pitch in his portrait of the swan caught in the ice, in *Le vierge, le vivace et le bel aujourd'hui.*[4]

Southey articulates disillusionment through the medium of fashion. He wrote to Joseph Cottle in May 1797 (*NL* I, pp. 125–26) concerning the second edition of his *Poems*, in which it had been suggested that he place illustrations:

> If you should think seriously of any ornaments of this kind, I would wish the frontispiece to be Gaspar Poussins exquisite landscape.

Kenneth Curry considers that the picture Southey refers to in *Musings* is Poussin's *The Cascade*,[5] which was engraved by Vivares[6] in 1785, and this would certainly seem to be the case. Southey uses fashion against itself, seizes upon a common idiom, for, at least in the circles of polite entertainment, books of prints of artists like Gaspar Poussin proliferated. That he chooses to inscribe this artist's landscape within his poetry is revealing because of its component parts, and because Gaspar, though taking on something of the mood-attributes of Claude Lorraine, particularly that which evokes repose and plenitude, also admits the roughness and unstable inhospitable danger of Salvator Rosa.[7] These artistic mood-traits feed into the metaphor of struggle in the poem itself.

It could be said that the struggle of 1795 was not merely that of a young poet, but of the whole nation. There had been a succession of bad harvests, in an almost unbroken line from 1789, a tendency which would continue until the Peace of Amiens in 1802. The burdens of war, taxation and the press-gangs became sharpened by the autumn of 1795, and, in addition to this, Pitt introduced his bills of repression to protect the King and to limit the gatherings of such as The Corresponding Society (responsible for circulating Paine's *Rights of Man*) to no more than fifty persons, without the permission of a magistrate. The king had heard cries of 'Bread! No War! No Famine!' on his way to Parliament as well as having the glass in his carriage broken. The King's son, the future George IV, added to his father's problems by pursuing the life of a libertine. On 9 May 1795 (*NL* I, p. 94), Southey writes to his brother Thomas:

> You must have heard that the King has applied to parliament to pay the Princes debts—700,000 pounds!!!!!!!! 180,000 are the annual expences of the United States of America.

The Prince's marriage of convenience (so that his debts would be paid) to Princess Caroline of Brunswick must have aroused not only the disgust of the young Pantisocrats (married themselves in 1795), but also of the whole nation. The 'dungeon bars' concluding the poem[8] try to express the entrapment of Liberty in a nation increasingly fearful of internal unrest and even civil war. They are the dungeon bars of Albion itself, an Albion imprisoned by war, fettered by social evils against which Southey had already flung his indignation in poetry.

How then does this text articulate the betrayal and unease pervading radical experience in the mid-1790s? The poem seems to me basically to re-read the taste of late eighteenth-century society in order to effect an ideological critique of that society. Southey's poem is furthermore a comment upon the debate around the Picturesque, some of whose major publications had arisen in 1794. The text also, on an autobiographical level, seems to draw together Southey's desire for escape to America, or for a home secure within contemporary fractured society, and to underline his ambivalent attitude towards Fancy. It is as if Fancy or imagination (he does not distinguish) is acting as a beautiful goad to the poet, showing him the true nature of the world outside the frame of the Poussin. There is also the sense of a profound mistrust of poetic Fancy as a liberating force. Southey faces the landscape in a line of readership, and recalls Poussin through Vivares, superimposing his own context upon an engraving of a phantom original. His poem is a series of apostrophes, to a dead artist, to the imagination or Fancy, and to what he calls the 'life of blessedness'. We overhear the poetic voice not just reading, but in the very act of self-constitution:

> We might posit, then, a third level of reading where the vocative of apostrophe is a device which the poetic voice uses to establish with an object a relationship which helps to constitute him. The object is treated as a subject, an *I* which implies a certain type of *you* in its turn. One who successfully invokes nature is one to whom nature might, in its turn, speak. Thus, invocation is a figure of vocation . . . that emphasises that voice calls in order to be calling, to dramatize its calling, to summon images of its power so as to establish its identity as poetical and prophetic voice.[9]

This process was an essential part of Southey's world in 1795, the attempt to bring the social and poetic self into being in a way that agreed with his developing beliefs and ideals. Helen Vendler in *The Odes of John Keats* says 'The fiction of the ode is that of a poet coming, in woe, to a work of art, interrogating it, and being solaced by it'.[10] Southey's approach to the Poussin is similarly troubled, being an apostrophic address to a dead master's work, trying to reconcile the coexistence of artificial or ideal beauty and a world of woe. Though the poem has aspects of a static representation, a mimesis of mimesis, whose matrix boundaries should, according to the poem's title, be on the picture itself, Southey attempts to make the scene live by imaginatively entering it, creating sound and movement and taking note of other travellers in the scene, being both 'on' and 'in' the scene. He represents himself neither simply as a watcher, nor the creator of a *mise en abîme*, but as a wanderer *in* the abyss, which is, by its very nature (a print, an oblong), purports to be both a given securing structure and visual prompt. But the security of the boundaries of Poussin's ideal landscape is decentred and destabilized by Southey's reading.

Helen Vendler, discussing Keats, claims that the 'constitutive trope of the *Urn* is interrogation, that trope of the perplexed mind'.[11] Southey's tropic mode is also questioning by contemplation introduced by apostrophe. He uses apostrophe in the poem with an enthusism of recognition for the mental landscape of art, a recognition of the enterprise of a fellow traveller, and is thus lured into a reading of the picture which mirrors his own condition and mimics his desires. The poem in the end seems to suggest that while art may sustain or fulfil the observer, it may also paradoxically reveal the boundary edges of that observer's entrapment, and engage the blinding forces of Fancy.

The poem's opening lines describe the lonely solitude in which 'musings' upon a picture carry the mind away from the 'foul haunts of herded humankind' (p. 154) to 'untainted air' around the eminence of 'mountain LIBERTY'.[12] It is through the rough imagery of the picturesque that Southey's mental flight takes place. He looks to a place where human beings are not 'herded' like cattle, where liberty is proclaimed in the very contours of the landscape. It is worth recalling that he ended his days surrounded by the mountains at Keswick, and that travellers like Gilpin had already made English and Welsh mountain landscapes fashionable places for tourism. The

implications are that touristic ideals (linked to ideal landscapes
like this one by Poussin) lent colour and articulation to the
landscapes of (political and poetical) desire. Southey's desire
for liberty beyond the herd in the realm of Fancy repeats the
motif of the herd or flock in the poem.[13] He transforms the
un-aesthetic image of overpopulation, the foul human herd,
by joyfully incorporating Poussin's goatherd depicted in *The
Cascade*. He watches

> . . . the goatherd down that high-bank'd path
> Urging his flock grotesque; and bidding now
> His lean rough dog from some near cliff to drive
> The straggler; while his barkings loud and quick
> mid their trembling bleat arising oft,
> Fainter and fainter from the hollow road
> Send their far echoes, till the waterfall,
> Hoarse bursting from the cavern'd cliff beneath,
> Their dying murmurs drown. (p. 156)

The noise and bustle of the city is supplanted by this pastoral
figure, the guardian and keeper of the flock whose upraised
left arm in *The Cascade* catches the eye of the observer and
urges it also into the centre of the picture where the road,
flock, and waterfall seem to converge. The goatherd is the
central figure in the narrative of the picture and a very
important figure in the poem itself. As guardian of the flock,
he represents the Arcadian lifestyle, a rugged self-sufficiency
as yet untainted by commerce. His are the liberty and
simplicity that Southey might have realized in the American
backwoods, but the poet depicts himself some way from the
action, making an ascent to look down upon the scene, like a
prospect-hunting tourist. Southey's aloofness extends to a
discussion of 'Fancy' which holds a strangely unstable
position in the poem, that of trusted-untrustworthiness. It is
'charmed FANCY', of 'faery flights', female-gendered per-
petrator of 'blessed witcheries' whose '. . . loveliest prospects
cheat the traveller / O'er the long wearying desart of the

world' (p. 154). Fancy here is nothing short of a purveyor of mirages, mimic othernesses which tantalize the 'traveller' thrust into the blank unreadability of a desert waste.

He distinguishes however between the 'witcheries' of Fancy, and the other magical powers (set in literature) of such figures as Merlin and Alquif.[14] The sorcerer's acts of vengeance and evil are different in quality to the effects of Fancy. But the sorcerers in this poem are rendered harmless servants of Fancy, themselves embedded in a static text awaiting readership, just like their victims 'Lisvart and Perion' (kings of England and Gaul respectively) represented as prisoners in 'the jacinth sepulchre'. Southey's little aside upon the sorcerers inhabits a textual space between two apostrophes to Fancy ('FANCY! best friend', p. 154, and 'Friend of my lonely hours!', p. 155), where the evil deceivers are themselves confined or imprisoned textually between apostrophic praise for Fancy itself. Southey goes on to distinguish Fancy from sorcery by linking the effects of Fancy to 'Nature':

> Friend of my lonely hours! thou leadest me
> To such calm joys as Nature wise and good
> Proffers in vain to all her wretched sons;
> Her wretched sons who pine with want amid
> The abundant earth, and blindly bow them down
> Before the Moloch shrines of WEALTH and POWER,
> AUTHORS of EVIL. Oh it is most sweet
> To medicine with thy wiles the wearied heart,
> Sick of reality. (p. 155)

Fancy leads the mind to Liberty, and also to the 'calm joys' which are like the joys found in the beneficent wisdom of 'Nature', a Nature linked here to flight and retreat. If, as Raymond Williams says:

> the idea of nature contains an extraordinary amount of human history. What is often being argued, it seems to me, in the idea of nature is the idea of man; and this not

> only generally, or in ultimate ways, but the idea of man
> in society, indeed the ideas of kinds of societies[15]

then Southey is, even when simply observing a picture,
constructing an idea of society. In this case, that society would
gain its health in retreat from crowds and commerce. 'Nature'
in this poem is of course not just an idea or a reality of open
green space, but a reading of a painting from the poet's own
nature, three dimensions attempting to force an entry into
two. Because Nature is female here, then, the flight to nature
becomes, as it were, a flight of desire to the mother, for
reassurance, for rebirth, for safety.

Southey's Fancy of 1795 is related to Coleridge's growing
dissatisfaction with Hartley and the empiricist concept of the
human mind. Southey appears to depict Fancy (pp. 154–55) as
an active power which 'makes / The lovely landscape live' and
which 'leadest' the mind to the calm joys which resemble the
available calmness of Nature. The poet's soul is a 'rapt' and
'willing' participant upon the flight undertaken with 'spirit
speed' via his 'best friend' into pure air, health, happiness and
Liberty. It is a minor Platonic visitation of the Muse. But it
does seem that Aristotle and Plato are both present in the
text—mimetic pleasure struggles with an imaginative flight or
possession somewhere upon the hazardous road to idealization or unification of elements.[16]

Like Wordsworth in *Michael*, Southey begins his wandering (a pleasurable tour) into the picture with an ascent, which
here is not only presaged by the whole tradition of prospect
poetry and Biblical allusion, but actually follows one of the
(un)natural lines taken by the eye in looking at the engraved
landscape. The eye is either drawn up the hill to look out into
the mountainous distance past the citadel, or, following the
one strenuous movement in the picture (the goatherd's arm),
rolls in a curve over the backs of his goats, up through the
boughs of the offset tree, and onto the citadel. Southey's poem
(p. 155) takes us straight to the citadel and then (p. 157) makes

the same journey a second time via the goatherd. The trapped eye rolls back and forth in the scene.

2
Southey Agonistes

However pleasant Southey the reader's initial wandering in his precursor's landscape is, its ideal contours throw him back upon 1795, forcing him, and us, to look away. The textual wanderer's phrase 'A little yet / Onward' (p. 156), as he reaches the top of the craggy hill, strongly recalls the opening line of Milton's *Samson Agonistes*,[17] where the blinded hero asks to be led to a bank where he can sit in sunshine or shade as he wishes, as a rest from prison toil, and, no doubt, from unseen but sensed prison darkness. Another precursor is therefore present in the text. Of course it is tempting to compare the hero Samson with the hero Milton, himself blind by 1651 with the collapse of the Commonwealth behind him. This adds to the poignancy of Southey's allusion here, linking his poem with the plight of republican politics in adverse times. Blindness, whether of an individual or of a nation, is an apt allusion when applied to Southey's poem, and an apt metaphor which recalls the lament for a society of 'wretched sons' (p. 155) who serve 'the Moloch shrines of WEALTH and POWER'. Again, the Miltonic voice is buried (alongside the Biblical root) within the poem. Moloch is well-represented in Milton's poetry—and notice that Southey uses Moloch rather than Mammon—as the idol to whom human sacrifice (the burning of children) is made:

> First Moloch, horrid King besmeared with blood
> Of human sacrifice, and parent tears . . .
> (*Paradise Lost* I, ll. 392–93)

And as Milton was aware, the name Moloch comes from the Hebrew 'molekh' (from 'melekh', meaning King). So in the

Southey poem 'WEALTH and POWER' recall the hated shrines of kingly or monarchical forces, Molochs that devour the children of the nation who are blind and wretched in their service.

The Prospect

Southey's imaginary ascent of the hill gives him a view of the mountain and its 'circling grandeur' (p. 157), an embracing landscape which expresses that desire in his nature for Liberty through Fancy. He imagines the 'traveller crossing his domain' and looking up at the dwelling he has chosen to inhabit, whose tower he suggests may be mistaken for 'the house of GOD':

> Nor would he err
> So deeming, for that home would be the home
> Of PEACE and LOVE, and they would hallow it
> To HIM. (p. 157)

Peace and love, two most fundamental Pantisocratic values, are inscribed in the poem upon the 'craggy hill' (p. 155) where the poet will live. His community of one upon the rough eminence enshrines the values of 'the house of God', a God whose own nature is reflected through the other eminence in the picture, the distant mountain perimeter, which forms the guardian barrier and limit of the idyll. But the idyll of plenitude becomes a cry of despair just at the moment when the poet accepts that the protective mountain:

> Should bound mine eyes; aye and my wishes too,
> For I would have no hope or fear beyond.
> The empty turmoil of the worthless world,
> Its vanities and vices would not vex
> My quiet heart. (p. 157)

In turning his back upon the world, the poet accepts the perimeter of vision here represented by the ever distant mountains of Liberty, but also has to accept the binding of the eyes, the guise of Southey Agonistes, which the idyll demands. The whole poem is undercut by a breaking of the idyll, a jolting foreclosure trapping the eye of Fancy in a Gothic image:

> Oh life of blessedness! to reap
> The fruit of honourable toil, and bound
> Our wishes with our wants! delightful Thoughts
> That sooth the solitude of maniac HOPE,
> Ye leave her to reality awak'd,
> Like the poor captive, from some fleeting dream
> Of friends and liberty and home restor'd,
> Startled, and listening as the midnight storm
> Beats hard and heavy thro' his dungeon bars. (pp. 157–58)

The Pantisocratic scheme is again brought to mind here in a brief picture of communal self-sufficiency, which like the perimeter of Southey's mimesis implies a bondage of a different kind, a material kind. What does it mean to 'bound / Our wishes with our wants'?[18] Is it a loose description of a Rousseauistic self-sufficient turning from the world? Southey has suddenly shifted from the first person singular to an admittance of community in the first person plural. At this point his misanthropy is forgotten, or at least reveals its true nature: he is thinking still of the community, or family, of like minds.

Southey's desire or 'maniac Hope', another female prime mover like Joan of Arc, feels the post-imaginative dismay which has sprung from this sour encounter with Fancy, which, far from being an idle day-dream, is in fact a political act of mind. Hope is likened to the 'poor captive' (a male) who cannot see out of his dungeon, but only hears the 'midnight storm' of darkness and strife, like the present qualities of Southey Agonistes' world. The cross-gendered female-Hope-as-male-captive is a peculiar example of literary transvestism which describes Southey's desperate attempt for a final joining with the picture. 'Hope' is the landscape itself and Southey the captive posing as Hope in prison.

The play of light over an evocatively beautiful landscape is finally viewed by the reader reading Southey's observations through a grid of dungeon bars—behind which the ideal, the idyll, remains in suspension. A landscape which had seemed welcoming to the politics of the eye closes down its perimeters, substitutes night for day and confines the victim. The 'GASPAR' of the title finds a terrible echo in the final word of the poem.

3
Quitting the Idyll:
Reflections on Having Left a Place of Retirement
Coleridge, a born editor, was also a born collaborator . . .[19]

Coleridge gravitated towards the post-Pantisocratic element of desire in Southey's work, revealingly emphasized here. He wrote to Joseph Cottle, on a Friday morning 6 January 1797, a few days after he arrived at Nether Stowey, making a detailed criticism of Southey's *Poems* 1797 which were out in their first edition by December 1796. He also singled out from these his own two favourite poems (*Griggs* I, p. 297):

> bye the bye what a *divine* poem his Musings on a Landscape after Gaspar Poussin is!—I love it almost better than the Hymn to the Penates.

He adds (*Griggs* I, p. 300) that the two poems 'deserve to have been published after the Joan of Arc, as proofs of *progressive* genius', suggesting that he also is fully aware of the sense of personal change therein, with some elements of which he perhaps had profound sympathies. C. G. Martin demonstrated some time ago[20] that Coleridge used William Crowe's *Lewesdon Hill* as a source for parts of *Reflections*. There are also intertextual similarities between Southey's poem and parts of Coleridge's *Reflections on Having Left a Place of Retirement* (*CP* pp. 106–08) which do not deserve the critical neglect to which they seem to have been condemned. Both poets surely knew Crowe's poem well. As we can see from Whalley's list of Bristol library borrowings, Coleridge had *Poetical Tracts* out (*WH* pp. 119 & 122) in March 1795 (and December 1795) which contained the poem, and it is hard to believe that Southey did not read it at some point. We might view Coleridge's poem as an answer to, or critique of, Southey's own—or vice-versa. Their titles suggest some inter-active impulses: after all, to muse and to reflect are verbs of meditation upon a subject, and Southey's poem, along with the *Hymn to the Penates*, it seems to me, has a place in the development of Coleridge's conversation genre.

I would place the writing of *Musings* around early September 1795, giving Southey the best part of two months to send a draught of it to Coleridge for criticism as was his wont with new work. A second period when the poem might have been communicated in this manner is between May 1796, when Southey returned from Portugal (and partially made up his quarrel with Samuel), and the publication of *Reflections* in the *Monthly Magazine* for October 1796. This period is close to the revised dating of *Reflections* that Kelvin Everest (*Everest* p. 236) suggests. The third scenario is that Coleridge first saw *Musings* on 27 December 1797, in the newly-printed volume of *Poems* which Southey had sent to him. He states (*Griggs* I, pp. 290–91) that 'The Musings on a Landscape' is a delicious poem but that the words 'TO HIM begin the line awkwardly to my ear' and that he had 'animadverted on those poems only which are my favourites'. His exclamation to Cottle above from January 1797 concerning *Musings* may be construed as the reactions of a reader to a new piece, or indeed the reactions of someone long-familiar with the poem. Here, I will read Coleridge's *Reflections* as if they were a comment upon

Southey's work, as a comment (*Everest* pp. 240–41) upon the 'wrong kind of retirement'.

Coleridge records the idyllic life at his Clevedon cottage or his 'Valley of Seclusion (*CP* p. 106) honeymooning with his new wife, but breaks from it to re-engage with the world, profoundly marked by the experience like his later character of the Mariner. What Crowe calls 'A blest condition',[21] Southey calls the 'life of blessedness' (*Musings* p. 157), and Coleridge echoes as the 'Blessed place' where he and Sara '*were* blessed'. Coleridge's 'wealthy son of Commerce with his 'thirst of idle gold' is actually softened, awakened, by exposure to the cottage's situation. The citizen of Bristowa is a servant of the 'shrines of Wealth and Power' to use Southey's phrase, execrated and pitied in his poem, one of society's 'wretched sons' (*Musings* p. 155) whom Southey would lead to 'Nature'. The two poets' depictions of 'Nature' differ in the sense that Coleridge avoids the abstract noun for particular description, setting the action in the locus of his own home, a marital home the like of which Southey did not then possess, a specific beloved place. Coleridge's citizen of Bristol recognizes the element of the divine in the focal point of the cottage, just as Southey's traveller figure, more distantly, looks up at the building upon the hill and thinks it sacred to God, 'TO HIM'.

Coleridge ascends a 'stony Mount' (*CP* p. 107) to look over a scene composed of details reminiscent of Southey's view from the 'craggy hill' within the Poussin of 'town-spires behind the castle towers' (*Musings* p. 157), but again, Coleridge responds to a living specific place rather than a work of art, and his detail is much finer. Both ascents are in the picturesque manner and the prospect tradition, which, in Coleridge's case, Everest (pp. 238ff) also relates persuasively to his reading of Crowe's *Lewesdon Hill*. The Coleridgean plenitude, or Claudian serenity,[22] encompasses the whole vista, a vista not entirely valorized by art and literary reference. Coleridge looks over a 'goodly scene' just as Southey had surveyed his 'goodly vale' (*Musings* p. 156), an echo,

perhaps, of Crowe's 'goodly fields',[23] but Coleridge's Unitarian vision pulls together the whole as an image of God's
temple, where the poet, feeling himself in the divine presence,
wishes for nothing but 'to be!':

> God, methought,
> Had built him there a Temple: the whole World
> Seem'd *imag'd* in its vast circumference:
> No *wish* profan'd my overwhelmed heart.
> Blest hour! It was a luxury,—to be! (*CP* p. 107)

Coleridge eschews Southey's reiterated 'wishes' (*Musings*
p. 157) as profane longings in the face of the Divine image
present to him in the surrounding plenitude. But for Coleridge
existence within the idyll, the mere glimpse of the eternal, is
incompleteness because he knows that outside in the political
and social arena his abilities could serve humanity. As Everest
notes (p. 122), Coleridge's vital radical audience, though
small, was in Bristol: at Clevedon it consisted of a handful of
friends. At Clevedon, Coleridge's sense of marginalization in
politics may have been increased. The idyll, though it displayed the face of the Divine, also seemed to show the poet
what he needed to achieve. Coleridge displaces his own vision
of the Divine:

> Was it right,
> While my unnumber'd brethren toil'd and bled,
> That I should dream away the entrusted hours
> On rose-leaf beds, pampering the coward heart
> With feelings all too delicate for use?

At least in the poem, Coleridge's persona is no misanthrope,
shunning as did Southey the 'empty turmoil of the worthless
world' (*Musings* p. 157), and the poem underlines a desire to
engage with the huge brotherhood, the extended family of
mankind, rather than to belong to:

> The sluggard Pity's vision-weaving tribe!
> Who sigh for Wretchedness, yet shun the Wretched,

Nursing in some delicious solitude
Their slothful loves and dainty sympathies!
(*CP* pp. 107–08)

Was this a criticism of Southey's avowed feelings for the 'wretched sons' (*Musings* p. 155) of the commercial world? A criticism of Southey's 'delightful Thoughts / That sooth the solitude of Maniac Hope'? Does the degeneration of *Reflections* towards the end into democratic trumpetings belie what its author really felt about leaving home? Is it a manoeuvre out-Southeying Southey?

Both men enshrine 'honourable toil' (*CP* p. 108 and *Musings* p. 157) in their individual poems, Southey as an essential part of his projected desire of the ideal life, and Coleridge as an idyll of the mind from which retrospective dreaming of the Clevedon Cot may spring. The Cot-idyll will remain for Coleridge as a faint image of God's Kingdom to be, something that (at least in 1795) he wishes upon 'all'. If *Reflections* is indeed a comment upon the world-weary dreaming in Southey's *Musings*, then we may also perceive the essential details of the two men's quarrelling, the vital differences of social outlook between them. The intertextual clues point in this direction—at the very least we have a plausible dialogue across two texts with similar concerns. If we reverse the reading and see Southey commenting upon Coleridge, having read his *Reflections* in the *Monthly Magazine*, then we could posit a Southeyan rejection of political and social involvement with 'Bristowa' itself as a place of failures.

Coleridge's regrets about leaving his flower-hung Cot, his sighing of 'fond wishes' (*CP* p. 108) replicates something of the tone of Southey's *Musings*, the sentiments of both poets being set in quietly moving blank verse. If Coleridge and Southey were not still intimates in collaboration by the end of 1795 and in 1796, they remained fully aware of each other's writings, sibling rivals in what would be called a sect of poets.

4

Glassy Sea, Deadly Swell:
Wordsworth's Re-painting of a Self
'Sea—Ship—drowned—Shipwreck—so it came'
(*WP* IV, p. 264)

In this line of ideal landscapes it may be worthwhile to include Wordsworth's own discussion of a picture, his *Elegiac Stanzas, Suggested by a Picture of Peele Castle, in a Storm, Painted by Sir George Beaumont*, which was exhibited by Beaumont at the Royal Academy Exhibition for 1806 where it was seen by Wordsworth. The castle was first observed in situ by Wordsworth during an anxious stay (just following the fall of Robespierre) at Rampside in the August of 1794 when the perfectly calm summer weather gave to the sea an aspect of gentleness upon which the trembling image of the castle was reflected, and by which the castle stood as one kind of presence, as a mark, then signifying sunny peacefulness. A gentle peacefulness informed in part, one imagines, by events in France. If the scene was not quite an ally of the 'shadow of the dome of pleasure' (*CP* p. 298) floating 'midway on the waves', the poet did make an idyll, a chronicle of heaven from what he saw, as if strife and toil had suddenly and miraculously been banished from the earth.

After his brother's drowning on 5 February 1805 in the wreck of the *Earl of Abergavenny*, the poet could never regard the sea (or French ideals) with that former narcissistic faith of illusion. His revisitation of the locus *via* the painting is set finally, as Hartman says, in words 'like the inscription on a tomb'.[24]

Whilst Southey in his reading of Poussin yearns for the ideal contours of the pictured landscape in thwarted flight from the world, Wordsworth, after acute personal grief, accepts the loss and embraces the re-shaping of the former idyll by Beaumont. Lying reflections upon water are banished forever

from the poet's active sympathies, yet remain inscribed in the
elegy. Both images, sun and storm, sit within the poem but the
castle, once merely a picturesque 'hoary pile', is re-marked
with that 'unfeeling armour' which only lived time settles
upon the comparative brevity of human grief. Wordsworth's
welcome to the picture is a welcoming of the human condition, of mortality and especially change via the anti-idyll,
encountered in Beaumont's romantic storm painting. Wordsworth relates his former memories of castle and sea to dreams
and blindnesses forged in solitude:

> Farewell, farewell the heart that lives alone,
> Housed in a dream, at distance from the Kind!
> Such happiness, wherever it be known,
> Is to be pitied; for 'tis surely blind. (*WP* IV, pp. 258–60)

These sentiments critique the escape-desires and the implied
misanthropy expressed in such poems as Southey's *Musings*,
or rather they surpass them with a stoicism (embryonic in
Southey's poem) which looks squarely at life in recognition of
the blindnesses of art. Wordsworth is upon the same road as
George Crabbe. He also aligns himself with Coleridge's 'habit
of accepting separation from joy as long as he can think of
participating in the joy of other persons',[25] which I have
discussed in relation to his quittal of the Clevedon cottage. To
live 'at distance from the Kind' is indeed pitiable in the views
of both men.

5
Cauda

> Come, Traveller, this hollow Rock beneath,
> While in the Leaves refreshing Breezes breath;
> Retire, to calm the Rage of burning Thirst,
> In these cool streams that from the Cavern burst.[26]

Some of the landscape components of Southey's *Musings* almost serve as archetypes of Coleridge's poem (*CP* pp. 295–98) *Kubla Khan*. I have already noted Coleridge's enthusiasm for Southey's poem and remain perplexed that critics such as John Livingston Lowes largely ignore Southeyan source-hunting as possible prompting for Coleridge's work. Southey's poem is bounded by the framing coordinates of the Poussin as Coleridge's is by the perimeters of the pleasure garden, and both poems strive for a stability which outside invasive forces deny to them. Both poems also use the work of others as a point of departure for explicit and implicit discussions of the imagination. Secret places, enfolded spots, clefts, chasms and bowered paths are parts of both poems, amplified greatly in Coleridge's work of course. Southey describes his 'close embowered' path up a wooded hill out of which a waterfall is rushing:

> craggy is the hill
> And steep, yet thro' yon hazels upward leads
> The easy path, along whose winding way
> Now close embowered I hear the unseen stream
> Dash down, anon behold its sparkling foam
> Gleam thr'o the thicket (*Musings* pp. 155–56)

The voice of the waters overwhelms the noise of the goatherd's dog and sheep:

> till the waterfall,
> Hoarse bursting from the cavern'd cliff beneath,
> Their dying murmurs drown. (p. 156)

Southey's verb 'bursting' along with 'cavern'd' is echoed in *Kubla Khan* and Coleridge also repeats the anthropomorphic nature of the waterfall: Southey's is 'hoarse', Coleridge's mighty fountain (*CP* p. 297) lives 'breathing'. Southey's spell-imprisoned contemplative blank verse is replaced in *Kubla Khan* by Coleridge's spell-binding incantatory mixture of short lines and couplet rhymes.

If, as Marilyn Butler says, Coleridge effects a re-reading of parts of Southey's *Thalaba the Destroyer* as a 'quietist maneuver',[27] may we not also include *Musings* in this overall process of re-reading of his more infamous peer, bearing in mind Coleridge's stated jealousy of Southey's fame? May we not regard *Kubla Khan* as a relative of *Musings on a Landscape of Gaspar Poussin*, come to us via *Reflections on Having Left a Place of Retirement*? Noting again Coleridge's enthusiasm about *Musings* and noticing the relative closeness of the dates of composition, could we not make a case for including Southey's poem as prototypical in discussions of contained gardens, idylls, or indeed 'false ideology'? Does Coleridge's applause (if it is genuine applause) for Southey's work in the phrase 'a *divine* poem' (echoing his famous comment upon Cowper's work) have any relevance to the visions of sacredness and holiness in *Kubla Khan*? Does Coleridge's 'quietism' re-echo and re-inscribe something of Southey's quietistic misanthropy of the 1795 *Musings*?

NOTES

1 William Taylor, 'Outlines of a Discourse on the History and Theory of Prospect-Painting', *Monthly Magazine*, xxxvii part I for 1814, p. 406.

2 William Haller, *The Early Life of Robert Southey, 1774–1803* (New York: Columbia University Press, 1917), p. 157.

3 *Die Lieden Des Jungen Werthers*, ed. E. L. Stahl (Oxford: Basil Blackwell, 1972), p. 84. Southey wrote to Horace Walpole Bedford: 'I need not tell you with what pleasure my frequent perusals of Werter have been attended. For six months I was never without it in my pocket—the character is natural—at least it appeared so when tried by the touch-stone of my own heart' (*NL* I, p. 44, 24 January 1794). Southey therefore uses literary models for his language of loss, posing here as the thwarted lover Werther. He repeated this motif of the void in the heart (this time from Schiller) when bringing about a reconciliation with Coleridge in 1796: 'Fiesco! Fiesco! thou

leavest a void in my bosom, which the human race, thrice told, will never fill up' (*Simmons* p. 65).

4 See Stephane Mallarmé, *Poésies* (Paris: Flammarion, 1983), p. 308.

5 'Gaspar Dughet, called Poussin, brother-in-law of Nicolas and associate of Claude, was enormously admired by the English, and much collected by them. His pictures show the training which he received from both Nicolas and Claude, and even at times, in his scenes of wild nature, have a suggestion of Salvator.' Elizabeth W. Manwaring, *Italian Landscape in Eighteenth Century England: A Study Chiefly of the Influence of Claude Lorraine and Salvator Rosa on English Taste 1700–1800* (London: Frank Cass, 1925, 2nd imp. 1965, p. v.). Hereafter 'Manwaring'.

6 Francis Vivares (1709–1780) was a Frenchman, who 'may be called the founder of the British school of landscape engraving' and who was, according to Manwaring (p. 80), 'especially known for his engravings after Claude'. Southey himself was listening to advice which told him that a few illustrations (see *NL* I, p. 129ff) would accelerate book sales.

7 Claude Lorraine (1600–82) and Gaspar Dughet, called Poussin (1615–75), belong loosely to the classical picturesque school of landscape painting and tend to evoke the serenity of the Virgilian world in their work. The other strain of the picturesque, the Romantic, derives essentially from the work of Adam Elsheimer (1578–1610) and Salvator Rosa (1615–73), in which the latter artist was seen particulary as the quintessential wild romantic. 'If for sixty or seventy years to come Claude is soft, Salvator dashes, and Poussin is learned, the responsibility is Thomson's. That stanza of his on landscape painting was a handy compendium of criticism for the general public . . .' (Manwaring p. 107). What can be added to this is the influence that both Dyer's Grongar Hill (with its Claudian expanses) and Bowles' own landscape painting in sonnet form had upon the young poet. Manwaring (p. 176) states also that 'In 1760, the influence of Salvator was reinforced by that of Ossian'. Southey's finale to the third act of *The Fall of Robespierre*, it could be said, was written in this sublimely dangerous mixture of Salvatorian Ossianics. The retreat from this position is self-evident in the present poem.

8 See *Poems* 1797, p. 158. All further references to the poem will give only the page number.

9 See Jonathan Culler, *The Pursuit of Signs* (London: Routledge and Kegan Paul, 1981), p. 142.

10 Helen Vendler, *The Odes of John Keats* (Cambridge, Mass. and London: The Belknap Press, 1983), p. 131.

11 *Ibid.*, p. 118.

12 This phrase occurs also in *Madoc* (F p. 500) where the hero dreams of a free kingdom as he wanders through the hills of Gwyneth.

13 In the chapter on Joan of Arc I drew attention to Burke's famous national idyll (B p. 181) in which the nation as cattle browse without supervision, save by the textual voice of Burke himself. Southey's/Poussin's goatherd is the pastor-figure, the overseer, the ordinary father, of the small post-Pantisocratic flock.

14 Merlin and Alquif are famous sorcerers of medieval romance. Merlin's tale is set out by Geoffrey of Monmouth in his *Vita Merlini* of circa 1150. Alquif appears in a sixteenth-century continuation of *Amadis of Gaul* called *Amadis of Greece* (actually the seventh book of *Amadis of Gaul*) by Feliciano de Silva. Southey himself translated *Amadis of Gaul*, which he published in an abridged form in 1803, but which he was working on at least as early as 1797 (*NL* I, pp. 146–47). 'Zarzafiel' I have been unable to trace.

15 Raymond Williams, *Problems in Materialism and Culture*, p. 71.

16 In some respects the poem is typical of the Romantic flight and return pattern found in poems such as Keats' *Ode to a Nightingale*. Keats recalls Southey's notion of cheating Fancy (p. 154) in the Ode.

17 *The Poetical Works of John Milton* (London: Oxford University Press, 1952), p. 509, l. 1.

18 The similar phrase 'bound my wishes' (F p. 510) occurs in *Madoc* in Llaian's tale about her enforced exile or retreat from political dangers with the child of Hoel.

19 Norman Fruhman, *Coleridge the Damaged Archangel* (London: George Allen and Unwin, 1971), p. 277.

20 See *Modern Language Review*, Vol. 62, 1967, pp. 400–06.

21 *Ibid.*, p. 404.

22 Manwaring (p. 229) sees suggestions of Claude in Coleridge's *Reflections* and his *Religious Musings*.

23 Martin, *op. cit.*, p. 403.

24 Geoffrey H. Hartman, *Wordsworth's Poetry 1787–1814* (New Haven and London: Yale University Press, 1964), p. 284.

25 *Ibid.*, p. 286.

26 Thomas Warton The Elder, 'On a Cave' from *Poems on Several Occasions* (New York: The Facsimile Text Society, 1930), p. 194.

27 Marilyn Butler, 'Plotting the Revolution: The Political Narratives of Romantic Poetry and Criticism' in *Romantic Revolutions: Criticism and Theory*, ed. K. R. Johnston, G. Chaitin, K. Hanson and H. Marks (Bloomington: Indiana University Press, 1990), p. 154.

Chapter Six

Hymn to the Penates

I
An Englishman in Portugal

With what enchantment Nature's goodly scene
Attracts the sense of mortals[1]

Hymn to the Penates, avowedly a poem of homecoming, a
renunciation of the muse, seeks to be autobiographical, and is
in fact a second poem of control in the mode of *The
Retrospect*. Between the writing of *Musings* and *Hymn to the
Penates* was Southey's experience of Spain and Portugal,
severance from his new bride (and the duties of marital vows)
and his first taste of travel outside England. Southey's often
uneasy intertextual sediment in this poem is composed primarily of events taken from his own life, his extensive reading,
and repeated images and themes from his own poetry, notably
as echoes of *Musings*. By holding the two poems in view,
regarding the *Hymn* as re-reading of the impasse of *Musings*,
we can draw out Southey's idea of home in England through
the iconography he employs in its description.

If Southey had almost entirely shrugged off the discourse of
the 'Crusader' (*NL* I, July 1796, p. 113),[2] for that of the
misanthropic prisoner, caught by the dungeon-bars of dejection in *Musings*, then after the trip to Portugal[3] another voice
may be discerned, that of the disillusioned idealist, the man
dedicated to the hearth and home, the votary of the Penates.
The journey to and from Spain altered his perceptions of
home. So before looking in detail at the *Hymn*, there are a few
important comments to be made about Southey's experiences

161

and writings about Spain and Portugal where he was plunged
into an otherness of extreme beauty and squalor.

*Letters Written During a Short Residence in Spain and
Portugal* is written as a travel book combining natural description, original poetry, humour and acute comparisons:

> Of the people, extreme filth and deplorable ignorance are
> the most prominent characteristics; yet there is a civility
> in the peasantry which Englishmen do not possess, and I
> feel a pleasure when the passenger accosts me with the
> usual benediction, 'God be with you.'(*S* p. 92)

Despite the fact that he suffered from the general dirtiness
of this encounter,[4] he was both appalled *and* fascinated
by another illustration of cultural difference. At Madrid,
Southey's party discovered that they would have to travel in
the wake of the Spanish court on its way to visit the
Portuguese court at Badajoz:

> You will wonder what difference their movements can
> possibly make to us, for in England, if his Majesty passes
> you on the road, you say, 'There goes the King,' and
> there's an end of it; but here, when the Court think
> proper to move, all carriages, carts, mules, horses and
> asses are immediately *embargoed*. Thank God, in an
> Englishman's Dictionary you can find no explanation of
> that word. (*S* p. 114)

Southey suddenly becomes 'an Englishman' critical of foreign
customs but nevertheless, enjoying the sheer picturesque
quality of his encounter:

> and never did I witness a more melancholy scene of
> devastation! His Most Catholic Majesty travels like the
> King of the Gypsies: his retinue strip the country,
> without paying for any thing, sleep in the woods, and
> burn down the trees. We found many of them yet
> burning . . . Mules, and horses, and asses lie dead along
> the road, and though they do not cry aloud in our ears

against the barbarity of thus destroying them by excess-
ive fatigue, yet they address themselves strongly to
another sense. The King is fond of inscriptions. Not a
ditch along the road has been bridged without an
inscription beginning, *Reinado Carlos IV*. I feel very
much inclined to indulge in a placard upon one of the
mutilated old trees. His Majesty's travelling exploits
would have furnished an excellent inscription for such a
monument of his journey. (*S* pp. 164–65)

Scenes like this could not be found in England, and if they
existed in writing, they belonged to a distant past. Home in
Georgian England was very far from this quasi-medieval,
picaresque, landscape. And Southey's idea of what he would
encounter in terms of landscape seems to have been informed
by none other than the subject of the last chapter:

The villages we passed through were mean and dirty, and
the houses are in that style of building, with which the
pencil of Gaspar Poussin had taught me to associate more
ideas of comfort than I found realized. (*S* pp. 33–34)

A few intertextual repetitions occur in this book which link
Southey's *Musings* with his *Letters*. It is as if he is still
searching for that ideal landscape, 'looking joyful on to that
abode / Where PEACE and LOVE await me'.[5] Spain's goats
and goatherds, seemingly born of that ideal, soothe the poet
(*S* p. 80) with 'comfortable feelings'. The pastoral figure of the
herdsman is readily adopted into the poetry in *Letters*, as the
guardian of the flock against the wolf (*S*, *Lines upon Christmas
Day*, p. 81), the good herdsman in surroundings that promote
the good life. Southey contrasts the good herd with the bad in
a poem (*S* pp. 332–34) called *Musings after Visiting the
Convent of Arrabida*. The landscape is the wellspring of
goodness:

And ye who tenant such a goodly scene
Must needs be good! here all is calm and fair,

And here the mirror of the mind reflects
Serenest beauty. (*S* p. 332)

The ideas expressed here link the main areas of Southey's implicit picture of England in *Musings on a Landscape of Gaspar Poussin* and the *Hymn*:

To have no cares,
To have no kindred with the reptile race
Of Man, no Wants to fetter down the soul
Amid the knaves and ideots of the world,
Almost, ye dwellers in this holy house
Almost I envy you! you never hear
The groans of Wretchedness; you never see
Pale Hunger's asking eye, nor roam around
Those huge and baleful sepulchres of Men,
Where WEALTH and POWER have rear'd their palaces,
And Vice with horrible contagion taints
The herd of human kind. (*S* pp. 332–33)[6]

If Southey had decided (*S* p. 65) that 'man is a Beast, and an ugly Beast' then at least there were certain places where this ugliness might be forgotten, where indeed 'the mirror of the mind' might reflect 'Serenest beauty' (*S* p. 332 above) in healing mimetic resonance. One of these places was Cintra (*S* p. 375):

I have now mentioned to you all that strangers usually visit at Cintra: but I cannot without a tedious minuteness describe the ever-varying prospects that the many eminences of this wild rock present, or the little green lanes over whose bordering lemon gardens the evening wind blows so cool, so rich![7]

Cintra was only a glimpse of the ideal, of light, beauty, in healthful landscape—but it was a living landscape. In a reading of the *Hymn* its luminosity might be borne in mind. If landscapes courting the ideal form of those by Gaspar Poussin truly existed, then only Wealth and Power (just two of Southey's dangerous metonymies) could prevent the poet from enjoying their boundaries, from being truly at home as it were. Of course Southey knew he had to return to those other homes, England, marriage, and Edith Southey, to compromise his desires. The *Hymn* describes the path of that compromise.

2
Abstract Domesticities

Southey's hymn of the hearth is, it cannot be denied, a very abstract affair. His vision of home, though it does include selective glimpses of autobiography, seems to constitute a fragmentary and fragmenting *gesture* towards an ideal, rather than a fully realized domestic blueprint. His appropriation of the learned Akensidian cosmos of neo-classical gods sits uneasily beside the Cowperian hearth scenes. His rather violent poetical reactions against the human mob of the world also create a tension with the passages which strive for a quiet contemplative tone. He poses as someone whose past behaviour has gone against the true grain of his desires. The hearth has, he states, always been central to his sense of lack:

> Nor did I cease to reverence you, when driven
> Amid the jarring crowd, an unfit man
> To mingle with the world; still my heart
> Sighed for your sanctuary, and inly pined . . . (p. 207)

Southey allies his notion of the world with Cowper's image in *The Task*, Bk III, ll. 675–83, of retreat from a 'jarring' engagement with the world:

> Oh blest seclusion from a jarring world
> Which he thus occupied, enjoys! Retreat
> Cannot indeed to guilty man restore

Lost innocence, or cancel follies past;
But it has peace, and much secures the mind
From all assaults of evil, proving still
A faithful barrier, not o'erleaped with ease
By vicious custom, raging uncontrol'd
Abroad, and desolating public life.[8]

Where Cowper in his flight as the stricken deer is found by
'one who had himself / Been hurt by the archers', that is,
Christ depicted in a natural image,[9] Southey finds the cheer-
less companionship of 'MISANTHROPY' (p. 212) born of
'SIMPLICITY' and 'BENEVOLENCE' (p. 211), but lives in
hope and patient faith (p. 220) that 'the pure song of
LIBERTY and TRUTH' remain as powers in his world.
Southey's hearth does not have the focal unity of Cowper's
interior world, and is veiled by the obtrusive literary allusiveness which disguises the poet. Nor of course is it the fully-
realized mountain home of Wordsworth's *Michael*, though
both works do include motifs of care. Southey has not yet
managed to humanize properly the inhuman personifications
and myths which we find in the *Hymn*. His hearthstone lacks
the imaginative force which in *Michael* emanates from the
straggling heap of stones to ensnare the reader's active responses. We glimpse the misanthropic persona in the *Hymn*
through learning, elevated language and literary allusion, but
we cannot warm to his plight as we might to the story of
Michael. Southey's hearth, his metaphorical sheep-fold, is in a
state of flux, and finally, in a state of expectancy in retreat.

3
Hope Long Deferred, Retrospection and Home:
Inside the *Hymn*

Southey shaped his poem around an analysis of the past, and a
vision of future events. Haller sees the poem as a 'farewell to

the muse as well as a pantisocratic palinode'.[10] To this assessment we could add Carnall's statement (*CA* p. 56) that:

> Southey's youthful jacobinism was turning into something a good deal more conformist. Probably the most important reason for this was the loss of direction suffered by radical politics after 1795. Unless one were simply to support the French, there was no hope to sustain those who had been excited by the prospect of a total renovation of society opened up by the French Revolution.

The advent of The Directory in France, from late 1795, a new government in which Bonaparte rose to prominence, brought out increasingly patriotic, or at least anti-Napoleonic, outbursts from Southey and eventually gave a name to the common enemy of both Pitt and Southey. Bonaparte became the enemy of English society, of English homes, a convenient focus of anti-French hatred. Southey presents 'society' (above) in the *Hymn* as a grave (when speaking of the city) and as the single hearth, when examining his own desire. Ideas of 'renovation' are not so much proclaimed any more as prophetically and passively left to chance. The *Hymn* is preceded (*Poems* 1797, p. 201) by an explanatory paragraph:

> THE title of the following Poem will probably remind the Reader of Akenside's Hymn to the Naiads; but the manner in which I have treated the subject, fortunately precludes comparison.

This is all very well, but in fact a few simple comparisons are illuminating. Akenside's optimistic and patriotic poem describes the evolution and function of the Naiads who are the imaginary motive force of the waterways which support empire and commerce. He relates them poetically to the natural and moral world, shows how they contribute to human health and how they are befriended by the Muses. This was the poetic cosmos of the Akenside of 1746, writing in the year of Culloden, the last doomed effort by the Stuarts to regain the English throne. Southey's *Hymn* also discusses the Muses, alludes to the question of empire, and his own place in it, to health and morality, but in a different key, with ruin and elegy, not victory, supplying the tone. The remains of the neo-classical commercial Whig paradise of Akenside is what became anathema to Southey in the post-Revolutionary years. It was this empire with its slaves and oppressors in which he was constrained to find a place.

However, both men link retreat and the poetic life. Akenside demands that 'all profaner audience far remove',[11] and this Horatian notion of *odi profanum vulgus* becomes the critical centre of Southey's own poem, Southey himself (p. 204) 'Shunning the polished mob of human kind'. Only the Penates are fit representatives of Southey's new age, their guardianship replacing the great failed hopes of the Revolution and Pantisocratic dreams. The *Hymn to the Penates*, as the *Anti-Jacobin* magazine forgot, coming at the end of the volume of *Poems* 1797, was both a comment and a seal upon the preceding poems. Southey states (*LC* I, p. 291, 29 August 1796), 'I have begun a hymn to the Penates, which will, perhaps, be the best of all my lesser pieces; it is to conclude the volume of poems'. It would be one of the 'chief pictures' (*NL* I, p. 116) of the volume and is in effect the manifesto of his desires.

The poem begins by an invocation to the Penates amidst a forest of apostrophes, in a mixture of allusive elements. The first line 'Yet one Song more! one high and solemn strain',[12] recalls both the opening of Book IV of Akenside's *The Pleasures of the Imagination*[13] ('One effort more, one cheerful sally more') and the first line of Milton's *Lycidas*, a pastoral elegy centred around the death of his friend Edward King. Southey's poem also contains an elegy to the shade of Edmund Seward, his lost paradigm. He wrote a second elegy to Seward (1771–1795) at Westbury in 1799, called *The Dead Friend*.

Seward, like the Penates (when they assume the guise of
benign departed spirits), becomes a guardian:

> And we have often said how sweet it were
> With unseen ministry of angel power
> To watch the friends we loved.
> Edmund! we did not err!
> Sure I have felt thy presence! Thou hast given
> A birth to holy thought,
> Hast kept me from the world unstain'd and pure.
> Edmund! we did not err!
> Our best affections here
> They are not like the toys of infancy;
> The Soul outgrows them not;
> We do not cast them off;
> Oh if it could be so,
> It were indeed a dreadful thing to die![14]

Seward occupies the role of a 'Lycidas' in Southey's *Hymn*,
becomes like Lycidas, a dead 'shepherd' of the virtuous ones.
In the retrospective passage from pp. 205–07, Southey recalls
his Balliol days and his retreat from the *Comus*-like 'noise /
of loud intemperance' (p. 206) of the other undergraduates from
which he and others including Seward fled. Their priggish-
sounding 'sober society' was formed at this time. Southey
wrote of Seward:

> I used to call him *Talus* for his unbending morals and iron
> rectitude, and his strength of body also justified the
> name. His death in the year 1795 was the first severe
> affliction that I ever experienced; and sometimes even
> now I dream of him, and wake myself by weeping,
> because even in my dreams I remember that he is dead. I
> loved him with my whole heart, and shall remember him
> with gratitude and affection as one who was my moral
> father, to the last moment of my life; and to meet him
> again will at that moment be one of the joys to which I

shall look forward in eternity. (*LC* IV, pp. 320–21, Keswick, 16 November 1818)

In the landscape of the Penates it is Seward, not Coleridge, who is Southey's moral father and guardian (p. 215), whose 'celestial ken' observes him and whose memory supports him at his most melancholy moments:

> When my sick Heart,
> (Sick with hope long delayed, than which no care
> Presses the crush'd heart heavier;) from itself
> Seeks the best comfort, often have I deemed
> That thou didst witness every inmost thought
> SEWARD! my dear dead friend![15]

Seward has, however, left Southey 'With strengthened step to follow the right path' (p. 215) and joins the Pantheon of the hearth in the highly unstable form of loss-as-presence, part of the double yearning for the past and for home. Seward, like Milton's Edward King, had been intended for the church, and he inhabits Southey's elegiac poem as a good shepherd, the herdsman of Southey's death-haunted text.

The opening lines of the poem re-empower the classical gods of Akenside's poetry, gods which had been struck dumb by Milton's Christ.[16] And it is amongst these gods that Southey purports to use the harp just once more before placing it upon the wall of the ruined temple of Paean. Paean, or Apollo, was the god of medicine, music, poetry, knowledge, a god who had served as a shepherd himself. He also had the gift of future sight, which is why Southey includes the olive tree (traditionally a sign of peace but also sacred to Apollo) in his own prophetic vision of the ruined city (p. 219), growing from the stones of the palace at the poem's end. But the combination of the ruin and the harp's 'melancholy music' (p. 203) in the opening lines draws the reader's ear away from the classical world to the legends of the North.

Once it is hung upon the wall, the (silent) instrument may

perform the passive and receptive function of an Aeolian harp
(p. 203) when the 'tempest shakes the aged pile'. Southey
appears to have appropriated this imagery from Macpherson's
Ossian fragments, where a footnote explains:

> It was the opinion of ancient times that, on the night
> preceding the death of a person worthy and renowned,
> the harps of those bards who were retained by his family
> emitted melancholy sounds. This was attributed to *the
> light touch of ghosts*, who were supposed to have a
> foreknowledge of events. The same opinion prevailed
> long in the north, and the particular sound was called *the
> warning voice of the dead.*[17]

Southey's harp (combining muse and prophetic warning
voice) was closely attuned to the political events of his world.
Coleridge made a fairly lengthy criticism of the *Hymn* trying
to work out for himself if Southey meant what he said:

> What if you *left* the harp in the fane of Vacuna? If these
> observations strike you as just, I shall be sorry, they did
> not strike me when you *read* the poem! But indeed the
> lines sound so sweet, and *seem* so much like sense, that it
> is no great matter. 'Tis a handsome & finely sculptur'd
> Tomb—& few will break it open with the sacrilegious
> spade and pick-ax of Criticism to discover, whether or no
> it be not a *Cenotaph*. (*Griggs* I, p. 290)

His purported farewell to the muse, the hanging up of the harp
in the 'rude tempest' (p. 203) leaves the melancholy voice of
warning wrung from the instrument for the ears of like hearts
only. The warning comes at the end of the poem, as I have
said, in a vision of apocalypse for city dwellers. But for the
present, Southey confines his quieted muse to the boundaries
of home, in:

> this better day, when on mine ear
> The uproar of contending nations sounds

> But like the passing wind, and wakes no pulse
> To tumult. (p. 205)

His muse will remain unmoved by the strife of war, unmoved because confused and dismayed by the fret of political and social hopes which have turned to dust. War is described as the wind of devastation, which once was the aery spirit of Liberty and Equality, which had not simply quickened Southey's pulse, but had appeared initially to bind his generation into millennium:

> You shall see one of these days what I say of that tempestuous age; few persons but those who have lived in it can conceive or comprehend what the memory of the French Revolution was, nor what a visionary world seemed to open upon those who were just entering it. Old things seemed passing away, and nothing was dreamt of but the regeneration of the human race.[18]

The *Hymn* is the major political and poetic statement in Southey's *Poems* 1797 of his reaction to the ebbing away of this visionary world. He portrays himself as the stranger and the exile of the hearth, one who has even so remained a lover of home:

> tho' from your rites
> Estranged, and exiled from your altars long,
> I have not ceased to love you, HOUSEHOLD GODS!
> In many a long and melancholy hour
> Of solitude and sorrow, has my heart
> With earnest longings prayed to rest at length
> Beside your hallowed hearth—for PEACE is there!
> (p. 204)

The hearth becomes that central point at which the poet sits in retirement and reflective thought (p. 204) upon 'All the recesses' of his 'wayward heart' and the 'strange unworldly feelings' therein, and rediscovers his self-respect, the 'best of lessons'. Southey's retrospective passage (pp. 205–07) details how the hearth retains its importance in the biographical progress of his life. He traces a mini-biography from 'the first dawn / Of reason' (p. 205) through his first break with his father's home (see *LC* I, p. 46) to his Oxford days, and to (p. 207) Pantisocratic or Cowleyan longings:

> And loathing human converse, I have strayed
> Where o'er the sea-beach chilly howl'd the blast,
> And gaz'd upon the world of waves, and wished
> That I were far beyond the Atlantic deep,
> In woodland haunts, a sojourner with PEACE.

As in *Musings on a Landscape of Gaspar Poussin*, the theme of entrapment re-appears. Southey presents his little biography as a picture of expulsion from home, concealment in his cave on the Avon (p. 206), retreat from the debauchery of undergraduate life, and longing for escape from his native country. He views himself as a person who is never in the right place, except when sitting by the hearth. The act of retrospection is a source of nostalgic pleasure to Southey, an escape from present problems into a past which he has now ordered and controlled.

> (for still I love
> To dwell with fondness on my childish years,
> Even as that Persian favorite would retire
> From the court's dangerous pageantry and pomp,
> To gaze upon his shepherd garb, and weep,
> Rememb'ring humble happiness.) (p. 205)

Again, the choice of imagery, though now eastern, recalls *Lycidas* and the humble guardianship of the shepherd. Coleridge objected to this simile:

> I have detected two faults only, that a Man amid the miseries of a struggling Life should look back on the quiet happiness of childhood bears no resemblance to a Persian Monarch leaving the Luxuries of a Palace to

revisit the cot where he had been a shepherd . . . (*Griggs* I, p. 290)

Coleridge seems to be missing the point. Southey's childhood, like his own, was not just quietly happy—and the Persian here is a 'favorite' not a 'Monarch', trying to reconcile the formative past with present events. Southey and Coleridge here seem to be thinking of two separate but connected characters, who inhabit the Eastern tales which William Collins used for his *Persian Eclogues*.[19] Southey's 'favorite' is based on the shepherd Alibez who weeps over his 'garb', not his 'cot' as Coleridge would have it.

The distinction is important. Southey, too, can weep over the 'garb' of the past, of memory, himself an exile. Like Alibez, with his private room containing only the 'shepherd garb', Southey has a private store of retrospective touchstones in the memories of home, admittedly an ideal 'cot'. The innocence and purity that he associates with his own past serves as a guide or measure of the present. And the guiding influence of the Household Gods within the history of poetry, a 'deep devotion' (p. 206), may be compared with that of the classical gods whose realm of beauty and 'local energies' (p. 208) have faded away:

> Yet was their influence transient; such brief awe
> Inspiring as the thunder's long loud peal
> Strikes to the feeble spirit. HOUSEHOLD GODS,
> Not such your empire!

The Household Gods according to Southey inhabit an empire of universal lococentrism. The classical gods mentioned here (Dryads, Oreads, Naiads) inhabit particular places, and in these places their power is dominant. The gods of home remain figureheads of the idea of home which moves as the poet moves. An apostrophe of philanthropical advice follows (pp. 208–09), in which some of the poet's own past problems may be recognized:

O ye whom YOUTH has wilder'd on your way,
Or VICE with fair-mask'd foulness, or the lure
Of FAME that calls ye to her crowded paths
With FOLLY'S rattle, to your HOUSEHOLD GODS
Return! for not in VICE'S gay abodes,
Not in the unquiet unsafe halls of FAME
Does HAPPINESS abide! O ye who weep
Much for the many miseries of Mankind,
More for their vices, ye whose honest eyes
Frown on OPPRESSION,—ye whose honest hearts
Beat high when FREEDOM sounds her dread tocsin;—
     . . . to your HOUSEHOLD GODS
Return . . .

If Southey had never been involved with any form of vice, he
had certainly been a wilder'd youth, a seeker of fame,
opponent of oppression and lover of freedom. These personifications or metonymies shout from the page at the reader, and
by their very unparticular nature do not satisfy our biographical questioning. The sheer textual noise of the above capital-
ized passage is in contrast to the later parts of the poem, where
Southey talks of the domain of the Penates (pp. 213–14, 218–
19) and his diction of quietness brings relief and solace. Even
so, he makes further use of personifications who are aspects of
the interior world (p. 209) of the Household Gods:

    . . . for by their altars VIRTUE dwells
And HAPPINESS with her: for by their fires
TRANQUILLITY in no unsocial mood
Sits silent, listening to the pattering shower;
For, so SUSPICION sleep not at the gate
Of WISDOM,—Falsehood shall not enter there.[20]

Unlike the access to Milton's paradise, the quiet hearth does
not admit wandering fallen angels, nor the worldly 'mob':

Grosvenor I despise the world. I hate the mob—I do not
love the soi-disant Philosophers—and I have a thorough

contempt for the aristocratic part. I shall mingle with the
world, but it will be only with the view of enabling
myself to get out of it. I must pass a very dirty road to get
into the path of a quiet life . . . Things will be better in
another world. Tell me Grosvenor is there not more real
pleasure in that belief—more consolation than in all the
systems and maxims of Philosophy? (*NL* I, p. 113, 26
July 1796)

Southey's hearth of the quiet life seems to have its basis in
violent recoil from aristocrats, philosophers and crowds. It is
the true test of virtue from whence (p. 210) he:

> will not quit,
> To mingle with the mob, your calm abodes
> Where, by the evening hearth CONTENTMENT sits
> And hears the cricket chirp; where LOVE delights
> To dwell, and on your altars lays his torch
> That burns with no extinguishable flame.

These two interior scenes evoke quiet retreat, where the
'pattering shower' and the chirp of the cricket are the only
sounds which break the silence of contentment. Southey
recalls Cowper's vocabulary from *The Cricket*:

> Little inmate, full of mirth,
> Chirping on my kitchen hearth;
> Wheresoe'er be thine abode,
> Always harbinger of good,
> Pay me for thy warm retreat,
> With a song more soft and sweet,
> In return thou shalt receive
> Such a strain as I can give.[21]

But there is to be a companion of the hearth, 'one / Must be
my inmate' (p. 210), the abstract 'Misanthropy', once a
philanthropist, a man of feeling taken in by the appearance of
the world, and now (pp. 211–12) sickened by it.

His mother was SIMPLICITY, his sire
BENEVOLENCE; in earlier days he bore
His father's name; the world who injured him
Call him MISANTHROPY. I may not chuse
But love him, HOUSEHOLD GODS! for we were
    nurst
In the same school.

So the poet-misanthrope appears to have arrived at the same point as other eighteenth-century anti-social solitaries (as in Johnson's *Rasselas* or Fielding's *Tom Jones*), rejecting the world to walk the liminal tangents of misanthropic sickness. Southey is again back with Cowley, shut away with his books, and the psychological presences of the dead. But just as the world of Milton's Adam is peopled with 'Millions of spiritual Creatures',[22] Southey's world of the hearth is watched over (p. 212) by the hallowed (if Ossianic) dead.

A dearer interest to the human race
Links you, yourselves the SPIRITS OF THE DEAD.
No mortal eye may pierce the invisible world,
No light of human reason penetrate
That depth where Truth lies hid. Yet to this faith
My heart with instant sympathy assents;
And I would judge all systems and all faiths
By that best touchstone, from whose test DECEIT
Shrinks like the Arch-Fiend at Ithuriel's spear,
And SOPHISTRY'S gay glittering bubble bursts . . .

The world of the hearth is the world of the heart, which overrides the reasoning of systems, and incorporates memories of childhood and associations with the safety of home. The heart, the core of feeling, is the 'touchstone' whose efficacy is illustrated by another Miltonic allusion.[23]

As I have said, Coleridge saw Southey as essentially the poet of feeling (*Griggs* I, pp. 293–94) who 'abjures thinking', and Southey's misanthropy appears connected to this 'abjuration' in the sense that he had generally rejected philosophy and makes a 'faith' (p. 212) from the idea of home itself.[24] Coleridge wrote to Southey (see *Griggs* I, pp. 290–92) on 27 December 1796:

> and now for the Penates, which if I were to abandon my judgement to the impulse of present Feelings, I should pronounce the most interesting poem of it's [sic] length in our Language.

Considering the importance of this statement, and the history of mutual (if stormy) interest that both poets shared, it is a great shame that Kelvin Everest's *Coleridge's Secret Ministry* makes no mention of the *Hymn to the Penates*, as its subject-matter allied to Coleridge's domestic interests would fit well into his discussion.[25] At least two of its passages, though marred by personification, show tonal values that suggest implicit connections with Coleridge's conversation poetry, especially the quiet contemplative voice perfected in *Frost at Midnight*. For example, from p. 213ff. Southey describes the guardian spirits of the dead as human souls shunning heaven, solicitous of the care of loved ones as a child is over a plant:

> Nor can the halls of Heaven
> Give to the human soul such kindred joy,
> As hovering o'er its earthly haunts it feels,
> When with the breeze it wantons round the brow
> Of one beloved on earth; or when at night
> In dreams it comes, and brings with it the DAYS
> And JOYS that are no more, Or when, perchance
> With power permitted to alleviate ill
> And fit the sufferer for the coming woe,
> Some strange presage the SPIRIT breathes, and fills
> The breast with ominous fear, and disciplines
> For sorrow, pour into the afflicted heart
> The balm of resignation, and inspires
> With heavenly hope. Even as a child delights

To visit day by day the favorite plant
His hand has sown, to mark its gradual growth,
And watch all anxious for the promised flower;
Thus to the blessed spirit, in innocence
And pure affections like a little child,
Sweet will it be to hover o'er the friends
Beloved; then sweetest if, as Duty prompts,
With earthly care we in their breasts have sown
The seeds of Truth and Virtue, holy flowers
Whose odour reacheth Heaven.[26]

This extract looks back to Pantisocratic guardianship of the children of the new age, and forward to Coleridge sitting by his baby's cot in Stowey in 1798. Southey has developed the image of the child's garden from its inclusion in *The Retrospect* (*Poems* 1795, p. 11) to this simile of care, which links the spirit-world with the home, involving the spirits of the dead with the living world. These spirit-guardians or living wanderers, servants of the Penates (p. 218), hearts 'made pure, and by domestic Peace and Love', gravitate towards the small community of 'goodly vales . . . cots and villages'. Southey himself tells of the experience of being shut out, an observer, longing to penetrate this communality, to belong:

Often at eve
Amid my wanderings I have seen far off
The lonely light that spake of comfort there;
It told my heart of many a joy of home,
And my poor heart was sad. When I have gazed
From some high eminence on goodly vales
And cots and villages embower'd below,
The thought would rise that all to me was strange
Amid the scene so fair, nor one small spot
Where my tir'd mind might rest and call it *home*.
There is a magic in that little word;
It is a mystic circle that surrounds
Comforts and Virtues never known beyond

The hallowed limit. Often has my heart
Ached for that quiet haven!—haven'd now
I think of those in this world's wilderness
Who wander on and find no home of rest
Till to the grave they go! (p. 218)

Here his blank-verse, nearly freed of personification, is
persuasive, yet it retains Miltonic and Biblical imagery ('eminence', 'world's wilderness') and a quasi-Spenserian picture of
'embower'd' homes. Southey is 'haven'd' inside the 'mystic
circle' (see Everest p. 87ff) of magical comfort supplied by
domestic peace, and from this point of vantage (a prospect
viewed from inside rather than from outside upon an 'eminence'), he expresses joy for himself and sorrow for those
beyond the boundaries of home.[27] Outside the circle Southey
lists the misfortunes (p. 219) which befall the individual, such
as 'POVERTY . . . the child of WEALTH and POWER',
'WANT', 'GUILT', and 'SLAUGHTER'. Such personified
evils are worthy of the poet in his most democratic manner,
but they hang back from the particularization which should be
a vital mode of writing in this kind of poem. This section of the
hymn ends with an appeal to the 'GOD OF ETERNAL
JUSTICE' to hold off his punishing thunderbolts.

Southey's hymn to the hearth finds its culminating point in
a playing off of the city against individual domesticity,
presumably of the cottaged hamlet. He states prophetically
that human happiness resides in the abandonment (pp. 219–
20) of the city:

then shall the city stand
A huge void sepulchre, and rising fair
Amid the ruins of the palace pile
The Olive grow, there shall the TREE OF PEACE
Strike its roots deep and flourish. This the state
Shall bless the race redeemed of Man, when WEALTH
And POWER and all their hideous progeny
Shall sink annihilate, and all mankind

Live in the equal brotherhood of LOVE.
Heart-calming hope and sure! for hitherward
Tend all the tumults of the troubled world,
Its woes, its wisdom, and its wickedness
Alike: so he hath will'd whose will is just.

There is a Biblical or apocalyptic flavour to this John Martin-esque vision of the abandoned city. But it is to Volney's *Ruins of Empires*, which was first translated in 1795, that Southey owes the most in finishing his *Hymn*. Here we should recall the first lines of the poem which used the image of Apollo's ruined temple from which to extend the metaphor of his own supposedly ruined muse. Volney's book, set around the ruins of Palmyra (see also *The Retrospect*, p. 9), contains an 'Invocation' which would certainly have impressed the young poet:

> SOLITARY ruins, sacred tombs, ye mouldering and silent walls, all hail! To you I address my Invocation. While the vulgar shrink from your aspect with secret terror my heart finds in the contemplation a thousand admirable recollections . . . Tombs, what virtues do you exhibit! Tyrants tremble at your aspect; you poison with secret alarm their impious pleasures; they turn from you with impatience, and, coward like, endeavour to forget you amidst the sumptuousness of their palaces. It is you that bring home the rod of justice to the powerful oppressor; it is you that wrest the ill-gotten gold from the merciless extortioner . . . The wise man looks towards you . . .[28]

There is also in Southey's ruined cityscape an undeniable Eastern flavour, 'the ruins of the palace pile' (p. 219) and the olive tree is itself not an English species. Volney's observations upon faded grandeur of the *sic transit* variety could of course make powerful poetic statements when blended with English elegists like Gray. Perhaps Southey's growing interest in

Eastern stories could not have resisted a passage such as this in which Volney, 'that Foucault of the day',[29] describes the Valley of Sepulchres:

> And now a mournful skeleton is all that subsists of this opulent city, and nothing remains of its powerful government but a vain and obscure remembrance! To the tumultuous throng which crowded under these porticos, the solitude of death has succeeded. The silence of the tomb is substituted for the hum of the market place. The opulence of a commercial city is changed into hideous poverty. The palaces of kings are become the lair of wild beasts, and obscene reptiles inhabit the sanctuary of the gods. What glory is here eclipsed, and how many labours are annihilated! Thus perish the works of men, and thus do nations and empires vanish away![30]

If Volney's polemic foregrounded the spells cast over humankind by political tyranny and religious superstition, and a way out of this via Nature and Reason, Southey's reading of this, through his *Hymn*, draws back from the revolutionary undertones in this discourse to preach the 'sacred power' (p. 219) of the hearth. When humanity goes home as it were, then the city, based as it is upon injustice and inequality (seen as 'WEALTH and POWER'), will crumble. But more appositely, the traveller-persona Don Manuel Alvarez Espriella, in Southey's later *Letters from England* of 1807, would give a glimpse of what the countryside itself had become under industrialization. It was industry rather than monarchy, or industry as part of monarchical power, that, in many cases, transformed the city into a picture of hell on earth.[31]

> The face of the country as we advanced was more hideous than can be described, uncultivated, black and smoking. I asked the coachman from whence the smoke proceeded, and he told me the whole earth beneath us was on fire; some coal-mines had taken fire many years ago and

still continued to burn. 'If you were to travel this road by night, sir,' said he, 'you would see the whole country a-fire, and might fancy you were going to hell!' This was in the vicinity of Birmingham.

Southey's position is now that of the wise man who watches and waits for a quiet revolution which may be as Coleridge (*Griggs* I, p. 158) said of Pantisocracy 'perhaps a miraculous millennium'. Now beyond Pantisocracy, he once again chooses domesticity, seeking out a poetical voice of the public in the private. As he says (*LC* I, p. 278, 12 June 1796): 'It is within doors, and not without, that happiness dwells, like a vestal watching the fire of the Penates'. Jean Raimond thinks (*RA* p. 523) that by 1797: 'Au culte de la nature, Southey préférait déjà . . . le culte du foyer'. Yet this had in many respects always been true. What had altered was the tonal quality of that language in which Southey's 'culte' became inscribed. After all, to publish a poem like the *Hymn*, Southey's Progress of Domesticity, alerts the reader again to that curious tension between misanthropic retreat and the commercial endeavour of publication. If Southey was to find a place in England, this quietistic tension would be concentrated around its hearth.

NOTES

1 *The Pleasures of the Imagination* in *The Poetical Works of Mark Akenside*, ed. George Gilfillan (Edinburgh: James Nichol/London: James Nisbet/Dublin: W. Robertson, 1857), p. 78.

2 'Allen agrees with me that Man is a Beast. He verges towards misanthropy and says that a years crusade to benefit mankind will cure any man of his prejudices in their favour. So say I—for I have been a Crusader . . .' (*NL* I, pp. 112–13). This passage of 26 July 1796 may be compared with an extract from p. 209 of the *Hymn:*

O ye who quit the path of peaceful life
Crusading for mankind—a spaniel race
That lick the hand that beats them, or tear all
Alike in frenzy—to your HOUSEHOLD GODS
Return . . .

This comparison may give a general date of composition for the poem.

3 See *NL* I, p. 104: Southey's six-month visit to Spain and Portugal (November 1795 to May 1796) may be traced chiefly through his *Letters Written During a Short Residence in Spain and Portugal* (1797; revised editions 1799 and 1808), which gives a detailed account of the tour through Spain to Lisbon.

4 Simmons' account of this holiday (*Simmons* ch. V) is short and informative, and he brings out well the atmosphere of the trip, and the fact that Southey had ample opportunities to study and write.

5 See *S* p. 40, *Lines Written on Monte Salguiero*. Peace and Love also inhabit the landscape of *Musings* (*Poems* 1797), p. 157.

6 This extract sits midway between *Musings on a Landscape of Gaspar Poussin* and *Hymn to the Penates*. In the former poem (p. 154) 'herded humankind' and (p. 155) 'WEALTH and POWER' are evils that go together. In the latter poem 'WEALTH and POWER' (p. 219 and p. 220) give way to a picture of the city in ruin.

7 See *Simmons* p. 61, and *NL* I, p. 248, after a second trip to Portugal in 1801: '. . . and for beauty—all English—perhaps all existing scenery must yield to Cintra . . .' In fact at Cintra (*LC* II, p. 162, Keswick, 6 September 1801) Southey found an ideal, for which ideal art such as Poussin's had prepared him: 'and for Cintra, my paradise!—the heaven on earth of my hopes; and if I ever should have a house at Cintra, as in earnest sincerity I do hope I shall, will you not give me one twelvemonth, and eat grapes, and ride donkeys, and be very happy? In truth, Grosvenor, I have lived abroad too long to be contented in England: I miss southern luxuries,—the fruits, the wines; I miss the sun in heaven . . . and if the nervous fluid be the galvanic fluid, and the galvanic fluid the electric fluid, and the electric fluid condensed light, zounds! what an effect must these vile dark rainy clouds have on a poor nervous fellow, whose brain has been in a state of high illumination for the past fifteen months!'

8 *The Works of William Cowper*, ed. Robert Southey, 8 vols (London: Henry G. Bohn, 1854), Vol. VI, p. 70.

9 *Ibid.*, *The Task*, Bk III, p. 54, ll. 108ff.

10 William Haller, *The Early Life of Robert Southey, 1774–1803* (New York: Columbia University Press, 1917), p. 184.

11 *The Poetical Works of Mark Akenside*, ed. George Gilfillan (Edinburgh: James Nichol, 1857), p. 247, the final line of the poem.

12 References to the *Hymn to the Penates* will simply give page numbers in *Poems* 1797.

13 *The Poetical Works of Mark Akenside, op. cit.*, p. 137.

14 *The Dead Friend*, stanza 3, *The Poetical Works of Robert Southey, Complete in One Volume* (London: Longman, Brown, Green and Longmans, 1853), p. 132. See the expression of Southey's 'passionate grief' for Seward in *LC* I, pp. 240–41.

15 Southey's reference in *Poems* to Statius (in the note to p. 215) is slightly garbled. It should run: 'qua non gravior mortalibus addita curis, / spes, ubi longa venit' (Statius, *Thebaid*, II, ll. 320–21). He quotes this line of Statius correctly in a letter (*NL* I, p. 98) of 1 September 1795 to Bedford. This book of the rather flashy poet Statius seems to have been favoured by both Southey and Coleridge, who quotes from it in his lectures. Southey also states in *Joan of Arc*, p. vii: 'I do not scruple to prefer Statius to Virgil . . .'

16 See Milton's *Hymn* forming a part of *On the Morning of Christ's Nativity*, where even '*Apollo* from his shrine / Can no more divine . . .' Southey's Penates are the gods addressed via the ruin of Paean's (Apollo's) temple.

17 James Macpherson, *The Poems of Ossian* (Edinburgh: Patrick Geddes, 1894), p. 305. See also p. 280 'Thou dweller between the shields, that hang on high in Ossian's hall! Descend from thy place, O harp, and let me hear thy voice!'; p. 353 'The blast came rustling through the hall, and gently touched my harp. The sound was mournful and low, like the song of the tomb'; p. 404 'My harp hangs on a blasted branch. The sound of its strings is mournful. Does the wind touch thee, O harp, or is it some passing ghost?'

18 *The Correspondence of Robert Southey with Caroline Bowles*, ed. E. Dowden (London: Longmans, 1881), p. 52 (13 February 1824).

19 In the notes concerning the third *Persian Eclogue* (*The Poems of Gray, Collins and Goldsmith*, ed. Roger Lonsdale [London: Longman, 1969/ 1976]), pp. 369–70, two versions of a similar tale are explained: 'Only for the third *Eclogue* has a specific narrative source been suggested . . . *The Free-Thinker* No. 128 describes how "CHA-ABBAS, king of Persia, making a Progress through his dominions" was "led by his Curiosity to see the simple, natural Life of the Peasants."—"Cha-Abbas eventually meets Alibez, a shepherd, whose beauty and virtue so impress him that he decides to take him back to court . . . *The Free-Thinker* No. 129 describes Alibez's eventual longing for the rural life he has left: On the death of Abbas, the new king inspects Alibez's strong-room to discover the extent of the treasure he had amassed as a royal favourite. It contained only "a Sheep-Hook, a Pipe, and a Shepherd's Habit . . . all which, he often took a pleasure in visiting privately, to remind him of his former Condition".' Coleridge seems to be

confusing Alibez with Abbas, and Southey obviously has Alibez in mind
here as an exemplary figure from the simple life whose rural origins
(therefore whose nature) revolt and fret against the danger and artifice of the
Court.

20 Southey's note in the poem refers to Milton, *Paradise Lost* III, ll. 686–
89. Satan, in the guise of a meaner angel anxious to see God's new Creation
and Man, deceives Uriel and alights on Mount Niphates. He juxtaposes the
allusion to the Satanic journey into Paradise, with the image of the 'way-
faring man' (pp. 209–10) looking from a huge eminence upon the further
reaches of his journey and longing for home, resolving to stray no more.

21 *The Works of William Cowper, op. cit.*, Vol. V, p. 259.

22 *Paradise Lost*, Bk IV, l. 677.

23 See *Paradise Lost*, Bk IV, ll. 810f, where the angel guardian Ithuriel
exposes Satan by the touch of his spear:

> Him thus intent *Ithuriel* with his Spear
> Touch'd lightly; for no falsehood can endure
> Touch of Celestial temper, but returns
> Of force to its own likeness: up he starts
> Discoverd and surpriz'd.

See also *Paradise Lost*, Bk IV, l. 788 and l. 868.

24 Coleridge had been attempting to bring him back into the religious
fold in 1795, when he told George Dyer (*Griggs* I, p. 153) that Southey is
'*Christianizing* apace'.

25 The 'private and domestic affections . . . were absolutely central to
Coleridge's happiness, not to speak of his philosophy' (*Everest* p. 210). 'The
conversation poems share as a group the same final atmosphere of quiet
intensity, a very powerful and beautifully understood sense of the private,
and local, and domestic values that Coleridge had come to regard . . . as
especially attractive' (*Everest* p. 220).

26 See *The Task*, Bk II, ll. 713–14: 'Learning grew / Beneath his care, a
thriving vigorous plant'. *The Works of William Cowper, op. cit.*, Vol. VI,
p. 47.

27 Southey leans upon Gray's famous *Elegy Written in a Country
Churchyard* for the essential tone of this passage, and the phrase 'often at
eve' both sets the conventional time of reflection and recalls Gray's 'Oft have
we seen him . . .' (*The Poems of Gray, Collins and Goldsmith, op. cit.*,
pp. 117, 135). Southey is again the elegiac voice at evening, but contemplat-
ing the living rather than the dead. The phrase 'Amid my wanderings' is
echoed by Wordsworth in *Tintern Abbey* as 'after many wanderings'
(*WP* II, p. 14) in 1798.

28 C. F. Volney, *The Ruins or a Survey of the Revolutions of Empires*,

revised trans. of 1795, introduced by George Underwood (London: The Pioneer Press, 1921), p. xi. Southey also wrote to Bedford concerning his imminent law-course in London (*LC* I, p. 295, 21 November 1796): 'However, I expect to be as comfortable as it is possible to be in that cursed city, "that huge and hateful sepulchre of men." I detest cities, and had rather live in Lincolnshire or on Salisbury Plain than in the best situation London could furnish.'

29 Marilyn Butler's phrase in 'Plotting the Revolution: The Political Narratives of Romantic Poetry and Criticism' in *Romantic Revolutions: Criticism and Theory*, ed. K. R. Johnston, G. Chaitin, K. Hanson and H. Marks (Bloomington: Indiana University Press, 1990), pp. 147–48.

30 Volney, *op. cit.*, p. 3.

31 Robert Southey, *Letters from England*, ed. Jack Simmons (Gloucester: Alan Sutton, 1951, repr. 1984), p. 203.

Chapter Seven

From the Sepulchre of Ages: Re-inscribing England

We are right glad to find ourselves in England, for we have learnt to know its value.[1]

1

Southey's *Hymn to the Penates* was an avowal of home-coming, return and reconciliation. That Southey chose to inscribe his return to England within a world of literary tensions is an indication of the dialogical continuance of Neo-classicism within Romantic discourse. Self-conscious classical pastiche is superimposed upon Ossianic, Miltonic and Biblical allusions, and a Southeyan self briefly appears in a language of quietness which we might only grudgingly recognize (because we have to recognize Southey not as himself but in the terms of other poets) as proto-conversational or Coleridgean. Southey chokes his own voice (we will say) by a voluntary invocation of the immortals and dead poets.[2]

We might decide that he had no aptitude for confessional poetry of mood or that the *Hymn* fails as poetic unity, tries to be too many things at once, or fails to be as Romantic as we want to recognize it to be. The passages of quiet confessional-ism in the *Hymn* constitute Southey's acknowledgement of the hearth as central to his view of the post-revolutionary world and also expose a Southey striving (uneasily) for the vocative mode, trying paradoxically to privilege his real voice (as truth) within his inscribed voice (the *Hymn*) and hence the strain. The touchstone of the real within the *Hymn* is the core

of domesticity (illustrated and reinforced by Southey's mini-
biography) to which the essential vow of the *Hymn* is
dedicated.

Yet if Southey, who in May 1796 as Carnall (*CA* p. 38)
reminds us, was 'still very much of a radical' and 'a violent
anti-militarist', proposes a return to his household gods, then
by implication he must also return to the tense landscape in
which the Penates have their place. This landscape is fragmen-
tarily mapped out in the project of response to English
landscape as Southey knew it. It is a selective act of salvage,
resembling his autobiographical methods, a rescuing of the
dangerous parts broken from a giant statue of Albion. The bias
of Southey's fragments serve political ends in which a shift of
views can be seen. Poetically this response was heightened and
informed particularly by his reading of Akenside's inscriptions, Bowles' *Sonnets, Written Chiefly on Picturesque Spots*,
and by the rise of the picturesque movement from about 1794.
From Akenside, Southey learnt to mingle politics, eminent
literary figures and place. From Bowles he learnt again how
feeling and place interact, how the particular spot on a
picturesque tour can form part of a re-mapping of England.
England could therefore be endlessly remade, endlessly re-
inscribed upon and within the most portable and convenient
object, a book of poems. The idea that an inscription can move
around with a reader (in a pocket, in a mind) divorced from its
place or its stone seems for a moment a contradictory idea. Of
course a book places heavy emphasis upon the reader's
inscriptive susceptibility. One poet's map may be another
reader's anathema: this was in fact what Southey discovered
when he published some of these poems. Yet they constitute
one of his longest, and most original, poetic projects.[3]

The earliest published poem which shows some of the
characteristic features of the inscription genre (a sense of place
and of history) is the sonnet in *Poems* 1795 (p. 61) called
Dunnington-Castle. There is a Donnington castle in Berk-

shire, which is close to Newbury, and which was described in Gilpin's *Observations on the River Wye*:

> As we approached Newberry, we had a view of Donnington Castle; one of those scenes, where the unfortunate Charles reaped some glory. Nothing now remains of this gallant fortress, but a gateway, and two towers. The hill on which it stands, is so overgrown with brushwood, that we could scarce trace any vestiges either of the walls of the castle; or of the works, which had been thrown up against it. This whole woody hill, and the ruins upon it, are now tenanted only by ghosts; which add much to the dignity of these forsaken habitations; and are, for that reason, of great use in description.[4]

Gilpin notes that the 'country about Newberry furnished little amusement. But it is not *picturesque*, it is very *historical*'.[5] Southey's sonnet appeared in *Poems* 1795, p. 61:

> THOU ruin'd relique of the ancient pile,
> Rear'd by that hoary bard, whose tuneful lyre
> First breath'd the voice of music on our isle;
> Where, warn'd in life's calm evening to retire,
> Old CHAUCER slowly sunk at last to night;
> Still shall his forceful line, his varied strain,
> A firmer, nobler monument remain,
> When the high grass waves o'er thy lonely site;
> And yet the cankering tooth of envious age
> Has sapp'd the fabric of his lofty rhyme;
> Though genius still shall ponder o'er the page,
> And piercing through the shadowy mist of time,
> The festive bards of EDWARD'S court recall,
> As fancy paints the pomp that once adorned thy wall.

This sonnet also has the epitaphic function evident in some of Southey's inscriptions. The bard Chaucer[6] is recalled as the father of English poetry, the ancestor of such as Southey. *Dunnington-Castle* transfers power from king and fortification to Chaucer's verse: the power of fancy remakes the context of the verse. Southey muses upon the power of the pen over the sword, a simple moral truth, barely political, but nevertheless we can see how easily such a poem might be made so. Castles form nodal points in a landscape which can be seen as Gothic or picturesque loci, or as relics of the exercise of oppressive power as in Southey's inscription on Marten. This chapter seeks to trace some of the main strands of Southey's inscription work, from its published origins in the sonnet above, to the inscriptions published in *Poems* 1797 and beyond.

2
The Manifesto

I have observed that touring Spain and Portugal directly provoked the poet into a re-assessment of the idea of home, here expressed as an interest in recording feelings and associations of place. He inserts several inscriptions into the *Letters Written During a Short Residence in Spain and Portugal* which was published in 1797.[7] A further clue to Southey's plan for his inscription project may be found (*S* pp. 170–71) in this volume:

> Our fathers have left us a rich inheritance, they have left us their experience; it has been accumulating from the creation of the world, and every day adds to the mass of knowledge. The voice of Reason speaks to us from the sepulchre of Ages, and bids us make their errors our wisdom. But the book of history is placed on the shelf of the student, and he is left to make those inferences in his study which should be forced upon the eyes of the public. Every spot that has been consecrated by a good action, or rendered notorious by being the scene of villainy should be marked out, that the traveller reflect-

ing on the past, might learn a lesson for the future. Not a church in England has been white-washed, in which the Churchwarden of the year has not inscribed his name; not an old woman has left twenty shillings for a sermon, and half a crown for the clerk, without being registered among the parish benefactors: yet there is no column in Smithfield where so many good men endured martyr-dom for their religion, and where the King and the Subject might alike be instructed by the life and murder of Wat Tyler.[8]

Southey's plan sounds like the sub-song of revolution. The sheer violence of this passage is intriguing if placed next to the tonally different *Hymn to the Penates*. History is a vast sepulchre from which Reason speaks to the student elect, and from that voice of reason the 'lesson for the future' should be 'forced upon' the public. The scurrilous implication of the phrase 'white-washed' gives the impression of an England which covers over its history, records the local petty acts of parishioners and ignores the titanic sufferings of the very people who strove on behalf of such. Southey seems to be saying that if clear historical information were readily avail-able to all, then tyranny would evaporate. Historical ignor-ance is political ignorance which enslaves.[9] His project would then seem to be that of an enlightenment dangerous to the established order, whether his inscribed information were accurate or not, and as I shall demonstrate, sometimes there was a twisting of the facts.

If points in the reader's landscape could be re-united with their histories, then the landscape in the text might be restored as text at liberty, open to all, albeit through the medium of the poet interpreter, who has chosen his textual places of inscrip-tion. All the 1797 inscriptions are poems of place (though in a book they are free from place), and number VIII looks to France and to Rousseau. Liberty, its bones and spirit evoked by the nature inscription, lives scattered across the field of view. Like Goethe's Wanderer stumbling over inhabited ruins, the poet reads the history of the landscape or endows a place of retreat in the heart of the landscape itself with healing and enlightening powers. Again, as in Goethe's *Der Wandrer*,[10] the poet acts as a remembrancer, waking up the people in the chance scattering of his texts. He helps them at once to become historically aware through his interpretation of the meaning of their environment, with its moral and intellectual voices.

Southey's inscriptions address the Stranger or Traveller or Passenger, and attempt to 'will a state of affairs'[11] by asking the implied reader to respond to a selection of imperatives such as: 'enter', 'repose', 'rest', 'go', 'think', 'feel', 'remember', 'reflect.' It is as if the reader were a somnambulist who must be embarrassed into wakefulness by the situational and intensifying trope of apostrophe. Southey's *Inscriptions* in *Poems* 1797 make up, to use another of Culler's phrases, 'a *now* of discourse, of writing' whose intent is to give information, to persuade, to awaken, to map out and even to 'constitute' the poet, whose 'invocation is a figure of vocation'.[12] It is certainly true that Southey was not embarrassed by the self-exposure that these poems involved, nor by the mock-vocative, or near-vocative of the apostrophic mode. Culler's statement that 'to the Romantics apostrophe was natural and insignificant'[13] is not exactly correct in this case. Southey's apostrophes denote the act of spreading the word of history to futurity. The grand desire for the vocative in the *Inscriptions* shows a poet in retreat (preaching through publication, not lecture) yet wanting to put across his views in a form as near to speech as possible. His project also meant a revival of inscriptional verse whose forerunners he freely acknowledged. In the preface to the third volume of his collected poetry he states:

> In a former Preface my obligations to Akenside were acknowledged, with especial reference to the *Hymn to*

the Penates; the earliest of my Inscriptions also originated in the pleasure with which I perused those of this favourite author.[14]

Southey's debt to Akenside will be considered briefly in relation to the subjects of the *Inscriptions* as we progress. Despite what Southey said in his 1837 *Preface*, it is possible to see the influence of Bowles alongside Akenside. Apostrophe abounds in Bowles—it is present in Akenside, Shenstone and Thomas Wharton certainly—but in Bowles it is coupled with a lachrymose sensibility. Bowles' sonnets, appropriately enough, are sonnets of the dismayed lover and Bowles imbues his poetry of place with a lightly melancholy moralizing voice. Southey sometimes follows the Bowlesian path of sensibility in his *Inscriptions*, but the influence of Akenside tempers this sensibility with classical and political themes, and a greater sense of historical events.

At times we are made to feel, on top of this, the pressure of the whole tradition of eighteenth-century prospect poetry bearing upon the inscription, and without doubt the giant shadow of Gray's *Elegy* must surely form a background to Southey's thoughts upon inscriptional or epitaphic writing.

> Can storied urn or animated bust
> Back to its mansion call the fleeting breath?
> Can Honour's voice provoke the silent dust,
> Or Flatt'ry soothe the dull cold ear of Death?[15]

Gray's triumph was to consider the anonymous poor and obscure, and to ponder a different historical course for their lives which had been confined under the erasure of poverty and obscurity. Southey, in his *Inscriptions*, examines the evils of kingship particularly, but leaves his poor common crowd more nebulous and obscure than Gray's own. But in every inscription he attempts what Gray considered impossible, loudly to call back to their mansions past events, past lives. His apostrophes to the stranger, the traveller or the passer-by, are the vocatives of chance; nothing is assured if the reader refuses to read, or indeed if s/he reads and scoffs. Southey is not at work in the realm of magic, nor can he invoke spellbinding Mariners to enslave his textual guests.

But the big advantage of the inscription is that it occupies a small space upon the page, the page itself replacing the stone of tomb, tablet or temple. If an apostrophe to a traveller implies the disadvantage (to the poet) of a moving audience, then this is cancelled out by the notion of the moving inscription, the portable weight of text. Inscriptional print gives liberty to the poet, who need not labour on the very spot to see the incision of his work, but might if he so wished re-inscribe England from anywhere he chose.

Perhaps too, the almost stanzaic shape (stanza being Italian for 'room') of the inscription (as in the sonnet) suggested that the poet was presenting the large within the small, creating room for thought, for imaginative power. We might see the inscription as a kind of funerary urn or 'mansion' (and there is a sense in which all poetry/writing is dead or funereal) asking for life from its readership, asking to be made larger than itself. But unlike the sonnet, these blank verse inscriptions do not have formal rhyme-schemes, they refuse to run on delicately as repetitive structures, and rather rest as fragments, incomplete stories, stanzas in shape only. They suggest that somehow they are tiny parts of a larger epical tapestry of interpretation, they are fragments gathered up by the poet serving as windows upon the past in a now of discourse and accompanied by the poet as guide hanging at our shoulders.

3
The Map

The eight *Inscriptions* in *Poems* 1797 are confined to southern England and Ermenonville outside Paris. The route of the poetry takes the reader from Oxford to Chepstow to Ermenonville, looking to France, to Rousseau. *Inscriptions* I, II, IV, V, and VI portray the effects of bad kingship and decayed power: II, VII and VIII look to natural images as healthful retreat from the world. Southey's new fragmentary map asks for both good and bad components of the historical landscape to manifest themselves in a confessional index. He begins this index with the story of a fallen woman, Rosamund Clifford. Such women were recurrent in much of the contemporary ballad-poetry and other genres of the 1790s, and Southey often places these figures in scenes of violence and death. His *Poems* 1797 contain a toadying and seductive sonnet (p. 3) *To Mary Wollstonecraft* (who was amongst the radicals he met in London in 1797), as of a lover apologizing for the way women have been depicted in verse, quoting from Gray's *The Progress of Poesy* in the first line, trying to ally his Joan of Arc with female Liberty taken from 'coward man'. But his unmemorable *The Triumph of Woman* (pp. 7–28), again vaunting ideas of liberty, gives way to poems about Widows and Outcasts, and to *Sappho* (pp. 121–25), who after Hamlet-like soliloquies, commits suicide by throwing herself from a precipice. Southey was, it appears, quite happy to have his poetical women in his power as heroines and victims. Rosamund Clifford was one of these.

For a TABLET at GODSTOW NUNNERY (*Poems* 1797, p. 55) seems to have grown from a visit to Godstow that Southey described back in 1793.[16] This visit seems to mark the beginning of the poet's serious analysis of place. He described his trip to Bedford:

> I have walked over the ruins of Godstow Nunnery with sensations such as the site of Troy or Carthage would inspire; a spot so famed by our minstrels, so celebrated by tradition, and so memorable in the annals of legendary, yet romantic truth. Poor Rosamond! some unskilful impostor has painted an epitaph on the chapel wall,

evidently within this century; the precise spot where she lies is forgotten, and the traces are still visible of a subterranean passage—perhaps the scene of many a deed of darkness; but we should suppose the best:—surely amongst the tribe who were secluded from the world, there may have been some whose motives were good among so many victims of compulsion and injustice. (*LC* I, p. 177)

He mentions the 'ruin'd convent tottering to its fall' in *The Retrospect* (*Poems* 1795, p. 10) and the notion of 'sacred ground' (*ibid.*) with regard to the memory of Corston in a telescoping of Oxford experiences and early memories. His sense of historical imagination was, it appears, already strongly developed—and it is noteworthy that the two cities he mentions are also famous for their heroines, Helen and Dido respectively, both associated with calamities originating in sexual disgrace. Southey's 'Rosamund' was Rosamond Clifford (d.1176?), probably the mistress of Henry II in 1174(?), who was buried in the choir of Godstow Abbey near Oxford. John Stow (1525–1605), following Ranulf Higden (d.1364), writes that she was kept by the king in a maze-like house where only he might find her and use her for his pleasure. The queen, Eleanor of Aquitaine, sought her out there and caused her death.

Southey does not mention Henry's name in the poem, but instead concentrates upon Rosamund's plight, her isolation even from the king's affections. The story was indeed a very well-known one. It may be found in a version by Deloney in *Percy's Reliques*, and in Samuel Daniel's *The Complaint of Rosamund* appended to his *Delia* of 1592. Daniel is mentioned by name in Spenser's *Colin Clout's Come Home Again* where Southey would certainly have come across him. Deloney's Rosamond is straightforwardly killed off in the ballad:

> Her body then they did entomb,
> When life was fled away,

At Godstowe, near to Oxford towne,
As may be seene this day.[17]

Daniel has the unfortunate woman speak to her audience as if she were a lingering ghost:

Then were my Funerals not long deferred,
But done with all the rites pompe could devise,
At Godstow, where my body was interred,
And richly tomb'd in honorable wise:
Where yet as now scarce any not descries
Unto these times, the memory of me,
Marble and Brasse so little lasting be.[18]

But Addison's opera *Rosamond* of 1707 differs slightly in storyline from the two previous examples in that the protagonist seems merely to have been drugged by the queen (or at least that is the story she tells her king), ready to be conveyed asleep to (we assume) a nunnery.

Queen Eleanor: Hear, and observe your Queen's commands
                [To her attendants]
                Beneath those hills a Convent stands,
                Where the fam'd streams of Isis stray;
                Thither the breathless corse convey,
                And bid the cloister'd maids with care
                The due solemnities prepare.[19]

Rosamond has been given over to the godly tenderness of the nuns, for her rehabilitation before the Almighty. Addison goes on further to illustrate the *Comus*-like sorcery of the wrathful Queen in thwarting her unrepentant husband— himself presented as a lord of misrule, the king of vice.

Queen Eleanor: The bowl with drowsie juices fill'd,
                From cold Egyptian drugs distill'd,
                In borrow'd death has clos'd her eyes:
                But soon the waking nymph shall rise,
                And, in a convent plac'd admire

> The cloister'd walls and virgin choire:
> With them in songs and hymns divine
> The beauteous penitent shall join,
> And bid the guilty world adieu,

King Henry: How am I blest if this be true![20]

Royalty here behaves with guile and with licence, the king like a Shakespearean Mark Antony, his moral code undermined by sexual zeal, and the queen, Cleopatra-like, forced to fight against him to keep him, with trickery. The world of the court and the world of the cloister are set in bold contrast. Queen Eleanor emphasizes the beauty of the nunnery and the beauty of the victim, now safe from the 'guilty world'. The final lines of Addison's play have the king and queen re-affirming morality in a harmonious statement:

> Who to forbidden joys would rove,
> That knows the sweets of virtuous love?[21]

Southey appears to have leant upon Addison's version of the story for the plot of the earlier *Rosamund to Henry Written After She Had Taken the Veil* from the 1795 volume of *Poems*. This was a long poem imitating Pope's *Eloisa to Abelard*, in which Southey spins out the extremities of misery with violent lines:

> Harlot! adultress! HENRY! can I bear
> Such aggravated guilt, such full despair!
> By me the marriage-bed defil'd, by me
> The laws of heaven forsook, defiled for thee!
> Dishonour fix'd on CLIFFORD'S ancient name,
> A father sinking to the grave with shame;
> There are the crimes that harrow up my heart,
> There are the crimes that poison memory's dart;
> For these each pang of penitence I prove,
> Yet these, and more than these, are lost in love. (p. 86)

Marriage and its vows, the dishonoured family name and the exposure of royal promiscuity are rehearsed by the voice of Rosamund who depicts herself as unfit to remain in a society which her behaviour threatens:

> Oft will remembrance, in her painful hour,
> Cast the keen glance to Woodstock's lovely bower;
> Recal each sinful scene of bliss to view,
> And give the soul again to guilt and you.
> Oh! I have seen thee trace the bower around,
> And heard the forest echo ROSAMUND;
> Have seen thy frantick looks, thy wildering eye,
> Heard the deep groan and bosom-rending sigh;
> Vain are the searching glance, the love-lorn groan,
> I live—but live to penitence alone;
> Depriv'd of every joy which life can give,
> Most vile, most wretched, most despis'd, I live.
> (pp. 93–94)

In the inscription, Southey effectively buries and silences the voice of the victim, by changing the first person to the third person: what was voice becomes observation of place. As in the earlier poem he extends the story imaginatively to describe Rosamund's life after Woodstock, which is one of wretchedness, her symbol being the beautiful but empty hazel nut. She herself can never bear fruit, as it were, because she is a political embarrassment to the court (a political prisoner), her shame being also their shame. Southey does not in fact mention the king in the poem, using his isolating technique again (as for example in *The Widow*), so that the beautiful victim's loneliness and distance even from the unvirtuous comfort of royal lust is amplified. He turns at last from a discussion of Rosamund to think about all male attitudes to women, urging 'reverence' above lust.

The closeness of sexuality to trauma, oppression or madness had of course well-known models in Shakespeare, and was again picked up by the poets of the 1790s, as Robert Mayo's essay on the *Lyrical Ballads* suggests.[22] The distressed female figure appealed to Southey's socially-concerned mind, and often the more hopeless her plight is (as in Mrs Radcliffe's work), the better. Rosamund is a glamorous yet dangerous female, who repels and fascinates the poet. The violence of her situation is mirrored in the rape-language of the poem; to visit Godstow the 'Stranger' must have 'forced' his 'bark / Up this strong stream', and the stream itself is 'broken waters' which yet impart pleasurable sounds to the ear. Southey builds his poem upon the glamour of misery and degradation, and though he earnestly wishes to champion his idea of virtue, one feels that yet again, as with Milton's Satan, the reader's interest may (to continue in the language of sex) lie more with a voyeuristic celebration of vice (like tabloid journalism) than in its correction. This may be borne out in Southey's later touristic prose on the subject:

> This place is celebrated for the ruins of a nunnery, wherein Fair Rosamund was buried, the concubine of King Henry II, a woman as famous for her beauty and misfortunes as our Raquel the Jewess, or the Inez de Castro of the Portuguese . . . The remains of the building are trifling, and only part of the chapel which is roofed, serves as a cow-house . . . The grave of Rosamund is still shown; a hazel tree grows over it, bearing every year a profusion of nuts which have no kernel. Enough of last year's produce were lying under the tree to satisfy me of the truth of this, explain it how you will.[23]

It is interesting to note how much Southey appears to have used the information collected in Percy for this passage. Yet he is able subtly to evoke the atmosphere of the Gothic, where Rosamund's grave is his focus, and growing from it the tree of barrenness. Southey makes a living ruin in the hazel tree symbol speak its moral to the contemporary world. The tragedy of Rosamund, dragging out her life in a Catholic nunnery,[24] is transformed to a marking of nature, a response from the natural world to the mutilating evil of monarchy. The tree, itself once a symbol of liberty for the French revolutionaries, adopted as the tree of peace in Southey's *Hymn to the Penates*, now represents confinement and blight, linked directly to the misrule of a king.

For a COLUMN at NEWBURY (Poems 1797, p. 56) gives another example of a bad king's work, using a battlefield as the marker of moral contemplation. It is perhaps worthy of note that the *Ordnance Survey*, begun in 1791, still includes the crossed swords and dates of Civil War battles. Two battles took place at Newbury in the English Civil War, but the first one on 20 September 1643 is where Lucius Cary, 2nd Viscount Falkland died. The year 1643 links his death with that of John Hamden or Hampden, who perished at Chalgrove Field[25] on 18 June of that year. Falkland, though indeed a famous royalist, really went along with Parliament in his convictions, but his love for the Church and his ideas of peace constrained him to fight for a king whom he mistrusted. At Great Tew near Oxford he was the centre of a literary circle which included Jonson, Earle, Suckling, Sandys, Godolphin, Chillingworth and Clarendon. Southey presents him as an early patriot, a friend to his country, as, he implies, is the poet himself.

Hampden was the leader of the Parliamentary opposition and later of the Long Parliament; he is famous for defying Charles I in refusing to pay the tax called the ship money hitherto only levied on seaboard towns. Hampden was tried for this in 1637–38, losing his case but gaining public support. Charles ordered his impeachment in 1642 but the Commons refused to order the arrest, and the king himself went with soldiers to the House only to discover Hampden, Pym, Haselrig, Strode and Holles had fled to London. This attempted arrest was one of the events that precipitated the Civil War itself. Later in the Restoration, the idea of divine right was supplanted by the moderate Parliamentarian regime which Pym and Hampden had aimed at, when all the acts of the Long Parliament to which Charles I had agreed were set in force.

Southey portrays both Falkland and Hampden as good men brought down by the actions of a tyrant. More explicitly than in the story of Rosamund, Southey critiques the monarchical system, and draws implicit parallels between the time of Cromwell and his own period of revolution. As Joseph Nicholes states, the 'English Romantics believed they were living in the fourth great epoch of republicanism', which gave them a frame of reference within which to articulate contemporary events.[26] From his study of poetry alone, Southey must have been long familiar with the names of both Falkland and Hampden, and here sets out a roll-call of patriots in this extract from a letter of 1792:

> . . . Milton, might he hear thy lyre
> Pour forth the flow of god-like fire,
> And hear thy Cromwell's praise, and sing
> How fallen—how mean a tyrant king!—
> While listening crowds in silence hear,
> And truths, unheard before, appear.
> But chief to hear thy patriot song,
> Hampden and Sidney, move along,
> And Brutus bends, thy voice to know—
> And Nature listens in Rousseau. (*W* I, pp. 11–12)

Falkland is literally immortalized by Ben Jonson in a Pindaric ode *To the Immortal Memory and Friendship of That Noble Pair, Sir Lucius Cary and Sir H. Morison*;[27] Hampden is mentioned in Gray's *Elegy* and in Thomson's *The Seasons*, both hugely popular poems. Writing about the 'rebel HAMB-DEN' Southey is compiling a patriotic tradition in verse, but bringing to it the idea that monarchical tyranny is the root cause of civil war and allying it to what remains of his revolutionary libertarian ideals.

In Thomson's *Summer* Southey would have read the panegyric upon England's 'sons of glory' who include notably Hampden, Milton, Spenser and Chaucer:

> A HAMPDEN too is thine, illustrious Land
> Wise, strenuous, firm, of unsubmitting Soul,
> Who stem'd the Torrent of a downward Age
> To Slavery prone, and bade thee rise again,
> In all thy native Pomp of Freedom bold.
> Bright, at his Call thy Age of *Men* effulg'd;
> Of Men on whom late Time a kindling Eye
> Shall turn, and Tyrants tremble while they read.[28]

Thomson's language uses some of the abstractions to talk of politics that Southey manipulated so willingly in *The Fall of Robespierre*, which itself made comparison, as Joseph Nicholes states),[29] between Robespierre and Cromwell. The inscription genre might help to recall those figures who made up a real tradition of national greatness, vexed and suppressed, in Southey's eyes, by monarchs, or those leaders such as Cromwell who became monarchs in every respect but name. His appeal in the inscription at Newbury 'to every honest Englishman' is a call for the response of like hearts to his re-writing of the canon of worthies, in a language of patriotism, which is not that of a pro-Gallican revolutionary nor that of a pro-Church and King patriot, but of the vexed patriot-reformer, the internal exile.

Gray also mentions Hampden, deepening the personal psychology of the *Elegy*, a pseudo-prospect poem, and even including an inscribed post mortem of the narrator's death. In a sense Gray's poem does what Southey's *Inscriptions* seek to do: it wakes up the musing mind to a sense of the past and tries to re-inscribe an idea of individual worth. The *Elegy*, like the *Inscriptions*, seeks to construct a community of like hearts in remembrance of the dead. Gray wanted to include examples of greatness in the English character which were also dangerous to the country:

> Some village-Hampden, that with dauntless breast
> The little tyrant of his fields withstood;
> Some mute inglorious Milton here may rest,
> Some Cromwell guiltless of his country's blood.[30]

'Hampden' in Gray was originally 'Cato' (in the Eton MSS.), who was himself a great opposer of Greek luxury, which he claimed would dissipate Roman valour and infect the stalwart simplicity of the Roman people. Gray's Civil War figures, then, perpetuate similar themes of moral stricture, in opposition to the corruption personified in Charles I. Southey's inscription attempts to reconcile the positions of Falkland and Hampden, showing them both as true servants of their country forced into opposing armies. Southey shows his own position clearly by referring to Charles I as a 'Tyrant'.

It could be argued that a civil war of sorts took place in England in the 1790s, essentially a war of books, allegiances and opinions, which, despite Pitt's provocative legislation, did not escalate into bloody war. As John Derry says:

> with the ascendancy of loyalism and the popular identification of radicalism with Jacobinism, radicals suffered more from the prejudices of the community than from the force of law ... If the period was a period of repression, this was brought about by a movement of public opinion rather than being opposed from above ... most historians would see radicalism as essentially law-abiding and constitutionalist, with only a tiny fringe of extremists being devoted to violence rather than persuasion as the means of achieving reform.[31]

Southey gradually adopts what the popular mind saw as the English language of self-control and reform in place of the radical language of French extremism.

His Civil War theme recurs in inscription number IV, *For the Apartment in CHEPSTOW-CASTLE where HENRY MARTEN the Regicide was imprisoned Thirty Years*. One can detect, creeping into this inscription, the Gothicization of the truth. Southey's castle here, as in other inscriptions he penned, works as a symbol of tyrannical power dressed for the literary market. Lewis's *Monk* was published in 1796 and so continued the popularization of the macabre Gothic mode upon which Southey leans. He gives the impression that Marten was locked away from light and the natural world in a dungeon; the word 'linger'd' supports this idea. Marten is portrayed as another good man defying tyranny, a good man suffering for his principles founded upon virtue, waiting, like Southey, for Christ the reformer's kingdom.

Marten was one of those who signed the death-warrant of Charles I, but who also quarrelled with Cromwell, when he suspected him of wanting to become king, and his life was probably spared at the Restoration because of this fact. He endured a fairly comfortable captivity (for twenty, not thirty years, until his death in 1680), with his wife and servants, being at times allowed out to visit gentry in the locality. Marten's Tower at Chepstow is in fact the largest of the round towers in the castle, and to give Southey his due, Marten did inhabit an 'apartment', though hardly 'secluded from mankind'.

This poem drew attention from the parodying hand of *The Anti-Jacobin* and Southey dropped it forever from his collected poems.[32] The *Anti-Jacobin* parody of this inscription *FOR THE DOOR OF THE CELL IN NEWGATE WHERE MRS. BROWNRIGG, THE 'PRENTICE-CIDE, WAS CONFINED PREVIOUS TO HER EXECUTION* takes Southey's earnest humanitarian and philosophical ideas to task. The parodist emphasizes the absolute rightness of the law, showing Brownrigg (executed at Tyburn in 1767 for wilful murder of one of her employees) as a drunken, low-bred and violent woman. He then uses her as an example of what could be unleashed by following French politics. Lycurgus, the Spartan ruler, mentioned in the parody beating Spartan children, was a double dig at Southey, or at least what the magazine considered to be his philosophical and political allegiance. Firstly Rousseau, in his *Discours sur l'origine de l'inégalité*,[33] advances the example of Lycurgus as the reformer. Rousseau[34] praises the Spartan regime as one 'where the laws were mainly concerned with the education of children, and where Lycurgus established such morality as practically made laws needless'. It is easy to see how antithetical such ideas of radical interference were to those of Burke, and how easily Rousseau, taken out of context, might fuel anti-French propaganda. And the Anti-Jacobin parody finish predictably in this vein, speaking (*M* p. 56) of a time when 'France shall reign, and Laws be all repealed!'

The emphasis upon Brownriggian flogging in the parody attacked Southey's supposed philosophies, but also brought to mind the publication against flogging which got Southey expelled from Westminster in 1793.[35] It implies that the poet perhaps suffered under the Lycurgan rod, along with Milton, portrayed in the parody not as any kind of heroic republican figure, but merely as a naughty schoolboy. Yet Southey vaunts Marten as a prophet of 'happiness on earth, / And peace and liberty'. He includes the man in his list of figures who have dared to have 'Wild dreams'! These wild dreamers Southey had already put together interestingly in a letter (Bodleian MSS. c. 22, f. 70) to Bedford of Saturday 26 October 1793:

> perhaps a city of philosophers would have gone beyond theory. I could rhapsodize most delightfully on [the] subject—plan out my city—no palaces no hovels—all simplex munditiis (my favourite quotation). But if you were with me—Southeyopolis would soon be divided into two sects—whilst I should be governing with Plato (correcting a few of Plato's absurdities with some of my own) & almost deifying Alceus Lucan and Milton—you (as visionary as myself—would be dreaming of Utopian things—possessed of the virtues of the Antonines—

> regulated by peers every one of whom should be a
> Falkland—& by a popular assembly where every man
> should unite the integrity of a Cato—the eloquence of a
> Demosthenes & the loyalty of a Jacobite.

By 1796, Southey was still not 'beyond theory' but trying to reconcile the England of that time with his household gods. Utopia (no place) was put alongside the Penates' hearth and the growing map of re-inscription.

Southey continues his critique of earthly powers in *For a MONUMENT at SILBURY HILL*.[36] Here he looks backwards in time (*Poems* 1797, p. 61) at the only remains of a 'Chieftain of the Age of Hills', a nameless individual, whose 'gallant deeds' lie forgotten, even though an equally nameless bard sang them; but 'one good deed' may, cryptically, never be 'wrought in vain'. Southey later invested this poem with a more Christian ending, which brought it into line with the longing for the coming of the kingdom of Christ in the previous poem.[37] The proud warrior romanticized in Southey's eyes is not, however, necessarily the performer of good deeds, merely 'gallant' ones. His displays of power now, eroded forever, were perhaps worthless and unvirtuous exercises of tyranny over the equally nameless multitude. Only the mound is the misread mark of his former existence.

Southey seems to be drawing upon earlier eighteenth-century poetic methods to put across his point. Silbury Hill takes the place of the more conventional Gothic ruin and the unreadable passage of time is evoked in a desolate landscape. Dyer's poem *Grongar Hill* strikes a similar note in looking at the ruined castles dotted around the prospect. The ruins become metaphors of ruined monarchical power:

> While ever and anon, there falls
> Huge heaps of hoary mouldered walls.
> Yet time has seen, that lifts the low,
> And level lays the lofty brow,
> Has seen this broken pile compleat,

Big with the vanity of state;
But transient is the smile of fate!
A little rule, a little sway,
A sun beam in a winter's day,
Is all the proud and mighty have
Between the cradle and the grave.[38]

Dyer had one advantage over Southey in that he understood
something of the purpose of the medieval fortifications he
surveyed. Southey believes he is looking at a grave (which is
untrue) and proceeds from that to his poetic message. Because
the inscription deals with such a remote period of history, he
has to invent the action, supply the writing as it were, to
convince his readers that ongoing moral and political truths
exist. The chieftain has left no 'storied urn' as in Gray's *Elegy*,
so Southey has to provide the text,[39] invent history. The
closeness of the inscription form to the prospect poem is an
obvious point about Southey's work here, but it is interesting
that he is promoting the erection of tablets and columns upon
the already extant ruin or historical place with a didactic, or
semi-didactic aim. The observer's freedom to muse is thus
intruded upon, but this was always the intention (as in S
p. 170), that 'the traveller reflecting on the past, might learn a
lesson for the future'.

This idea of a legacy for the future is continued by
Inscription VI, *For a MONUMENT in the NEW FOREST*
(*Poems* 1797, p. 62), yet another picture of the tyrant king at
work, an image of power gone mad. King William drives the
peasant farmers from their 'little cottages' to reduce them to
utter homelessness, causing a desolation synonymous with
negative rule. Southey seems to join together political power
with Judgement Day conflagration here:

Think thou then
What cities flame, what hosts unsepulchred
Pollute the passing wind, when raging Power
Drives on his blood-hounds to the chace of Man . . .

The vision of cities as sepulchres (as in the *Hymn to the Penates*), purged by some 'raging Power', is shown as a kind of apocalypse ravaged by the misuse of power and then by an angry God. But Southey's choice of King William is not arbitrary, it perpetuates the popular notion of the Norman Yoke which 'had long provided English radicalism with its own fanciful version of history and a validation of its claim to be doing no more than seeking a return to a purer and more democratic past'.[40] Paine also makes several comments upon the Norman invasion:

> The English government is one of those which arose out of a conquest, and not out of society, and, consequently it arose over the people; and though it has been much modified from the opportunity of circumstances since the time of William the Conqueror, the country has never yet regenerated itself, and is therefore without a constitution.[41]

Another of Paine's remarks on this subject may have fed into Southey's inscription plan:

> Conquest and tyranny transplanted themselves with William the Conqueror from Normandy into England, and the country is yet disfigured with the marks.[42]

Southey insists on re-inscribing these *disfiguring marks*, for the education of all. In 1791 Paine looked to France for the impetus of regeneration in *Rights of Man*: Southey, by 1796, had no further trust in revolutionary force. His inscription ends:

> And as thy thoughts anticipate that day
> When God shall judge aright, in charity
> Pray for the wicked rulers of mankind.

The disfiguring marks of Norman rule (set around homelessness) may extract 'curses' from the 'Passenger' of feeling, but now prayers and charity supplant revolutionary unrest, which

in Paine reproduced the divisions of the English Civil War.
Southey was content to point out society's shortcomings from
a position of retirement. By mid-1797 his position was clear:

> There was a time when I believed in the persuadibility of
> man, and had the mania of man-mending. Experience has
> taught me better. After a certain age the organs of voice
> cannot accommodate themselves to the utterance of a
> foreign pronunciation; so it is with the mind, it grows
> stiff and unyielding, like our sinews as we grow older.
> The ablest physician can do little in the great lazar house
> of society; it is a pest-house that infects all within its
> atmosphere. He acts the wisest part who retires from the
> contagion; nor is that part either a selfish or a cowardly
> one; it is the ascending of the ark, like Noah, to preserve
> a remnant that may become the whole. As to what is the
> cause, of the incalculable wretchedness of society, and
> what is the panacea, I have long felt certified in my own
> mind. The rich are strangely ignorant of the miseries to
> which the lower and largest part of mankind are aban-
> doned . . . (*LC* I, p. 317)

4
The Nature Inscriptions

Three inscriptions in *Poems* 1797 (II, VII and VIII) are
explicitly concerned with a nature that constructs an image of,
and critiques the nature of, human society. The act of re-
inscription embraces (and penetrates) the landscape it purports to describe, seeking to bind the individual parts of the
natural world together. The landscape is employed as if it were
(like the hearth of the Penates) a touchstone of life, health and
purity. Southey's inscribed pictures resemble emblems from
the old moral didactic tradition for the instruction of the

reader.[43] But the Southeyan reader (in retreat) is persuaded to enter, explore or recline in a textscape of feeling which is set up to clean off the poison of the world.

Inscription VII, *For a Tablet on the Banks of a Stream*, invites the Stranger to quiet repose in retreat, in an attitude which has a long history in poetry. Ideas of retreat from the crowd proliferate amongst the Latin poets, where 'the image is frequently presented of the poet lying at full length under a large tree, upon soft grass, and usually beside a gently flowing stream'.[44] This represents not indolence but a form of pleasure which is simple and healthful.[45] The revision of the old melancholic pose by Milton was continued in Akenside, whose Naiads, Reed feels,[46] are 'filled with Greek joy in nature rather than English melancholy'. Perhaps this joy was what Gray called 'Leucocholy' or white melancholy,[47] similar to the feelings engendered by the positive seclusion in Southey's nature inscriptions. Here, as in all the *Inscriptions*, the vocative address is to one person, calling that individual into the arms of the landscape, reclaiming from the ill-health of society, remaking the reader.[48] Southey's remaking also recalls Rousseau's savage, alone for the present in a society of one:

> I see him satisfying his hunger at the first oak, and slaking his thirst at the first brook: finding his bed at the foot of the tree which afforded him a repast; and, with that, all his wants supplied.[49]

Rousseau's written fantasy of the origins of the human race here depicts the individual subsisting in the world of the forest, possessing nothing, remaining physically strong and untainted in a world without writing. Southey's reclining Stranger, perhaps a readerly descendant of the savage in a world where writing thrives, is invited to see and feel the harmony and beauty around him, to deplore the taint of the city, and is urged, as a kind of nostalgic reunion with nature, to 'sojourn in the woodland cot / Of INNOCENCE' where happiness resides in simplicity. Southey's word 'cot' is suggestive of a civilization, a culture, of greater sophistication than Rousseau's savage beneath the tree. The city, 'the haunts of man', and nature (the mossy bank, stream, the woodland), become terms which struggle for supremacy in the midst of which hides the 'cot'. This is obviously a gesture of desire for retreat into the (female-gendered) 'HAPPINESS', within the yielding arms of the landscape. And it was in such a cot that his Joan of Arc was born to set right the wrongs of the city and the monarchy. Southey's desire to get inside the embrace of nature is most explicitly illustrated by inscription III, *For a CAVERN that overlooks the River AVON*, another poem[50] which dwells upon city/country polarities and the tensions aroused.

Bernard Blackstone describes the cave or cavern as a 'complex symbol', as 'the Romantic symbol *par excellence*', and goes on to list its attributes, some of which apply to this discussion:

> The cave is a womb and tomb, it is a place of refuge and a haunt of terror, it is the witch's den, the prophetic antrum of the Sibyl, the Sage's contemplative cell, the locus of divine birth, and the repository of ancient wisdom.[51]

Blackstone might have added in Southey's case the locus of formative memory and play. Suggested in Southey (see also *Poems* 1795, p. 51, where Arthur is the 'patriot monarch'), and explicit in many tales of romance, the cave is the place whence the sleeping hero will return to liberate the land or restore ancient rights to the people after their conquest by an alien power. Southey's cave puts the reader in touch with such a power that can re-adjust the mind, restore its powers, heal over the scarring of city life. Moreover, this cavern is not just literary device, but a place that was visited by the youthful

poet. Sóuthey places the cave in the short autobiographical
passage of *Hymn to the Penates* in *Poems* 1797, pp. 205–06:

> As I grew
> In years and knowledge, and the course of Time
> Developed the young feelings of my heart,
> When most I loved in solitude to rove
> Amid the woodland gloom; or where the rocks
> Darken'd old Avon's stream, in the ivied cave
> Recluse to sit and brood the future song . . .[52]

The cave, cavern and grotto may be found strewn throughout
literature from ancient times, often containing a power in
direct contact with the earth, or earth magic, or an oracular
power. Akenside's inscription, *For A Grotto*,[53] dedicates the
poem to Actea, a Nereid, who inhabits a sea-side cave. Noon
is the time to enter this cave in solitude, as it is also in
Southey's own poem. Akenside has the poet 'Here at noon, /
Lull'd by the murmur of my rising fount'. The escape from
noontide heat is a poetic convention, which exists in the
inscriptions of the Greek Anthology, and passes through
Thomson's *Seasons* to Wordsworth's *Excursion*, where the
reclining man reposes before a cave mouth out of the heat and
dreaming, whilst listening to the wren's magnified song.
Thomson's *Summer* (1727) shows a reclining figure[54] escaping
from the Italianate noonday sun, serving an emblem of virtue:

> Thrice happy he, who on the sunless side
> Of a romantic mountain, forest-crowned,
> Beneath the whole collected shade reclines;
> Or in the gelid caverns, woodbine-wrought
> And fresh bedewed with ever-spouting streams
> Sits cooly calm; while all the world without,
> Unsatisfied and sick, tosses in noon.
> Emblem instructive of the virtuous man,
> Who keeps his tempered mind serene and pure,

And every passion aptly harmonized
Amid a jarring world with vice inflamed.

Wordsworth seems to follow Thomson closely, re-appropri-
ating the reclining man in the summer heat:

> To him most pleasant who on soft cool moss
> Extends his careless limbs along the front
> Of some huge cave, whose rocky ceiling casts
> A twilight of its own, an ample shade.
> (*WP* Vol. V, p. 7, ll. 9–11)

Southey's apostrophic directions to the reader of his *Inscriptions* aim to involve the reader directly in the act of feeling, so
that reading is no longer (as in Thomson) an observation of
emblematic virtue, but participation in a hidden community,
if not communion itself. In number III, the 'clasping' arms of
the ivy around the 'rude portal' embrace the reader as they
embrace the cavern. The approach to the cavern 'Is long and
steep and toilsome', marking it out as a special place (like the
special place in Wordsworth's *Michael*) reached only by the
persistent. It is the home of the 'Power who prompts the
song', the Muse of the poetic and philosophic mind that asks
the reader (*Poems* 1797, p. 57 ff.) to:

> Gaze Stranger here!
> And let thy soften'd heart intensely feel
> How good, how lovely, Nature! When from hence
> Departing to the City's crowded streets,
> Thy sickening eye at every step revolts
> From scenes of vice and wretchedness; reflect
> That Man creates the evil he endures.

The sentiments of this final line might be compared with a
stanza from the poem *The Miser's Mansion* in *Poems* 1795,
p. 33:

> Thou melancholy mansion! much mine eye
> Delights to wander o'er thy sullen gloom,

And mark the daw from yonder turret fly,
And muse how man himself creates his doom.

The moral quality of this pronouncement recalls Epictetus'
belief that 'Men are disturbed not by Things, but by the
Principles and Notions, which they form concerning Things'.
Adverse conditions are therefore self-created.[55] Geoffrey
Hartman notes the interpretative design of Southey's *Inscriptions* and also a greater interest in natural detail:

> Southey's Inscriptions of which eight were published in
> the first edition of his Poems (1797), often assume the
> bardic and officious voice of the interpreter instead of
> letting the genius loci speak directly to us. In this respect
> they do not differ from the odic or iconic modes of nature
> poetry in which the poet addresses the landscape in his
> own person, asking woods and valleys to mourn or
> rejoice or show their splendours or perform in one way
> or another. Yet the Hellenic originals, or intermediate
> models, chasten Southey's verse into pictures of nature
> almost completely free of penseroso chimeras and alle-
> gorical personifications . . .[56]

Southey's 'bardic and officious voice' (tempered by Epictetan
stoicism) is as necessary to his original plan for the *Inscriptions*
as is the space allowed to the reader witnessing the re-
inscription of England. He must avoid the temptation to bully
in his quest for the kindred spirits he tries to awaken with his
new map. Joshua Scodel[57] notes the apparent futility of the
bullying voice in a brief note on inscription VIII (*Poems* 1797,
p. 64), *For the CENOTAPH at ERMENONVILLE*, where
communion between Rousseau's spirit and the stranger will
only take place if 'that stranger has the requisite sensibility to
mourn the deceased'. Southey is, in other words, in this case
asking for something already there, trying to awaken the
metaphorical sleeping hero/ine in every reader through the
medium of feeling. Rousseau was to the youthful Southey the

'Guide of my life',[58] the 'MAN OF NATURE' as the inscription states, in whose sensibility he was deeply interested.

Ernest Kabisch[59] notes that the poem is a protest about the action of Paris Convention in 1794 who transferred Rousseau's remains to the Pantheon. The inscription is indeed a 'CENOTAPH', designed to save its subject from his increasingly assumed association both with Voltaire and with the 'giddy throng' of the revolution. The poet is not interested in the veneration of relics (as in certain church practices) but rather venerates the life of feelings and ideas, conjured up by the inscriptive naming of the genius loci. Corpse and inscription here part company, but the discourses of feeling endure. In fact the obvious point is that 'Ermenonville' is as movable, as portable, and ready to be filled up (a stanza of prompts) by the reader, as the book of poems in which it is imprinted. The reader (somewhere in England perhaps) looks to 'Ermenonville' empathically through the text. Kabisch[60] states that for Southey 'the particular appeal of the cenotaph lay in its implicit Platonic-Gnostic (and by then quite orthodox) de-emphasis of the body'. In the previous chapter, I noted how Southey thought of his dead friend Seward as freed from the body, a paternal spirit guardian of Penates' hearth, and thought of Rousseau similarly here. At 'Ermenonville' the textual pilgrim may be cleansed, purified by contact with the 'SPIRIT' of the man:

> If in thine eye the tear devout should gush,
> His SPIRIT shall behold thee, to thine home
> From hence returning, purified of heart.

Indeed the lachrymose contact with the ghost in the wandering genius loci of Southey's poem shares close connections with the extreme emotional responses in Mackenzie's *The Man of Feeling*, where nature, change and death provoke elegiac thoughts about the whole act of being. Harley, the weeping hero, sheds tears for others and for the effects of change he observes. After he has died the narrator, his friend, concludes the story:

> He was buried in the place he had desired. It was shaded by an old tree, the only one in the churchyard, in which was a cavity worn by time. I have sat with him in it, and counted the tombs. The last time we passed there, methought he looked wistfully on that tree: there was a branch of it, that bent towards us, waving in the wind; he waved his hand, as if he mimicked its motion. There was something predictive in his look! perhaps it is foolish to remark it; but there are times and places when I am a child at those things. 'I sometimes visit his grave; I sit in the hollow of the tree. It is worth a thousand homilies! every noble feeling rises within me! every beat of my heart awakens a virtue!—but it will make you hate the world—No: there is such an air of gentleness around, that I can hate nothing; but, as to the world—I pity the men of it.[61]

Southey is asking for a similar (though perhaps not as extreme) correspondence of grief between reader and text. The act of purification takes the reader upon an inscribed journey and then back to the point of home. Southey's eight inscriptions in *Poems* 1797 end on a reconciliatory note, at the cleansing of the reader, but this cathartic finale did not mean the end of the poet's project. His inscription work continued through 1798 and 1799, during which period further reconciliation with the map of England took place. If England was not perfect, it was at least a better place to live in than it had been in the past and Southey's *Inscriptions* foster an active remembrance of past mistakes as one indignant gesture towards reform of the present.

5
Southey's Englishness Revisited:
The Calm Collected Public Voice

The poet's motto became 'let the future expiate the past' (*AA* I, p. 69), as he wrote in *For a Monument at Oxford, opposite Balliol gate-way*, written at Bath in 1797. Southey had studied at Balliol not far from the spot where Latimer and Ridley were martyred for the Protestant cause in 1555 after the return to Catholicism. His anti-Catholic views also had been strengthened by his trip to Spain and Portugal in 1795–96. True patriotism in England had been linked with Protestantism before and since the Civil War and the execution of Charles I, against whom figures like Hampden and Marten stood. Charles I, in Southey's poetry, is rather like a latter-day King John, who paid with his life for 'Norman' tyrannies. Southey continued to attack the idea of the Norman Yoke, but it was a pressure that did not always agitate and seemed also to give thanks for concessions.

This can be seen in *The Epitaph on King John* (*AA* I, p. 71), written at Westbury in 1798, which portrays the ruler as an infamous tyrant who nevertheless gave back something of the 'Saxon' birthright to his subjects:

> Englishman!
> Curse not his memory. Murderer as he was,
> Coward and slave, yet he it was who sign'd
> That charter that should make thee morn and night
> Be thankful for thy birthplace: Englishman!
> That holy charter, which, should'st thou permit
> Force to destroy, or Fraud to undermine,
> Thy children's groans will persecute thy soul,
> For they must bear the burthen of thy crime.

Southey has intensified Akenside's idea of the debt of freedom owed to our ancestors in his *For a Column at Runnymede*[62]

into a poem which celebrates national identity. Where Akenside urges the instruction of England's freedom to be passed
from father to son, Southey urges the Englishman to be
vigilant for the sake of all children. He picked up this notion of
Englishness again in *For a MONUMENT at OLD SARUM*
(*AA* I, p. 208 and *MP* p. 148, for 1 May 1799), an uneasy and
xenophobic poem celebrating 'the privileges of English subjects' (*CB* IV, p. 197), and particularly those of 'the old
pauper' who 'sends two Members to Parliament'. The poem
addresses the 'Reader' who might 'boast the noble name / Of
Englishman', and consoles the 'foreigner' who may not enjoy
such pre-Norman privileges of freedom and political representation. He extends his idea of Englishness further back in
history to include the notion of Britishness. In *For a Monument in the Vale of Ewias*, first published in *The Morning Post*
on 21 December 1798, describing St David's exploits, he looks
for a quickening of the pulse as a reaction born of the
'authentic' reader. This extension of English national pride
back into British national pride encompasses not only
Southey's interest in Welsh history, but, set in the context of
the war against France, acts as a propaganda which unites the
nation through blood-ties:

> and if that in thy veins
> Flow the pure blood of Britain, sure that blood
> Hath flow'd with quicker impulse at the tale
> Of David's deeds, when through the press of war
> His gallant comrades follow'd his green crest
> To victory. (*F* p. 428)

Warrior kings who emblematized Celtic and Saxon freedom
are adopted to emblematize threatened contemporary freedom in time of war which must be both revered and preserved.
King Arthur, and then King Alfred feature in the *Inscription
for the Ruins of Glastonbury Abbey* (*MP* pp. 113–14), in a
mingling of romance and Saxon patriotism:

Here rest his mortal relics, round whose board
The heroes sat, ARTHUR, heroic King,
The prowest [sic] Monarch, he whose deeds adorn
The country's ancient annals. Dost thou love
Thy country, and the freedom once her boast?
Here was it, in these moors, that ALFRED lay.
Like to the couching lion, and beheld
Th' invading danes, and rush'd to victory.
This fabric, Englishmen! may emblem well,
The noble structure of the laws he built,
Like this majestic once, and ruin'd now!

After the sentiments of the above, it might be thought that Southey's *Inscription for a Column in Smithfield where Wat Tyler was killed* (*MP* pp. 31–32, for 12 February 1798) was a return to the Jacobinical views of 1794. But it bears out the design of the long passage (*S* pp. 170–71) quoted earlier in this chapter, to give information to all as an education for the future. If 'England's injur'd sons' had found their king's 'yoke was grievous' then (*MP* p. 32):

Here the Citizen should think
That not by tumult and mad violence
Can Peace be forc'd, and Order and Reform,
But by the calm, collected public voice
Marking our father's errors, be we wise!

Southey exhorts the reader to thank 'thy God that thou were born / In better days' (*MP* pp. 40–41) in *For a Monument at Corfe Castle* where 'King Edward the martyr' was murdered. And again in the *Inscription for a Monument where the battle of Barnet was fought* he exhorts the traveller (*MP* p. 84, for 25 July 1798) to be 'thankful for a lot / Humbler, and happier, and in better days'. The poet therefore softens and changes the focus of his language. And he is in line with the English Jacobins such as Thelwall, who as Carnall (*CA* p. 39) says after the Acts of the winter of 1795–96, fell into an attendant silence 'to wait and hope for better days'. A version of English history is presented to the reader that has two main implications, the possibility of further reform and partial political reconciliation. We can also sense that this examination of fragments of the past is a way in from the cold for Southey, a way for him to identify with England itself or to create a version of England for himself, from little potent episodes in the entire tapestry of historical discourse. These inscriptive fragments persisted in Southey's work from observations upon the Peninsular War, to praise of public works, the 'great British work' (*F* p. 444) of building the Caledonian Canal.

6
An Emblem of his Own Unfruitful Life: Caverns, Rivulets and Yew Trees

> Mr. Falkland was sometimes seen climbing among the rocks, reclining motionless for hours together upon the edge of a precipice, or lulled into a kind of nameless lethargy of despair by the dashing of the torrents . . . delighted with that uproar of the elements which partially called off his attention from the discord and dejection of his own mind.[63]

Geoffrey Hartman's essay upon inscription poetry showed amongst other things how Wordsworth made the nature-inscription into a free-standing lyric, and Hartman gave Southey a muted, yet significant, place in the increasingly direct voicing born of this metamorphosis. Southey's political stridency and sententiousness, coupled with its borrowings from the classical models, differs from the inscriptive Words-worthian voice of the mid to late 1790s. Southey generally makes use of well-known or even glamorous historical episodes and personages to make moral and political points in which he acts as master of ceremonies. He also trades off the fact that the inscription form was both familiar and fashionable in circles of readership, so that in his hands it becomes almost a scurrilous disguise, a passport into the establishment he criticizes. Hartman seems to place Southey's nature-inscriptions somewhere between his second and third categories, between the tradition of iconic verse and the plain speaking voice of the genius loci. He also shows[64] how Wordsworth in his *Lines left upon a Seat in a Yew-Tree* uses the 'traditional *Siste Viator* of the epitaph' to inscribe his poem 'before our eyes' involving the reader actively in the process, rather than merely pointing out information with imperatives. Wordsworth's natural scene is composed of a rugged barrenness and distant beauty, and it contains natural description lifted from wandering experience which opposes loco-descriptive clichés deliberately placed within the poem.

The poem is an answer to depictions of nature found in precursor-poems such as Southey's *Inscription* III on the Avon Cavern. Though Southey's poem has a pleasant sharpness and brightness about it, its landscape details are too easily found, and it implies that recourse to nature is *always* beneficial against unstated city evils. Wordsworth's poem *Yew-Tree Lines* seeks to 'combat the melancholy use of nature'[65] and critiques merely literary inscription fashion. Wordsworth writes like a man indignantly defending natural landscape from the bookish writer, someone trying to wake up the reader to the realization that Classical ideal landscape casually slipped into inscription poetry is as false a path as the selfish tendency of making nature merely a mirror of individual mood. Some passages in *Yew-Tree Lines* may be compared with Southey's work, which was published by December 1796, and to which, I believe, Wordsworth responds. His opening lines emphasize the simple solitary isolated yew, the graveyard tree far from an actual graveyard, in acute contrast to the attributes of the ideal retreat-environment that he then lists in negative:

Nay, traveller! rest. This lonely yew-tree stands
Far from all human dwelling: what if here
No sparkling rivulet spread the verdant herb?
What if these barren boughs the bee not loves?
Yet, if the wind breathe soft, the curling waves,
That break against the shore, shall lull thy mind
By one soft impulse saved from vacancy.[66]

He got these elements from Southey's work, drawing out details from the three nature-inscriptions in Southey's 1797 *Poems*. Wordsworth picks on the way Southey uses bookish natural imagery to cast the natural world in the role of pleasure-garden or soothing anodyne, and questions the optimistic quality of the encounters of traveller with nature. Wordsworth's 'sparkling rivulet' and 'verdant herb' echo the 'rivulet' that 'sparkles o'er the shallows' and the 'healthful herb' of *For a TABLET on the Banks of a Stream*,[67] and his bee-less 'barren boughs' over 'curling waves' draw upon the 'wild Bees' murmuring over 'dark green branches' and the 'tide below' found in the Avon Cavern inscription. Wordsworth's soft breathing wind is mildly parodic of the softening effects of nature, the 'soft rustling' of the correspondent breeze in Southey's *For the CENOTAPH at ERMENON-VILLE*.[68] Wordsworth continues his use of Southeyan material to describe the actions of the reclusive figure. Again he plunders the Avon Cavern inscription:

And, lifting up his head, he then would gaze
On the more distant scene—how lovely 'tis
Thou seest—and he would gaze till it became
Far lovelier, and his heart could not sustain
The beauty, still more beauteous![69]

Wordsworth's repetition of the word 'gaze' and his amplification of 'lovely' to 'lovelier' and 'beauty' to 'more beauteous' is surely a borrowing and a criticism of Southey's instructions for the 'Stranger' to be healed by exposure to nature:

> Gaze Stranger here!
> And let thy soften'd heart intensely feel
> How good, how lovely, Nature!
>   (*Poems* 1797, pp. 57–58)

Wordsworth's recluse follows Southey's instructions, but instead of being soothed by what he sees, he is thrown into a mounting agony of yearning for the loveliness he cannot enjoin or endure in contrast to himself. His panic is powerfully observed. The man can perceive the loveliness of the scene, but cannot 'let' his 'soften'd heart' move beyond envy for the happiness of others, or break the psychological reflecting mirrors of his mind (grievously broken in *Peele Castle*) which make his surroundings into a mere emblem of his own barren life. Nature is not a guarantor of health for one whose own nature is cauterized against humanity. Wordsworth follows Gray under the elegiac shadow of the yew to present his lost man, a man who has even lost his name—he is no Hampden or Marten—and unlike Gray's illiterate buried swains we sense that this man's anonymity is the result of his own writing out of the self from society, from community, from friendship. His failed, panic-ridden attempts to inscribe what he sees in nature upon his own nature, do not exactly regain that lost health, that lost name, save that his ghostly presence is rehearsed as a warning to each reader.

Southey's purposes are heavily political in the 1797 inscriptions; even the evocations of his idea of nature function as criticism of city life and of city sensibility. It is no surprise that Wordsworth should wish to correct him or build upon his work; this was of course a thriving aspect of literary life. In fact we catch glimpses of an interactive discourse between the two within other inscription poems.[70] Southey dated his *In a FOREST* (*AA* I, p. 72) 'Westbury 1798' and published it in the *Morning Post* on 13 April 1799:

> Stranger! whose steps have reach'd this solitude,
> Know that this lonely spot was dear to one

Devoted with no unrequited zeal
To Nature. Here, delighted he has heard
The rustlings of these woods, that now perchance
Melodious to the gale of summer move,
And underneath their shade on yon smooth rock
With grey and yellow lichens overgrown,
Often reclined, watching the silent flow
Of this perspicuous rivulet, that steals
Along its verdant course, till all around
Had filled his sense with tranquillity,
And ever sooth'd in spirit he return'd
A happier, better, man. Stranger, perchance
Therefore the stream more lovely to thine eye
Will glide along, and to the summer gale
The woods wave more melodious. Cleanse thou then
The weeds and mosses from this letter'd stone.

Priestman sees the poem wholly as a Southeyan imitation which reverses the rule in Wordsworth's later *Preface* of 1800 that the 'feeling therein developed gives importance to the action and the situation and not the action and the situation to the feeling'. Southey had seen *Lyrical Ballads* by early September 1798,[71] and Priestman argues, *In a Forest* is a poem imitating the *Yew-Tree Lines*, which indeed is most strongly borne out by Southey's words 'verdant' and 'rivulet' which do take Wordsworth's third line into account. But Southey *also* looks back to his own nature-inscriptions for rustling trees, shady rocks, invitations to recline, rivulets, soothed minds returning home and lovely vistas. From Wordsworth's *Yew-Tree Lines*, he *takes back* the very elements which that poem had itself incorporated for criticism from his own 1797 *Inscriptions*. It is a gentle tug of war, not simply a one-sided re-rendering of poetic style. And Southey's sheer optimism is intriguing. He does not look to present the unhealable courses that life sometimes can take: there is no Wordsworthian misanthrope present. Nature in the poem is both reflected in the external details inscribed here and is a reflection of the poet's own stoical character. He has moved from the earlier more dogmatic position of giving information, to a growing delight in landscape detail, doubtlessly encouraged by Coleridge's and Wordsworth's example. The request to the reader to cleanse the inscription implies that a joining of nature (as weeds and mosses) with the human text ('this letter'd stone') has already taken place. Our poet-inscriber pretends to risk obliteration, or asks fellow strangers to come to him (the stone, the inscribed word) through nature, through the moss and weeds. Conversely, this cleansing could more appropriately be seen as the reader's act of purification, the re-inscription of the self before the beautiful loneliness of the text. Southey wrote down the blueprint for this inscription in a section of his *Commonplace Book* (p. 194) entitled *Subjects for Little Poems*:

> INSCRIPTION in a forest, near no path; who reads it has most like been led by the love of nature, and he may enjoy the beauties of scenery more by knowing another has felt them. If it has pleased thee to be told of this, cleanse the moss and weeds from the tablet!

This conversational process (and the Southeyan self-recycling process) can also be seen in the parodic *Inscription Under an Oak* (*MP* pp. 139–40) of 27 February 1799, where Southey re-uses the phrase 'if the sun ride high' which is almost identical to part of the second line of his *For a TABLET on the Banks of a Stream*, and again includes the clichés of natural loveliness, the wind as motive force, fruitful boughs and the softening feelings of place. However, he goes on to use the motif of retreat under trees per se, as a good-humoured parodic gesture (like a painting by George Morland in fact) not just at Wordsworth's expense, but at his own, using materials ready to hand for the speedy manufacture of magazine verse.

7
The Nature Inscription and *Joan of Arc* 1798

Southey's second edition of *Joan of Arc*, which emerged early
in 1798 amidst an atmosphere fraught with fears of an invasion
by France, is an interestingly revised text which, I suggest,
responds directly to English landscape as observed by the poet
as well as to literary models. In Book 9, Southey again
includes the picture of regenerate France imported from *The
Fall of Robespierre*, Act III, but now the quotation reads
(p. 216): 'she shall wield / The thunder—she shall blast her
despot foes'. France will no longer by its example 'liberate the
world' as before. Liberty in the revised version would appear
to be represented by the Maid's somewhat misanthropic
veneration of the natural world, which resembles much of the
staple comments upon city and country made already in the
nature-inscriptions. There is the sense of a return to Rousseau
in the epic—Joan's father is even called 'Jaques'. Fairchild
comments thus:

> In the first edition, Southey, out of deference to epic
> traditions, lets his heroine's actions be guided in part by
> the miraculous intercession of the Christian Olympus;
> but in the second edition, which appeared in the great
> naturalistic year of 1798, all this machinery is stripped
> away, and Joan appears as a true child of nature. She is
> akin to Lucy, for her faith is due to the benign influence
> of the forests in which she was reared. She is a Noble
> Savage, for she owes her spiritual power to her ignorance
> of those rationalistic subtleties which have corrupted
> religion. (*N* p. 435)

I would like to view Southey's revisions in his 'great naturalistic year' as part of the continuing process of the re-inscription
of England when he was, as Bernhardt-Kabisch (*K* p. 34) says:
'at the height of his productiveness as a lyrical poet'. And if
Joan is akin to a prototypical 'Lucy', then Southey's misan-

thropic notions of Englishness are perhaps also represented within the text. Joan's own misanthropy is strikingly presented by the Lord of Vaucouleur:

> she frequents
> The loneliest haunts and deepest solitude,
> Estranged from human kind and human cares
> With loathing most like madness. (p. 96)

As in the inscriptions, country/city opposition is re-emphasized as the opposition between God and human evil. It is hard to believe that Coleridge did not play some part in this Christianizing process, which Bernhardt-Kabisch (*K* p. 35) calls 'Deism':

> It were as easy when I gaze around
> On all this fair variety of things,
> Green fields and tufted woods, and the blue depth
> Of heaven, and yonder glorious sun, to doubt
> Creating wisdom! when in the evening gale
> I breathe the mingled odours of the spring,
> And hear the wild wood melody, and hear
> The populous air vocal with insect life,
> To doubt God's goodness! there are feelings Chief
> That may not lie; and I have oftentimes
> Felt in the midnight silence of my soul
> The call of GOD. (pp. 98–99)

Southey's little idylls have the aspect of inscriptive prospects reflecting the divine, reminiscent of parts of Coleridge in *Reflections on Having Left a Place of Retirement*. In his revisions, Southey had amplified the importance of natural description and cut down or cut out supernatural intervention. *The Monthly Review* for January 1799 noted that:

> The Maid's *call* is divested of preternatural agency, and made the result of natural enthusiasm . . . On the whole we believe that the poem in its present state will please

more readers than before; though some, we doubt not, will regret those higher efforts of fancy which displayed themselves in the preternatural machinery of the first draft. Its present character is sentimental, pathetic, and descriptive; and perhaps modern epic poetry cannot safely soar higher. (pp. 59–62)

Landscape description therefore assumes an importance it did not exactly have in the earlier version. It is given increased aesthetic, religious and political status. The text also contains passages which continue my illustration of the poet's self-plundering tendency. Joan begins her life as a shepherdess in the arms of the landscape:

> I have laid me down
> Beside yon valley stream, that up the ascent
> Scarce sends the sounds of waters now, and watch'd
> The tide roll glittering to the noon-tide sun,
> And listened to its ceaseless murmuring,
> Till all was hush'd and tranquil in my soul,
> Filled with a strange and undefined delight
> That pass'd across the mind like summer clouds
> Over the lake at eve . . .
> Here in solitude
> My soul was nurst, amid the loveliest scenes
> Of unpolluted nature. (p. 108)

Line 3 takes the reader back once more to the Avon Cavern *Inscription* III: 'The tide below / Scarce sends the sounds of waters to thine ear' and also to *Inscription* VII with its notion of polluting mankind. Another passage from *Joan* illustrates Southey's growing ability in the presentation of natural description, and again his re-use of phrases from his own inscription work of *Poems* 1797 ('the passing wind' from nos VI and VIII, and from the *Hymn to the Penates* p. 205; 'scarce-heard' waters again from no. III):

Lonely the forest spring: a rocky hill
Rises beside it, and an aged yew
Bursts from the rifted crag that overbrows
The waters . . .
                The adder's tongue
Rich with the wrinkles of its glossy green
Hands down its long lank leaves, whose wavy dip
Just breaks the tranquil surface. Ancient woods
Bosom the quiet beauties of the place,
Nor ever sound profanes it, save such sounds
As Silence loves to hear, the passing wind,
Or the low murmuring of the scarce-heard stream.
(Bk I, pp. 127–28)

Southey's nature-religion, if it can be called such, is linked
closely to his misanthropic attitudes to the city and to the
established church. Streams, fountains and the motive force of
the wind, motifs common enough in the period, gain an
increasing foothold in his nature-poetry. All these motifs
serve as links between the natural landscape and the man-made
landscape, both literally and metaphorically. Streams and
rivers of course are the veins of Albion itself, so that even in
retreat situations some contact with a larger theatre of life is
maintained.

Inscription VII, *For a Tablet on the Banks of a Stream*, is the
emblematic blueprint for many Southeyan idylls which
endlessly repeat antipathies to the city, but another poem, the
hymn-like *Written On SUNDAY MORNING*, of 1795
(*Poems* 1797, pp. 129–31) explicitly links woods, waters and
natural sounds with God, rather than God with 'the House of
Prayer'. The woods become a natural temple where (p. 129)
one may 'in lovely Nature see the GOD OF LOVE'. This
poem has direct connections with Southey's portrayal of Joan
baffling her questionners:

Methinks it not strange then, that I fled
The house of prayer, and made the lonely grove

My temple, at the foot of some old oak
Watching the little tribes that had their world
Within its mossy bark; or laid me down
Beside the rivulet whose murmuring
Was silence to my soul, and mark'd the swarm
Whose light-edged shadows on the bedded sand
Mirror'd their mazy sports; the insect hum,
The flow of waters, and the songs of birds
Making most holy music to mine ear:
Oh! was it strange, if for such scenes as these
Such deep devoutness, such intense delight
Of quiet adoration, I forsook
The house of worship? (pp. 211–12)

Joan's religion is innate, as she says, like the spontaneous warblings of the birds, needing no priest-craft to instil or guide its joy. This attitude to the established church was condemned by another poet of the period, an anonymous 'Lady' who re-asserts the position of orthodoxy. She published her poem in *The Gentleman's Magazine* 1799 (i, 237) and took Southey's misanthropy in *Written On SUNDAY MORNING* to task:

And when, among the wise and good, the time
That man refused to join in holy worship?
The heathen temple, and the Turkish mosque,
The Jewish synagogue, and Christian church,
Have all resounded with a *social* praise.
Shall I then go like thee, in churlish, wild,
Or solitary mood, to the lone vale,
The silent glen, or unfrequented grove,
When from the neighbouring spire the cheerful bells
Call us in sweet society to join,
And offer holy prayer?[72]

This was another instance of the poet's aptitude for audience aggravation. That a woman poet took the trouble to correct

Southey in 1799, over two years after the publication of *Poems* 1797, says something about his notoriety, and something about how seriously his views on the divine were regarded by those who saw themselves as members of the established order. If his misanthropy was not atheistic, it was suspect, because anti-social and anti-traditional, and had not *The Anti-Jacobin* already marked him out as a blackguard?

However insensitive Southey appears to parts of his audience, his misanthropic themes are not pure churlishness as his critic above suggests. Southey developed a deep interest in social reform after Pantisocracy, which grew in 1797 and in the years following. The nature-inscriptions are mild invitations to the reader to reflect upon society, to step outside and observe. That is of course the initial position of the reformer. In the attempt to rouse the reader by his inscription work, Southey would always run the risk of arousing antipathy from those satisfied with society as it was. Southey's positive retreat-motifs then become subversive. His repeated idyll by the stream nearly always includes some critique of society, or as here in an extract from *For the Banks of the HAMPSHIRE AVON*, also invokes the journey of life.

> the river here
> That, like a serpent, thro' the grassy mead
> Winds on, now hidden, glittering now in light.
> Nor fraught with merchant wealth, nor fam'd in song,
> This river rolls; an unobtrusive tide
> Its gentle charms may soothe and satisfy
> Thy feelings. Look! how bright its pebbled bed
> Gleams thro' the ruffled current; and that bank
> With flag leaves borderd, as with two-edged swords!
> See where the water wrinkles round the stem
> Of yonder water lily whose broad leaf
> Lies on the wave,—and art thou not refresh'd
> By the fresh odour of the running stream?
> Soon Traveller! does the river reach the end

Of all its windings: from the near ascent
Thou wilt behold the ocean where it pours
Its waters and is lost. Remember thou,
Traveller! that even so thy restless years
Flow to the ocean of eternity. (*AA* I, pp. 67–68, *MP*
p. 122, 19 November 1798)

He based the poem upon an idea jotted down in his *Commonplace Book*, another little poem of place:

> INSCRIPTION for a tablet by the Hampshire Avon.
> The flags' sword-leaves; the six-legged insect; the freshness of running water, noticed. From the near hill you see the ocean, to which the river is running. The trite allusion,—where'er we go, we're journeying to the tomb. But this is not the less true for being trite. (*CB* p. 192)

Southey's evocation of the passage of time in the allegorical motif of the river of life lifts the reader from the locus of the inscription to near-transcendence. The poet allows the reader further into the poem by giving a greater impression of being himself absent from the place. What Southey evokes in the early chapters of *Joan* 1798 is the idea of the natural world as a prompt for those who commune with it. Withdrawal into this communion for someone like Southey, is actually the emblem of the open mind, the mind of the critic of society and the reformer of society. This openness is given one major inscriptive image in the poem:

> There is a fountain in the forest call'd
> The fountain of the Fairies: when a child
> With most delightful wonder I have heard
> Tales of the Elfin tribe that on its banks
> Hold midnight revelry. An ancient oak,
> The goodliest of the forest, grows beside,
> Alone it stands, upon a green grass plat,
> By the woods bounded like some little isle.

> Fancy had cast a spell upon the place
> And made it holy . . .
> The strange and fearful pleasure
> That fill'd me by that solitary spring,
> Ceas'd not in riper years . . . (pp. 126–27)

This fountain by the ever-attendant (British) oak[73] represents among other things the irrational, playful, responsive and active principles which are generally lost in adulthood, but which in *Joan* (as perhaps in the later voice of *Tintern Abbey*) endure. Southey's new heroine remains receptive to these life-giving or imagination-feeding powers, and even reaches a kind of Ossianic negative capability at this spot in the midst of a storm, becoming herself like an Aeolian harp:

> and the rush
> Of winds that mingled with the forest roar,
> Made a wind music. On a rock I sat,
> The glory of the tempest fill'd my soul.
>   . . . annihilate was every thought,
> A most full quietness of strange delight
> Suspended all my powers, I seem'd as tho'
> Diffused into the scene. (pp. 129–30)

This passage with its echo of Marvell's garden,[74] tries to restore an idea of the close interaction of human and natural life which, as Rousseau had stated, was eroded by the intrusion of sophisticated civilization.[75] But what kind of a readership could Southey expect for the inscription of his 'natural enthusiasm' which is badly integrated into a war-torn epic? Perhaps we can guess the reaction of many readers by bearing in mind the comments of the anonymous 'Lady'. The *Critical Review* for June 1798 thought the poem's conclusion 'too tame and spiritless' because unaltered from the first edition (p. 200), nor did they regret the deletion of Coleridge's lines (p. 197) from the poem. The *Monthly Review* for January 1799 (p. 58) claimed that 'the present abrupt beginning . . . is rather unsuitable to the dignity of an epic poem, and too much in the ballad style'. There it seems lies the conflict of styles in *Joan of Arc* 1798. Southey the ballad-writer, the writer of epic and the inscription-writer, all pulling in different directions, trying to shock, subvert, amaze, or arouse a sleeping Albion?

NOTES

1 See *Letters of William and Dorothy Wordsworth*, ed. E. De Selincourt; *The Early Years, 1787–1805*, revised by C. L. Shaver (Oxford: Oxford University Press, 1967), p. 259. Wordsworth to Cottle, c.20 May 1799.

2 Marilyn Butler, in *Romantics, Rebels and Reactionaries* (Oxford: Oxford University Press, 1981), p. 6, embraces this mixture of styles by the implications of her statements (on art) here: 'The attraction of this alternative proposition, which permits a redefined Neoclassicism to go on co-existing with Romanticism, is that it allows for a dialogue within the arts, for conflict and even contradiction. Almost every attempt to represent *one* artistic new wave, *one* Romanticism is hopelessly subverted by the richness of art in the period.'

3 His published poems called 'inscriptions' date from between 1796 and 1828. Southey's pronouncements on the genre are few, but two extracts from his letters after he had settled at Keswick, show the progress of his thought upon inscription-writing: 'The *Lapidary style* is, of all others, the most difficult . . . In my own judgement, the shorter such things are the better,—*all* cannot be said upon stone; comprehension, therefore, should be aimed at,—not discrimination' (*W* I, p. 405, 27 January 1807). He added: '. . . I am persuaded that, as pieces of composition, they will more completely exhibit my skill as an *artist*, than any other of my poems . . .' (*W* III, p. 85, 6 January 1818).

4 Gilpin, *Observations on the River Wye* (Richmond: Richmond Publishing Company, 1973), pp. 96–97.

5 *Ibid.*, p. 98.

6 Southey was not alone in his remembrance of Chaucer. In Anderson's *The Works of the British Poets* Vol. 11 (London: J. & A. Arch/Edinburgh: Bell & Bradfute, & J. Mundell & Co., 1795), Thomas Penrose has a poem called *Donnington Castle* which also links Chaucer 'the prime of bards'

(p. 622) with Gothic and picturesque elements, and it is also an anti-civil war poem. Akenside's inscription *For a Statue of Chaucer at Woodstock* (*The Poetical Works of Mark Akenside*, ed. George Gilfillan [Edinburgh: James Nichol, 1857], p. 256) is the forerunner of Southey's sonnet in the sense that he too depicts the bard as 'him who first with harmony inform'd / The language of our fathers'.

7 See (*S*) 'Epitaph on an Astrologer, from the Spanish', pp. 29–30, *Lines Written on Monte Salgueiro*, pp. 39–40, *Inscription for a Monument where Juan de Padilla Suffered Death*, pp. 107–08, *Inscription for a Column at Truxillo*, p. 171, *Inscription for a Tablet at the bottom of the path leading to the Arrabida Convent*, p. 325. Southey's interest in Juan de Padilla (who led the increasingly radical uprising of the comuneros 1520–21) is tinged with radicalism. 'It was here too Padilla triumphed, and we have perhaps this day trod over the ground where this martyr of Freedom suffered. With Padilla expired the liberties of Spain: her despotism . . . is now become as despicable abroad for its imbecility, as it is detestable for its pernicious effects at home' (*S* pp. 106–07). At Truxillo, Southey wrote of the exploits of Francisco Pizarro (1470–1541) the conqueror of the Incas of Peru, giving information to the common reader and exhorting the reader to 'thank the gracious GOD / Who made you, that you are not such as he!' (*S* p. 171). Pizarro is shown as the glorious successful soldier, a servant of 'Wealth and Power' and an early example of one of Southey's tyrant-figures.

8 *Wat Tyler* was of course the short play that Southey had written in the summer of 1794, and which returned to haunt him in 1817. See especially *LC* IV, pp. 236–42, 251–55, and appendix 372ff.

9 The political implications of information-possession are examined in Jean-Francois Lyotard's *The Postmodern Condition*, trans. G. Bennington (Manchester: Manchester University Press, 1984/1991): 'data banks of hitherto unimaginable proportions, whose control or even ownership is, as Herbert Schiller and others have warned us (and as Lyotard is very well aware), one of the crucial *political* issues of our own time' (pp. xii–xiii). 'It is conceivable that the nation-states will one day fight for control of information, just as they battled in the past for control over territory . . .' (p. 5). Southey's inscription project was the elegant forerunner of an information technology that would give back information to the public.

10 See Goethe's *Der Wandrer*, trans. William Taylor of Norwich, *The Monthly Magazine*, Vol. IV, August 1798, pp. 120–23.

11 Jonathan Culler, *The Pursuit of Signs* (London: Routledge and Kegan Paul, 1981), chapter 7, *Apostrophe*, p. 139.

12 *Ibid.*, pp. 142, 152.

13 *Ibid.*, p. 137.

14 The quotation runs on: 'Others of a later date bear a nearer

resemblance to the general character of Chiabrera's epitaphs. Those which relate to the Peninsular War are part of a series which I once hoped to have completed. The epitaph for Bishop Butler was originally composed in the lapidary style, to suit the monument in Bristol Cathedral: it has been remodelled here, that I might express myself more at length, and in a style more accordant with my own judgement' (*PW* III, p. xi).

15 *The Poems of Thomas Gray, William Collins and Oliver Goldsmith*, ed. Roger Lonsdale (London: Longman, 1969), p. 125.

16 See Bodleian MSS. Eng. Letters, c. 22, f. 50, received by Bedford 16 January 1793. Later in the year (8 June) Southey writes desirously: 'you Bedford are peculiarly fortunate in escaping the four year purgatory of an University. to [sic] live so many months with-out seeing one female being, or rather without speaking to one—totally confined to the intercourse of men or boys your own age, is miserable.'

17 *Reliques of Ancient English Poetry Collected by Thomas Percy* (London: H. Bohn, 1845), p. 127. The historical accounts of Rosamund's life are given here on pp. 124–26. The *Reliques* were in their fourth edition by 1794.

18 *The Complete Works in Verse and Prose of Samuel Daniel*, ed. Rev. Alexander B. Grosart, 4 vols (London: Hazell, Watson & Viney, 1885), Vol. I, p. 112. Spenser's reference to Daniel may be found in *Spenser's Poetical Works*, ed. J. C. Smith and E. De Selincourt (Oxford: Oxford University Press, 1970/1979), p. 540.

19 *The Miscellaneous Works of Joseph Addison*, ed. A. C. Guthkelch MA, vol. I (London: G. Bell and Sons, 1914). *Rosamund*, II, vii, ll. 96–101, p. 319.

20 *Ibid.*, III, iii, ll. 79–83, p. 236.

21 *Ibid.*, III, iv, ll. 30ff, p. 328.

22 Robert Mayo, *The Contemporaneity of The Lyrical Ballads* (*PMLA* lxix, 1954, pp. 495ff).

23 *Letters from England: by Don Manuel Alvarez Espriella*, ed. Jack Simmons (Gloucester: Alan Sutton, 1951/1984). Letter xxxiv, pp. 184–85.

24 William Bowles' sonnet *At a Convent* appeared in the first edition of his *Fourteen Sonnets* 1789 (Oxford and New York: Woodstock Books, 1991), which lamented the fate of one Matilda, locked away like Rosamund.

25 The status of Chalgrove Field as battlefield *or* field of skirmish is being debated in a modern 're-mapping'. See *The Independent* for Friday 15 July 1994, p. 10.

26 See Joseph Nicholes, 'Revolutions Compared: The English Civil War as Political Touchstone in Romantic Literature' in *Revolution and English Romanticism*, ed. Keith Hanley and Raman Selden (Hemel Hempstead: Harvester Wheatsheaf, 1990), Chapter 13, p. 261.

27 See *Ben Jonson, Poems*, ed. Ian Donaldson (London: Oxford University Press, 1975), pp. 233–38.

28 James Thomson, *The Seasons*, ed. James Sambrook (Oxford: Clarendon, 1981): *Summer*, ll. 1514–21.

29 Nicholes, *op. cit.*, p. 262.

30 *The Poems of Thomas Gray, William Collins and Oliver Goldsmith, op. cit.*, pp. 127–28 and notes.

31 John Derry, *Politics in the Age of Fox, Pitt and Liverpool: Continuity and Transformation* (London: Macmillan, 1990), p. 98.

32 The poem in full with its parody appeared in the *Anti-Jacobin* no. I, for 20 November 1797. It also appears in the suppressed poems section of the French edition of Southey's works. See *The Poetical Works of Robert Southey Complete in One Volume* (Paris: A. & W. Galignani, 1829).

33 'In spite of the endeavours of the wisest legislators, the political state remained imperfect . . . and as it had begun ill . . . the original faults were never repaired. It was continually being patched up, when the first task should have been to get the site cleared and all the old materials removed, as was done by Lycurgus at Sparta . . .' G. H. Cole's translation (London: J. M. Dent, 1973, revised 1988), p. 101.

34 *Ibid.*, p. 109.

35 *The Flagellant* no. V (London: T. & J. Egerton, 1792), p. 89: 'Now, since there is but one God, whosoever floggeth, that is, performeth the will of Satan, committeth an abomination: to him, therefore, to all the consumers of birch, as to the priests of Lucifer, ANATHEMA. ANATHEMA. *GUALBERTUS.*'

36 Compare this poem with the already quoted extract from *Joan* Bk X, pp. 372–73, ll. 61–68.

37 Go, Traveller, and remember that when the pomp
     Of earthly Glory fades, that one good deed,
     Unseen, unheard, unnoted by mankind,
     Lives in the eternal register of Heaven. (*PW* III, p. 105)

38 John Dyer, *Poems* MDCCLXI (Menston, Yorkshire: The Scolar Press, 1971), p. 13.

39 See also Ernest Kabisch, 'The Epitaph and the Romantic Poets. A Survey', in *The Huntingdon Library Quarterly*, Vol. XXX, 1966–67, p. 124.

40 Derry, *op. cit.*, p. 91

41 See *Rights of Man* introduced by Eric Foner (Harmondsworth: Penguin, 1984), p. 72. See also William Godwin's *Enquiry Concerning Political Justice* (Harmondsworth: Penguin, 1985), p. 95, where Godwin deplores the feudal system.

42 *Ibid.*, p. 75.

43 Southey was fond of the *Emblems* of Quarles, and quotes from him in *LC* I, p. 323, 22 September 1797.

44 Amy Louise Reed, *The Background of Gray's Elegy: A Study in the Taste for Melancholy Poetry (1700–1751)* (New York: Russell and Russell, 1962), p. 41.

45 Milton employs this emblematic trope in *Il Penseroso*. See *The Poetical Works of John Milton*, ed. H. C. Beeching (London: Oxford University Press, repr. 1952), p. 27. A. L. Reed says of Milton's poem that it is a reaction against Burton, 'and while keeping the word melancholy to describe the thoughtful mood of the man who loves to be alone by night . . . or who by day courts the brown shadows in the close coverts of a wood by the brook, he deliberately rejects all the associations of the word with disease, madness, suicide and fear' (*op. cit.*, p. 19). She gives a list of new connotations for the word, including: saintliness, wisdom, beauty, leisure, poetry, philosophy and music.

46 Reed, *op. cit.*, p. 210.

47 Gray to Richard West on 27 May 1742. *The Correspondence of Thomas Gray*, ed. P. Toynbee and L. Whibley, 3 vols (Oxford: Clarendon, 1935), Vol. I, p. 209: 'Mine, you are to know, is a white Melancholy, or rather Leucocholy'.

48 See David Trotter, *The Making of the Reader* (Hong Kong: Macmillan, 1984), p. 6: 'the making of readers has often involved the making of moral and political dissidents. Thus we might regard the obsessive patrolling of margins and thresholds in poetry since Wordsworth, the journeys outward from centre to periphery, as part of an attempt to marginalise the reader.'

49 *Jean-Jaques Rousseau: The Social Contract and Discourses*, trans. G. D. H. Cole (London: J. M. Dent, 1973, repr. 1988), p. 52. Joseph Wright of Derby had painted Sir Brooke Boothby in 1781, holding a double-bent tome of Rousseau. William Vaughan, *Romantic Art* (London: Thames and Hudson, 1978), pp. 27–28 states: 'When he made emotion the guide to reason, Rousseau endowed it with a peculiar optimism. The image of a golden age, a state of innocence from which man had fallen, was hardly a novel one; yet no one had asserted before that this lost world could be rediscovered through the exploration of one's own natural predilections. Reflection led to liberation; and when the English editor of Rousseau's *Dialogues*, Sir Brooke Boothby, had himself portrayed by Joseph Wright of Derby, the result was a new image of contemplation. For while Sir Brooke Boothby seems at first glance to show all the traditional attributes of melancholy . . . there is no despair in his gestures.'

50 In the preface to *Joan of Arc*, Southey writes: 'Upon showing it to the friend in conversation with whom the design had originated, he said, "I am

glad you have written this: it will serve as a store where you will find good passages for better poems" ' (*PW* I, p. xviii). This is borne out by several passages which bear similarities to poems that Southey wrote between 1794 and 1796. Compare this inscription with a passage already quoted from *Joan*, p. 128 using the familiar 'retreat' motifs and the music of the bees and the 'waters' to signify the music of the harmony between the person in retreat and the external world. It is an early example of Southeyan revisionism.

51 Bernard Blackstone, *The Lost Travellers* (London: Longman, 1962), pp. 36 and 39.

52 In 1793 Southey wrote to Bedford (Bodleian MSS. Eng. Letters, c. 22, f. 75): 'I am doomed to be pestered by wasps—the other day I was posting to my cave to sit half an hour in the sun & eat blackberries—I had got within five yards & found a thousand devils with stings in their tails flying about me—like a prudent general when it is impossible to advance I retreated— now were not this so far off & and were poor Shad well we would sally forth & exterminate the invaders.'

53 *The Poetical Works of Mark Akenside*, ed. George Gilfillan (Edinburgh: James Nichol, 1862), p. 255.

54 *The Complete Poetical Works of James Thomson*, ed. J. Logie Robertson (London: Oxford University Press, 1951), p. 70.

55 See *All The Works of Epictetus*, trans. Elizabeth Carter (London: Millar, Rivington, J. & R. Dodsley, 1758).

56 Geoffrey Hartman, 'Wordsworth, Inscriptions, and Romantic Nature Poetry', in *From Sensibility to Romanticism, Essays Presented to Frederick A. Pottle*, ed. F. W. Hilles and Harold Bloom (New York: Oxford University Press, 1965), p. 395.

57 In *The English Poetic Epitaph* (Ithaca and London: Cornell University Press, 1991), p. 327, note 41.

58 See *Romance* in *Poems* 1795, p. 149:

> Fain would the grateful Muse to thee, ROUSSEAU,
> Pour forth the energic thanks of gratitude;
> Fain would the raptur'd lyre ecstatic glow,
> To whom Romance and Nature form'd all good:
> Guide of my life, too weak these lays,
> To pour the unutterable praise;
> Thine aid divine for ever lend,
> Still as my guardian sprite attend:
> Unmov'd by Fashion's flaunting throng,
> Let my calm stream of life smooth its meek course along.

59 Ernest Kabisch, 'The Epitaph and the English Romantic Poets', *The Huntingdon Library Quarterly*, Vol. XXX, 1966–1967, p. 122.

60 *Ibid.*, p. 122 and note 25.

61 *The Man of Feeling*, ed. Brian Vickers (London: Oxford University Press, 1967), pp. 132–33.

62 *The Poetical Works of Mark Akenside*, ed. George Gilfillan (Edinburgh: J. Nichol/London: J. Nisbet/Dublin: W. Robertson, 1857), pp. 258–59.

63 William Godwin, *Caleb Williams*, ed. David McCracken (Oxford: Oxford University Press, 1986), p. 124.

64 Hartman, *op. cit.*, pp. 393, 400.

65 *Ibid.*, p. 398.

66 *Lyrical Ballads*, ed. Michael Mason (London and New York: Longman, 1992), p. 112.

67 *Ibid.*, p. 63.

68 *Ibid.*, p. 64.

69 See also Jonathan Wordsworth, *The Music of Humanity* (London: T. Nelson, 1969), p. 196.

70 Donald G. Priestman suggests that by 1799 Southey was imitating and parodying Wordsworth's poetry. In *Notes and Queries* 224 (1979), pp. 229–31.

71 D. F. Foxon, 'The Printing Of Lyrical Ballads', *The Library*, Fifth Series, Vol. IX, no. 4, December 1954, pp. 221–41.

72 See *Eighteenth Century Women Poets*, ed. R. Lonsdale (Oxford: Oxford University Press, 1989), pp. 507–09, and p. 538.

73 This tree almost comes to represent Southey's audience or country in silent attendance of his poetical metamorphoses.

74 See *The Poems & Letters of Andrew Marvell*, ed. H. M. Margoliouth, 2 vols (Oxford: Clarendon, 1967), Vol. I, p. 49.

75 The passage also recalls Bowles' *Sonnet* XX:

> There is strange music in the stirring wind,
> When low'rs the autumnal eve, and all alone
> To the dark wood's cold covert thou art gone.

Sonnets With Other Poems, 3rd edn (Bath: R. Crutwell, 1794), p. 23.

Chapter Eight

The Westbury Experience

... nothing lasts, Nature seems to delight in disorganizing to reproduce. Not only does every thing change around us but we change ourselves—the oak indeed was contained in the acorn but it is not to the human eye that the resemblance is visible. (*NL* I, p. 179, 3 January 1799)

1
Westbury and *The Morning Post*

Early in 1798, Southey contracted to supply poems for *The Morning Post*, a paper to which Coleridge had been a contributor since 1797. Daniel Stuart, the editor, was not entirely pleased with the frequency of Coleridge's contributions,[1] but found that Southey supplied all the quantity of poetry he needed, and that it was often work of reasonable quality to include in a newspaper. Southey composed with 'extreme rapidity' and 'punctuality'[2] and greatly valued the income from his work:

> My engagement as your Poet-Laureate did not commence till 1798; and the quantity which I supplied was never intended to be considered as making up Coleridge's deficiency. I never think of that Laureateship without satisfaction. The guinea a week, while I held it, came every quarter very reasonably in aid of slender means; and a very considerable part of those Minor Poems which I have thought worth preserving, and upon which much careful correction has recently been bestowed, were written in your employ, and otherwise would not have been written.[3]

245

Here perhaps was born the version of Southey the literary magpie and literary pirate, as the pressure to obtain copy sometimes drove him to a plundering of other poets' work, as well as to the self-plundering I have noticed in regard to the *Inscriptions*. But this hackwork was certainly more congenial than the law. Southey had been studying law since 1797, in a rather hopeless attempt to fix his talents upon employment which would be a steady support for him and his family. It became increasingly obvious that he was not destined to follow law as a career, and the fact that he had to carry out his studies at Gray's Inn in London exacerbated his distaste for the whole venture. The *Metrical Letter* to his cousin Margaret (*Poems* 1799, p. 87) displays something of his longing for domestic bliss in retreat:

> In a narrow sphere
> The little circle of domestic life
> I would be known and loved; the world beyond
> Is not for me . . .
> We would have a faery ship,
> Ay, a new Ark, as in that other flood
> Which cleansed the sons of Anak from the earth,
> The Sylphs should waft us to some goodly isle . . .

Early in 1798 he left London, taking Edith back to Bath, and spent the spring at Bath and Bristol. Later on, in May, he escorted his younger brother Henry to Norfolk, to put him under the tuition of George Burnett, ex-Pantisocrat and comrade from Balliol days, and it was on this trip that he met William Taylor of Norwich, an authority on German literature. Taylor had already translated Bürger's *Lenore*, Lessing's *Nathan the Wise*, Goethe's *Iphigenia in Tauris* by 1790, and he entered into a long exchange of letters with Southey, fostering his interest in eclogues and ballads with German models in mind. This meeting was one important event within a very busy period in Southey's life. That domestic stability was ever on the poet's mind is illustrated by a poem sent to Edith (*LC* I, pp. 336–37, 4 June 1798):

> Edith, it ever was thy husband's wish,
> Since he hath known in what is happiness,
> To find some little home, some low retreat,
> Where the vain uproar of the worthless world
> Might never reach his ear; and where, if chance
> The tidings of its horrible strifes arrived,
> They would endear retirement, as the blast
> Of winter makes the sheltered traveller
> Draw closer to the hearth-side, every nerve
> Awake to the warm comfort. Quietness
> Should be his inmate there; and he would live
> To thee, and to himself, and to our God.
> To dwell in that foul city,—to endure
> The common, hollow, cold, lip-intercourse
> Of life; to walk abroad and never see
> Green field, or running brook, or setting sun!
> Will it not wither up my faculties,
> Like some poor myrtle that in the town air
> Pines on the parlour window?

The most fortuitous point of the year came when Southey took a lease on a house in Westbury outside Bristol. Edith Southey's father had had connections (*L* p. 23) with Westbury, and perhaps that was one reason why that village was chosen. He was then able to enjoy many of the things that the above poem desired, to realize the longings embedded long ago in the melancholy ideologies of *The Retrospect*. Southey said of this period (see *PW* IV, pp. ix–xi):

> This was one of the happiest portions of my life. I never before or since produced so much poetry in the same space of time. The smaller pieces were communicated by letter to Charles Lamb, and had the advantage of his animadversions.

The Westbury house became the centre of a web of writing from which Southey spun out his newspaper poetry and much other literary work. In 1798 a new edition of *Joan of Arc* emerged, and in 1799 Southey finished *Madoc*, published a second volume of *Poems*, and the first volume of *The Annual Anthology*. His 'first perfect year' (*G* p. 18), the summer-to-summer residence at Westbury 1798–99, was thus incredibly productive, yet at the back of this was the knowledge that this security would be all too brief. If the Westbury experience was not exactly on a par with the experience of Nether Stowey, it, too, had at its core the sense of domestic happiness so vital to Coleridge and Wordsworth, and it freed up something of Southey's lyrical and descriptive abilities which can be observed in his journalistic short poems with natural themes. Southey told John May (*W* IV, p. 503) in 1837 that he wanted to arrange his poetry chronologically for his *Collected Works*, which he did. Added to this in many cases is an indication of the place of composition, and a considerable quantity of his poetry has Westbury as its place of origin. My small selection of poems from some of the publications of the 1798–99 period is an attempt to describe aspects of a poet's year and his social attitudes informed by an experience of partial domestic security. But in the case of *The Morning Post* it is not a full description: translations, inscriptions, epitaphs and other poems have been marginalized to allow the poetry of home or natural description as a reaction to, or celebration of, home to surface, to centre around the spectral core of Westbury.

Southey wrote to John May on 15 June 1798 (*NL* I, p. 167) from Bath, where he was helping his mother wind up her household affairs: 'I had hoped to have given you an account of our settling by this time, but we are still on the hunt'. By late June (*LC* I, p. 340), however, a house had been secured at Westbury:

> Martin Hall, Westbury, June 27 1798. To Thomas Southey.

Here we are, and you see have christened the house
properly, I assure you, as the martins have colonized all
round it, and doubly lucky must the house be on which
they so build and bemire. We hesitated between the
appropriate names of Rat Hall, Mouse Mansion, Vermin
Villa, Cockroach Castle, Cobweb Cottage, and Spider
Lodge; but as we routed out the spiders, brushed away
the cobwebs, stopped the rat holes, and found no
cockroaches, we bethought us of the animals without,
and dubbed it Martin Hall.

I am sorry, Tom, you could not have seen us settled,—
you would like the old house; and the view from the
drawing-room and garden is delightful; we have turned
to most notably. But once the house was an inn, or
alehouse, so we have had application to sell beer, and buy
a stock of tobacco-pipes. Much has been done, and much
is yet to do. The rooms are large, the garden well
stocked; we cut our own cabbages, live upon currant
puddings, and shall soon be comfortably settled.

I wish you had been here, you might have been up to
your eyes in dirt and rubbish.

We have bespoke a cat, a great carroty cat.

There is an obvious sense of mirth and relief in this account of
Southey's first real domestication as a writer, and also the
sense of a poet ensconced in the landscape, along with his
books and extended family. This personal trope was of course
replicated at Keswick a few years later under different circum-
stances. At Westbury, Southey achieved a kind of self-
sufficiency and set the pattern of work which essentially
characterizes the rest of his life. He wrote to John May on
8 July 1798:

It was not until the Thursday evening preceding quarter
day that a house was found at all suitable for us, and you
can hardly conceive in what perpetual occupation I have

been since we took possession, pulling down and putting up; upholsterer—carpenter—mason—painter—paperer in succession, till of a filthy, old, barn-looking house we have made a clean and comfortable dwelling. It is at Westbury, a village two miles from Bristol, in the pleasantest part of this country. There is a tolerable garden behind the house, in which excepting some half dozen rose bushes, every thing is calculated for use. The view over the garden is very beautiful, a fertile and woody vale, bounded on each side by hills, and terminated by a range of hills ten miles distant. The most interesting parts of the country are near at hand, and ten minutes walk would convey me to one of the most beautiful glens I ever saw.

Here I begin to feel myself at home and am already enough acquainted with the house to go about in the dark; this is the criterion I think of intimacy with a dwelling place. To day my books are to arrive; two windows that have been blocked up on account of the tax form two convenient recesses for them, I have knocked up some shelves there, and when my box arrives from Cottles I shall need no other society. (*NL* I, p. 169)

The view from the house at Westbury, and the beauty of the locality, would appear to supply many of the images for the poetry written there. This new sense of rest and mirth is continued in his letter to G. C. Bedford, 20 July 1798 (*W* I, p. 58):

Write, and thou shalt hear from me, as how I am dwelling in house—which, to the great titillation of thy risible nerves, is christened 'Martin Hall.'

Southey remained in good humour about the whole regime at Westbury, despite having to accommodate his mother and 'a female cousin', constrained not merely to the rigours of DIY, but also to the journeywork of writing from which he never escaped. The above phrase 'I shall need no other society' was indeed a prophetic one—his books were vital to his work, books from which he often plundered and extracted and revised. But it should not be forgotten that he was capable of accurate and beautiful observation of the natural world, of the landscapes and creatures he encountered: he *was* a bookish poet, but not *simply* that.

Southey wrote to John May on 23 July (*J* pp. 34–35), telling him that his daily routine began like clockwork at a quarter past five in the morning, and that this time was given to the writing of *Madoc*, doubtless undertaken to the sound of the birds outside. The 'martins' became the badge of the Westbury house, and metaphorically the poet's emblem as his year's lease coincided with two migratory years:

> Their tails are forked; they flutter at their nests before they enter, showing their white bodies, and often rise up and hover there, then dart away on arrowy wing. Their notes are even musical sometimes. At evening, when looking from the window, the murmuring of their young is pleasant—a placid sound, according with the quietness of all around. (*CB* pp. 105–06)

His magazine poem, *Ode: The Martins* (*MP* pp. 88–90), puts the above extract into the poem's first four stanzas, giving an example of how immediately and directly (and lucratively) his observations aided his work. Southey describes the evening flight and the sound of the birds, but extends beyond this to imagine the 'clay-built nests' (*MP* p. 89) lying empty, the soothing bird-music silent. Migration homewards is inevitable for the martins, who are instinctively in key with the cycle of the year. The poet too wishes that he could follow them from 'the tempest and the windy storm / and be at rest'. He too observes the seasonal and metaphorical 'evil time', but is forced to remain, trapped, in his present state:

I, too, the signal know,
And know the evil time;
But where shall Peace and Liberty be found?
Where should the wanderer rest? (*MP* pp. 89–90)

Southey referred to himself as 'the wanderer' (*Poems* 1797,
p. 46) in an earlier piece about his straying into the paths of
poetry as a child. The reference to 'Peace and Liberty' gives
the poem a mild political twist, drawing attention to the larger
issues beyond the Westbury circle. Southey continues his
theme of entrapment in a sonnet, written in 1798, and
published in *The Morning Post* on 29 May 1799. *O thou sweet
Lark* (*F* p. 380) is an observation of the bird in flight, the poet
himself wishing for similar wings, as in the previous poem, to
take him not into the ether, but quickly back to 'that loved
home' which he implies is ever the object of his desires:

O Thou sweet Lark, who in the heaven so high
Twinkling thy wings dost sing so joyfully,
I watch thee soaring with a deep delight,
And when at last I turn my aching eye
That lags below thee in the Infinite,
Still in my heart receive thy melody.
O thou sweet Lark, that I had wings like thee!
Not for the joy it were in yon blue light
Upward to mount, and from my heavenly height
Gaze on the creeping multitude below;
But that I soon would wing my eager flight
To that loved home where Fancy even now
Hath fled, and Hope looks onward through a tear,
Counting the weary hours that hold her here.

In the Westbury year, home was synonymous with the duty
of writing. By the end of 1798 Southey had become unwell, no
doubt from the debilitating excess of work that his literary
endeavours had driven him to. On top of this, the winter at
Westbury was a cold one:

> We are enduring something like a Kamtschatkan winter
> here, I am obliged to take my daily walk, & go wrapped
> up in my great coat almost like a dancing bear in hirsute
> appearance still the wind pierces me. we are very
> deficient in having no face dress for such weather as this.
> (*J* p. 40, 14 December 1798)

A severe winter provoked Southey into images of the poet
comfortably sheltered at home yet thinking in metaphors of
retreat, isolation, oppression and privacy. The sonnet 'O
God! have mercy in this dreadful hour' (*F* p. 382) has the
storm-tossed mariner melodramatically trying to imagine the
prayers of his wife. A more comfortable poem published in
The Morning Post on 17 December 1798, and much-antholo-
gized, *The Holly Tree* (*F* p. 343), looks to venerable old age as
its goal. Southey would 'emblems see' (st. 3) of himself in the
holly, with its natural defences and its softer leaves out of
reach (st. 4) of predatory cattle. The poet wishes to temper the
frivolity of youth and to be supple and cheerful as the holly in
his own winter of life:

> Thus, though abroad perchance I might appear
> Harsh and austere,
> To those who on my leisure would intrude
> Reserved and rude,
> Gentle at home amid my friends I'd be
> Like the high leaves upon the Holly Tree.

Most appealing is the simple and delightful cheerfulness (st. 6)
of the autobiographical holly in the midst of winter, when all
else is barren. We might read this as a combination of stoicism
and a trace of Godwin's recommendation of that very humour
in *An Enquiry Concerning Political Justice*:

> A habit peculiarly favourable to corporeal vigour is
> cheerfulness. Every time that our mind becomes morbid,
> vacant and melancholy, our external frame falls into
> disorder. Listlessness of thought is the brother of death.

> But cheerfulness gives new elasticity to our limbs, and
> circulation to our juices. Nothing can long be stagnant in
> the frame of him whose heart is tranquil, and his
> imagination active.[4]

Although Southey had thrown off Godwin's ideas by 1795, he
perhaps recalled this maxim, as perhaps does Wordsworth
when he speaks of the cheerful faith inscribed within *Tintern
Abbey*. Southeyan tranquillity thrived in domestic harmony,
even if his imagination, especially when it encountered strong
emotions, was kept closely in check. Southey's habitually
cheerful aspect was as much a defence as anything. His
defensive nature is summed up most effectively in this poem,
and if we contrast this picture of the holly and cattle with
Burke's famous oak and cattle, we almost immediately arrive
at the emblem of an internal exile, a man among the 'cattle' of
England, flourishing in an English political landscape and
presenting to the world a harshness which conceals domestic
warmth:

> Below, a circling fence, its leaves are seen
> Wrinkled and keen;
> No grazing cattle through their prickly round
> Can reach to wound;
> But as they grow where nothing is to fear,
> Smooth and unarm'd the pointless leaves appear. (st. 2)

These aspects of retreat are made more explicit in the playful
poem *The Filbert* which appeared in *The Morning Post* on 28
February 1799. His disgust with the political sphere is
obvious, and his use of the word 'Jacobines' heartfelt:

> It were a happy metamorphosis
> To be enkernelled thus: never to hear
> Of wars, and of invasions, and of plots,
> Kings, Jacobines and Tax-commissioners,

> To feel no motion but the wind that shook
> The Filbert Tree, and rock'd me to my rest;
> And in the middle of such exquisite food
> To live luxurious! the perfection this
> Of snugness! it were to unite at once
> Hermit retirement, Aldermanic bliss,
> And Stoic independance of mankind. (*AA* I, p. 130)

Life at Keswick would eventually fulfil Southey's wishes for retirement, 'enkernelled' in a wilderness of his own making, and if his life there would never be 'luxurious' or entirely free from political concerns, it would indeed rock him to his 'rest'. But his longing for a 'happy metamorphosis' into the realization of a domestic barrier between him and the world was only briefly resolved at Westbury, where hospitality, domesticity and poetry worked together harmoniously. This idealization of home produced a recurring poetical picture of old age amid the family which I have previously observed in *Joan of Arc* of 1796.

The irregular sonnet on winter (*AA* II, p. 148) comments upon the usual personified depiction of Winter as an old man muffled against the cold struggling along in the snows. Southey simply translates this picture (he was himself 'knee-deep' in snow in the winter of 1798–99 [*NL* I, p. 181]) into something kinder by bringing the old man inside:

> A wrinkled crabbed man they picture thee
> Old Winter, with a ragged beard as grey
> As the long moss upon the apple-tree;
> Close muffled up, and on thy dreary way,
> Blue lipt, an ice drop at thy sharp blue nose,
> Plodding alone thro' sleet and drifting snows.
> They should have drawn thee by the high-heapt hearth
> Old Winter! seated in thy great arm'd chair,
> Watching the children at their Christmas mirth,
> Or circled by them as their lips declare
> Some merry jest or tale of murder dire,

Or troubled spirit that disturbs the night,
Pausing at times to move the languid fire,
Or taste the old October brown and bright.

Winter is no longer the outcast, the liminal figure essentially
cut off from other human contact, but the centre of a family
group, a circle of children, the missing element of the Westbury
house. Fire and ale are close at hand to complete the sense of
well-being. Southey inserts another picture of Christmas
plenty into *The Old Mansion-House* (*Poems* 1799, pp. 183–93)
and sets up a conversation between a stranger and an old man.
The old man breaking stones is fearful of the changes going
on in the house he has known for so long. The stranger (the
new owner) takes the old man inside and convinces him that
whatever the changes to the outside, inside the house hospitality is still enshrined. This obviously serves as a metaphor
for the enduring domestic quality loved by the poet.

Southey continues his patriotism of the hearth in the poem
To a Friend (*MP* p. 135), no doubt with his Portuguese and
Spanish experiences in mind. The traveller's tale of wild and
beautiful landscapes is seen as a lure to the 'friend' who the
poet considers is in danger of feeling the isolation of being
alone in a foreign land. This isolation is seen as a negative
aspect of travel:

Delightful, sure, it is at early morning,
To see the sun-beam shine on scenes so fair,
And when the eve, the mountain heights adorning,
Sinks low, empurpling the luxurious air.
At times like these, thou might'st love to roam;
But would'st thou not at night, confin'd within
Thy comfortless and lonely Inn,
Remember with a sigh the joys of home?

Southey implies that his friend should let the traveller's tale
suffice, make the journey in his mind perhaps, with the
knowledge that travel, like Fancy itself, is fraught with

deceitful joys. The poet's interest in the poetry of the home landscape did indeed remain strong. His *Sonnet* (*MP* p. 141), published on 12 March 1799, seems, according to Curry's note, to be a little picture of the Bristol area. Southey returns again to the haunts of his boyhood which, as in *The Retrospect*, recall the past and present, and the 'deeper joy' of this reading of the landscape. Familiar scenes 'satisfy and fill' the poet's 'soul'. Memories of childhood play, like the semi-humorous metaphor of *The Filbert*, protect and re-invigorate the present. On the same day that the previous poem was published, he wrote to William Taylor:

> Of America we have sad accounts here. The English emigrants complain bitterly. That they should feel the want of cultivated society is not to be wondered at, but it is their own fault that they do not cluster together. Priestley writes that he is to the full as obnoxious to the people there as ever he was in England. Their Sedition Bill had for its first clause, that all persons who had fled their country on charges of treason or sedition, and had taken refuge in the United States, should be delivered back to their respective governments. This clause was indeed thrown out, but what a spirit does it show when it could be proposed! England is certainly the best place now. (*R* I, p. 265)

Even America, which had seemed to Southey in 1794 to be a land of freedom for such men as Priestley, Paine, and himself, was no longer that wild arena of the imagination: laws and prejudices had interfered. The suggestion that the emigrants should 'cluster together', coming from an ex-Pantisocrat, sounds rather lame. Retreat in England, rather than emigration, had become Southey's lot. He had not taken the political and symbolic step of emigration to America, but had remained in England to emerge as a poet of some consequence, earning money by his own pen, which had been a proposed aspect of the American scheme. So in writing the good-

humoured poem *To a Spider* (*F* pp. 386–87, which appeared
in *The Morning Post* of 23 March 1799), appropriate for a
house nearly named 'Spider Lodge', Southey unwittingly
predicted the course of his life, and the mental decay of his
final years:

> Thou busy labourer! one resemblance more
> May yet the verse prolong,
> For, Spider, thou art like the Poet poor,
> Whom thou hast help'd in song.
> Both busily our needful food to win,
> We work as Nature taught, with ceaseless pains:
> Thy bowels thou dost spin,
> I spin my brains. (*F* p. 387)[5]

Overwork was a recurrent problem for Southey, which
strained his faculties and often produced poor-quality verse.
But such stuff would do very well for a moment's amusement
in a magazine or newspaper, and his duty to *The Morning Post*
each week was one more burden upon an excitable mind. In a
letter of March 1799 we get a glimpse of the nervous state
which sometimes assailed the poet:

> I wish these March winds were over. By day I feel
> nothing but a general relaxation, but at night every sound
> startles me. It has hung on me a long while and God
> knows when I shall shake it off. (*NL* I, p. 183)

There is no doubt that Southey's natural playfulness was one
antidote to the strain of keeping house by his literary efforts,
and it is a great shame that Edith Southey's published
correspondence should be so minimal; it would have been
interesting to hear more of her accounts of life with Southey.[6]
His burlesque voice in poetry (further developed in the
domestic sphere) provided stimulus and critique upon current
fashionable attitudes and poses, which he himself had on
occasion adopted. He published some of the *Amatory Poems*

of Abel Shufflebottom (see *G* pp. 66–73) which, as Grigson
notes (*G* p. 16), make fun of the magazine verse of the day.

Another example of this can be drawn out of a brief
comparison between two sonnets, the first of which (*MP*
pp. 143–44, 3 April 1799) creates its comedy by over-alliter-
ation and tautology. Southey sends up the melancholy pose of
the nightingale-beleaguered night-wanderer:

> OH! 'tis a soft and sorrow soothing sight
> The mellow moon at ev'ning to behold
> Lay on the level lake her liquid light,
> And gild the green grove with her yellow gold.
> Sweet to the lonely wand'rer then to walk
> With none but SOLITUDE, and only talk
> Of his own sorrow, by himself, alone;
> To hear poor Philomela's plaintive tale,
> And hearken oft upon the dank night gale,
> In sudden whiz the drowsy beetle's drone.
> Sweet then to hear the owlet, in the dale,
> Hoot from the hollow of her hallowed throne;
> And trace so tranquil by her track of trail,
> Slow sliding o'er her slime, the slipp'ry, sleek, slug snail.
>
> (*MP* p. 144)

Southey's ludicrously amusing sonnet is followed by another
of 15 April 1799 on a gooseberry bush, where the poet closely
observes the new growth on the bush and anticipates summer.
Southey is burlesquing the kind of magazine poems which
sprang up from Joseph Warton's *The Enthusiast or the Lover
of Nature* of 1740,[7] whose 'love-sick Philomel' and 'lone
night-wanderers' antithesize the stable security of the domestic interior which Southey's sonnet implies. If this may be
given as a true picture of the poet's views, or part of that
picture in 1799, it may be one small part of the evidence for the
distance between Southey and the Stowey collaborators
(though of course Coleridge himself could write in this
humorous vein too):

THAT gooseberry bush attracts my wand'ring eyes,
Whose vivid leaves, so beautifully green,
First opening in the early spring art seen.
I sit and gaze, and cheerful thoughts arise
Of that delightful season drawing near,
When those gray woods shall don their summer dress
And ring with warbled love and happiness;
I sit and think that soon th' advancing year
With golden flow'rs shall star the verdant vale.
Then may th' enthusiast youth, at eve's lone hour,
Led by mild Melancholy's placid pow'r,
Go listen to the soothing nightingale,
And feed on meditation; while that I
Remain at home, and feed on gooseberry pie.

(MP pp. 145–46)

Domesticity and comfort supplant the food of meditation in this sonnet, and one cannot fail to be reminded of Dr Johnson's burlesques of Thomas Wharton's poetry, where the comfort and food of society replace lone contemplation. Southey inevitably courted this kind of semi-Johnsonian conservatism by his worship of the domestic gods, mockery replacing any serious extension of the idea of the poetic life through the nightingale motif, which in itself was enormously popular in magazine verse.[8] In *Poems* 1795, Southey had himself published a sonnet *To the Nightingale* (p. 71), a 'SAD songstress of the night', whose song ceases when her family is fledged.

   Southey's *To Lycon*, also in the volume of *Poems* 1795, had included a vignette of a similar but more positive encounter with the 'night-bird' and the phrase 'sorrow-soothing' (p. 81) which begins the first sonnet example as well. And before we leap to the further conclusion that Southey in these poems was just attacking the baby-soothing moon and other elements in Coleridge's *The Nightingale* from *Lyrical Ballads*, two stanzas of *To Lycon* need to be quoted:

Oft when my steps have trac'd the secret glade,
What time the pale moon glimmering on the plain
Just mark'd where deeper darkness dyed the shade,
Has contemplation lov'd the night-bird's strain:
Still have I stood, or silent mov'd and slow,
Whilst o'er the copse the thrilling accents flow,
Nor deem'd the pensive bird might pour the notes of
    woe.

Yet sweet and lovely is the night-bird's lay,
The passing pilgrim loves her notes to hear,
When mirth's rude reign is sunk with parted day,
And silence sleeps upon the vacant ear;
For staid reflection loves the doubtful light,
When sleep and stillness lull the noiseless night,
And breathes the pensive song a soothing sad delight.

> (*Poems* 1795, p. 82)

Southey's poem had found a positive rather than melancholy aspect to the 'night-bird's' song years before Coleridge wrote his poem in April 1798. He appears, then, to be including part of his own poetical production in his burlesques, mocking the urge to wander around at night outside *at all*. If any malice was directed at Coleridge's poem, it may be that it was born out of Southey's envy of the portrayal of Coleridge's new friendship in *The Nightingale*, with its own return to domestic bliss after the encounter with the nightingales.

But in some of his poetry of natural description he does evade the cynicism about the relationship of poet to landscape that the above burlesques imply. A sonnet in *The Annual Anthology* (p. 138), *Thou lingerest, spring!*, returns Southey's attention to the details of external nature reflecting human nature. This poem was published in *The Morning Post* on 21 May 1799, and is basically another sonnet of the Shakespearean type, but it has the rhyming couplet which would usually end the poem occurring after the second quatrain, and signalling the poem's concluding points.

Thou lingerest, spring! still wintry is the scene,
The fields their dead and sapless russet wear,
Scarce does the glossy pile-wort yet appear,
Starring the sunny bank, or early green
The elder yet its circling tufts put forth.
The sparrow tenants still the caves-built nest
Where we should see our martins' snowy breast
Oft darting out. The blasts from the bleak north
And from the keener east still frequent blow,
Sweet Spring, thou lingerest! and it should be so—
Late let the fields and gardens blossom out!
Like man when most with smiles thy face is drest,
'Tis to deceive, and he who knows ye best,
When most ye promise, ever most must doubt.[9]

His observation of the retarded spring is a kind of rueful and wishful thinking. His anticipation of the year's changes suggests anxiety about further changes in his own domestic affairs. When the martins return, the Southeys will soon have to quit the house. The sonnet is nevertheless awkwardly worded. Southey seems to mean by 'lingerest' that the spring is late, that the landscape remains wintry and that this lack of 'promise' in the year's physical appearance has bearing upon some metaphorical truth. Friendly appearances (the usual blooms of spring), like friendly human faces, often betray the observer. But with the summer he reclaims his natural cheerfulness to greet the prospect of the next house move and the next stage in his literary career. As the lease on Martin Hall was to expire at midsummer, Southey had to look around for somewhere to live, a move which would take him away not only from Westbury, but the Bristol area itself:

> The time of removal is so near at hand, that I begin to wish every thing were settled and over. This is a place which I leave with some reluctance after taking root here for twenty-five years . . . (LC II, p. 19)

A series of events occurred around this time, which may in some part be indicative of the underlying stresses to which he was subject. In a letter of 30 March 1799, he states: 'The Pneumatic Institution is just opened here. I am acquainted with the young man who manages it.' Curry writes (*NL* I, p. 183n) that this is:

> The first reference to Sir Humphry Davy (1778–1829) who had come to Bristol at the invitation of Dr. Beddoes to superintend experiments in the medical powers of certain gases. In addition to his scientific interests Davy had written poems, some of which Southey published in the *Anthology*.

The young poet now proceeded to help Davy with his experiments:

> Davy, the Pneumatic Institution experimentalist, is a first-rate man, conversible on all subjects, and learnable-from . . . I am going to breathe some wonder-working gas, which excites all possible mental and muscular energy, and induces almost a delirium of pleasurable sensations without any subsequent dejection. (*LC* I, p. 19, 5 June 1799)

Southey seems to have been fighting off some form of 'dejection' with a little help from Davy's gases, and it implies that he had experienced that very state by recourse to other substances. If he had 'Laudunum visions' (*CP* p. 29), however, they did not result in addiction, and his domestic tranquillity was not affected by breathing in a little laughing-gas.

He set out for Burton in Hampshire house-hunting on 28 June (*Simmons* p. 81), leaving Edith in Bristol, and discovered that he would have to wait for the house to be made ready. Therefore he and Edith made their base in Bristol once more with an old friend of Southey's, Charles Danvers, now a wine-merchant. Southey was excited by and proud of the mass of poetry he had seen into print in this year. Poetry had become a duty, a necessity: if he wanted to eat, he had to write. He sums this up in a grimly cheerful (and rather medical) poem of 24 June 1799 called *The Poet Perplexed* (*MP* p. 157):

> BRAIN! thou must work! begin, or we shall lose
> The day, while yet we only think upon it.
> The hours run on, and yet thou wilt not chuse
> The subject, come, Ode, Elegy, or Sonnet.
> You must contribute, Brain! in this hard time
> Taxes are high, food dear, and you must rhyme.
>
> 'Twere well if when I rubb'd my itchless head,
> The fingers, with benignant stimulation,
> Could thro' the medullary substance spread
> The motions of poetic inspiration.
> But scratch, or knock, or shake my head about,
> The motions go in but nought comes out.
>
> The nat'ral head, consider good my brain,
> To the head politic bears some allusion;
> The limbs and body must support your reign,
> And all, when you do wrong, is in confusion.
> But CAPUT mine, in truth I can't support
> A head as lazy as if born at Court.
>
> The verse goes on, and we shall have, my friend,
> A Poem, ere the subject we determine—
> But ev'rything should have some useful end—
> That single line itself is worth a sermon.
> The moral part, as obvious is as good,
> So, gentle BRAIN! I thank thee, and conclude.

Southey had finished his cherished epic project *Madoc* by 11 July 1799, as he told his brother Tom in a letter (*LC* II, p. 21), but had resolved to alter it radically before he published. On the evening of 12 July, in the same letter, and in a state of excited relief, he continues:

> Oh, Tom! such a gas has Davy discovered, the gaseous oxyde! Oh, Tom! I have had some; it made me laugh and tingle in every toe and finger tip. Davy has actually invented a new pleasure, for which language has no name. Oh, Tom! I am going for more this evening; it makes one strong, and so happy! so gloriously happy! and without any after-debility, but instead of it, increased strength of mind and body. Oh, excellent airbag! Tom, I am sure the air in heaven must be this wonder-working gas of delight! (*LC* II, pp. 21–22)

It is very rare for Southey to speak in such superlative terms about pleasure and glorious happiness, but for a young writer whose natural disposition hovered between good-humoured dutifulness and a painful excitability it must have been a very welcome experience. This may be set alongside Coleridge's contemporary use of opium, which by 1798 was producing for him enjoyable reveries, but which would lead on to addiction and eventually to ruin. Of course it was Southey, amongst others, who looked after his wife and his children when he no longer could. And Southey's literary duty followed him even to the realms of the 'excellent air-bag'. As Alethea Hayter says:

> Davy tried to get Southey to include in his *Thalaba* (finished by July 1800) one of these nitrous oxide visions, of 'a paradise wholly immaterial—trees of light growing in a soil of ether—palaces of water refracting rich colours'; a version of this did finally find its way into Southey's *Curse of Kehama*.[10]

The Westbury period seems to have achieved a balance in the tensions between these fleeting translucent and immaterial visions and the banal necessities of home. His valedictory sonnet at the end of this productive year, with its rather Coleridgean title, *On Leaving a Place of Residence*,[11] appeared in *The Morning Post* for 13 July 1799:

FAREWEL, my home, my home no longer now,
Witness of many a calm and happy day;
And thou, fair eminence, upon whose brow
Dwells the last sunshine of the ev'ning ray.
Farewel! mine eyes no longer shall pursue
The west'ring sun beyond thy utmost height,
When slowly he forsakes the field of light.
No more the freshness of the falling dew,
Cool and delightful, here shall bathe my head,
As from this western window dear I lean,
List'ning the while I watch the placid scene,
The martins twitt'ring underneath the shed.
Farewel, my home! where many a day has past,
In joys whose lov'd remembrance long shall last.

How appropriate is the sense of setting light in this (uncon-
ventional) Shakespearean sonnet. Southey links together his
badge of luck, the martins, with the calmness and joy of the
home spot from which he observes the sunset that brings to an
end his 'first perfect year', to use Grigson's phrase. The sonnet
marks the farewell, like a wreath of 'remembrance' set around
the 'brow' of the anthropomorphized landscape. Kenneth
Hopkins[12] believed that Southey found his 'true home' in the
Lake District where he was hemmed in by mountains and by a
study full of books, but it was only at Westbury, during his
annus mirabilis, that Southey glimpsed a happiness in literature and place, a kind of personal re-inscription, which he
never truly recaptured.

2
Southey and *Lyrical Ballads* 1798

The Lyrical Ballads are by Coleridge and Wordsworth.
The Nightingale, the Dungeon, the Foster Mothers Tale,
and the long ballad of the Old Mariner are all that were

written by Coleridge. The ballad I think nonsense, the Nightingale tolerable. The other two are pieces of his tragedy. For Wordsworths poems, the last pleases me best, and tho the Idiot Boy is sadly dilated, it is very well done. I reviewed them two months ago. (to Charles Wynn, *NL* I, pp. 176–77, 17 December 1798)

There is still an amusing sense of outrage in the way in which some critics write about Southey's attitudes to and borrowings from Coleridge and Wordsworth, particularly when *Lyrical Ballads*, one of our cultural icons, is examined. Yet Southey, Coleridge and Wordsworth all indulged in the textual interactivity which was part of the late eighteenth-century literary scene, and which remains one of the chief accusations against Southey at the time of *Lyrical Ballads'* publication.

If Coleridge is seen as the covert plagiarist, Southey is the unabashed textual pirate. But all three men had given themselves to that natural exchange of poetical ideas since 1795,[13] and it would be fair to say that Southey's small poems, especially inscriptions, ballads and poems on popular superstitions, supply Wordsworth and Coleridge in part with models for their joint collaboration in *Lyrical Ballads*. And Southey's lean and flashy poems were one of the major goads to which Wordsworth in particular responded.

I would not wish to defend Southey's methods in his ruthless drive for publications in 1798–99, the urgency of which I have tried to sketch in the previous section. He was supporting a household by his pen and therefore all sources of copy were fair game in the struggle. One of the additional reasons for his exploitation of the *Lyrical Ballads* volume of 1798 would have been Southey's personal interest in the ballad form, and certainly in the stories and situational events therein. The 1797 *Poems* included (pp. 163–98) three ballads; *Mary, Donica* and *Rudiger*. They lie amongst the variety of forms and styles of the volume and illustrate Southey's early preoccupation with stories of frisson and horror popularized

by Matthew Lewis and others. Southey's attitude to *Mary* is
ambivalent:

> The 'Maid of the Inn' you selected for censure, and in my
> own mind it values little; yet how popular it has become!
> and where one person reads the 'Hymn to the Penates,'
> unquestionably the best piece in the volume, fifty can
> repeat that foolish ballad. (*W* I, pp. 69–70, 9 April 1799)

He obviously still valued his most domestic poem, *Hymn to
the Penates*, in which, as Fairchild says:

> Southey represents himself as a disillusioned idealist who
> heals his soul by cultivating the domestic affections in
> their appropriate environment of natural simplicity. And
> this simplicity is not, as in pantisocratic days, regarded as
> an initial step forward to a higher perfection: it is in itself
> perfection. (*N* p. 201)

But during the Westbury period, the commercial aspects of
writing began to gain an increasing hold upon his work. In
1798–99, the popularity of the 'foolish ballad' was exploited
by the poet to the full. Southey could not afford to scoff at its
potential for pleasing an audience. He began to take a more
serious view of the ballad for commercial reasons alone, and
he enjoyed rooting out his bizarre stories from avowedly
authentic antiquarian sources. Under his enduring contempt
for *Mary*, which (*JAC* p. 216) 'provides an obvious parallel
for *The Thorn*', we can perhaps discern a certain amazement
about its vulgar fame as late as 1809:

> They have made a melo-drama of 'Mary the Maid of the
> Inn,' at one of the Strand theatres. Did I ever tell you that
> the story is in Plott's 'Staffordshire?' The scene of it was
> the Black Meer of Morridge, near Leek; the chief
> personage a man, and the murder not discovered, but
> prevented. If you have the book, you will find it on page
> 291. I verily believe that at least half my reputation is

owing to that paltry ballad, which is bad enough to spoil a very fine story. The strolling players recite it here about the country. (*W* II, p. 181, December 1809)

Southey obviously loved the source-hunting and the story-moulding, but held the medium of ballad-metre in some disdain, despite linking it to part of his poetical reputation. This rather careless or insensitive attitude to metrical work (which can also be seen in the 1799 volume of *Poems*) had already cost him dear. But in 1798–99 if the ballad could be used as a popular vehicle for saleable work, then he would continue to use it. It was an easy container for social comment, and for the old tales that he and Charles Lamb loved. Something of the continuing popularity of the form is evident here in the fate of *The Old Man's Comforts*, which had originally appeared in *The Morning Post* on 17 January 1799:

I have met a very odd person, by name Worgan . . . He does wonders on the pianoforte. Oddly enough, he played and sung The Old Man's Comforts in a large company; and after praising the music, they fell to praising the poetry, which nobody knew to be mine. He himself fancied it was Bowles's; so I set him right. (*W* I, p. 289, 27 November 1804)

The trite moral reassurance which closes *The Old Man's Comforts* and the love of antiquarian tales of horror, is characteristic of much of Southey's work in the more stylistically coherent 1799 volume of *Poems*, and here he seems to function best when he is dramatic, dialogic, idiomatic and vernacular. If he saw himself as something of a proven pioneer, an experimenter, and an authority in 'ballad-work' by the time of the publication of *Lyrical Ballads*, this might account, in another sense, for the corrective strain in his borrowings, a wish to show his peers how it should be done. Mary Jacobus and others[14] provide us with a list of Southey's borrowings from *Lyrical Ballads*, the manuscript of which

was in Cottle's hands by the end of May 1798 and which
Southey seems to have read very soon after, because his
Morning Post poem *The Idiot*, based around Wordsworth's
The Idiot Boy,[15] appeared on 30 June 1798. Over half of the
Jacobus list of borrowings, to which I have made several
additions (see Table 1), appeared initially in *The Morning
Post*; other borrowings were re-vamped for inclusion in the
1799 volume of *Poems* and beyond.

I have noticed similarities between *The Complaint of a
forsaken Indian Woman* (spring 1798?) and Southey's *The
Song of the Old American Indian* (*MP*, 16 July 1799)—
Southey wrote several more *Songs of the American Indians* at
Westbury and Exeter in 1799. He alters Wordsworth's abandoned female to a male lamenting old age, and he imitates the
short couplet lines of his model to produce a rather sentimental poem showing how Indian society rejects the old hunter.
There is nothing of the blank desertion found in his model,
though, simply the imitative refrain 'Alas the burthen of old
age', which also makes links between Southey's poem and
Simon Lee (spring 1798?)—compare Southey's lines 'when I
was young, / My heart was glad, my arm was strong' and 'the
burthen of old age' with Wordsworth's 'When he was young
he little knew / Of husbandry or tillage' and 'Of years he has
upon his back / No doubt a burthen weighty'.[16] Southey's
poem does not of course catch the reader up in the intervening
mattock-blow that brings out the lamentable gratitude of the
struggling Simon Lee, crippled by aristocratic servitude. We
remain at a distance, listening to a lament for a man who
cannot even bend a bow, reinforced in the notion that old age
in itself is a bad thing because it renders us useless, rather than
being implicated ourselves as readers in the idea that society
itself, to which we all belong and have responsibilities in, can
produce versions of old age which are lamentable. It is a
general involvement with suffering, as Mary Jacobus notes[17]
when speaking about his version of *The Ruined Cottage*, that
Southey avoids here and in much of his other work:

Table 1 Southey's borrowings from *Lyrical Ballads* and other works in 1798–99

W. WORDSWORTH AND S. T. COLERIDGE	ROBERT SOUTHEY
Yew-Tree Lines (from 1797)	*Henry the Hermit* (*Poems* 1799, p. 177)
The Idiot Boy (written spring 1798)	*The Idiot* (*MP*, 30 June 1799)
We Are Seven (spring 1798)	*The Battle of Blenheim* (*MP*, 9 August 1798)
Old Man Travelling (late 1796–98)	*The Sailor's Mother* (*Poems* 1799, p. 206, circa 27 December 1798)
Goody Blake and Harry Gill (first half of 1798)	*The Witch* (Westbury 1798, *Poems* 1799, p. 216)
The Thorn (March/April/May 1798)	*The Circumstance on which the following Ballad is Founded Happened Not Many Years Ago in Bristol* (*MP*, 11 June 1799), and *Annual Anthology* Vol. II, p. 70 as *The Mad Woman* (*MP*, 11 June 1799) and it also supplied material for *A Landscape* (*MP*, 26 October 1799)
The Ryme of the Ancyent Marinere (winter and spring 1797–98)	*The Sailor who had served in the Slave Trade* (from an actual event in September 1798, Westbury 1798, *Poems* 1799, p. 107), *The Murderer* (*MP*, 14 July 1798)
The Complaint of a forsaken Indian Woman (spring 1798?) and *Simon Lee* (spring 1798?)	*The Song of the Old American Indian* (*MP*, 16 July 1799)
Simon Lee (spring 1798?)	*The Old Mansion-House* (*Poems* 1799, p. 183)
Expostulation and Reply	*Night* (*MP*, 26 September 1798)
Expostulation and Reply & *The Tables Turned*	The conversational form/metre of *The Morning Mists* (*MP*, 11 October 1798), *Stanzas* (*MP*, 28 September 1798)
Outside *Lyrical Ballads:*	
Peter Bell of the summer of 1798	*The Secret Expedition* (*MP*, 17 August 1799)
The Ruined Cottage begun in 1795	*The Ruined Cottage* (*Poems* 1799, p. 226), *Henry the Hermit* (*Poems* 1799, p. 177)
Frost at Midnight (February 1798)	*Night* (*MP*, 26 September 1798), and influenced *To A Friend* (*MP*, 18 September 1798), *Stanzas* (*MP*, 28 September 1798)

Southey's adaptation of material from *Lyrical Ballads* is, however, of two sorts. Despite the evidence of his 'Ruined Cottage' one has to concede the possibility that his other borrowings represent a deliberate attempt to put right what he had criticised in his review. In some cases, poems from *Lyrical Ballads* are returned firmly to the level of the magazine poetry from which they had been raised, stripped of their new thematic depth and narrative sophistication. In other cases, what is idiosyncratic or disturbing in the poetry of Wordsworth and Coleridge is replaced by topical or humanitarian interest of a quite straightforward kind: the poems become not simply shallower, but more public.

It is true that Southey converts the disturbing open-endedness of Wordsworth and Coleridge's work to sententious, clearcut, rapidly-moving stories, or emblems of suffering. Yet one other aspect of Southey's own writing needs to be included in this analysis of his corrective borrowing, and that is the famous summary of his poetical character by his friend William Taylor:

> You have a mimosa-sensibility, which agonizes in so slight a blast; an imagination excessively accustomed to summon up trains of melancholy ideas, and marshal funeral processions; a mind too fond by half, for its own comfort, of sighs and sadness, of pathetic emotions and heart-rending woe. You miss-see the dangers in expectation through the lens of a tear. (*R* I, p. 256, 4 March 1799)

Southey's reply is equally famous, *R* I, p. 262, 12 March 1799:

> Once, indeed, I had a mimosa-sensibility, but it has long been rooted out: Five years ago I counteracted Rousseau by dieting upon Godwin and Epictetus; they did me some good, but time has done more. I have a dislike to all

strong emotion, and avoid whatever could excite it; a book like 'Werter' gives me now unmingled pain. In my own writings you may observe that I dwell rather upon what affects than what agitates. (12 March 1799, *LC* I, p. 13)

Mary Jacobus is certainly correct in representing the borrowings as stolen copy for magazine poetry (though the borrowing was not always one way), and to notice the removal of idiosyncrasies and disturbing qualities from the borrowings, but the above adds another dimension to her appraisal. The way in which Wordsworth draws the reader into imaginative involvement with his subject time and again is exactly what Southey shies away from. His borrowings may *affect* the magazine or anthology audience, but they do not powerfully *agitate* in the way that the poems in *Lyrical Ballads* still do. Southey rejects the crucial sense of involvement in poems like *The Ryme of the Ancyent Marinere* and *The Idiot Boy* and replaces this with an immediacy which is as Mary Jacobus says of a shallower and more public kind.

William Taylor's summary of Southey's imaginative tendencies show the latter as a poet of sensibility, whose use of Godwin and Epictetus has not quite obscured the apparently habitual turmoil which strong emotions wrought upon him and Southey's reply appears contradictory. If he had 'rooted out' his 'mimosa sensibility' then surely he could read Werther without 'unmingled pain'? I suggest, then, another hidden aspect of Southey's borrowings, which lies in the corrective diffusing of this agitatory involvement demanded by the *Lyrical Ballads* experiment. Southey takes a step back from the intensity of the subjects which he claims to have found uninteresting whilst plundering what he could re-use.

He was much easier with poems deriving from Cowperian domestic interiors or conversations of advice. In *Night* (*MP* pp. 103–04), Southey apparently combines elements of

Coleridge's *Frost At Midnight* with part of Wordsworth's
Expostulation and Reply[18] and extracts from *CB* p. 106,
describing poplar trees and a sunset which corresponds
roughly to lines 18–21 (*MP* p. 103) of his poem. His phrase
'The lovely landscape' is a stock-in-trade lifted (*Poems* 1797,
p. 154) from his own *Musings on a Landscape of Gapsar
Poussin*.

In *Night* (*MP* pp. 103–04), Southey emphasizes the absolute quiet of evening, suggesting the evening of human life, and
his poem, with its resigned passivity, looks to the stoical
wisdom of old age, rather than retrospectively upon his own
life and forward into his child's life as does Coleridge's. Here
in fact lies the great distance between *Frost At Midnight* and
Southey's *Night*. The real nucleus of domesticity, a child, is
absent from *Night* which evokes the acceptance of rest,
tranquillity or death. Echoes of Coleridge's phrasing and
vocabulary, as well as the attempt to convey an extreme
stillness link the two poems strongly:

> HOW calm, how quiet all! still, or at times
> Just interupted by such stirring sounds
> As harmonise with stillness; even the bark
> Of yonder watch-dog, heard at intervals,
> Comes from the distance pleasantly. Where now
> The lovely landscape! hill and vale and wood,
> Broad oak, high tufted elm or lighter ash,
> Green field and stubble meadows sapless grey,
> Or brown variety of new plough'd land?
> A dim obscurity o'ermantles all,
> An undistinguished greyness, save that near
> The church tower seems in heavier gloom to rest
> More massy, and those light leaved poplars rise
> Dark as a Cypress grove. How fair at morn
> It opened on the eye as the grey mists
> Roll'd off, how bright at noon, how beautiful

Its evening glories, when more radiant,
Of majesty more visible, the Sun
Beyond the brow of yonder western hill
Blazed o'er the cluster'd clouds! nor charmless now
The scene so dim, nor idly wanders there
The unprofitable eye; earth, air and heaven,
Earth so o'ershadowed, air thus void of sounds,
And yonder moonless vastity of heaven,
With all its countless worlds, all minister
To fill with soothing thoughts the ready mind.
No dissipating objects now distract
Her calm employ; the stir of this low earth
Is silenced, and the bodily powers subdu'd
By the day's business, leave her tranquiliz'd,
And aptest for such feelings as this hour
Inspires, nor light, nor fruitless; for as now
The lively hues of nature are all fled,
Gone with the light that gave them; so the toys
The puppetry of life have lost their glare,
Their worthless splendour. Wise is he who lets
The influence of this spirit-soothing hour
Fill all his thoughts, who passively receives
The calmness that descends upon his soul,
That like the sober wisdom of old age,
Softens and purifies the hallow'd heart.

Southey's phrase 'save that near / The church tower' recalls
Gray's *Elegy* line 9[19] 'Save that from yonder ivy-mantled
tower' and brings Coleridge's line 'save that at my side / My
cradled infant slumbers peacefully' back in line with its literary
source. Coleridge's living domestic vignette is returned to its
graveyard cliché. Southey's *Night* by comparison with *Frost
At Midnight* is a childless, Godless, tranquillized, passivity.
Inchoate feeling takes the place of wandering thought, in a
kind of stoical melancholy without past or future reference.

Two years earlier, in October 1796, he had described a similar existential inertia to Bedford:

> If you were married, Grosvenor, you would know the luxury of sitting indolently by the fireside . . . There is a state of complete mental torpor, very delightful, when the mind admits no sensation but that of mere existence. (*LC* I, pp. 292–93)

Southey's phrase 'hill and vale and wood' echoes the Coleridgean 'Sea, and hill, and wood' (*CP* p. 240) and seems to have been a favourite borrowing as it occurs in *To A Friend*[20] (*MP*, 18 September 1798) as 'hill, vale, and wood, art hidden from thy sight' and also in *Stanzas* (*MP*, 28 September 1798) as 'Hill, vale, and wood, and the broad sea'. He also extracts the beneficial depiction of passivity from Wordsworth's *Expostulation and Reply* st. 6, so that where Wordsworth writes about 'wise passiveness', Southey incorporates this as:

> Wise is he who lets
> The influence of this spirit-soothing hour
> Fill all his thoughts, who passively receives
> The calmness that descends upon his soul,
> That like the sober wisdom of old age,
> Softens and purifies the hallow'd heart.

Night has a rather terrifying blankness, a joyless quality, where home becomes synonymous not just with rest after toil, but with an isolation from the community quite different in quality to that found in *Frost At Midnight*. Wisdom and purification are high goals, but comfortless housemates and the evocation of calm in this poem is the silence of absolute retreat. It is as if Southey could not disentangle 'nature' from the contemporary social life he so mistrusted. In sum, this is an excellent example of Southey's working methods, which are not simply 'borrowings', in the production of magazine verse, and other poetry.

3
Southey on *Lyrical Ballads* in
the *Critical Review* xxiv, October 1798

Derek Roper's comments upon *Lyrical Ballads* by way of
contemporary reviewers' opinions show once and for all that
the volume did not emerge into an entirely antagonistic critical
atmosphere:

> *Lyrical Ballads* came before the critics as a small anony-
> mous volume of no particular prestige. Its 'Advertise-
> ment' was somewhat provocative, and its contents
> uneven in quality. Wordsworth had not yet, to use his
> own phrase, created the taste by which he was to be
> relished. Nevertheless, the reviews given to *Lyrical
> Ballads* average six pages in length, much more than was
> usually given to volumes of verse—twice the space given
> to Rogers's *Pleasures of Memory*, or Moore's *Thomas
> Little* volume. All reviewers expressed strong interest,
> and their reaction was generally favourable. The *Monthly*
> bestowed praise and blame in roughly equal proportions,
> the *Analytical* was preponderantly favourable, and the
> *British Critic* gave almost nothing but warm praise. The
> only review in which adverse criticism predominated was
> that in the *Critical*, written by the third member of the
> supposed Lake School, Robert Southey. His was the
> earliest review to appear; but except for one comment on
> 'The Ancient Mariner' repeated in the *Analytical*, no
> critic seems to have followed his lead. (*RO* p. 95)

Southey (pp. 197–204) disliked the experimental poems in the
volume including what he saw as the wasted effort (p. 200) of
The Idiot Boy, and 'tiresome loquacity' of *The Thorn*. In the
case of *The Idiot Boy*, this did not stop him from quoting
sixteen stanzas and giving a full synopsis of the events in the
poem. But he thought it, and other poems, 'bald in story'. In
Southey's eyes *Goody Blake* was 'perhaps a good story for a

ballad' in the sense that it was a well-known tale and would have had an immediate popular appeal. But he criticized the poem by casting doubts upon its authenticity and because it might promote superstitious belief in witchcraft. This, in the light of his own (often obscure and supernaturally horrific) ballad-work sounds very hypocritical, even if he had in *The Witch* shown up the brutal stupidity of persecution with (humorous) reason. He also attacked *The Rime of the Ancyent Marinere* because it did not conform to his idea of authenticity (it claimed to display the style and spirit of the elder poets), and affronted Southey's confidence in his own reading. He had not seen its precursor in the 'early English poets', therefore it was a bad poem. It seemed to him 'perfectly original in style as well as in story' with many 'laboriously beautiful' stanzas which were unfortunately 'absurd or unintelligible' when put together.

In dealing with both *The Idiot Boy* and *The Rime of the Ancyent Marinere* Southey makes the point that genius (a word very much in vogue with reviewers) has produced worthlessness. On *The Idiot Boy* he pronounces:

> No tale less deserved the labour that appears to have been bestowed upon this. It resembles a Flemish picture in the worthlessness of its design and the excellence of its execution. From Flemish artists we are satisfied with such pieces: who would not have lamented, if Corregio or Rafaelle had wasted their talents in painting Dutch boors or the humours of a Flemish wake? (p. 200)[21]

On *The Rime of the Ancyent Marinere* he admits:

> We do not sufficiently understand the story to analyse it. It is a Dutch attempt at German sublimity. Genius has here been employed in producing a poem of little merit. (p. 201)

So Wordsworth, referred to in this rather brilliant painterly allusion, has metaphorically left the path of the high art of

Corregio (c.1489–1534) and Raphael (1483–1520) for imitations of the low genre scenes of the seventeenth century Netherlandish painters. Continuing this thread, Coleridge has put aside the authentic and successful models from German ballad-work, to substitute his own 'Dutch attempt', whose storyline is unintelligible, double-Dutch, a verdict (*RO* p. 100) 'voiced by every contemporary critic except Charles Lamb'. Southey was at least consistent in his opinions, as this extract from a letter of September 1798 to William Taylor indicates:

> Coleridge's ballad of 'The Ancient Mariner' is, I think, the clumsiest attempt at German sublimity I ever saw. Many of the others are very fine; and some I shall re-read, upon the same principle that led me through Trissino, whenever I am afraid of writing like a child or an old woman. (*R* I, p. 223, 5 September 1798)

Overall, both authors, it is implied, are damned for quitting the poetical renaissance for a failed experiment upon the 'uninteresting subjects' (p. 204) of genre-painting. I say both authors. Southey writes 'ill as the *author* has employed his talents' (my emphasis) in an apparent attempt to cover the fact that he knew there to be two authors when he reviewed the volume.

All in all, his verdict upon *Lyrical Ballads*, though hard upon certain poems, does indeed give praise for *The Foster-Mother's Tale*, *The Dungeon*, the *Yew-Tree Lines*, *The Female Vagrant* and *Tintern Abbey*, of which he said:

> the author seems to discover still superior powers in the Lines written near Tintern Abbey. On reading this production, it is impossible not to lament that he should ever have condescended to write such pieces as the Last of the Flock, the Convict, and most of the ballads. In the whole range of English poetry, we scarcely recollect any thing superior to a part of the following passage. (p. 204)

Southey quotes lines 66–112 of *Tintern Abbey* which delineate
the change in Wordsworth's character from youthful wildness
in nature to profound sobriety informed by nature. Perhaps
here we might recall the earlier passage in which Southey
explains the chastening of his own Rousseauistic impulses and
the purported calming of his own character. He responds to
that dignified tone of wisdom in Wordsworth's poem suggestive of a similar maturity, if not of a similar frame of mind.

That Southey was so quick to blame and praise *Lyrical
Ballads* is another factor in his own lost poetical reputation,
another instance of self-injury. His praise for *Tintern Abbey*
and other poems in the volume is buried under the fact that he,
who should have been sympathetic to the aims of the two
collaborators, failed to respond properly to the experiment
and went so far as to scorn *The Rime of the Ancyent Marinere*,
a poem which retains its spellbinding powers of fascination to
this day. It is not hard for the reader to take an immediate
dislike to Southey on these grounds alone, and to cast him, as
so many critics do, as the black sheep of the Lakers. But
Wordsworth came to believe that *The Rime of the Ancyent
Marinere* had hindered the sales of the volume for similar
reasons to the ones Coleridge himself had already stated here,
(*Griggs* I, pp. 332–33) in July 1797 in a letter to Southey, who
was editing Chatterton:

> You are acting kindly in your exertions for Chatterton's
> sister: but I doubt the success. Chatterton's or Rowley's
> poems were never popular—the very circumstance which
> made them so much talked of—their *ancientness*—pre-
> vented them from being generally read—in the degree, I
> mean, that Goldsmith's poem or even Rogers's thing
> upon memory has been.—The sale was *never* very great.

In the light of the above comment it does seem slightly
perverse that Coleridge should have set the poem in a mock
ancient English, especially when Wordsworth was so keen for
the volume to succeed. Wordsworth, who was easily put off

the idea of publication altogether, was rightly put out by the review:

> ... Southey's review I have seen. He knew that I published those poems for money and money alone. He knew that money was of importance to me. If he could not conscientiously have spoken differently of the volume, he ought to have declined the task of reviewing it.
>
> The bulk of the poems he has described as destitute of merit. Am I recompensed for this by vague praises of my talents? I care little for the praise of any other professional critic, but as it may help me to pudding . . .[22]

Seen in this very un-romantic light, it is not impossible to regard Southey's review of *Lyrical Ballads* as the tactics of someone already in the ballad market as I have suggested, also in pursuit of 'pudding' and quite prepared to put the opposition in its place, and even damage it a little. If Southey could not have been expected to write the puff that Wordsworth seemed to want, his review was certainly not what one would have expected from a friend. One further negative aspect here is that Coleridge and the Wordsworths were away in Germany[23] whilst Southey's review came out, so that his behaviour would appear both hostile and sneakish.

4
The World of *Poems* 1799

Then with a deep heart-terrifying voice,
Exclaim'd the Spectre, 'Welcome to these realms,
'These regions of DESPAIR! O thou whose steps
'By GRIEF conducted to these sad abodes
'Have pierced; welcome, welcome to this gloom
'Eternal, to this everlasting night,
'Where never morning darts the enlivening ray,
'Where never shines the sun, but all is dark,

'Dark as the bosom of their gloomy King.
          (*The Vision of the Maid of Orleans, Poems* 1799,
                                          pp. 11–12)

Geoffrey Carnall (*CA* p. 54) speaks of Southey's poetry as having a joyless quality which sets him apart from Wordsworth. Though this is by no means completely true, it may serve as a general comment upon this volume:

> There is little joy in Southey's poetry. When one turns from him to Wordsworth, it is the warmth and tenderness which is more welcome than anything. Southey is obsessed by insecurity and death—the obsession makes his idiot poem extremely powerful.

Yet the volume of *Poems* 1799 has to be viewed largely in this light, because there is indeed a fascination with death and horror which vies with 'Monk' Lewis and the German ballads. One of these strands of horror takes its cue from *The Idiot* (*MP*, 30 June 1798) in which the son Ned digs up his mother's coffin, takes out the corpse and seats it by the fire:

> He plac'd his mother in her chair,
> And in her wonted place,
> And blew the kindling fire, that shone
> Reflected on her face;
>
> And pausing now, her hand would feel,
> And now her face behold,
> 'Why, mother, do you look so pale,
> 'And why are you so cold?'

This scene, with its motif of a kind of return from death (worthy of Hitchcock's film *Psycho*), is one keynote of the volume with its expected quota of social protest, parody and experimentation. In some ways the volume is Southey's answer to *Lyrical Ballads*, and I will explore the poems with this in mind. His idea of interesting subjects, it appears, hinged primarily around outrage, horror and death, a kind of poetical extremis, which usually draws attention by shock.

Both *The Vision of the Maid of Orleans* (pp. 5–69) and *The Rose* (pp. 75–80) which begin the volume, contain violent scenes where young women are about to be burnt, but are presented as heroines with miraculous events surrounding their lives. Presumably Southey thought that supernatural was admissible as long as it appeared to have a reliable source and narrative coherence understandable to the reader.

In his anxiety to please an audience, the poet dilutes the depth of his work, as in *The Complaints of the Poor* (pp. 81–84), which is, as Carnall (*CA* p. 53) notices, is a distant observation of frozen, diseased and ragged poverty from the vantage point of the well-dressed. It is obvious why the 'old bare-headed man' (p. 81), the 'young bare-footed child' (p. 82), the woman with the baby (p. 82) and the girl with the sunken eyes (p. 83) are out in the streets in bad weather, but Southey's questions to each character provoke a restatement of their plight from each character's own mouth. He acts as the tour-guide of misfortune, and points out to the 'rich man' that (p. 84) 'these have answered thee'. It is not possible to misunderstand his message, but it is hard to engage any feelings for the sufferers.

The eight 'Ballads' forming the central section of *Poems* 1799 are a mixture of entertainments of varying seriousness, including poems of social protest, inscripsive epitaphs, horror-stories and a parody of the same genre. Southey's fascination with authenticity is again revealed, as in his epigraph to *The Cross Roads* (pp. 93–102):

> The circumstance related in the following Ballad happened about forty years ago in a village adjacent to Bristol. A person who was present at the funeral, told me the story and the particulars of the interment, as I have versified them.

This ballad is one extra dig at the superstitious notions of witchcraft found particularly in village life. Southey borrows the nightingale motif contained in William Taylor's translation of *The Lass of Fair Wone*,[24] signifying death and sorrow:

> I have past by about that hour
> When men are not most brave,
> It did not make my heart to fail,
> And I have heard the nightingale
> Sing sweetly on her grave. (p. 97)

He sets out a dialogue (on a hot day) between an old man breaking stones and a passing soldier who covets the post against which the old man leans as a resting place. When the old man has moved for the soldier, he reveals:

> There's a poor girl lies buried here
> Beneath this very place.
> The earth upon her corpse is prest
> The stake is driven into her breast
> And a stone is on her face. (p. 96)

The post is the rather grisly mode of contact with the dead girl's story and it transpires that she was a servant to some wicked farming folk, and was found 'hung up one day' behind a stable door. But it is the method of burial that Southey wishes to expose:

> And there were strange reports about
> That the coroner never guest.
> So he decreed that she should lie
> Where four roads meet in infamy,
> With a stake drove in her breast. (p. 100)

This was of course the traditional way to bury witches, vampires and other unfortunates in order to prevent them from returning to trouble the living. The way that the soldier edges away from the post is intended to show not just the superstitious nature of soldiers perhaps, but that superstitious persons do not really have any faith in their own barbaric methods against the victims of their fears. The old man, however is quite unafraid of the dead girl, fearing instead her killer, 'one who like a Christian lies' (p. 97) in hallowed ground. Superstition has led to social injustice, and the girl assumes the symbolic quality of slighted Justice herself, remaining in the last line of the ballad with the metaphorical stake in her heart and the stone on her face.

This sense of outrage is continued in *The Sailor who had served in the Slave Trade*, where again, by epigraph, Southey protests the authenticity of his story:

> In September, 1798, a Dissenting Minister of Bristol, discovered a Sailor in the neighbourhood of that City, groaning and praying in a hovel. The circumstance that occasioned his agony of mind is detailed in the annexed Ballad, without the slightest addition or alteration. By presenting it as a Poem, the story is made more public, and such stories ought to be made as public as possible.

This then, is one answer to *The Ryme of the Ancyent Marinere*: an intelligible, authentic story of contemporary social concern publicly told without embellishment, with the reinforcing statement that such tales need publicity. In this, it continues the anti-slavery theme of *Poems* 1797, and is one more example of the very common trope of violence against women in Southey's work. He regularized the rather shifting metre of Coleridge's poem and gave a picture of a sailor cursed, not because he had shot an albatross, but because, more understandably, he had been forced to whip a female slave until she perished from her wounds. But the parallels between the two poems are obvious, and here is just one very Coleridgean example from the guilt-ridden sailor's story:

> Oh I have done a wicked thing!
> It haunts me night and day,

And I have sought this lonely place
Here undisturbed to pray. (p. 108)

Following Coleridge's cue of the haunted mariner, Southey
captures very well the agonized grief of the man who is
followed everywhere by 'the wicked one' (p. 109) waiting for
his soul, and then goes further by explicitly describing the
flogging:

> She groan'd, she shriek'd—I could not spare
> For the Captain he stood by—
> Dear God! that I might rest one night
> From that poor woman's cry!
> She twisted from her blows—her blood
> Her mangled flesh I see—
> And still the Captain would not spare—
> Oh he was worse than me! (p. 112)

After the exposure of the brutality from the superior ranks
which has in its turn brutalized the sailor and the slave,
Southey's dismissal of the man by the Minister to 'the house of
prayer', transfers the man's problem to God, and rather ruins
the effect. This is also true of *The Victory* (pp. 174–76), which
is nevertheless a touching poem based upon a true story of a
midshipman who was killed serving alongside Southey's
brother Tom on the *Mars*. Southey told Wynn that: 'he was
pressed into the service' (*W* I, p. 55), and left behind a wife and
family. In the poem he contrasts the way that 'Old England
triumphed!' (p. 174) with the description of the man, his
family and his horrific death. The poem falls into the category
of epitaph rather than ballad, and the central part would have
made a successful blank-verse inscription:

> There was one who died
> In that day's glory, whose obscurer name
> No proud historian's page will chronicle.
> Peace to his honest soul! I read his name,

'Twas in the list of slaughter, and blest God
the sound was not familiar to mine ear.
But it was told me after that this man
Was one whom lawful violence had forced
From his own little home and wife and little ones,
Who by his labour lived; that he was one
Whose uncorrupted heart could keenly feel
A husband's love, a father's anxiousness,
That from the wages of his toil he fed
The distant dear ones, and would talk of them
At midnight when he trod the silent deck
With him he valued, talk of them, of joys
Which he had known—oh God! and of the hour
When they should meet again, till his full heart
His manly heart at last would overflow
Even like a child's with very tenderness.
Peace to his honest spirit! suddenly
It came, and merciful the ball of death,
For it came suddenly and shattered him,
And left no moment's agonizing thought
On those he loved so well. (pp. 174–76)

The sentiments here have direct connections with those in *Joan of Arc* 1796 upon the effects of war, and with some of the poems ridiculed by the *Anti-Jacobin*. The sailor's wife is another war-widow, handed over to the divine for comfort. Southey does not exactly blame Old England for this situation, nor does he praise it wholeheartedly—he is content to tell the story plainly and let the reader draw his or her conclusions, which are not difficult to come to. He underlines the cost of patriotism to the English cause in the struggle against France.

If the above pieces were claimed as authentic stories, then the ballads *Jaspar* and *Lord William* were by contrast stated to be products of imagination:

The stories of the two following ballads are wholly imaginary. I may say of each as John Bunyan did of his Pilrim's Progress,

> It came from my own heart, so to my head,
> And thence into my fingers trickled;
> Then to my pen, from whence immediately
> On paper did I dribble it daintily.

In *Jaspar*, Southey again uses the nightingale motif as a prelude firstly to a murder, and then as a signal of the dénouement. Jaspar's victim is thrown into the water, and years pass. Later he tries to persuade an honest but financially troubled man, Jonathan, to kill his landlord, but Jonathan fears God's all-seeing eye and the revealing supernatural light which suddenly appears leads to the madness of Jaspar:

> His cheek is pale, his eye is wild,
> His look bespeaks despair;
> For Jaspar since that hour has made
> His home unshelter'd there.
>
> And fearful are his dreams at night
> And dread to him the day;
> He thinks upon his untold crime
> And never dares to pray. (pp. 129–30)

Southey's echo of the opening lines of Wordsworth's *The Mad Mother* is set into a much more straightforwardly cause and effect ballad. Hidden crime is revenged by divine intervention, unlike the loose ends which inhabit the psychologies of real life situations. This neatness of plot, by no means out of place in the fragmentary nature of the traditional ballad, is repeated in *Lord William*. William is also a murderer, who does away with his brother's orphan and is visited by the spirits of both brother and child. The child Edmund is drowned by William, so it is fitting that at the poem's end, William himself, escaping from a flood drowns also. He goes to rescue a child who turns out to be the ghostly boy:

Then William shriek'd; the hand he touch'd
Was cold and damp and dead!
He felt young Edmund in his arms
A heavier weight than lead.

The boat sunk down, the murderer sunk
Beneath the avenging stream;
He rose, he scream'd, no human ear
Heard William's drowning scream. (p. 141)

These descriptions of supernatural justice, as a way of explaining and punishing guilt, are similar to the events in George Crabbe's later account in *The Borough* of the violence and murder perpetrated by Peter Grimes. Grimes suffers persecution by the ghostly forms of the boys he has beaten and drowned:

There were three places where they ever rose,—
The whole long river has not such as those,—
Places accursed, where, if a man remain,
He'll see the things which strike him to the brain;
And there they made me on my paddle lean,
And look at them for hours;—accursed scene![25]

Crabbe continues in his own way the neat revenges of the ballad-scene of the 1790s. Southey, though, has a flashy jocularity in his ballad work which is quite unlike the sombre tones of Crabbe's heroic couplets.

Southey's adaptation of a story from Olaus Magnus, *A Ballad, shewing how an old woman rode double, and who rode before her*, is another supernatural revenge, a fashionable abduction story, like William Taylor's version of the *Lenore* of Bürger. Again, and unlike the heroine Bürger's ballad, the old woman has committed horrible deeds, and is punished accordingly:

I have suck'd the breath of sleeping babes,
The fiends have been my slaves,

> I have nointed myself with infant's fat,
> And feasted on rifled graves.

> And the fiend will fetch me now in fire
> My witchcrafts to atone,
> And I who have rifled the dead man's grave
> Shall never have rest in my own. (p. 151)

The old woman of Berkeley's coffin is chained down, and mass is sung to keep off the powers of evil, until at last the Fiend prevails. The old woman's corpse rises and groans, and then:

> She followed the fiend to the church door,
> There stood a black horse there,
> His breath was like red furnace smoke,
> His eyes like a meteor's glare.

> The fiend he flung her on the horse
> And he leapt up before,
> And away like lightning's speed they went
> And she was seen no more. (p. 160)

Southey's parody of this poem, *The Surgeon's Warning*, following this supernatural romp, reduces superstitious beliefs in the undead to the level of simple rational explanation. Graves do not open by themselves, but by the agencies of body-snatchers, in this case with the help of the Surgeon's own zealous 'Prentices. Southey inserts a ludicrous feature into the ballad about 'patent coffins' which seems to fascinate him enough to allude to this invention in the epigraph, alongside an anti-popish dig:

> Respecting the patent coffins herein mentioned, after the manner of Catholic Poets, who confess the actions they attribute to their Saints and Deity to be but fiction, I hereby declare that it is by no means my design to depreciate that useful invention; and all persons to whom this ballad shall come, are requested to take notice, that

nothing here asserted concerning the aforementioned Coffins is true, except that the maker and patentee lives by St. Martin's lane.

Southey's surgeon initially inhabits a deathbed scene, as did the old woman of Berkeley, but is then buried with much fuss in a patent coffin, being wrapped in lead and being watched over by three men who are on the look out (p. 168) for the 'resurrection man'. The Surgeon retells his crimes in the cause of anatomical research:

> I have made candles of infants fat
> And the Sextons have been my slaves,
> I have bottled babes unborn, and dried
> Hearts and livers from rifled graves.
>
> And my Prentices will surely come
> And carve me bone from bone,
> And I, who have rifled dead man's graves
> Shall never rest in my own. (p. 165)

His apparent scientific interest in the uses and abuses of the human bodies he has stolen is made to seem like the work of a witch. The men who guard the body are bribed after three attempts by Joseph the rogue prentice to release the Surgeon's corpse:

> The watchmen as they past along
> Full four yards off could smell,
> And a curse bestow'd upon the load
> So disagreeable.
>
> So they carried the sack a-pick-a-back
> And they carved him bone from bone,
> But what became of the Surgeon's soul
> Was never to mortal known. (p. 173)

So the Surgeon, who has not sold his soul to the devil as did the old woman, finds himself anatomized in the rational quest for knowledge, with the consequent (but not proven) dispersal of his soul. It is a tale almost worthy of Voltaire's pen, and lively, if revolting, entertainment. *Jaspar, Lord William, The Surgeon's Warning* and the 'old woman of Berkeley' all fall into this category of entertainments, lively episodic tales which begin *in medias res* and swiftly run their course. They are quite different from most of the poetry of *Lyrical Ballads,* and if their details are not instantly forgotten, because they are disturbing or vile, they do not make the same demands upon the reader that Wordsworth's poems do. But then that was not their intention. They do, however, reflect part of the fashionable taste of the period and indicate something of Southey's ideas about what was marketable verse.

But in the last section of *Poems* 1799, Southey moves much closer to the world of *Lyrical Ballads* with his experimental *English Eclogues* that largely centre around themes of domestic unrest. Southey's too-honest epigraph, like the introductory paragraph in *Poems* 1797, has a kind of hauteur and belligerence peculiar to the poet, claiming originality. His third paragraph might stand as an answer to Wordsworth's 1798 *Advertisement*:

> The following Eclogues, I believe, bear no resemblance to any poems in our language. This species of composition has become popular in Germany, and I was introduced to attempt it by an account of the German Idylls given me in conversation. They cannot be properly styled imitations, as I am ignorant of the language at present, and have never seen any translations or specimens of this kind.
>
> With bad Eclogues I am sufficiently acquainted, from Tityrus and Corydon down to our English Strephons and Thyrsises. No kind of poetry can boast of more illustrious names, or is more distinguished by the servile dulness of imitated nonsense. Pastoral writers, 'more silly than their sheep,' have like their sheep gone

on in the same track one after another. Gay stumbled
into a new path. His eclogues were the only ones which
interested me when I was a boy, and did not know they
were burlesque. The subject would furnish matter for a
long essay, but this is not the place for it.

How far poems requiring almost a colloquial plainness of language may accord with the public taste, I am
doubtful. They have been subjected to able criticism, and
revised with care. I have endeavoured to make them true
to nature. (p. 183)

To Wordsworth's announcement in his 1798 *Advertisement* to
Lyrical Ballads that 'the following Poems are to be considered
as experiments', Southey responds with an explanation of
experimental originality. To Wordsworth's interest in ascer-
taining 'how far the language of conversation in the middle
and lower classes of society is adapted to the purposes of
poetic pleasure',[26] Southey responds with open doubts about
'public taste' and 'colloquial plainness of language'. In this, he
goes beyond his statements in the *Critical Review* that:

The 'experiment,' we think, has failed, not because the
language of conversation is little adapted to the 'purposes
of poetic pleasure,' but because it has been tried upon
uninteresting subjects. (p. 204)

He now appears very doubtful about the employment of plain
or conversational speech altogether in the face of the 'public
taste' which, like Wordsworth, he is actively courting. In what
senses the subjects of his *Eclogues* have *interesting* subjects, I
will explain. Southey responds to Wordsworth's demand that
the reader search *Lyrical Ballads* for 'a natural delineation of
human passions, human characters, and human incidents', by
merely stating of his own poems: 'I have made them true to
nature'. His linking together of the idea of originality and his
open comments on his German models, are perhaps a direct
slap in the face for Coleridge whose *Rime of the Ancyent*

Marinere Southey thought 'perfectly original in style as well as story' (p. 200) but a clumsy adaptation of other German models. This seems an instance of Southey trying to correct Coleridge's methods of presentation.

The *English Eclogues* begin with *The Old Mansion-House*, a poem in blank-verse continuing Southey's interests in old mansions and hospitality which he first published in the 1795 volume of *Poems*. The eclogue also contains a central trope explored in *The Retrospect* of 1794, the changing fortunes of a mansion reflecting the changing fortunes of humankind. Southey's method however is the conversational method of the German idylls, such as the famous *Der Wandrer* (1774) of Goethe (between Woman and Wanderer) which was translated by William Taylor and appeared in the *Monthly Magazine* xxxv, pp. 120–21, for August 1798. The poem's central character, the Old Man (p. 185) nearly 'threescore and ten', is reminiscent of Wordsworth's Simon Lee, not just in terms of age, but in the sense that he is doing hard physical work (breaking stones) and he has served the local aristocrats all his life. His greatest fear is that now the old occupants of the mansion have both died, that the new squire will change everything he is familiar with. This work is already under way. The Old Man is, however, talking to the new Squire without knowing it, and the new occupant generously assures him that though the exterior of the house is changed, inside the old hospitality still reigns:

OLD MAN
I remember
All this from a child up, and now to lose it,
'Tis losing an old friend. There's nothing left
As 'twas;—I go abroad and only meet
With men whose fathers I remember boys;
The brook that used to run before my door,
That's gone to the great pond; the trees I learnt

To climb are down; and I see nothing now
That tells me of old times, except the stones
In the church-yard. You are young Sir and I hope,
Have many years in store,—but pray to God
You mayn't be left the last of all your friends.

STRANGER

Well! well! you've one friend more than you're aware of.
If the Squire's taste don't suit with your's, I warrant
That's all you'll quarrel with: walk in and taste
His beer old friend! and see if your old Lady
E'er broached a better cask. You did not know me,
But we're acquainted now. 'Twould not be easy
To make you like the outside; but within—
That is not changed my friend! you'll always find
The same old bounty and old welcome here.

Again the familiar pattern emerges. Where Simon Lee's plight is left as an unresolved state, the Old Man's fears are soothed, and his agitations are smoothed over by the new order. Despite being childless like Simon Lee, his attachment to the aristocracy has not resulted in him being left as useless in old age. It is, however, a patronizing solution to the problem. Could mere hospitality make up the loss of the Old Man's intimately-loved world? Or is Southey criticizing the new Squire as a second version of Gay's profligate in *The Birth of the Squire. An Eclogue*?

This same cheerful and superficial answering of problems is found in *The Sailor's Mother*, another blank-verse eclogue which picks up the journey to hospital theme of Wordsworth's *Old Man Travelling*. Here Southey has a dialogue between a Woman and a Traveller about the woman's son now in Plymouth hospital. And here more doubts begin to arise again about Southey's trite answers. The Traveller cheerfully tries to rouse the Woman by offering her food and rest and then launches into a consolatory speech:

TRAVELLER
Perhaps your fears
Make evil worse. Even if a limb be lost
There may still be enough for comfort left
An arm or leg shot off, there's yet the heart
To keep life warm, and he may live to talk
With pleasure of the glorious fight that maim'd him,
Proud of his loss. Old England's gratitude
Makes the maim'd sailor happy. (pp. 207–08)

This speech could be viewed as a piece of patriotic jingo, or as a ludicrous satire upon the way government forces try to justify war-wounds to the maimed. The same kind of nervous conversation is echoed in Edward Thomas's poem[27] *As the Team's Head-Brass*:

I could spare an arm. I shouldn't want to lose
A leg. If I should lose my head, why, so,
I should want nothing more.

The sailor's wounds are more horrific than simply losing limbs; he has lost his eyes in a sea-fight from some appalling secret weapon (p. 208) used by the French forces, 'some cursed thing / which bursts and burns'. Southey inserts a footnote:

The stink-pots used on board the French ships. In the engagement between the Mars and L'Hercule, some of our sailors were shockingly mangled by them: One in particular, as described in the Eclogue, lost both his eyes. It would be policy and humanity to employ means of destruction, could they be discovered, powerful enough to destroy fleets and armies, but to use any thing that only inflicts additional torture upon the victims of our war systems, is cruel and wicked.

This footnote undercuts the entire poem altogether, indeed the subject is scarcely fit for genteel poetry at all because it is so explicit. At the side of *Old Man Travelling*, which draws back from the particularities of horrific detail, Southey's poem reads like an item on the agenda of the Cabinet of War. The Woman pours out her grief to the Traveller, telling him how this is her only child, the history of the boy's life, and the fact that he was forced into service because of his love of trapping animals:

> He did what he should not when he was older:
> I warn'd him oft enough; but he was caught
> In wiring hares at last, and had his choice
> The prison or the ship. (p. 213)

His replies about the leniency of the sentence, about patriotic glory and the fact that the country takes care of its bereaved mothers, set against the Woman's plight read like stark insensitivity or intended burlesque. It is a sophisticated attempt at another anti-war poem, which seems to sit on the fence of possible readings. It could be seen as either a patriotic gesture for king and country, or born of a patriotism which rests upon a concern for humanity. Southey is hedging his political bets, whilst feeling for the victim.

A similar kind of conversation occurs in *The Witch*, but here the interpretation of the poem is more obvious. This poem is Southey's answer to *Goody Blake and Harry Gill* which he condemned in his review. The characters of Nathaniel and his Father discuss old Margery, who is thought to be a witch, with a Curate. Nathaniel thinks it a shame that 'in a Christian country they should let / Such creatures live!' (p. 219) and the Father sees his 'proof' of witchcraft:

> And when there's such plain proof!
> I did but threaten her because she robb'd
> Our hedge, and next night there came a wind
> That made me shake to hear it in my bed!
> How came it that that storm unroofed my barn,
> And only mine in the parish? look at her

And that's enough; she has it in her face—
A pair of large dead eyes, sunk in her head,
Just like a corpse, and purs'd with wrinkles round,
A nose and chin that scarce leave room between
For her lean fingers to squeeze in the snuff,
And when she speaks! I'd sooner hear a raven
Croak at my door! (p. 219)

Goody Blake's hedge-robbing is repeated here and also the righteous indignation of Harry Gill, which is ever the voice of the haves against the have-nots. Southey's solution to the situation comes from reason and pity. There is no possibility that Margery can bring down curses by prayer, although Wordsworth's poem only hints at that possibility, and Harry Gill's Lear-like discovery of what wretches feel is replaced by the ridicule of country thickheads like Nathaniel and his father. The Curate's depiction of the old woman is rational:

Poor wretch! half blind
And crooked with her years, without a child
Or friend in her old age, 'tis hard indeed
To have her very miseries made her crimes!
I met her but last week in that hard frost
That made my young limbs ache, and when I ask'd
What brought her out in the snow, the poor old woman
Told me that she was forced to crawl abroad
And pick the hedges, just to keep herself
From perishing with cold, because no neighbour
Had pity on her age; and then she cried,
And said the children pelted her with snow-balls,
And wish'd that she were dead. (pp. 221–22)

Wordsworth's rather rollicking metre is put aside for the relative calm of blank verse, where the situation is taken away from any hint of moonlit superstition into the light of day to plainly expose the yokels' stupidities. And the poem's comic finale rubs in the message. When the Curate leaves to visit the dying old woman the Father insists (p. 225) that Nathaniel 'drive t'other nail in!' to the horseshoe which is set up against witches, after all 'She may recover'. The kind of brutality that these yokels are only inches away from is explored more fully in *The Grandmother's Tale*, which is another tale of murder and revenge focused upon a female victim, though this time she is not a defenceless old woman.

This poem, Southey's second *Eclogue*, is far from just being the tale for children which it purports to be. It concerns the story of a woman, Moll, who because of her ugliness had, in one escapade, passed for a man when the press-gang arrived and saved her husband from military service. She now kept asses, which she loved tenderly, and when she threatened a smuggler that if he molest them again she would inform upon him, he murdered her:

> he provoked her,
> she laid an information, and one morn
> They found her in the stable, her throat cut
> Form ear to ear, 'till the head only hung
> Just by a bit of skin. (p. 199)

The man suffers in the same way that the slave-sailor did, namely he is haunted by the sight and the cries of the woman until at last he confesses his crime. He is 'Hung and anatomized' in the words (p. 201) of the Grandmother. Southey's footnote relates the truth of the events:

> There must be many persons living who remember these circumstances. They happened two or three and twenty years ago, in the neighbourhood of Bristol. The woman's name was Bees. The stratagem by which she preserved her husband from the press-gang, is also true.

True horrors are then represented alongside horrors in the fictive gothic mode. The explicit nature of the poems is indeed shocking or harrowing, and Southey no doubt had confidence in his market when he published this volume. As Robert Mayo has shown,[28] the distress-ridden situations which centre around female figures in the magazine verse of this period were very saleable indeed. The subject-matter of *Lyrical Ballads* was therefore in line with this fashion, but the poetical treatment of its subjects was different. Mayo draws attention to Southey's *Hannah, A Plaintive Tale*, which had appeared in the *Monthly Magazine* for October 1797 (pp. 286–87) as a classic example of the kind of poem to which later works like *The Thorn* or *The Mad Mother* were closely related. Southey's blank-verse poem re-titled *The Funeral*, appeared as one of the *English Eclogues* in the 1799 volume. Hannah, like Martha Ray, is left alone as an unmarried mother to endure the scorn of the local community and Southey's speaker, as Mayo points out, resembles the narrator of *The Thorn* in having 'a kind of character of his own'.[29] We may deduce that the poem grew from one of Southey's experiences when he was living in Burton near Christchurch in Hampshire in 1797:

> It is proper to remark that the story related in this Eclogue is strictly true. I met the funeral, and learnt the circumstances, in a village in Hampshire. The indifference of the child was mentioned to me; indeed no addition whatever has been made to the story. I should have thought it wrong to have weakened the effect of a faithful narrative by adding any thing. (p. 202)

These constant protestations of truth about local events are in a sense analogous to the use of political and historical material in some of the *Inscriptions*. As if the *Inscriptions* had gone more completely commercial. In poems like *The Funeral*, Southey seems to extend his inscription-work to local popular tales, another form of historical reference. *Hannah* was a creation from the period before Southey's exposure via William Taylor to the varieties of German literature. Mary Jacobus (*JAC* pp. 169–72) attaches considerable importance to the poem which she feels 'can find room only in the meditative mind' and which despite Southey's 'limited ability to portray suffering' does mark 'the transition between the pathetic episodes of the eighteenth century and Wordsworth's poetry of suffering'. The poem is really a blank-verse epitaph, drawing somewhat upon the inscription voice of *Poems* 1797, a vivid episode of contemplation in a tone of extreme meditative quietness, much different from many of the other *Eclogues* in the volume. Its political elements are muted into allusions to poverty. Southey manages to create a kind of immediacy of narration in the poem's opening lines: 'The coffin as I past across the lane / Came sudden on my view' (p. 202) which he sustains for most of the poem. He disappoints only in the areas where the description of suffering is wanted, and in the final lines where God's mercy lifts the poem away from the human context and abruptly closes down any imaginative sympathies.

In a similar blank-verse vein *The Ruined Cottage* which closes the volume treats another widow's plight alongside the humiliation of her daughter Joanna (a name echoing 'Hannah') and the consequent ruin of her home. It is the end of a long list of tales which loosely chart the ruin of domesticity and community, the obverse of the quest for home. The poem found an able and attentive critic in Charles Lamb, who said:

> I find no fault in it, unless perhaps Joanna's is a catastrophe too trite, and this is not the first or second time you have cloth'd your indignation in verse in a tale of ruined Innocence. The Old lady spinning in the Sun, I hope would not disdain some kindred with old Margaret.[30] (29 October 1798)

Lamb's critiques spotted Southey's hidden and indignant social agendas, noticed how Southey had responded to the details of his own *Rosamund Gray* of 1798, and went on:

> but the old Lady is so great a favourite with me, I want to hear more of her, and of Joanna you have given us still

less.—But the picture of the rustics leaning over the
bridge & the old Lady travelling abroad on summer
evenings to see her garden water'd, are images so new and
true, that I decidedly prefer this ruin'd cottage to any
poem in the book. Indeed I think it the only one that will
bear comparison with your Hymn to the Penates in a
former vol.—I compare dissimilar things, as one would a
rose & star for the pleasure they give us. (15 March
1799)[31]

Lamb's connection of this poem with the *Hymn to the Penates*
makes an interesting oblique link between the domestic
centres of both poems, and exposes the radical point of
departure for much of Southey's work. He is not simply
fascinated by death and horror, but by the twists and turns of
domestic fortune which suffer the impact of those adverse
events. The poem's opening has the gravity of an inscription:

Aye Charles! I knew that this would fix thine eye,
This woodbine wreathing round the broken porch,
Its leaves just withering, yet one autumn flower
Still fresh and fragrant; yon holly-hock
That thro' the creeping weeds and nettles tall
Peers taller, and uplifts its column'd stem
Bright with broad rose-blossoms. I have seen
Many a fallen convent reverend in decay,
And many a time have trod the castle courts
And grass-green halls, yet never did they strike
Home to the heart such melancholy thoughts
As this poor cottage. Look, its little hatch
Fleeced with that grey and wintry moss; the roof
Part moulder'd in, the rest o'ergrown with weeds,
House-leek and long thin grass and greener moss;
So nature wars with all the works of man,
And, like himself, reduces back to earth
His perishable piles. (pp. 226–27)

The details of the ruined cottage bear some comparison with those in Wordsworth's poem of the same name, for example:

> this poor hut
> Stripped of its outward garb of household flowers,
> Of rose and jasmine, offers to the wind
> A cold bare wall whose earthy top is tricked
> With weeds and the rank spear-grass.[32]

But it is not enough to merely restate the fact that Southey's poem fails to travel across the range of emotions discovered in Wordsworth's *The Ruined Cottage*. Again, it would be more appropriate to view Southey's work in the light of his own poetic developments, especially his *Inscriptions*. This poem is another example of his epitaphic and elegiac mode, given a kind of lapidary polish in places with reference to predecessors like Akenside. Southey inscribes the tale like a man working against stone, marking a monument. But, again, *The Ruined Cottage* is a direct relation of nature inscriptions like *For the Banks of the HAMPSHIRE AVON* (*MP*, 19 November 1799), where Southey's own abilities for the recording of natural details are manifest.

His attempt to lump together the range of styles and subjects in his *English Eclogues* is rather amateurish, and he is wrong to say that poems such as *The Funeral* and *The Ruined Cottage* 'bear no resemblance to any poems in our language' (p. 183) because firstly *The Funeral* had already been published before his German-influenced phase, and secondly the poems bear resemblances to his own inscription work.

This, then, is how Southey stands in regard to the experiment of *Lyrical Ballads*—not simply as a kind of precursor-poet, nor simply as piratical hack who shamelessly borrowed, but as an established commercial writer and social commentator eager to maintain his own growing literary reputation in the experimental cutting-edges of the poetry of the 1790s, a man inside the debate, not upon its periphery.

NOTES

1 Wilfrid Hindle, *The Morning Post 1772–1937* (London: Routledge, 1937), p. 91.

2 *Letters from the Lake Poets to Daniel Stuart* (London: West, Newman and Co., 1889), p. 384.

3 Hindle, *op. cit.*, p. 345, 3 May 1838.

4 William Godwin, *An Enquiry Concerning Political Justice* (Harmondsworth: Penguin, 1985), p. 772.

5 This poem bears great similarities to a piece also called *The Spider* (1720) by Edward Lyttleton:

> And as from out thy tortured body
> Thou draw'st the slender strings with pain,
> So does he labour like a noddy
> To spin materials from his brain.

See *The New Oxford Book of Eighteenth-Century Verse*, ed. Roger Lonsdale (Oxford: Oxford University Press, 1987), pp. 150–51.

6 An example of Edith Southey's letter-writing can be found (*W* I, p. 335), to a Miss Barker. Edith sounds very lively and playful, and totally involved with Southey's own sense of fun.

7 See *The Three Wartons*, ed. Eric Partridge (London: The Scholartis Press, 1927), p. 73.

8 See Robert Mayo, 'The Contemporaneity of the Lyrical Ballads', *PMLA* lxix (1954), p. 494.

9 Here the word 'caves' was corrected to 'eaves' (*F* p. 380) and 'martins' to 'martin's' in the final edition of the poems.

10 See Alethea Hayter, *Opium and the Romantic Imagination* (London: Faber and Faber, 1968), p. 75. She is quoting from *CB* IV, p. 185. See also *The Curse of Kehama* VII, 10.

11 My grateful thanks go to Elizabeth Freebairn of the Special Collections Department of the Newberry Library, Chicago, for sending a copy of this sonnet reproduced from *The Morning Post*, of a page apparently unavailable on microfilm in Britain. The actual title of the sonnet *as printed in The Morning Post* differs slightly from the title Professor Curry gives in his *Morning Post* chronology (*MP* p. 23). Thanks are also due to Professor Curry himself for giving clues to the whereabouts of this poem.

12 Kenneth Hopkins, *English Poetry: A Short History* (London: Phoenix House, 1962), p. 313.

13 Southey even supplied Wordsworth with lines for a satire in imitation of Juvenal, *PW* I, p. 302.

14 Grevel Lindop (*Times Literary Supplement*, 12 October 1984, p. 1170).

15 See B. R. McElderry, 'Southey, and Wordsworth's "The Idiot Boy" ', *Notes & Queries* NS II (November 1955), pp. 490–91 and Elizabeth Duthie, 'A Fresh Comparison Of "The Idiot Boy" and "The Idiot" ', *Notes & Queries* Vol. 223 (June 1978), pp. 219–20, and *MP* pp. 67–69. Carnall (*CA* p. 54), in his discussion of the *Morning Post* poetry, states: 'There is little joy in Southey's poetry. When one turns from him to Wordsworth, it is the warmth and tenderness which is more welcome than anything. Southey is obsessed with insecurity and death—the obsession makes his idiot poem extremely powerful.'

16 *Lyrical Ballads*, ed. Michael Mason (London: Longman, 1992), pp. 147–48.

17 Mary Jacobus, 'Southey's Debt to *Lyrical Ballads* (1798)', *Review of English Studies*, n.s. 22, 1971, p. 24.

18 *The Morning Mists* (*MP* pp. 112–13) with its addressee, 'William' may possibly be one William Bowyer Thomas, a friend Southey had made in Portugal, and with whom he and Edith stayed in the autumn of 1798, in Hereford (*Simmons* p. 75, and *NL* I, p. 175), but it also strongly recalls the 'William' of *Expostulation and Reply*.

19 *The Poems of Gray, Collins and Goldsmith*, ed. Roger Lonsdale (London: Longman, 1969), p. 119.

20 *Lines. To A Friend* (*MP* p. 128), makes the point that his friend should rouse himself from despair, strive to achieve against the negative current of the world, because age does not spring back from the shocks of life as does the strength of youth. Southey urges a change of attitude to adversity, recalling the Epictetan maxim from the *Enchiridion* translated by Mrs Elizabeth Carter: 'The Condition and Characteristic of a vulgar Person is, that he never expects either Benefit or Hurt from himself; but from Externals. The Condition and Characteristic of a Philosopher is, that he expects all Hurt and Benefit from himself.' *All The Works Of Epictetus* (London: S. Richardson, 1758), pp. 460–61.

21 Lamb may have influenced Southey's review by his phrase 'Fleming painter' in a letter to the poet, 29 October 1798. See Edwin J. Marrs Jr (ed.), *The Letters of Charles and Mary Lamb*, 3 vols (Ithaca and London: Cornell University Press, 1975–78), Vol. I, p. 137.

22 *The Letters of William and Dorothy Wordsworth: The Early Years 1787–1805*, 2nd edn, ed. E. de Selincourt and C. L. Shaver (Oxford: Oxford University Press, 1967), pp. 267–68. To Cottle, summer 1799.

23 During this period Coleridge particularly was on Southey's mind because of the tragic death of his son Berkeley. Sara Coleridge wrote to Thomas Poole on Monday 11 February 1799 (*Minnow Among Tritons*, ed. Stephen Potter [London: Nonesuch Press, 1934], p. 1): 'Oh! my dear Mr Poole, I have lost my dear child! . . . Southey has undertaken the business

of my babe's interment and in a few days we shall remove to his house at
Westbury which I shall be rejoiced to do for this house at present is quite
hateful to me.'

24 See Mary Jacobus, *Tradition and Experiment in Wordsworth's Lyrical
Ballads* (Oxford: Clarendon Press, 1976), appendix II, p. 284.

25 Howard Mills (ed.), *George Crabbe: Tales, 1812 and Other Selected
Poems* (Cambridge: Cambridge University Press, 1967), p. 114, ll. 338–43.

26 *Lyrical Ballads*, ed. Michael Mason (London and New York: Longman, 1992), p. 34.

27 *Collected Poems*, with a foreword by Walter De La Mare (London and
Boston: Faber, 1981), p. 29.

28 'The Contemporaneity of the *Lyrical Ballads*' *PMLA* 69 (1954), pp.
486–522, p. 496ff.

29 Robert Mayo, *op cit.*, p. 496.

30 Edwin J. Marrs, Jr (ed.), *The Letters of Charles and Mary Lamb*, 3
vols (Ithaca and London: Cornell University Press, 1975–78), Vol. I,
p. 137.

31 *Ibid.*, p. 162.

32 *The Ruined Cottage and The Pedlar*, ed. James Butler (Ithaca and
New York: Cornell University Press, 1979), p. 50, ll. 159–62.

Chapter Nine

Madoc:
Southey's Reputation or a
Melancholy Memento?

The poetical powers of Mr. Southey are indisputably very superior, and capable, we doubt not, of producing a poem that will place him in the first class of English poets. He is at present, he tells his readers, engaged in the execution of *Madoc*, an epic poem, on the discovery of America by that prince. We cannot, therefore, help expressing our wish, that he would not put his future poem to so hazardous an experiment as he has this, by assigning himself so little time for its completion.[1]

1

This chapter seeks to sketch out the growth of a poem, the hazardous experiment, by which Robert Southey wanted to secure his reputation as a writer for all time. It was a poem brought to an end simultaneously with the end of the Westbury year, and represents a further comment upon *Lyrical Ballads* in the sense that Southey valued the epic above every other poetic genre. His own small poems are therefore also implicated in this veneration of the epic form. I want to draw attention firstly to the way Southey spoke of his work in progress and to give a brief reading of the epic in the light of its critical reception.

It was Kenneth Curry who back in 1943 produced an article[2] on the *Madoc* of 1794, a fragment of two books only, apposite to the disturbed nature of the times, with its theme of emigration to America, civil war amongst the Welsh (evoking

307

ideas of authentic Britishness), Saxon tyranny—seen in the
1790s in the spectral form of the Hannoverian kings—and the
consequent ruin of domestic, familial values. Southey added a
note to the end of this fragment: 'Thus far in 1794. I began to
revise Feby 22. 1797, and finished the revisal March 1799.'[3]
The exact date of finishing was 12 July 1799 (*PW* IV, p. xi),
according to Southey. He tells a short history of the poem in
October 1803 (*NL* I, p. 332) to Charles Danvers:

> The poem has hung so long upon my hands and during so
> many ups and downs of life that I had almost become
> superstitious about it and could hurry thro it with a sort
> of fear. Projected in 1789 and begun in prose at that time,
> then it slept till 1794 when I wrote a book and a half—
> another interval till 97 when it was corrected and carried
> on to the beginning of the fourth book and then a gap till
> the autumn of 1798. From that time it went fairly on till it
> was finished in your poor mother's parlour on her little
> table. Book by book I had read it to her and passage by
> passage as they were written to my mother and to Peggy.
> This was done in July 99—four years! I will not trust it
> any longer least more changes befall and I should learn to
> dislike it as a melancholy memento.

But as Curry's *New Letters* show, Southey was thinking of
Madoc in May of 1795 also, describing it merely as 'a good
poem' (I, p. 96). After the Portuguese holiday in July 1796 he
lets slip his idea of what *Madoc* will really signify to him, and
he hopes, to the nation:

> No Grosvenor when I come to London I will live to
> myself and to you. I will enter into no clubs, no literary
> societies. I will use no literary arts. When I have done
> with the world I will give *Madoc* to posterity. I shall get
> the applause of the present generation which I care not
> for—but believe that I may benefit the future. (*NL* I,
> p. 113)

The project then was long-term and ambitiously, if not conceitedly, stated. In November 1796 (*NL* I, p. 117) Southey could proclaim:

> Poor Madoc! . . . is it not damned hard Bedford that the booksellers should make so much of that poem when I am rotten, and that I should make so little?

He was serious in his belief that 'On a great work like *Madoc* I should think ten years labour well bestowed' (*NL* I, p. 181, February 1799), especially since he hoped that he might (*NL* I, p. 206, November 1799) 'Leave that as a post-obit bond for my family'. By December 1803, Southey had the idea that he would publish the poem the following winter and try to have the whole of the profits for himself. He writes gloomily in 1807 (*NL* I, p. 457):

> I have received my account from Longman—the total profit from *Madoc* is 25£. There is little likelihood that the remaining quarto copies will ever sell, unless at trade sales for a fourth part of their price. The small edition will go off drop by drop—by *leakage* not by a run; in about two years time it will perhaps begin to send in some returns, and then produce some yearly five or ten pounds. The laws of copy-right are singularly hard, twenty or thirty years hence it is probable that this poem will have made its way, and settled into a steady and regular sale, and then when the returns would be valuable, the property becomes common. 'Sic vos nobis!' Surely this deserves to be amended, and men of letters ought not to be the only persons whose children are not to reap the fruit of their fathers labours.

Later, in a letter to Sir Walter Scott, Southey (*NL* I, p. 513), discussing *The Curse of Kehama*, states: 'The only question therefore seems to be in what form to print. 180 *Madocs* in the warehouse plead I am afraid strongly against the quarto . . .' He seemed to have been looking rather dismally upon his whole epical enterprise by 1809, commenting to Bedford in October:

> Scribo-scribo-scribo quid hunc? populus non emit. Ego abstergam meum tergum-latus cum Thalaba, cum Madoco, cumque Kehama nil dubito . . . Ego haurio et haurio super Longum Hominem. Longus Homo est bonus homo, ille sinit me haurire, nil contradicens. Habet satis in manibus suis [facere] omne liquidare ad finem. Hoc vero inconveniens est, quod credo alii bibliopolae darent me bonum summum pecuniae pro quolibet opere novo, et ego nonopossum ire ad eos, quia hoc modo obligatus sum ad Hominem Longum.[4]

The once vaunted and valued *Madoc* remaindered or used as toilet-paper? Southey's most valued long-term project become merely one of his 'unsaleables'?[5] How could this happen? Several answers suggest themselves.

A glance at *Madoc* in Southey's *Complete Poetical Works* in the rather condensed form of the posthumous new edition of 1853 shows one thing very clearly, simply that the poem is incredibly well annotated. The notes are generally of a scholarly antiquarian nature, attesting to the vast effort of reading and research of which Southey was capable. But are they a vital part of the presentation of a poem? Would they not be better employed in prose history or literary studies? Southey seemed to enjoy displaying his abstruse researches in this way, apparently believing that his readership would enjoy, as much as he did, the exhumation and perusal of his sometimes scurrilous textual relics. In the production of *Madoc*, he wanted to create as authentic an atmosphere as possible. In March 1797 (*NL* I, p. 122), he states:

> My mornings are devoted to Law; I allow the evening for pleasanter employments, and divide it between German Grammar and *Madoc*, with both of which I am getting forwards. I am fond of learning languages. Nothing

exercises a man's ingenuity more . . . It is my intention
to learn Welsh. I shall find it almost necessary to render
Madoc as I intend to. They who understand the language
say it is a fine one.

How he expected a poem to flourish between law and German
grammar is not clear: that he was *manufacturing* poetry
(against the laws of such as Shelley's *The Defence of Poetry*)
was very clear. He was also on the lookout for authentic-
sounding names for his characters. He tells his friend Wynn
(*NL* I, pp. 137–38) in July 1797 that all 'long speeches,
catalogues of armies or navies, geographical descriptions,
shield paintings, lists of killed and wounded' and other aspects
of Homeric and post-Homeric epic will be excluded from
Madoc, but:

> I wish you would pick me out from the Royal Commen-
> taries of Peru if you meet with them or indeed where ever
> you can, a Peruvian mans name fit for poetry. I have
> enough Mexican ones, and am somewhat puzled to lick
> the ladies into shape. What think you of Atotoztli and
> Tziltomiauh? These are perfect beauties compared with
> Tlacapantzin and Ilancueith etc. I must spell it Ziltomia
> and its physiognomy is bearable.

It is easy to sense Southey's real, playful, delight in this kind of
pursuit, his sheer enjoyment of the strangeness of names and
indeed the naming process. But these prototypes do not augur
well for readability, as they slow down or halt the eye on the
page—and they do not sound well either. Southey's quest to
create a poem of convincing authenticity, carried with it the
danger of leading him away from poetry itself, relying too
much upon external information in the process of creation.

> I long to see North Wales and to become familiar with its
> scenery. The first sketch of *Madoc*, for I look upon it as
> not much more, draws to its conclusion, and I may
> perhaps have the whole outline to show you in May. In

the first books I have spoken of Snowden and Cader Idris, and that is all. Careless and hasty as I am thought in my writings I would willingly go to Orleans to enable myself to describe its situation—and take the journey from Aberffraw to Mathrafal—thence to Dinevor and back to Aberffraw for the same purpose. (*NL* I, p. 183, March 1799)

Southey in fact spent the latter part of September 1801 walking with Wynn around the Welsh countryside in which part of *Madoc* is set. This touring impulse was perhaps not so detrimental to the making of a poem as is the plundering of books[6] and archives, whose lack the poet had lamented in September 1797 (*NL* I, p. 145) whilst writing the third book of the epic.

2
Southey's Tropes:
The Broken Nation as Broken Family
Woe for the house of Owen! (*F* p. 462)

I would open a reading of *Madoc* by saying that no one who perseveres with the poem is likely to forget the experience. The narrative is full of vivid and striking passages, and also contains barbaric horrors (previously noted in respect to *Poems* 1799) which Southey seemed to delight in and excel at. Unspeakable horror gives licence to the annihilating sword and cause of the hero. What Southey has created in *Madoc* is in fact a remarkable film-script, over a century before such film plots could be captured and replayed. Just as Bantok made a musical score from *The Curse of Kehama*, we have to acknowledge the film industry's witting or unwitting debt to epic adventure tales like *Madoc*. Perhaps this says something about Southey's way of writing, relying heavily upon a *visuality* which is the subtext of the poetry. Many encounters with the Aztecs or Indians found in *Madoc* are now clichés that moving pictures have long employed: drunken natives, the ordeal of the hero or the hero as sacrifice, unfamiliar or bloodthirsty religious rites, violent battle-scenes, volcanic conflagration, and overall, contemporary ideology set within the narrative.

In *Madoc*, we can still perceive the typical interests of the poet expanded upon an epic stage, which may be interpreted as comments upon the backdrop of revolution and war, and indeed, the spectre of personal longings, over the period 1794–1805. By 1800, after Bonaparte's climb to power, Southey could say 'Damn the French!' (*CA* p. 55), and after the Peace of Amiens of 1802, he was famously returned (*W* III, p. 302) to sympathy with his country, and increasingly an implacable foe of Bonaparte's empire which had finally translated France into an aggressive imperial nation bent upon massive conquest. The bloody Revolution and its piles of heads was really a savage precondition of absolute power of this Napoleon I, who by 1805 had crowned himself Emperor of the French and made himself King of Italy.

The family of the deceased Owen Gwynaeth king of North Wales suggests the struggle of the factions during the French Revolution and beyond. The new king David hunts down, kills and imprisons his fraternal rivals in the struggle for succession. He then proceeds to marry a Saxon woman ('the Plantagenet!', *F* p. 462) in order to unite the two nations, a manoeuvre seen as political suicide by *Madoc*. 'Saxon yoke' (*F* p. 500) is then really Norman yoke in *Madoc*. The 'sword of civil war' (*F* p. 468) has fractured the family ties of the true Britons, the Welsh, and if we bring to mind epic forbears of this poem, we might remember the anathema in which the Roman writers of the age of Augustus held civil war.

If David's 'Saxon' bride (like another Homeric Helen) is seen as the metaphorical wooden horse which will complete the overthrow of the Welsh, then Madoc himself is like another Aeneas looking for his new nation home. Civil war is 'impious', a favourite Southeyan word (*F* p. 467, l. 28), recalling the *pietas* typical of Aeneas himself in opposition to this. Madoc, like the Roman/Trojan founding father, is a 'perfect Prince' (*F* p. 522), appalled at the 'shame and guilt of that unhappy strife, / Briton with Briton in unnatural war' (*F* p. 468), but unlike Aeneas is also (*F* p. 533) a 'Christian Prince'. The plight of the Welsh is romantically drawn:

> Alas, our crimes
> Have drawn this dolorous visitation down!
> Our sun hath long been westering; and the night
> And darkness and extinction are at hand.
> We are a fallen people! . . . From ourselves
> The desolation and ruin come;
> In our own vitals doth the poison work . . .
> The House that is divided in itself,
> How should it stand? (*F* p. 492)

The sense of ruin is compounded by the scenes where Madoc stands by his brother Yorwerth's grave (p. 496) and by his meeting with a war widow Llaian (p. 510), his brother Hoel's mistress. Madoc disinters his father Owen in order to take his body to America as a gesture of the preservation of freedom (p. 514) symbolized by the king himself, like the idealized king (p. 470) 'immortal Arthur', who upheld freedom in the idealized ancient kingdom. Madoc, being of 'Arthur's line', must uphold this freedom, or surrender his birthright.

Pantisocratic Spectres, True Pariots

Madoc's return to Wales at the beginning of the epic, gives Southey the chance to make stirring tales about the crossing of the ocean and the American lands themselves. Distance, danger and unfamiliarity conspire with the fact that a contingent of known Welsh people await his return to America in setting up a kind of yearning in the text for reunification of the parties. Madoc describes America thus:

> Many moons
> Have wax'd and waned, since from that distant world,
> The country of my dreams and faith,
> We spread the homeward sail: a goodly world
> My Sister! thou wilt see its goodliness
> And greet Cadwallon there . . . (*F* p. 466)

The spectre of the Pantisocratic nation is here enshrined in the text, transformed and retold in the historical settings chosen for it by the poet. Southey's 'worlds beyond the sea' (p. 467) set into *Madoc* are essentially the topics of 1794–95 pushed into narrative. Cadwallon gave Madoc the desire for voyage:

> What meanest thou?
> I cried . . . That yonder waters are not spread
> A boundless waste, a bourne impassable! . . .
> That man should rule the Elements! . . . that there
> Might manly courage, manly wisdom find
> Some happy isle, some undiscovered shore,
> Some resting place for peace . . . Oh that my soul
> Could seize the wings of Morning! soon would I
> Behold that other world, where yonder sun
> Speeds now, to dawn in glory! (*F* pp. 471–72)

This land is further celebrated by druidical conversation after the Gorsedd in I, XI, as the place where 'Plenty dwelt with Liberty and Peace', the opposite image of Britain both in the 1790s and under Madoc's brother David. Madoc assesses the cost of this second expedition in terms of total exile (p. 506) from 'the Green Isle' of Britain.

The first meeting of the Hoamen and the Welsh is painted as an idyll of admiration and wonder, but holds within it the tension associated with narratives of exploration and conquest. Southey appears to be interested in ideas of racial purity:

> To the shore
> The natives throng'd; astonish'd, they beheld

Our winged barks, and gazed with wonderment
On the strange garb, the bearded countenance
And the white skin, in all unlike themselves.
I see with what enquiring eyes you ask
What men were they? Of dark brown colour, tinged
With sunny redness; wild of eye; their brows
So smooth, as never yet anxiety
Nor busy thought had made a furrow there;
Beardless, and each to each of lineaments
So like, they seem'd but one great family,
Their loins were loosely cinctured, all beside
Bare to the sun and wind; and thus their limbs
Unmanacled display'd the truest forms
Of strength and beauty. Fearless sure they were,
And while they eyed us grasp'd their spears, as if,
Like Britain's injured but unconquer'd sons,
They too had known how perilous it was
To let a stranger, if he came in arms,
Set foot upon their land. (*F* p. 476)

The analogy is drawn between Welsh authenticity and Indian strength, beauty and apparent familial harmony. The Indians are what the Pantisocratic family could have been. True Britishness seems to overflow its Welshness and spread out into a Southeyan patriotism which his Madoc articulates.

. . . Madoc replied, Barbarians as we are
Lord Prelate, we received the law of Christ
Many a long age before your pirate sires
Had left their forest dens; nor are we now
To learn that law from Norman or from Dane,
Saxon, Jute, Angle, or whatever name
Suit best your mongrel race! (*F* p. 512)

Racial purity is here emphasized, in what can be regarded as a xenophobic passage. Is this Southey's or Madoc's? The anti-papal sentiments further in the same speech against 'the yoke /

Of Rome' certainly smack of the poet's own views. Indeed it is from this 'foul indignity of Romish pride' (*F* p. 533) that the body of king Owen, the dead father, is transported away. The Welsh, or true British, kingdom is shown as the polluted land, a cadaverous body of ruined fatherhood, unfit for the bones of Owen's line. Hence Madoc's desire for a new kingdom, where at one stroke he will cleanse away family feuds, civil war, the blood of brothers and friends, and all the threats of slavery under the various yokes of Rome and the invader.

Southey's happy land recalls his earliest reveries upon the Kentucky backwoods, but it is translated into 'Caermadoc' the militarized stronghold of the emigrant Welsh:

> Here had the Chief
> Chosen his abiding place, for strength preferr'd,
> Where vainly might an host in equal arms
> Attempt the difficult entrance; and for all
> That could delight the eye and heart of man;
> Whate'er of beauty or of usefulness
> Heart could desire, or eye behold, being here.
> What he had found an idle wilderness
> Now gave rich increase to the husbandmen,
> For Heaven had blest their labour. Flourishing
> He left the happy vale; and now he saw
> More fields reclaim'd, more habitations rear'd,
> More harvests rising round. The reptile race,
> And every beast of rapine, had retired
> From man's asserted empire; and the sound
> Of axe and dashing oar, and fisher's net,
> And song beguiling toil, and pastoral pipe,
> Were heard, where late the solitary hills
> Gave only to the mountain-cataract
> Their wild response. (*F* p. 523)

How changed is Southey's solitary Cowleyan reverie and his desire to emancipate black slaves associated with the proto-typical Pantisocratic scheme. Axe and snake remain from the earlier vision, but community or indeed 'asserted empire' has replaced individual retreat, with the additional military capabilities, crops, houses, and the promise of expanding fortunes. What in 1794 was seen as a simple assertive act of buying land in order to farm and write books, now looks like a maturer vision of military expansion, colonization, with the Christian God as guarantor that every drop of blood shed for the righteous cause will not count against the invader. If we can view *Madoc* as not merely a good adventure story, but as the poem Southey held closest to his heart, is it fair to interpret the tale as his epical political and social manifesto, as I have begun to do? It is very difficult to rescue the tale from the teller without losing a large area of valid interpretative possibility.

Southey interests us by his historical researches, his vivid epical tableaux. He revolts and appalls by some of his episodes of barbarity. Madoc the hero fails to persuade us into sympathy with his cause, mainly because, as the critics have indicated, he largely remains psychologically aloof ready to exact his punishments and revenges. One feels as if Southey drew Madoc not objectively as a fully-formed character with an individual life, but from a selection of laws or principles. Madoc, as hero, is a series of unjoined dots composed of prejudices and reactions, and of melodramatic postures. Whatever Southey meant by Madoc, his hero's actions leave the reader uneasy. It is no longer acceptable to condone invasion, religious conversion, or meddling in the military struggles of other races because our world picture is steeped in the bloodshed and misery resulting from similar ideological and anti-ecological ventures. Nowhere is safe, as Jonathan Bate in his excellent *Romantic Ecology* has shown.[7] Even the massive American land in which Southey, Coleridge and Madoc were to flourish, is no longer a grand image of natural ecological permanence; it has already been conquered and plundered. Madoc's American colony begins by seeing Nature as pure and bountiful, supplying trees, birds and fish for the taking—nearly two centuries later we have lists of extinct animals and birds to set against this, not to mention the names only of lost and brutalized Indian tribes. The 'heroic Spaniard's unrelenting sword' (*F* p. 608) was of course already well-known to the poet, and is Southey's remedy to the 'foul idolatry' of the Aztecs who are now vanished forever. Southey's epic leaves the reader sick and uneasy. If Madoc's flight from Wales has optimism, Madoc's barely disguised imperial agenda is in the late twentieth century a story which does not warrant rehearsal. The rise and fragmentation of empires is a human trope which has outlived its validity. Other tales need to be told.

The Imperial Trope and the Fascination of Horrors

> he placed
> The falchion in my hand, and gave the shield,
> And pointed south and west, that I should go
> To conquer and protect. (*F* p. 478)

In the above passage, Lincoya urges Madoc to vengeance for the Aztecan religious and military tyranny over the Hoamen. He is essentially asking the Welsh colonists to act as mercenaries, as did the Saxon pirates in post-Roman Britain, to emulate what Madoc purportedly abhors (*F* p. 512): 'Saxon, Jute, Angle, or whatever name / Suit best your mongrel race!' Madoc assumes the anti-Pantisocratic role of being God's sword against the religion and culture of the barbarian. Admittedly the Aztecas practise human sacrifice, but does that mean that they must be exterminated or converted? Whose ideology is the right one? This question is also central to Conrad's *Heart of Darkness*, and is part of the serious challenge of that novel. Is it possible for western readers to make the imaginative leap into a state in which human sacrifice is a normal event? How many readers would dare to do that? Very few indeed. The question cannot be seriously asked because our society recoils from it or laughs at it. But this is

exactly the point where human sacrifice in the disguise of
imperialism or war comes into being.

Madoc's foes are shown militarily and culturally as having
great strength, imperial strength against which the small
numbers of Welsh and Indians are opposed. This fact is
supposed to add to Madoc's righteous cause:

> There Aztlan stood upon the farther shore:
> Amid the shade of trees its dwellings rose,
> Their level roofs with turrets set around,
> And battlements all burnish'd white, which shone
> Like silver in the sunshine. I beheld
> The imperial city, her far-circling walls,
> Her garden groves and stately palaces,
> Her temple's mountain-size, her thousand roofs;
> And when I saw her might and majesty
> My mind misgave me then. (*F* p. 481)

Here is a complete civilization set up for the hero to fight his
holy war against. Not only that, once inside Aztlan, Madoc
gains inspiration from his God, toying with the idea of
presenting himself as an immortal before the Aztecas (*F*
p. 482), relishing the effect this has upon his audience, but in
the end claiming not divinity but 'knowledge' as his power.
Madoc is no Mr Kurtz. The piles of human skulls and heads in
the city are one deciding factor for the Prince to take arms
against this (ideologically incorrect) civilization. Faint echoes
of the French Revolutionary Terror spring to mind here—
Robespierre's near-religious head-hunting lust perhaps.
Robespierre's desire to cleanse the state of France is also
echoed in Madoc's crusade against the black arts of Aztecan
religion. Madoc offers the king of Aztlan friendship (*F* p. 483)
once the Aztecan religion has been purged clean. War is
inevitable, and the Welsh boast of their advantage:

> . . . what the thin gold hauberk, when opposed
> To arms like ours in battle? What the mail

Of wood fire-harden'd, or the wooden helm,
Against the iron arrows of the South,
Against our northern spears, or battle-axe,
Or god sword, wielded by a British hand? (*F* p. 484)

This passage could be seen either as poetry or as propaganda. It is one small step from seeing 'British' as Welsh to British as those people in the British Isles who are enemies of Napoleon, 'iron men, impassable' (*F* p. 485) suddenly united against one person rather than chimerical Revolutionary principles. Southey seems to take a pride in his descriptions of the 'bowmen of Deheubarth' and the spearmen of Gwyneth. He inadvertently draws attention to the essential place that Welsh archers had in later English victories such as Agincourt. And as in Shakespeare's propagandizing of that campaign, the Welsh in this epic use God as the scourge of 'impiety' (*F* p. 489), as the guarantor of victory. America is the chosen land, whether the indigenous people like it or not, for the Aenean impulse focuses upon the prize of 'nature' which those people possess:

There I return, to take thee to our home.
I love my native land; with as true love
As ever yet did warm a British heart,
Love I the green fields of the beautiful Isle,
My father's heritage! But far away,
Where nature's booner hand has blest the earth,
My lot has been assign'd; beyond the seas
Madoc hath found his home; beyond the seas
A country for his children hath he chosen,
A land where their portion may be peace. (*F* p. 491)

If at the core of this picture is the spectre of the Pantisocratic venture, then the unfolding of *Madoc* suggests the real cost of such a venture. Madoc's new home may be far from the paternal heritage of the beautiful Isle, with its 'cold king-craft' (*F* p. 492), but it may also bring the longed-for peace which

Southey's hero desires. Though the emigrants do free the
Hoamen from their 'wretched yoke' (F p. 525), they are
unabashed 'colonists' (F p. 527), whose 'Ocean Prince' has the
'Beloved Teacher' (F p. 529) on his side and in the heads and
hearts of the converted Hoamen.

The enemy-god is a snake that demands an endless supply of
human blood, described with relish by the poet:

> Whereat from that dark temple issued forth
> A Serpent, huge and hideous. On he came,
> Straight to the sound, and curl'd round the Priest
> His mighty folds innocuous, over-topping
> His human height, and arching down his head,
> Sought in the hands of Neolin for food;
> Then questing, rear'd and stretch'd and waved his neck,
> And glanced his forky tongue. Who then had seen
> The man, with what triumphant fearlessness,
> Arms, thighs, and neck, and body, wreathed and ring'd
> In those tremendous folds, he stood secure,
> Play'd with the reptile's jaws, and call'd for food,
> Food for the present God! (F p. 537)

Southey here partly recalls the horror of the Laocoon episode
from Virgil's *Aeneid* Bk II, where the priest and Neptune's
sons are devoured by serpents who enfold them all in their
coils. This allusion is continued when (F p. 538) an eight-year-
old boy is whirled around by the snake-man Neolin and
thrown to the serpent who carries him off to eat him in its den.
This is only one example of what we might call Southey's
literary child abuse.[8] The snake-god draws together Edenic
symbolism and classical Python myths, evoking a fundamental human loathing and, of course, in post-Freudian terms it
suggests Southey's covert sexual symbolism. He devotes the
best part of one chapter *The Snake God* to the description of
the annihilation of this reptile. Initially (piling symbol upon
symbol) Madoc bends his sword upon the beast's 'unyielding
skin' (F p. 540), and has to pursue it into 'Cave within cave'

(*F* p. 541) where a snake-idol is situated and beyond which the real serpent hides. The pursuers vote to 'hem him in with fire' and 'crush him'. Madoc drives out the beast with arrows, posing like Apollo in Bk I of Ovid's *Metamorphoses* at the slaying of Python. Once trapped under boulders the snake is helpless:

> In suffocating gulps the monster now
> Inhales its own life-blood. The Prince descends;
> He lifts another lance; and now the Snake,
> Gasping, as if exhausted, on the ground
> Reclines his head one moment. Madoc seized
> That moment, planted in its eye the spear,
> Then setting foot upon his neck, drove down
> Through bone and brain and throat, and to the earth
> Infixed the mortal weapon. Yet once more
> The Snake essay'd to rise; his dying strength
> Fail'd him, nor longer did those mighty folds
> Obey the moving impulse, crush'd and scotch'd;
> In every ring, through all his mangled length,
> The shrinking muscles quiver'd, then collapsed
> In death. (*F* p. 542)

If this is entertainment, an epical set-piece, then it is overdone, cruel, appealing to rather sadistic depths in Southey's readership. But the snake is a necessary manifestation of the kind of paganism that he wants us to abhor, and who could possibly have sympathy for a serpent or those who worshipped such a monster? Was not a snake responsible for the fall of mankind? Southey's allusive parade continues after the ceremony of purification to where the Hoamen are converted to Christianity. Madoc has 'hyacinthine locks' (*F* p. 543) just like Milton's Adam of *Paradise Lost* Bk IV, l. 301. The new Adam, converting a tribe of Indians? There is something faintly ridiculous about this but it does fit very well with the residue of millennial hopes in *Madoc*. American soil represented as a new Eden over which the 'righteous sword' (*F* p. 545) of the

Prince is waved. This Eden, is, as an Aztec captive states, not easily kept. Peace will have to be bought in blood:

> Seek ye peace? . . .
> Not with the burial of the sword this strife
> Must end, for never doth the Tree of Peace
> Strike root and flourish, till the strong man's hand
> Upon his enemy's grave hath planted it. (*F* p. 546)

Even the 'British women' (*F* p. 571) are forced to join in the fight when Madoc's party is away on the campaign and the camp is attacked. Again, this is true movie-style action, with the maid Goervyl supporting the injured Malinal, drawing out an arrow from his arm, then stabbing the same arrow through the hand of a savage from a treacherous band of Hoamen led by the drink-loving Amalahta. Southey indulges his violent imagination in a further description (*F* p. 572) of Goervyl wielding a spear at Amalahta, which 'plough'd up / The whole scalp-length'. Amalahta is hamstrung, throttled, and finally stabbed in the groin by Malinal who wields Madoc's sword. Goervyl is then told:

> Yea, daughter of Aberfraw, take thou hope!
> For Madoc lives! . . . he lives to wield the sword
> Of righteous vengeance, and accomplish all. (*F* p. 573)

Madoc's force takes its 'righteous slaughter' (*F* p. 580) to the very temple precincts 'so often which had reek'd with innocent blood', smashing their idol Mexitli. It might have ended there, but Southey drags out his tale further to show the crowning of a new Aztecan king in II, XIX, and the arrival of a maniacal priest Tezozomoc, who demands human sacrifices to 'purify the nation' (*F* p. 585) like some Robespierrian villain. The idol Mexitli magically reforms itself (*F* p. 587) as if to suggest the ever-present principle of evil in Madoc's blood-soaked world. The destructive nature of the Welsh Prince's initiative is well described:

Aztlan, meantime, presents a hideous scene
Of slaughter. The hot sunbeam, in her streets,
Parch'd the blood pools; the slain were heap'd in hills;
The victors, stretch'd in every little shade,
With unhelm'd heads, reclining on their shields,
Slept the deep sleep of weariness. Ere long,
To needful labour rising, from the gates
They drag the dead; and with united toil,
They dig upon the plain the general grave,
The grave of thousands, deep and wide and long.
Ten such they delved, and o'er the multitudes
Who levell'd with the plain the deep-dug pits,
Ten monumental hills they heap'd on high.
Next horror heightening joy, they overthrew
The skull-built towers, the files of human heads,
And earth to earth consign'd them. To the flames
They cast the idols, upon the wind
Scatter'd their ashes; then the temples fell,
Whose black and putrid walls were scaled with blood,
And not one stone of those accursed piles
Was on another left. (*F* p. 588)

Madoc is now given the title of the 'White King' (*F* p. 592) a
title based around an uneasy racial difference, as the 'Cross of
Christ' is raised over Aztlan's towers. But it is clear that one
city taken is only a fraction of the Aztecan empire. Madoc is
offered terms of settlement but is defiant. A fleet is constructed of 'British barks' (*F* p. 595), aping in some degree the
British sea-power of the early nineteenth century, giving rise
to a gruesome fight on a lake (*F* p. 594ff) in which 'the strong
bark of Britain over all / Sails in the path of death'. Perhaps it is
at this point that the modern reader becomes exhausted.
Southey's plot could presumably continue until every Aztecan
life is over. Is there also some indication of the poet's own
fatigue with his creation? The volcanic eruption (used so often
in modern film-sequences) in II, XXVI, which annihilates

Tezozomoc and his thousands, seems to indicate the necessity
of a deus ex machina which will save Madoc the trouble of
raising his over-weary sword-arm again. Madoc emerges in
the last chapter of the epic out of an apocalyptic lava landscape
worthy of the painter John Martin. The Aztecan remnants of
the eruption crawl from the lake water and regroup like Satan
and his subordinates upon Hell's burning marl. King Yuhid-
thiton watches the refugees (*F* p. 604) and accepts that the
'Gods are leagued' with Madoc's forces, and he decides to
migrate with the remainder of his folk. Tlalala the warrior falls
upon his javelin in true epic style, though unlike Turnus in the
Aeneid he is not killed *by* the hero but is a suicide. This death
in the final moments of *Madoc* adds to the unsatisfactory tone
of the whole. It is merely a badly-staged convenience.

Southey's Barbarous Romanticism: Some Doubts

Madoc tells the tale of the fragmentation of an ancient royal
house of Wales, the discovery of America, and the initial
military struggles to conquer the Indians and Aztecas, to
convert them to Christianity, and to secure Welsh colonial
interests in their lands. That is Southey's tale told in a few lines
and I have assumed in my brief reading that Southey condoned
his hero's actions. I have also implied that *Madoc* reflects
Southey's own political development and mixes his ideas and
hopes from 1794 onwards. Having tried to discover what
Southey meant by *Madoc*, I have of course to admit that this
may be the very thing that eludes the critic forever. Bernhardt-
Kabisch believes that *Madoc* is instantly available to the
exegete:

> The celestial gleam of Pantisocracy, after first retreating
> from America to Wales, not only faded to the light of
> common domesticity and the bourgeois symbiosis of
> Greta Hall but gradually turned into the glare of an
> unabashed colonialism . . . [*Madoc* is] Southey's epic of

foundation—his answer to the *Aeneid* and particularly to the *Lusiad*, then recently translated by Julius Mickle and recommended by him to English readers as 'The Epic Poem of the Birth of Commerce' and colonialism. (*K* p. 111)

Is it as straightforward as this? Is *Madoc* a demonstration of belief in the expansion of empire and the condonement of all that entails? Is the epic just a historical tale of adventure and horror to thrill Southey's readership by their respective firesides? What does Southey mean when he remarks (*NL* I, p. 113) in July 1796 that by *Madoc* he 'may benefit the future'? Does he merely expect financial gain by the work, as I have already shown, or was there another facet to his expectations? Are we, because of historical hindsight alone, forced into a reading of *Madoc* as a *cautionary tale*, a story which, far from condoning the colonial/imperial tendencies of human civilizations and their use of religions to condone atrocities, exposes the never-ending human and natural cost of inter-cultural struggles for territories and resources? Was that what Southey intended? Do Southey's Welsh colonists in *Madoc* show the struggle of a God-fearing band of emigrants against the barbarous practices of Aztlan, or do they show how one set of beliefs brings war and ruin to another set of beliefs?

Adding to these doubts, Southey's textual allusiveness in at least two points in the epic is drawn from very inappropriate sources. The blind Cynetha (*F* p. 489) asks the Aztecas whether or not they recognize the Christian God: 'Know ye not Him who laid / The deep foundations of the earth?' It is an odd detail, because it echoes Milton's Satan in *Paradise Lost* IV, ll. 827–28: 'Know ye not then said Satan, filld with scorn / Know ye not me?' Whether this can be seen to undermine Southey's intentions in his portrayal of the divine is questionable, but it remains odd that Satanic pronouncements should inform the discourse of a Welsh emigrant speaking about his

God. Similarly inappropriate is the discourse of the intended
sacrifice to the Snake-god, Ayayaca:

> At once all eager eyes were fix'd on him,
> But he came forward calmly at the call;
> Lo! here am I! quoth he; and from his head
> Plucking the grey hairs he dealt them round . . .
> Countrymen, kinsmen, brethren, children, take
> These in remembrance of me! (*F* p. 538)

The final sentence here directly echoes part of the Anglican
communion service at its most sacred point, the sharing out of
the symbolic bread and wine:

> Hear us, O merciful Father, we most humbly beseech
> thee; and grant that we receiving these thy creatures of
> bread and wine, according to thy Son our Saviour Jesus
> Christ's holy institution, in remembrance of his death
> and passion, may be partakers of his most blessed Body
> and Blood: who, in the same night that he was betrayed,
> took Bread; and when he had given thanks, he brake it,
> and gave it to his disciples saying, Take, eat, this is my
> Body which is given for you: Do this in remembrance of
> me.[9]

Southey's apparent impiety here is at odds with the Christian
righteousness of Madoc and his followers, even if he wants to
show Ayayaca as the final (and passive) victim of Aztlan,
someone going meekly to death like Christ himself. Perhaps
finally we have to take the poet's word about his creation, and
accept that he intended to show the Aztecas in a bad light:

> The plan upon which I proceeded in Madoc was to
> produce the effect of machinery as far as was consistent
> with the character of the poem, by representing the most
> remarkable religion of the New World such as it was, a
> system of atrocious priest-craft. (*PW* VIII, p. xv)

3
Reviews

The review articles which greeted the publication of the poem drew some attention, as here (*M* p. 103) in the *Monthly Review* for October 1805, to Southey's choice of names:

> *Goervyl* and *Ririd* and *Rodri* and *Llaian* may have charms for Cambrian ears, but who can feel an interest in *Tezozomoc*, *Tlalala*, or *Ocelopan*? . . . how could we swallow *Yuhidthiton*, *Coanocotzin*, and, above all the yawning jaw-dislocating *Ayayaca*? . . . Mr. Southey's defence . . . is that the names are conformable to history or analogy . . . but it is not requisite to tread so closely in the traces of barbarity. Truth does not constitute the essence of poetry: but it is indispensably necessary that the lines should be agreeable to the ear, as well as to the sense.

Ferriar went on to damn the whole poem as a waste of exertion and as the most severe trial his patience ever endured. But as an obvious follower of Pope, what else could he have said? Bridling at barbarity and at the foreign or alien quality of the poem's nomenclature indicates an unwillingness to engage with the rather savage world of the poem. Indeed, the *Eclectic Review* for December 1805 (*M* pp. 106–07) thought that the 'leading character of the poem is *horror*' and that 'Mr. S. seems enamoured of any thing either very old, or very new-fashioned, so that it be only out of the common way'. The reviewer expresses disgust at the primitive societies described by Southey:

> The manners, and minor historical facts, are most barbarously romantic. At so much snake-worship; so much human sacrifice; at such diabolical painting of savages; and such deification of a marauder, possibly almost as savage as the Indians themselves; at such eulogia on

human nature in one case, and such libels on it in the other, we turn away disgusted . . . The poem closes with an act of the most premeditated suicide by an American chief; a very favourite catastrophe with modern poets: and the hero, Madoc, being thus delivered from his last implacable foe, is left with his followers, in peaceable possession of a domain, which the natives had been miraculously deterred from attempting to recover . . .

It is as if Southey's shock-tactics have scored against polite society to the extent that the reviewer has had to look away. If the poet wanted in this way to show war and conquest in terms of horror, then he succeeded in some measure. The Words-worths enjoyed the poem, however. William (*M* p. 100) repeatedly praised the 'beautiful pictures and descriptions' but thought *Madoc* failed both imaginatively and in the real understanding of the human heart, and that 'Southey's mind does not seem strong enough to draw the picture of a hero'. Dorothy Wordsworth was delighted with *Madoc*, but could not respond to the hero in the way that she sensed the author wished. She thought (*M* pp. 101–02) that Southey's characters did not claim that 'separate after-existence' in her affections that she desired.

As you observe the descriptions are often exceedingly beautiful,—they are like resting-places both for repose and delight. The language occasionally, nay frequently gave me pain, and mostly in cases where it seemed that a very little trouble might have removed the faults. I have not the Book here or I would take down a few of those expressions which I complain of. They are a sort of barbarisms which appear to belong to Southey himself.[10]

The *Literary Journal* (*M* pp. 100–10) thought of these barbarisms as 'blemishes in the language' or 'unusual and forced expressions', the effect of simplicity running into vulgarity not in contextual harmony with the moment, and amounting to stylistic incorrectness. Southey's subject, language and style had therefore acted against his cherished *Madoc* and put barriers between him and his poetic audience. *Madoc* was further evidence of the bizarre road Southey had taken away from the intentions of *Lyrical Ballads* and the linguistic clarity of that volume, especially in Wordsworth's productions. His comments to Bedford (*NL* I, p. 418, 22 March 1806) are scarcely believable in the textual light of *Madoc*:

> When you and I dispute about poetry we argue from different premises. I wish you would buy *Lyrical Ballads*—if you have them not already. You will see in the Preface and Postscript my critical creed. Since the days of Pope our poetical language has been systematically barbarized.

Southey had gone his own way, whatever he told Bedford, down a strange and unique literary path.

NOTES

1 *Critical Review*, June 1796, *M* p. 45, on *Joan of Arc*.

2 Kenneth Curry, 'Southey's *Madoc*: The Manuscript of 1794', *Philological Quarterly* XXII, IV, October 1943, pp. 347–69.

3 *Ibid.*, p. 369.

4 *NL* I, p. 520. Curry translates this as 'I write-write-write to what end? The public did not buy. I'll no doubt wipe my backside with Thalaba, Madoc and Kehama . . . I borrow and borrow from Longman. The Long Man is a good man, he allows me to borrow, denying nothing. He has enough in his hand to settle everything at last. It is certainly inconvenient, but I believe that other booksellers would give me a good sum of money for any new work, but I am not able to go to them because I am obligated in this way to the Long Man.'

5 See *Byron's Letters and Journals*, ed. Leslie A. Marchand (London: John Murray, 1973/1981), Vol. III, p. 101. Byron is commenting upon Southey's eastern epics.

6 See also *LC* II, p. 14: 'I have picked up an epic poem in French, on the discovery of America, which will help out in the notes to *Madoc* . . .'

7 See Jonathan Bate, *Romantic Ecology: Wordsworth and the Environmental Tradition* (London and New York: Routledge, 1991), p. 34.

8 Another example of this is the placing of the child Hoel in a cave in Part II, XII. Hoel is left to die by the Aztecas, but rescued by one Coatel. The horror of the situation is quite unpleasantly protracted as the woman has to leave the child before fetching help.

9 See *The Book of Common Prayer* (London: Cambridge University Press, as proposed 1928), p. 349.

10 Examples of Southey's 'barbarisms' include: 'Fitlier habilments of javelin-proof!' (*F* p. 465, l. 49), 'These were lip-lavish of their friendship now' (p. 525, l. 145), 'his dizzy eyes / Roll'd with a sleepy swim.' (p. 532, ll. 122–23), 'aknee they fell before / the Prince' (p. 542, l. 230). We might also include in this list such unpoetical words as 'dight', 'volant', and 'gossampine' from the early lines of chapter XV (p. 566) of 'Madoc in Aztlan'.

Epilogue

1

Witold Rybczynski's survey of the idea of home[1] draws attention to the fact that by 1800, a household interior had become a personal retreat for the occupants. For Robert Southey, personal retreat included space for books, a study in which he could write poetry, prepare editions, reviews, articles and produce any other work he could fit in. Perhaps his greatest unspoken fear was of being subjected to an English revolution in which his books and his personal space were taken from him and destroyed. This kind of fear was present even after at least twenty-five years of retreat at Keswick:

> I was born during the American Revolution, the French Revolution broke out just as I grew up, and my latter days will, in all likelihood, be disturbed by a third revolution, more terrible than either. (*LC* VI, p. 75)

What would Southey have been without his books? That he was sentenced to spin out his brains by writing, I have tried to indicate in my study: no home for Southey might literally mean no livelihood, no place, no intellectual space or property in post-revolutionary England. What I have also hinted at is the political upheavals which a servant of the Penates, 'whose inclinations cling so obstinately to the hearth-stone' (*W* I, p. 232), endured. Southey's home, his territory, especially after his Laureatship was conferred, linked him, however tenuously, to Burke:

> The Burkean positives are family affections and loyalties, hearth and home, a hierarchy with the king at its head; and continuity with the past, especially with the inherited creed which it is the Church's business to preserve.[2]

Longing for, and achieving, the continuity or stability of a home in time of revolution, is the first step towards a reconciliation with the grander domestic politics of a nation. If Burke stood for national stability in the face of revolution, Southey sought personal stability in spite of it. Southey's psychology needed the enkernelling of retreat but harboured desires to lash out. If he had, as William Taylor of Norwich (*R* I, p. 256) believed, 'a mimosa-sensibility, which agonises in so slight a blast', it was not the only predominant aspect of the poet's character:

> I intend to be a hedge-hog and roll myself up in my own prickles: all I regret is that I am not a porcupine, and endowed with the property of shooting them to annoy the beasts who come near enough to annoy me. (*CB* p. 44, 18 January 1798)

This is the householder's voice, full of fear and suspicion (and humour), blustering, but perhaps not dangerous, once the outer defences are down. Southey extended his metaphors of self to a representation of the state:

> The holly-tree, an emblem, and somewhat in Quarles's way. Kingdoms should be like it, fenced well, but only strict there; men gentler at home than anywhere else. (*CB* p. 193)

Even his other emblem of the self, the boiling well, has this forbidding duality (*W* I, pp. 270–71, 1804), but in reverse:

> Coleridge is gone for Malta, and his departure affects me more than I let it be seen. Let what will trouble me, I bear a calm face; and if the Boiling Well could be drawn (which, however it heaves and is agitated below, presents a smooth, undisturbed surface), that should be my emblem.

This emblem is also descriptive of the stoical curb upon action, in order to bear misfortune, or fear, without flinching.

Southey's rigid impassivity (like a neo-classical facade), when extended to his desires on the political scene after settling at Keswick, recalls again that implicit conservatism detected at the root of the Pantisocratic scheme and at the core of *Joan of Arc*. We could say cynically that after Southey had got his desired home, or its surrogate at Keswick, then anyone violently disturbing the peace was condemned by him. It seems as if he wanted the political stage to become as calm and untroubled as the way he presented himself to the world. But his desire for peace and stability provoked remarks like the following:

> But to return to the Luddites. The danger is of the most imminent kind. I would hang about a score in a county, and send off ship loads to Botany Bay; and if there were no other means of checking the treasonable practises which are carried on in the Sunday newspapers, I would suspend the Habeas Corpus. Shut up these bellows-blowers, and the fire may, perhaps, go out. (*W* II, p. 274, 12 May 1812)

Southey's desire for the domestic hearth seems, then, to have courted the metaphor of burial, stasis, death, and introspection. His own fire had gone out after he had himself once been among 'bellows-blowers' (as Shelley found when he visited him at Keswick), although Southey had perhaps sided more with the Girondists, the reformers, than the violent revolutionaries. The poet of the *Botany Bay Eclogues* of 1794, the man who, as Jonathan Wordsworth notes in his introduction to the facsimile of *Poems 1797* was then wondering what it *felt like* to be transported, had by 1812 apparently withdrawn this empathy. Southey's desirably static picture of England seen from Keswick, could do without the Luddites.

In the years between the end of the chronology of my study and Southey's residence at Keswick, an emergent sense of conservative and xenophobic Englishness (already glimpsed in some of his remarks from the Portugal trip of 1795–96) is plain in his attitudes to other nations. When in 1801 he took a post as private secretary to a Mr Corry, Chancellor of the Exchequer for Ireland,[3] he viewed the Irish as little better than savages and compared his experience with what he knew of Portugal:

> The filth of the houses is intolerable,—floors and furniture offending you with Portuguese nastiness. (*LC* II, p. 169, 16 October 1801)

He saw the Irish as comic aboriginals, dangerously uncivilized, yet worthy of a social experiment to bring them into line. This was perhaps a harsher Southey than the man of the Westbury period, his great naturalistic year. In the autumn of 1802, Southey was still wandering, looking for a permanent home, and had left the Irish post:

> Now then for egotism. You know, or ought to know, that I am no longer secretary to the Irish Chancellor, losing a foolish office and a good salary. The salary I might have kept, if I would have accepted a more troublesome situation, that of tutor to his son: all this was transacted with ministerial secrecy and hints, but with respectful civility: so much for that. Moreover, you know that I have an additional reason for ceasing to be a wanderer on the face of the earth, having now a nursery as well as a library to remove. I am in treaty for a house in Glamorganshire eight miles from Neath, in the Vale of Neath, between high mountains,—a beautiful spot, almost the most beautiful that I have seen in this island: the treaty will in all probability end to my wishes, and in the spring I shall probably be R.S. of Maes Gwyn. To live in the country is my choice . . . One of the motives for fixing there is the facility afforded of acquiring the Welsh language. (*R* I, pp. 426–27)

Chrystal Tilney's article[4] on the eventual refusal of the landlord, a Mr Williams, to allow Southey to rent the house, ostensibly because the poet wanted to alter the kitchen, is interesting. Tilney demonstrates that, because Southey was best known by his republican writings, Williams saw him in 1802 as a dangerous prospective tenant. She quotes from Elijah Waring's *Recollections . . . of . . . Iolo Morgannwg*:

> It is not a little curious, viewed in connexion with Southey's change in political opinions, that the real cause of Maesgwyn not having been made a desirable abode for him, was the democratic bias of his writings then best known to the public. The agent and legal adviser of the Aberpergwm family was a staunch Tory of the old school, and entertained such a dread of bringing 'a republican poet' into the Valley, that he discouraged the proposed improvements, and thus warded off the danger.[5]

Southey was rejected not (as would have been appropriate considering his own apparent xenophobia) because he was English, but because of his recent political past haunting him. The picture of Southey established in the then famously picturesque Vale of Neath, perhaps as English Laureate (with different political overtones), makes fascinating speculative material. Tilney[6] notes the poet's interest in Welsh history and topography, encouraged by his friend from Westminster days, Charles Watkin Williams Wynn.[7] Southey put great faith in the epic *Madoc* as the keystone to his enduring poetical reputation, a faith not shared by many. Yet if Southey's unquestionable zeal for Welsh historical research and Welsh literature had been focused at Maes Gwyn, he may have produced some huge work in this area, and perhaps altered the relationship between notions of Englishness and Welshness which burden the present. But of course this did not happen, Southey immured himself at Keswick and went through his 'period of hardening', as Fairchild (*N* p. 227) termed it.

What this book has partially uncovered is the wealth of literary allusiveness in Southey's work, the conflict between politics and the quest for home expressed as poetic tension, and hints as to how the student of Romanticism might re-assess Southey's position. His fight to the death with writing was frequently an important influence upon other writers, irritated by his fame, but constrained to react within or against his language and his poetic genres. We have to go further than Jean Raimond who decided:

> Southey n'est ni classique ni romantique: il se situe, pour ainsi dire, au confluent de deux mondes, celui du romantisme et celui du classicisme. (*RA* p. 577)

Critical anxiety to compartmentalize poetry shuts down tight proper consideration of historical and linguistic discourse. The labels 'classical' and 'Romantic' applied to one man suggest a struggle of terms which perhaps at the time of the writing, the 1790s, felt easy enough. If the poet was at home with his influences and styles, then the critic, if honest, must follow suit.

In tracing Southey's selected poetry of home from the melancholy optimism of *The Retrospect* to the recovery and first domestic closure at Westbury, essentially the struggle against banishment-love, one thing is clear, that there is room for a new selection of his poetry to be added to debate about the 1790s. Southey's natural voice in poetry centred around the domestic core as I have tried to emphasize. His other voice, which he sometimes entangled and misused in poetry, was the prose voice, of unequalled clarity. In concentrating on the short poems, or short passages of larger works, I have tried additionally to allow Southey's natural voice in poetry to surface, to allow him a canon of his own, which, though linked intimately to his peers, is not Coleridge's, which does not lead naturally to Wordsworth's.

Kenneth Hopkins[8] laments that Southey 'chose to consider as mere trifles' the shorter poems 'in which he had so clear and single a voice'. Part of this voice was the brevity, even stoical brevity, which seems to have been a Southeyan characteristic,

not only in his gem-like short passages, but in conversation, as
de Quincey noticed:

> A sententious, epigrammatic form of delivering opinions
> has a certain effect of *clenching* a subject, which makes it
> difficult to pursue it without a corresponding smartness
> of expression, and something of the same antithetic point
> and equilibrium of clauses . . . He seeks, indeed, to be
> effective, not for the sake of display, but as the readiest
> means of retreating from display . . .[9]

Grigson's selection of Southey's shorter pieces (G pp. 9–20)
drew attention to the 'verge of self-parody' (p. 15) which he
considered made up the thrust of many of these poems.
Southey himself said to Taylor, who had been criticizing his
poetry (R II, pp. 133–34, Keswick, 27 May 1806):

> I wish you had drawn out for notice the 'Pig,' the
> 'Filbert,' and the 'Dancing Bear,' because there is a
> character of originality in them,—a sort of sportive
> seriousness, which is one of my predominant moods of
> mind.

In presenting a study of what I think of as Southey's serious
work, I have perhaps run the risk at times of coming close to
this 'sportive' quality, but that should not detract from the
genuine sense of his early struggle towards home. The year at
Westbury freed up the Southeyan laughter which is so
dangerous to our serious notions of high Romanticism, and
which he accommodated so naturally within his broad canon
of writing. The poetry of home was perhaps the most serious
centre of that laughter.

2
Against Diasparactivity: Southey's Reputation

The difficulty I find in every subject that has occurred to
me is to make enough of it. I cannot wire draw a story.
(*W* I, p. 67, 5 April 1799)

I must spur you to something, to the assertion of your
supremacy; if you have not enough to muster, I will aid
you in any way—manufacture skeletons that you may
clothe with flesh, blood, and beauty. (*LC* II, p. 150,
11 July 1801, to Coleridge)

Lionel Madden's volume on Southey in *The Critical Heritage*
series gives a reasonably full picture of the progress of
Southey's literary reputation, but is rather thin upon the early
period. If Derek Roper's account of the early years is added to
this, a fuller picture emerges:

It is clear that the short poems Southey published
between 1797 and 1800 damaged his reputation with the
reviewers, and called forth the kind of criticism that is
noticeably absent from reviews of *Lyrical Ballads* . . .
when Jefrrey came to work up his collective caricature of
the 'new school of poetry' in the *Edinburgh Review* for
October 1802, most of the materials were ready to his
hand. It is virtually certain that he knew Ferriar's articles,
and not only because they appeared in the leading Review
of the day. Some time in the spring of 1802 Jeffrey had
himself joined the staff of the *Monthly*, and had been
given *Thalaba* to review; and it was almost certain that he
should look up earlier articles on Southey to see what line
the *Monthly* had taken . . . The existence of a school of
poets subversive both in politics and literature was
postulated as early as 20 November 1797, in the first
number of the *Anti-Jacobin*. (*RO* pp. 108–09)

So Southey's early political views, as well as the stylistic experiments in his volumes of 1797 and 1799 (and of course the *Joan of Arc*), were hauled forward as the basis for critical attitudes in the early nineteenth century. Southey was seen not just as politically suspect, but to be leading a suspect school of poets who followed Rousseau's attitude to society, and the poetical doctrines of a slovenly, uncouth simplicity. This summary of course put the poet's reputation before a wider audience, but it also linked his name forever with Wordsworth's own. Southey's rather disingenuous letter to Bowles[10] of 21 February 1815 remarked upon the 'school' theory:

> I am indebted to you for many hours of deep enjoyment, and for great improvement in our common art,—for your poems came into my hands when I was nineteen and I *fed* upon them. Our booby critics talk of *schools*, and if they had common discernment they might have perceived that I was of your school. But they are as deficient in judgement as they are in candour and common honesty.

It was forgotten that Southey had himself dealt rather harshly with the volume of *Lyrical Ballads*, though perhaps it was assumed that such behaviour automatically sprang from jacobinical poets. Southey's work had gone far beyond the tentative wistfulness of Bowles to inspire poets like Shelley for example, an admirer of Southey's eastern epics—but of course it was Scott who profited from the writing of popular epic, not the revivalist pioneer Southey.

It is a tendency in criticism to use Southey as the butt of (old) jokes, or as the ideal example of the transitional poet, or to revere him as the dutiful man of letters. Looking at Southey's own progress of poetry, we can see how the predominant picture of Southey the laughable Laker-villain has arisen. In many ways, the poet set himself up as a poetical or political target to be shot at, in ways that Wordsworth never did. A string of serious career mistakes, and sheer bad

luck, give us one version of Southey: the *Anti-Jacobin*
parodies which are still to this day highly amusing; Southey's
adverse review of *Lyrical Ballads*, which sets him at odds with
his sibling poets, who are, like their poetry, cultural icons, and
sets him at odds with the taste of later readers; his hasty and
little-known reply to *Lyrical Ballads*, *Poems* 1799, which fails
to convince in terms of stylistic seriousness alone; *Madoc*,
which failed to secure his reputation; Southey's acceptance of
the post of Poet Laureate in 1813, a post which he restored to
credence, but which resulted in the consequent depictions of
him as a political turncoat; the *Wat Tyler* furore of 1817, in
which Southey's jacobinical political past was held up in
parliament against his seemingly royalist present; the destructive involvement with Byron over notions of a 'Satanic School'
of poets in 1821, and Macaulay's devastating 1830 review of
the *Colloquies*. These events alone, hovering around
Southey's career, are strong advocates against any regard for
the writer or the man, and are not really offset by biographical
works in the Edward Dowden or Jack Simmons vein. Southey
more than most seems dogged by anecdotes of failure. His
readers are often introduced to him through his humiliations
and failures. But as Marilyn Butler says:

> Nevertheless, it is surely one of the injustices of literary
> history that Hazlitt has on the whole got away with his
> trivializing and his nastiness—which are not replied to in
> lasting literature—while the less malicious Southey
> attracts such very devastating and memorable literary
> fire . . .[11]

Alongside this we might place (*RA* p. 581) Jean Raimond's
comment:

> On ne dira jamais assez combien Byron a fait tort à
> Southey. Aujourd'hui encore, Southey n'est guère . . .
> qu'un poète lauréat que Byron a tourné en dérision.
> Byron a immortalisé Southey en l'embaumant dans le

ridicule, et c'est une sorte du momie travestie qui est parvenue jusqu'à nous.

Byron had a secret regard for Southey, whilst in public he vilified him. He noted (*M* p. 157) that 'His prose is perfect' and predicted that posterity would select from the poems in which there were '*passages* equal to anything'. But the student is likely to approach a Southey travestied through the more outrageous and damning pronouncements of such as Byron and Shelley, without ever looking at such 'passages'. Even Coleridge's account in the third chapter of the *Biographia Literaria* (public praise concealing private dislike) is not calculated to send anyone to Southey's poetry despite its adulatory tone. Coleridge does however remark upon the 'abuse and indefatigable hostility' (*M* p. 258) of Southey's critics, presenting him as a good man rather than a good poet:

> In poetry he has attempted almost every species of composition known before, and he has added new ones; and if we except the highest lyric, (in which how few, how very few even of the greatest minds have been fortunate) he has attempted every species success-fully . . .

In a much more open and intelligent appraisal which strikes directly at the root of the matter, Wordsworth saw poetical composition as something which descended upon the writer and totally absorbed that writer. This absorption he noted was absent in Southey's method, and this he deduced was intima-tely linked with the effect which Southey's poetry had upon its readership. It simply did not engage with or remain in the mental impressions of the reader:

> no man can write verses that will live in the hearts of his Fellow creatures but through an overpowering impulse in his own mind, involving him often times in labour that he cannot dismiss or escape from . . . Observe the

difference of execution in the Poems of Coleridge and
Southey, how masterly is the workmanship of the
former, compared with the latter; the one persevered in
labour unremittingly, the other could lay down his work
at pleasure and turn to any thing else. But what was the
result? Southey's Poems, notwithstanding the care and
forethought with which most of them were planned after
the material had been diligently collected, are read once
but how rarely are they recurred to! how seldom quoted,
and how few passages, notwithstanding the great merit of
the works in many respects, are gotten by heart.[12]

This, surely, when we leave aside all the hostility to Southey's
career in politics and writing, is the most profound and
enduring verdict of all, even when we add to this Mrs Thrale's
perceptive remarks from August 1808:

The fashionable poetry of Southey & Scott will fall into
Decay—it will never be Classical—It leaves too little
behind it—Handel and Milton must be forever *felt*;
Bach's Lessons & Pope's moral Essays must be forever
recollected; *Madoc* and *Thalaba*, *Teviot Dale* and
Marmion depend too much on their colouring: In a
hundred Years People will wonder why they were so
admired. (*M* p. 129)

Southey had the unfortunate tendency to be continually in the
vanguard of poetical fashion, even admired as Mrs Thrale says;
the experimental poet, who set trends, as in his epics, but then
gave ground to such as Scott or Byron who profited from
them. Fashion in poetry, when devoid of poetic depth, results
in the effect described by Wordsworth of instantaneous loss of
impression. To attempt to restore Southey's reputation as a
poet would go against this enduring verdict by his successor as
Laureate, which holds true. At the side of Wordsworth's
poetry, Southey's speaks a different language, in a discourse
often fogged by just that 'gaudy and inane phraseology' which

the *Lyrical Ballads* experiment had tried to combat, though Southey's smaller poems often escape this trap successfully.

If he is to be reinstated as a poet then this process might begin by using his work properly in detail and in chronological sequence, rather than cursorily, and in context with the studies of *Lyrical Ballads* alone. A second and much more important step might involve the presentation of Southey as intimate collaborator amongst the literary friendships of the 1790s in which he played such a centrally important part. Too often his name is entirely (and incredibly) absent from the studies of his peers, and even when it is included, Southey's active part in the remaking of the poetical voice of the late eighteenth century is never acknowledged. His poetical works, even if they cannot sustain a readership, form an enormous cultural index of fashions, allusions, voices and prompts, in whose light the other poets of the time need to be fully contextualized. To this end it is obvious that a new edition of the poems needs to be assembled.

NOTES

1 Witold Ribczynski, *Home: A Short History of an Idea* (New York: Viking Penguin, 1986), p. 111.

2 Marilyn Butler, *Romantics, Rebels and Reactionaries* (Oxford: Oxford University Press, 1981), p. 180.

3 See Tom Paulin, *Minotaur: Poetry and the Nation State* (Cambridge, Mass.: Harvard University Press, 1992), for an account of Southey's reactions to Ireland at this time: 'Southey Landing', pp. 32–46.

4 Chrystal Tilney, 'Robert Southey at Maes-Gwyn', *National Library of Wales Journal* 15, 1968, pp. 437–50. Note also that William Gilpin makes advertising reference to the area around Neath in his *Observations on the River Wye* (Richmond: Richmond Publishing Co., 1973), pp. 72–74.

5 Tilney, *op. cit.*, p. 442.

6 *Ibid.*, p. 437.

7 Biographical information on Wynn (1775–1850) and other friends of

the poet may be found in Curry's *NL* pp. 481–508. Southey dedicated his poem about the Welsh colonizers of America, *Madoc*, to Wynn in 1805.

8 Kenneth Hopkins, *English Poetry: A Short History* (London: Phoenix House, 1962), p. 307.

9 Thomas De Quincey, *The Collected Writings of Thomas De Quincey*, ed. David Mason, 14 vols (Edinburgh: Adam & Charles Black, 1889–1890), Vol. II, pp. 328–29.

10 *A Wiltshire Parson and his Friends*, ed. Garland Greever (London: Constable, 1926), p. 150. Southey was not always so kind in his opinions of Bowles.

11 Butler, *op. cit.*, p. 145.

12 See *The Letters of William and Dorothy Wordsworth, 1841–50*, ed. E. De Selincourt (Oxford: Oxford University Press, 1939), p. 1231.

Bibliography

Editions of Southey's Poetry

Poems: Containing The Retrospect, Odes, Elegies, Sonnets, &c. by Robert Lovell, and Robert Southey, of Baliol College, Oxford (Bath: R. Crutwell, 1795).

Poems by Robert Southey, 1st & 2nd edns (Bristol: N. Biggs for J. Cottle and G. G. & J. Robinson, London, 1797) and facsimile (Oxford: Woodstock Books, 1989).

Poems by Robert Southey: The Second Volume (Bristol: Biggs and Cottle, 1799).

Joan of Arc (Bristol: Cottle & Robinson, 1796).

Joan of Arc: 2nd edn, 2 vols (Bristol: Biggs for Longman London, and J. Cottle Bristol, 1798).

Wat Tyler, A Dramatic Poem in Three Acts (London: Sherwood, Neeley, And Jones, 1817).

The Annual Anthology, vols I & II (Bristol: Biggs for Longman, 1799 and 1800).

The Poetical Works of Robert Southey, Complete in one Volume (Paris: A. & W. Galignani, 1829).

The Poetical Works of Robert Southey Collected by Himself, 10 vols (London: Longman, Brown, Green, and Longmans, 1843–45).

Southey's Poetical Works. Complete in one Volume (London: Longman, Brown, Green & Longmans, 1845).

The Poetical Works of Robert Southey: Joan of Arc, Ballads and Minor Poems (London: G. Routledge & Sons, 1894).

Poems of Robert Southey, ed. M. H. Fitzgerald (London: Oxford University Press, 1909).

A Choice of Southey's Verse, ed. G. Grigson (London: Faber, 1970).

The Contributions of Robert Southey to the Morning Post, ed. Kenneth Curry (Alabama: University of Alabama Press, 1984).

Correspondence in Chronological Order

A Memoir of the Life and Writings of the Late William Taylor of Norwich, ed. J. W. Robberds (London: John Murray, 1843).

The Life and Correspondence of Robert Southey, ed. C. C. Southey, 6 vols, 2nd edn (London: Longman, Brown, Green and Longmans, 1849–50).

Selections from the Letters of Robert Southey, edited by his son-in-law John Wood Warter, in four vols (London: Longmans, 1856).

The Correspondence of Robert Southey with Caroline Bowles, ed. E. Dowden (London: Longmans, 1881).

Letters of Robert Southey. A Selection, ed. M. H. Fitzgerald (London: Oxford University Press, 1912).

New Letters of Robert Southey, 2 vols, ed. Kenneth Curry (New York & London: Columbia University Press, 1965).

The Letters of Robert Southey to John May 1797 to 1831, ed. Charles Ramos (Austin, TX: Jenkins Publishing Company, The Pemberton Press, 1976).

Prose, and Editions by Southey and Others in Chronological Order

Letters Written During a Short Residence in Spain and Portugal, 2nd edn (Bristol: Cottle, 1799).

The Works of William Cowper, 15 vols (London: Baldwin & Cradock, 1835–37), and 8 vols (London: Henry G. Bohn, 1854).

Southey's Commonplace Book, 4th series, ed. John Wood Warter (London: Longman, Brown, Green, and Longmans, 1849–51).

Amadis of Gaul, translated from the Spanish version of Garciodonez De Montalvo, by Robert Southey, in 3 vols (London: John Russell Smith, 1872).

Life of Nelson, ed. H. B. Butler (London: Oxford University Press, 1911).

Robert Southey: Journals of a Residence in Portugal 1800–1801, ed. Adolfo Cabral (Oxford: Clarendon, 1960).

Letters From England, ed. Jack Simmons (Gloucester: Alan Sutton, 1951, repr. 1984).

Southey Biographies and Studies in Alphabetical Order by Author or Editor

Bernhardt-Kabisch, Ernest, *Robert Southey* (Boston: Twayne, 1977).

Carnall, Geoffrey, *Robert Southey and his Age* (Oxford: Clarendon, 1960).

——, *Robert Southey*, British Council (London: Longmans, 1964).

Curry, Kenneth, *Southey*, Routledge Author Guides (London: Routledge & Kegan Paul, 1975).

Dowden, Edward, *Southey*, English Men of Letters (London: Macmillan, 1888).

Haller, William, *The Early Life of Robert Southey 1774–1803* (New York: Columbia University Press, 1917).

Houtchens, C. W. and L. H., eds., *The English Romantic Poets and Essayists: A Review of Research and Criticism* (Published for The Modern Language Association of America by New York University Press, and London: University of London Press, 1957, 1966, repr. 1968).

Madden, Lionel, ed., *Robert Southey: The Critical Heritage* (London: Routledge, 1972).

Raimond, Jean, *Robert Southey: L'Homme et son Temps. L'Oeuvre. Le Rôle* (Paris: Didier, 1968).

Roe, Nicholas, *The Politics of Nature* (Basingstoke: Macmillan, 1992), chapter 2, 'Robert Southey and the Origins of Pantisocracy', pp. 36–55, and appendix 1.

Simmons, Jack, *Southey* (London: Collins, 1945).

Articles on Southey in Alphabetical Order

Barber, Giles, 'Poems, by Robert Southey, 1797', *Bodleian Library Record* vol. VI, 1957–61, pp. 620–24.

Curry, Kenneth, 'Southey's *Madoc*: The Manuscript of 1794', *Philological Quarterly*, XXII, IV, October 1943, pp. 347–69.

——, 'The Contributors to the Annual Anthology', *The Papers of the Bibliographical Society of America* XLII, 1948, pp. 50–65.

——, 'The Published Letters of Robert Southey: A Checklist', *New York Public Library Bulletin* 71, 1967, pp. 158–64.

——, *Robert Southey: A Reference Guide* (Boston, MA: G. K. Hall, 1977).

——, 'Robert Southey's Contributions to the Monthly Magazine and the Athanaeum', *The Wordsworth Circle* 11, 1980, pp. 215–18.

————, 'The Text of Robert Southey's Published Correspondence: Misdated Letters and Missing Names', *Papers of the Bibliographical Society of America*, 1981, V. 75(2).

Jacobus, Mary, 'Southey's Debt to *Lyrical Ballads* (1798)', *Review of English Studies*, n.s. 22, 1971, pp. 20–36.

Knowlton, E. C, 'Southey's Eclogues', *Philological Quarterly* 7, 1928, pp. 231–41.

————, 'Southey's Monodramas', *Philological Quarterly* 8, 1929, pp. 408–10.

Paulin, Tom, 'Southey Landing', in *Minotaur: Poetry and the Nation State* (Cambridge, MA: Harvard University Press, 1992), pp. 33–46.

Raimond, Jean, 'Southey's Early Writings and the Revolution', *Yearbook of English Studies*, 1989, V. 19.

Sternbach, Robert, 'Coleridge, Joan of Arc, and the Idea of Progress', *English Literary History*, vol. 46, 1979, pp. 248–60.

Whalley, George, 'Coleridge, Southey and "Joan of Arc" ', *Notes & Queries*, vol. CXCIX, 1954, pp. 67–69.

The Wordsworth Circle, Southey Special Number, vol. V, 2, Spring 1974.

Coleridge, Samuel Taylor.
Editions and Studies in Alphabetical Order

Coburn, Cathleen, ed., *The Notebooks of Samuel Taylor Coleridge*, 5 vols (London: Routledge, 1957–1990).

Coleridge, E. H., ed., *The Letters of Samuel Taylor Coleridge* (London: William Heineman, 1895), 2 vols.

————, *The Complete Poetical Works* (Oxford: Henry Frowde, Clarendon, 1912).

Coleridge, Samuel Taylor and Robert Southey, *The Fall of Robespierre* (Cambridge: Benjamin Flower, 1794).

Everest, Kelvin, *Coleridge's Secret Ministry: The Context of the Conversation Poems 1795–1798* (Sussex: The Harvester Press, 1979).

Fruhman, Norman, *Coleridge the Damaged Archangel* (London: George Allen & Unwin, 1971).

Griggs, E. L., ed., *The Collected Letters of Samuel Taylor Coleridge*, 6 vols (Oxford: 1956–71).

Haven R. and J., and M. Adams, eds., *Samuel Taylor Coleridge: An Annotated Bibliography of Criticism and Scholarship*, vol. 1: 1793–1899 (Boston, MA: G. K. Hall, 1976).

Holmes, Richard, *Coleridge: Early Visions* (London: Hodder and Stoughton, 1990).

Martin, C. G., 'Coleridge and William Crowe's "Lewesdon Hill" ', *Modern Language Review* 62 (1967), pp. 400–06.

Patton, Lewis and Peter Mann, eds., *Lectures 1795: On Politics and Religion* (London: Routledge, 1971) (*The Collected Coleridge* vol. I).

Potter, Stephen, ed., *Minnow among Tritons*, Mrs S. T. Coleridge's Letters to Thomas Poole 1799–1834 (London: Nonesuch Press, 1934).

Sayre, Robert, 'The Young Coleridge: Romantic Utopianism and the French Revolution', *Studies in Romanticism*, vol. 28, 1989, pp. 397–415.

Schulz, M. F., *The Poetic Voices of Coleridge* (Detroit: Wayne State University Press, 1963).

Whalley, George, 'Coleridge and Southey in Bristol, 1795', *Review of English Studies*, N.S. 1, no. 3, July 1950, pp. 324–40.

Woodring, Carl R., *Politics in the Poetry of Coleridge* (Madison, WI: The University of Wisconsin Press, 1961).

Wordsworth: Editions and Studies in Alphabetical Order

Bate, Jonathan, *Romantic Ecology: Wordsworth and the Environmental Tradition* (London and New York: Routledge, 1991).

Butler, James, ed., *Wordsworth, William, The Ruined Cottage and The Pedlar* (Ithaca, NY: Cornell University Press, 1979).

De Selincourt, E. and Helen Darbishire, eds., *The Poetical Works of William Wordsworth*, 5 vols (Oxford: Clarendon Press, 1940–49).

De Selincourt, E. and C. L. Shaver, eds., *The Letters of William and Dorothy Wordsworth: The Early Years 1787–1805*, 2nd edn (Oxford: Oxford University Press, 1967).

Foxon, D. F., 'The Printing of Lyrical Ballads', *The Library*, Fifth Series, vol. IX, no. 4, December 1954, pp. 221–41.

Gill, Stephen, *William Wordsworth: A Life* (Oxford: Clarendon, 1989).

Hartman, Geoffrey H., *Wordsworth's Poetry 1787–1814* (New Haven, CT and London: Yale University Press, 1964).

———, 'False Themes and Gentle Minds', *Philological Quarterly* XLVII, 1, January 1968, pp. 55–68.

———, *The Unremarkable Wordsworth* (London: Methuen, 1978).

Havens, R. D., *The Mind of a Poet* (Baltimore: The Johns Hopkins Press, 1941).

Jacobus, Mary, *Tradition and Experiment in Wordsworth's Lyrical Ballads* (Oxford: Clarendon, 1976).

Sheats, Paul D., *The Making of Wordsworth's Poetry, 1785–1798* (Cambridge, MA: Harvard University Press, 1973).

Smith, Nowell C. and Howard Mills, eds., *Wordsworth's Literary Criticism* (Bristol: Bristol Classical Press, 1980).

Turner, John, *Wordsworth: Play and Politics* (Basingstoke: Macmillan, 1986).

Watson, George, 'The Revolutionary Youth of Wordsworth and Coleridge', *Critical Quarterly*, vol. 18, no. 3, 1976, pp. 49–66.

Wordsworth, Jonathan, *The Music of Humanity* (London: Thomas Nelson, 1969).

Wu, Duncan, *Wordsworth's Reading 1770–1799* (Cambridge: Cambridge University Press, 1993).

General Works, in Alphabetical Order by Author or Editor

Abrams, M. H., *The Mirror and the Lamp* (New York: W. W. Norton, 1958).

———, *Natural Supernaturalism* (New York and London: W. W. Norton, 1973).

The Poetical Works of Mark Akenside, The Aldine Edition of the English Poets (London: G. Bell, 1886).

Anderson, Robert, ed., *The Works of the British Poets* (London: J. & A. Arch/Edinburgh: Bell & Bradfute, & J. Mundell & Co., 1795).

The Anti-Jacobin or Weekly Examiner, in two vols, 4th edn (London: J. Wright, 1799).

Arthos, John, *The Language of Natural Description in Eighteenth Century Poetry* (Ann Arbor, MI: The University of Michigan Press and London: Geoffrey Cumberledge, Oxford University Press, 1949).

Ayer, A. J., *Thomas Paine* (London and Boston: Faber and Faber, 1988).

Baldick, Chris, *The Social Mission of English Criticism 1848–1932* (Oxford: Clarendon, 1987).

Barrell, John, *English Literary History 1730–80: An Equal Wide Survey* (London: Hutchinson, 1983).

Bate, Jonathan, *Shakespeare and the English Romantic Imagination* (Oxford: Clarendon, 1986).

Beeching, H. C., ed., *The Poetical Works of John Milton* (London: Oxford University Press, 1906, repr. 1952).

Bernhardt-Kabisch, Ernest, 'The Epitaph and the Romantic Poets. A Survey', *Huntingdon Library Quarterly*, vol. XXX, 1966–1967.

Bernier, Oliver, *Words of Fire, Deeds of Blood* (London, Boston and Toronto: Little, Brown & Co., Canada, 1989).

Blackstone, Bernard, *The Lost Travellers* (London: Longmans, 1962).

Bloom, Harold, *The Anxiety of Influence* (London, Oxford & New York: Oxford University Press, 1973, 1975).

Boswell, James, *The Life of Samuel Johnson*, vol. I, ed. Roger Ingpen (Bath: George Baytun, 1925).

Boulton, James T., ed., Edmund Burke, *A Philosophical Enquiry into the Origin of our Ideas of the Sublime and Beautiful* (London: Routledge and Kegan Paul, 1958, repr. 1967).

Bowles, William Lisle, *Fourteen Sonnets* 1789 (Oxford and New York: Woodstock, 1991).

Bowles, William, *Sonnets, Written Chiefly on Picturesque Spots During a Tour*, 2nd edn (Bath: R. Cruttwell, 1789).

————, *Sonnets With other Poems*, 3rd edn (Bath: R. Crutwell, 1794).

Bronson, Bertrand H., *Facets of the Enlightenment* (Berkeley, CA: University of California Press, 1968).

Browne, Alice, *The Eighteenth Century Feminist Mind* (Sussex: The Harvester Press, 1987).

Burke, Kenneth, 'Four Master Tropes', in *A Grammar of Motives* (Berkeley, CA: California University Press, 1969).

Butler, Marilyn, *Romantics, Rebels and Reactionaries* (Oxford: Oxford University Press, 1981).

———, ed., *Burke, Paine, Godwin and the Revolution Controversy* (Cambridge: Cambridge University Press, 1984).

Clayden, P. W., *The Early Life of Samuel Rogers* (London: Smith, Elder & Co., 1887).

———, *Rogers and his Contemporaries*, 2 vols (London: Smith, Elder & Co., 1889).

Cobban, Alfred, *A History of Modern France*, 2 vols (London: Jonathan Cape, 1962).

Cohen, Ralph, *The Unfolding of the Seasons* (London: Routledge, 1970).

Cottle, Joseph, *Poems*, 2nd edn (Bristol: Bulgin and Rosser, 1796).

———, *Reminiscences of Samuel Taylor Coleridge and Robert Southey* (Highgate: Lime-Tree Bower Press, 1970).

Courtney, Winifred F., *Young Charles Lamb 1775–1802* (London: Macmillan, 1982).

Culler, Jonathan, *Saussure* (London: Fontana Modern Masters, 1976).

———, *The Pursuit of Signs* (London: Routledge and Kegan Paul, 1981).

Curran, Stuart, ed., *The Cambridge Companion to Romanticism* (Cambridge: Cambridge University Press, 1993).

Darwin, Erasmus, *The Botanic Garden 1791* (Yorkshire and London: The Scolar Press, 1973).

Davy, John, ed., *Fragmentary Remains, Literary and Scientific, of Sir Humphry Davy, Bart.* (London: John Churchill, 1858).

D'Herbelot, Barthelemy, *Bibliothèque Orientale* (Maastricht: J. E. Dufour and P. H. Roux, 1776).

De Man, Paul, 'Autobiography as Defacement', *Modern Language Notes* 94, 1979, pp. 919–30.

———, *Blindness and Insight: Essays in the Rhetoric of Contemporary Criticism*, Theory and History of Literature vol. 7 (Minneapolis: University of Minnesota Press, 1971, 1983).

————, *The Rhetoric of Romanticism* (New York: Columbia University Press, 1984).

Derry, John W., *Politics in the Age of Fox, Pitt and Liverpool* (London: Macmillan, 1990).

Doyle, William, *The Oxford History of the French Revolution* (Oxford: Clarendon, 1989).

Duffy, Edward, *Rousseau in England* (Berkeley, CA and London: California University Press, 1979).

Dyce, A., ed., *Recollections of the Table-Talk of Samuel Rogers*, 3rd edn (London: Edward Moxon, 1856).

Dyer, John, *Poems 1761* (Menston, Yorkshire: Scolar Press, 1971).

Elwin, Malcom, *The First Romantics* (London: Macdonald, 1947).

Everest, Kelvin, *English Romantic Poetry* (Milton Keynes: Open University Press, 1990).

————, ed., *Revolutions in Writing* (Milton Keynes: Open University Press, 1991).

Fairchild, Hoxie Neale, *The Noble Savage. A Study in Romantic Naturalism* (New York: Russell and Russell, 1928).

————, *The Romantic Quest* (Philadelphia: Albert Saifer, Columbia University Press, 1931).

Feiling, Keith, *Sketches in Nineteenth Century Biography* (London: Longmans, Green and Co., 1930).

Froude, J. A., ed., *Reminiscences*, by Thomas Carlyle, 2 vols (London: Longmans, Green & Co., 1881).

Frye, Northrop, *Romanticism Reconsidered* (New York and London: Columbia University Press, 1963).

————, *A Study of English Romanticism* (New York: Random House, 1968).

Gibbon, Edward, *The Decline and Fall of the Roman Empire*, 6 vols (London and New York: Everyman, 1977).

Gilfillan, George, ed., *The Poetical Works of Beattie, Blair & Falconer* (Edinburgh: James Nichol/London: James Nisbet/Dublin: W. Robertson, 1854).

————, *The Poetical Works of Goldsmith, Collins & T. Warton* (Edinburgh: James Nichol/London: James Nisbet/Dublin: W. Robertson, 1854).

————, *The Poetical Works of William Lisle Bowles*, 2 vols (London, Paris and New York: Cassell, Petter, Galpin & Co., 1855).

————, *The Poetical Works of Mark Akenside* (Edinburgh: James Nichol/London: James Nisbet/Dublin: W. Robertson, 1857).

Godwin, William, *Enquiry Concerning Political Justice* (Harmondsworth: Penguin, 1985).

————, *Caleb Williams* (Oxford and New York: Oxford University Press, World's Classics, 1986).

Gosse, Edmund, 'Two Pioneers of Romanticism: Joseph and Thomas Warton', Warton Lecture on English Poetry VI, *From the Proceedings of the British Academy*, vol. VII (London: Oxford University Press, 1915).

Grant, Douglas, *James Thomson: Poet of 'The Seasons'* (London: The Cresset Press, 1951).

Greever, Garland, ed., *A Wiltshire Parson and his Friends. The Correspondence of William Lisle Bowles* (London: Constable, 1926).

Grigson, Geoffrey, *The Harp of Aeolus* (London: Routledge, 1947).

Grosart, Alexander, *The Complete Works of Samuel Daniel*, 4 vols (London: Hazell, Watson and Viney, 1885).

Hanley, Keith, ed., *Walter Savage Landor: Selected Poetry and Prose* (Manchester: Carcanet, 1981).

Hanley, Keith and Raman Selden, eds, *Revolution and English Romanticism* (Hemel Hempstead: Harvester Wheatsheaf, 1990).

Harris, R. W., *Romanticism and the Social Order 1780–1830* (London: Blandford, 1969).

Harvey, A. D., *English Poetry in a Changing Society* (London: Alison & Busby, 1980).

Hayter, Alethea, *Opium and the Romantic Imagination* (London: Faber and Faber, 1968).

Hilles, F. W. and H. Bloom, eds, *From Sensibility to Romanticism: Essays Presented to Frederick A. Pottle* (New York: Oxford University Press, 1965).

Hindle, Wilfrid, *The Morning Post 1772–1937* (London: George Routledge & Sons, 1937).

Hogan, Charles Beecher, *Shakespeare in the Theatre, 1701–1800* (Oxford: Clarendon, 1957).

Howe, P. P., ed., *The Complete Works of William Hazlitt*, 21 vols (London and Toronto: J. M. Dent, 1930–34).

Hyslop, Beatrice F., 'The Theater During a Crisis: The Parisian

Theater during the Reign of Terror', *Journal of Modern History* vol. XVII, London, 1945.

Jackson, J. R. de J., *Poetry of the Romantic Period: The Routledge History of English Poetry*, vol. 4 (London, Boston and Henley: Routledge and Kegan Paul, 1980).

————, *Historical Criticism and the Meaning of Texts* (London and New York: Routledge, 1989).

Jarret, Derek, *Pitt the Younger (British Prime Ministers)* (London: Weidenfield and Nicholson, 1974).

Jeffrey, Francis, *Essays on English Poets and Poetry* (London: Routledge, no date).

Johnson, Samuel, *The Works*, 9 vols (Oxford: Talboys and Wheeler/ London: W. Pickering, 1825).

Johnston, K. R., G. Chaitin, K. Hanson and H. Marks, eds, *Romantic Revolutions: Criticism and Theory* (Bloomington: Indiana University Press, 1990).

Jones, A. R. and W. Tydeman, eds, *A Pedestrian Tour through North Wales, in a Series of Letters (1795)* by Joseph Hucks (Cardiff: University of Wales Press, 1979).

Jowett, B., trans., *The Dialogues of Plato*, 4 vols (Oxford: Clarendon, 1953).

Ketton-Cramer, R. W., 'Lapidary Verse', Warton Lecture on English Poetry, 50, *From the Proceedings of the British Academy*, vol. XLV (London: Oxford University Press, 1959).

Knight, R. P., *The Landscape: A Dramatic Poem in Three Books*, 2nd edn (London: W. Bulmer, 1795).

Kristeva, Julia, *Desire in Language*, ed. Leon S. Roudiez, trans. Thomas Gora, Alice Jardine and Leon S. Roudiez (Oxford: Basil Blackwell, 1989).

La Cassagnere, Christian, ed., *Romantisme Anglais et Eros* (Clermont-Ferrand: Université de Clermont-Ferrand II, 1982).

Lange, Victor, *The Sorrows of Young Werther by J. W. Goethe* (New York: Holt, Rinehart and Winston, 1949).

Lefebure, Molly, *The Bondage of Love* (New York and London: W. W. Norton, 1987).

Levinson, M., M. Butler, J. McGann and P. Hamilton, eds, *Rethinking Historicism* (Oxford: Basil Blackwell, 1989).

Lister, Raymond, *British Romantic Art* (London: G. Bell, 1973).

Lodge, David, ed., *20th Century Literary Criticism* (London and New York: Longman, 1972, 1981).

———, *Modern Criticism and Theory* (London and New York: Longman, 1988, 4th impression, 1990).

Lonsdale, Roger, ed., *The Poems of Gray, Collins and Goldsmith* (London: Longman, 1969).

———, *Eighteenth Century Women Poets* (Oxford and New York: Oxford University Press, 1989).

Lovejoy, Arthur O., *Essays in the History of Ideas* (Baltimore: The Johns Hopkins University Press, 1948), 'On the Discrimination of Romanticisms'.

Lyotard, Jean-Francois, *The Postmodern Condition: A Report on Knowledge*, trans. Geoff Bennington (Manchester: Manchester University Press, 1984, 1991).

Macpherson, James, *The Poems of Ossian*, with notes and introduction by William Sharp (Edinburgh: Patrick Geddes and Colleagues, 1896).

Mainwaring, Elizabeth Wheeler, *Italian Landscape in Eighteenth Century England* (London: Frank Cass, 1925/1965).

Marrs, Edwin J., Jr, ed., *The Letters of Charles and Mary Lamb*, 3 vols (Ithaca, NY and London: Cornell University Press, 1975–78).

Mason, David, ed., *The Collected Writings of Thomas De Quincey*, 14 vols (Edinburgh: Adam and Charles Black, 1889–1890).

McFarland, Thomas, *Romanticism and the Forms of Ruin* (Princeton: Princeton University Press, 1981).

McGann, Jerome J., *The Romantic Ideology* (Chicago and London: Chicago University Press, 1983).

Mills, Howard, ed., *George Crabbe: Tales, 1812 and other Selected Poems* (Cambridge: Cambridge University Press, 1967).

Nussbaum, Felicity A., *The Autobiographical Subject* (London: The Johns Hopkins University Press, 1989).

Park, T., ed., *Joseph Warton: The Poetical Works*, John Sharpe's edn of Poets (London: Stanhope, 1805).

Parker, Noel, *Portrayals of Revolution* (London: Harvester Wheatsheaf, 1990).

Partridge, Eric, ed., *The Three Wartons: A Choice of their Verse* (London: The Scholartis Press, 1927).

Patrides, C. A., ed., *Milton's Lycidas: The Tradition and the Poem* (New York: Holt, Rinehart and Winston, 1961).

Percy, Thomas, *Reliques of English Poetry* (London: Bohn, 1845).

Polwhele, Richard, *The Idyllia, Epigrams, and Fragments, of Theocritus, Bion, and Moschus* (Exeter: R. Thorn, 1786).

Popper, Karl, *The Poverty of Historicism* (London: Routledge, 1991).

Prance, Claude, *Companion to Charles Lamb* (London: Mansell, 1983).

Price, Uvedale, *An Essay on the Picturesque* (London: J. Robson, 1794).

Priestley, Joseph, *The Present State of Europe compared with Antient Prophecies* (London: J. Johnson, 1794).

Quarles, Francis, *Emblems*, Cassell's Library Edition of British Poets (London: Cassell, Petter, Galpin & Co., 1871).

Raknem, Ingvald, *Joan of Arc in History, Legend and Literature* (Bergen: Universitetsforlaget, 1971).

Renwick, W. L., *English Literature 1789–1815* (Oxford: Clarendon, 1963).

Riffaterre, Michael, *Semiotics of Poetry* (London: Methuen, 1978).

Rivers, Isabel, ed., *Books and their Readers in Eighteenth Century England* (New York: St Martin's Press, 1982).

Robertson, J. Logie, ed., *Thomas Campbell: The Complete Poetical Works* (London: Oxford University Press, 1907).

———, *The Complete Poetical Works of James Thomson* (London: Oxford University Press, 1951).

Rodway, Allan, *The Romantic Conflict* (London: Chatto and Windus, 1963).

Rogers, Samuel, *The Pleasures of Memory with Some Other Poems*, 5th edn (London; T. Cadell and C. Dilly, 1793).

———, *Poems* (London: Moxon, 1839).

Roper, Derek, *Reviewing before the Edinburgh* (London: Methuen, 1978).

Rousseau, Jean-Jacques, *The Social Contract and Discourses*, trans. G. D. C. Cole (London: J. M. Dent, 1973).

Rybczynski, Witold, *Home: A Short History of an Idea* (New York: Viking Penguin, 1986).

Salvesen, Christopher, *The Landscape of Memory: A Study of Wordsworth's Poetry* (London: Edward Arnold, 1965, 1970).

Sambrook, James, ed., *James Thomson: The Seasons* (Oxford: Clarendon, 1981).

Samuel, Ralph, ed., *Patriotism: The Making and Unmaking of British National Identity*, Vol. 1 (London/New York: Routledge, 1989).

Sandford, Mrs Henry, *Thomas Poole and His Friends*, 2 vols (London: Macmillan, 1888).

Sayers, Frank, *Poems, Containing Dramatic Sketches of Northern Mythology & C.*, 4th edn (Norwich, 1807).

Schama, Simon, *Citizens: A Chronicle of the French Revolution* (London: Viking, 1989).

Scodel, Joshua, *The English Poetic Epitaph* (Ithaca, NY and London: Cornell University Press, 1991).

Smith, Olivia, *The Politics of Language 1791–1819* (Oxford: Clarendon, 1984).

Southey, Caroline Bowles, *The Poetical Works* (Edinburgh: William Blackwood and Sons, 1867).

Stuart, Mary, ed., *Letters from the Lake Poets to Daniel Stuart* (London: West, Newman & Co., 1889).

Thacker, Christopher, *The Wildness Pleases: The Origins of Romanticism* (London and Canberra: St Martin's Press, 1983).

Thomas, Brook, *The New Historicism and other Old-Fashioned Topics* (Princeton: Princeton University Press, 1991).

Thompson, E. P., *The Making of the English Working Class* (Harmondsworth: Penguin, 1962/1972).

Thompson, J. M., *Leaders of the French Revolution* (Oxford: Basil Blackwell, 1988).

Todd, Janet, *Feminist Literary History: A Defence* (Oxford: Polity Press/Blackwell, 1991).

Todd, Janet and Marilyn Butler, eds, *The Works of Mary Wollstonecraft* (The Pickering Masters), 7 vols (London: William Pickering, 1989).

Toynbee, P. and L. Whibley, eds, *The Correspondence of Thomas Gray*, 3 vols (Oxford: Clarendon Press, 1935).

Trotter, David, *The Making of the Reader* (Hong Kong: Macmillan, 1984).

Vaughan, William, *Romantic Art* (London: Thames and Hudson, 1978).

Veeser, H. Aram, ed., *The New Historicism* (New York and London: Routledge, 1989).

Vendler, Helen, *The Odes of John Keats* (Cambridge, MA and London: The Belknap Press of Harvard University Press, 1983).

Vickers, Brian, ed., *The Man of Feeling* by Henry Mackenzie (London: Oxford University Press, 1967).

Voisine, Jacques, *J-J. Rousseau en Angleterre à L'Epoque Romantique* (Paris: Didier, 1956).

Warner, Marina, *Joan of Arc: The Image of Female Heroism* (New York: Alfred A. Knopf, 1981).

Warton, Thomas the Elder, *Poems on Several Occasions* (New York: The Facsimile Text Society, 1930).

Watson, J. R., *Picturesque Landscape and English Romantic Poetry* (London: Hutchinson, 1970).

Widdowson, Peter, ed., *Re-Reading English* (London: Methuen, 1982).

Wilburn, Raymond, ed., *John Locke: An Essay Concerning Human Understanding* (London and New York: J. M. Dent, E. P. Dutton, 1948).

Willey, Basil, *The Eighteenth Century Background* (London: Chatto and Windus, 1965).

Williams, Orlo, *Lamb's Friend the Census-Taker: Life and Letters of John Rickman* (London: Constable/Boston: Houghton Mifflin, 1912).

Williams, Raymond, *Problems in Materialism and Culture* (London: Verso, 1980).

Wilton, Andrew and Anne Lyles, eds, *The Great Age of British Watercolours 1750–1880* (London: Prestel, 1993).

Wittkower, Rudolf and Margot, *Born Under Saturn* (London: Weidenfield and Nicholson, 1963).

Woodring, Carl P., *Politics in English Romantic Poetry* (Cambridge, MA: Harvard University Press, 1970).

Wright, Elizabeth, *Psychoanalytic Criticism* (London and New York: Routledge, 1984, repr. 1991).

Index of Proper Names and Works